T0321683

Collaborative Filtering Using Data Mining and Analysis

Vishal Bhatnagar
Ambedkar Institute of Advanced Communication Technologies and Research, India

A volume in the Advances in Data Mining and
Database Management (ADMDM) Book Series

Published in the United States of America by
　　Information Science Reference (an imprint of IGI Global)
　　701 E. Chocolate Avenue
　　Hershey PA, USA 17033
　　Tel: 717-533-8845
　　Fax: 717-533-8661
　　E-mail: cust@igi-global.com
　　Web site: http://www.igi-global.com

Library of Congress Cataloging-in-Publication Data

Names: Bhatnagar, Vishal, 1977- author.
Title: Collaborative filtering using data mining and analysis / Vishal
　　Bhatnagar, editor.
Description: Hershey, PA : Information Science Reference, [2017] | Includes
　　bibliographical references and index.
Identifiers: LCCN 2016012755| ISBN 9781522504894 (hardcover) | ISBN
　　9781522504900 (ebook)
Subjects: LCSH: Data mining. | Recommender systems (Information filtering) |
　　Multiagent systems.
Classification: LCC QA76.9.D343 C747 2017 | DDC 006.3/12--dc23 LC record available at https://lccn.loc.gov/2016012755

This book is published in the IGI Global book series Advances in Data Mining and Database Management (ADMDM)
(ISSN: 2327-1981; eISSN: 2327-199X)

British Cataloguing in Publication Data
A Cataloguing in Publication record for this book is available from the British Library.

All work contributed to this book is new, previously-unpublished material. The views expressed in this book are those of the
authors, but not necessarily of the publisher.

For electronic access to this publication, please contact: eresources@igi-global.com.

Advances in Data Mining and Database Management (ADMDM) Book Series

David Taniar
Monash University, Australia

ISSN: 2327-1981
EISSN: 2327-199X

MISSION

With the large amounts of information available to organizations in today's digital world, there is a need for continual research surrounding emerging methods and tools for collecting, analyzing, and storing data.

The **Advances in Data Mining & Database Management (ADMDM)** series aims to bring together research in information retrieval, data analysis, data warehousing, and related areas in order to become an ideal resource for those working and studying in these fields. IT professionals, software engineers, academicians and upper-level students will find titles within the ADMDM book series particularly useful for staying up-to-date on emerging research, theories, and applications in the fields of data mining and database management.

COVERAGE

- Data warehousing
- Sequence Analysis
- Quantitative Structure–Activity Relationship
- Profiling Practices
- Data Analysis
- Neural Networks
- Database Testing
- Cluster Analysis
- Web-based information systems
- Information Extraction

IGI Global is currently accepting manuscripts for publication within this series. To submit a proposal for a volume in this series, please contact our Acquisition Editors at Acquisitions@igi-global.com or visit: http://www.igi-global.com/publish/.

Titles in this Series

For a list of additional titles in this series, please visit: www.igi-global.com

Intelligent Techniques for Data Analysis in Diverse Settings
Numan Celebi (Sakarya University, Turkey)
Information Science Reference • copyright 2016 • 353pp • H/C (ISBN: 9781522500759) • US $195.00 (our price)

Managing and Processing Big Data in Cloud Computing
Rajkumar Kannan (King Faisal University, Saudi Arabia) Raihan Ur Rasool (King Faisal University, Saudi Arabia)
Hai Jin (Huazhong University of Science and Technology, China) and S.R. Balasundaram (National Institute of
Technology, Tiruchirappalli, India)
Information Science Reference • copyright 2016 • 307pp • H/C (ISBN: 9781466697676) • US $200.00 (our price)

Handbook of Research on Innovative Database Query Processing Techniques
Li Yan (Nanjing University of Aeronautics and Astronautics, China)
Information Science Reference • copyright 2016 • 625pp • H/C (ISBN: 9781466687677) • US $335.00 (our price)

Handbook of Research on Trends and Future Directions in Big Data and Web Intelligence
Noor Zaman (King Faisal University, Saudi Arabia) Mohamed Elhassan Seliaman (King Faisal University, Saudi
Arabia) Mohd Fadzil Hassan (Universiti Teknologi PETRONAS, Malaysia) and Fausto Pedro Garcia Marquez
(Campus Universitario s/n ETSII of Ciudad Real, Spain)
Information Science Reference • copyright 2015 • 500pp • H/C (ISBN: 9781466685055) • US $285.00 (our price)

Improving Knowledge Discovery through the Integration of Data Mining Techniques
Muhammad Usman (Shaheed Zulfikar Ali Bhutto Institute of Science and Technology, Pakistan)
Information Science Reference • copyright 2015 • 391pp • H/C (ISBN: 9781466685130) • US $225.00 (our price)

Modern Computational Models of Semantic Discovery in Natural Language
Jan Žižka (Mendel University in Brno, Czech Republic) and František Dařena (Mendel University in Brno, Czech
Republic)
Information Science Reference • copyright 2015 • 335pp • H/C (ISBN: 9781466686908) • US $215.00 (our price)

Mobile Technologies for Activity-Travel Data Collection and Analysis
Soora Rasouli (Eindhoven University of Technology, The Netherlands) and Harry Timmermans (Eindhoven Uni-
versity of Technology, The Netherlands)
Information Science Reference • copyright 2014 • 325pp • H/C (ISBN: 9781466661707) • US $225.00 (our price)

DISSEMINATOR OF KNOWLEDGE

www.igi-global.com

701 E. Chocolate Ave., Hershey, PA 17033
Order online at www.igi-global.com or call 717-533-8845 x100
To place a standing order for titles released in this series, contact: cust@igi-global.com
Mon-Fri 8:00 am - 5:00 pm (est) or fax 24 hours a day 717-533-8661

Editorial Advisory Board

Table of Contents

Foreword xv

Preface xvi

Acknowledgment xxiv

Section 1
Data Mining Techniques and Analysis: An Overview

Chapter 1
Review of Data Mining Techniques and Parameters for Recommendation of Effective Adaptive
E-Learning System.. 1
    Renuka Mahajan, Amity University UP, India

Chapter 2
Modified Single Pass Clustering Algorithm Based on Median as a Threshold Similarity Value 24
    Mamta Mittal, G. B. Pant Govt. Engineering College, India
    R. K. Sharma, Thapar University, India
    V.P. Singh, Thapar University, India
    Lalit Mohan Goyal, Bharati Vidyapeeth College of Enineering, India

Chapter 3
Dimensionality Reduction Techniques for Text Mining.. 49
    Neethu Akkarapatty, SCMS School of Engineering and Technology, India
    Anjaly Muralidharan, SCMS School of Engineering and Technology, India
    Nisha S. Raj, SCMS School of Engineering and Technology, India
    Vinod P., SCMS School of Engineering and Technology, India

Section 2
Collaborative Filtering: An Introduction

Chapter 4
History and Overview of the Recommender Systems 74
    Venkatesan M., Government Arts College (Autonomous), India
    Thangadurai K., Government Arts College (Autonomous), India

Chapter 5
A Classification Framework Towards Application of Data Mining in Collaborative Filtering 100
  Neeti Sangwan, Maharaja Surajmal Institute of Technology, India
  Naveen Dahiya, Maharaja Surajmal Institute of Technology, India

Chapter 6
Collaborative Filtering Based Data Mining for Large Data 115
  Amrit Pal, Indian Institute of Information Technology Allahabad, India
  Manish Kumar, Indian Institute of Information Technology Allahabad, India

Chapter 7
Big Data Mining Using Collaborative Filtering 128
  Anu Saini, G.B. Pant Engineering College, India

Section 3
Applications of Data Mining Techniques and Data Analysis in Collaborative Filtering

Chapter 8
Collaborative and Clustering Based Strategy in Big Data 140
  Arushi Jain, Ambedkar Institute of Advanced Communication Technologies and Research,
  * India*
  Vishal Bhatnagar, Ambedkar Institute of Advanced Communication Technologies and
  * Research, India*
  Pulkit Sharma, Ambedkar Institute of Advanced Communication Technologies and Research,
  * India*

Chapter 9
Association Rule Mining in Collaborative Filtering 159
  Carson K. Leung, University of Manitoba, Canada
  Fan Jiang, University of Manitoba, Canada
  Edson M. Dela Cruz, University of Manitoba, Canada
  Vijay Sekar Elango, University of Manitoba, Canada

Chapter 10
A Classification Framework on Opinion Mining for Effective Recommendation Systems 180
  Mahima Goyal, Ambedkar Institute of Advanced Communication Technologies and
  * Research, India*
  Vishal Bhatnagar, Ambedkar Institute of Advanced Communication Technologies and
  * Research, India*

Chapter 11
Combining User Co-Ratings and Social Trust for Collaborative Recommendation: A Data
Analytics Approach 195
  Sheng-Jhe Ke, National Sun Yat-Sen University, Taiwan
  Wei-Po Lee, National Sun Yat-Sen University, Taiwan

Chapter 12
Visual Data Mining for Collaborative Filtering: A State-of-the-Art Survey 217
  Marenglen Biba, University of New York Tirana, Albania
  Narasimha Rao Vajjhala, University of New York Tirana, Albania
  Lediona Nishani, University of New York Tirana, Albania

Chapter 13
Data Stream Mining Using Ensemble Classifier: A Collaborative Approach of Classifiers 236
  Snehlata Sewakdas Dongre, Ghrce Nagpur, India
  Latesh G. Malik, Ghrce Nagpur, India

Chapter 14
Statistical Relational Learning for Collaborative Filtering a State-of-the-Art Review 250
  Lediona Nishani, University of New York Tirana, Albania
  Marenglen Biba, University of New York in Tirana, Albania

Compilation of References 270

About the Contributors 302

Index 307

Detailed Table of Contents

Foreword xv

Preface xvi

Acknowledgment xxiv

Section 1
Data Mining Techniques and Analysis: An Overview

Chapter 1

Review of Data Mining Techniques and Parameters for Recommendation of Effective Adaptive
E-Learning System 1
    Renuka Mahajan, Amity University UP, India

This chapter revolves around the synthesis of three research areas- data mining, personalization, recommendation systems and adaptive e-Learning systems. It also introduces a comprehensive list of parameters, extricated by reviewing the existing research intensity during the period of 2000 to October 2014, for understanding what should be essential parameters for adapting an e-learning. In general, we can consider and answer few questions to answer this body of literature 'what' can be adapted? What can we adapt to? How do we adapt? This review tries to answer on 'what' can be adapted. Thus, it advances earlier personalization studies. The gaps in the previous studies in building adaptive e-learning systems were also reviewed. It can help in designing new models for adaptation and formulating novel recommender system techniques. This will provide a foundation to industry experts and scientists for future research in adaptive e-learning.

Chapter 2

Modified Single Pass Clustering Algorithm Based on Median as a Threshold Similarity Value 24
    Mamta Mittal, G. B. Pant Govt. Engineering College, India
    R. K. Sharma, Thapar University, India
    V.P. Singh, Thapar University, India
    Lalit Mohan Goyal, Bharati Vidyapeeth College of Enineering, India

Clustering is one of the data mining techniques that investigates these data resources for hidden patterns. Many clustering algorithms are available in literature. This chapter emphasizes on partitioning based methods and is an attempt towards developing clustering algorithms that can efficiently detect clusters. In partitioning based methods, k-means and single pass clustering are popular clustering algorithms but they have several limitations. To overcome the limitations of these algorithms, a Modified Single Pass Clustering (MSPC) algorithm has been proposed in this work. It revolves around the proposition of a threshold similarity value. This is not a user defined parameter; instead, it is a function of data objects left to be clustered. In our experiments, this threshold similarity value is taken as median of the paired distance of all data objects left to be clustered. To assess the performance of MSPC algorithm, five experiments for k-means, SPC and MSPC algorithms have been carried out on artificial and real datasets.

Chapter 3

Dimensionality Reduction Techniques for Text Mining 49
Neethu Akkarapatty, SCMS School of Engineering and Technology, India
Anjaly Muralidharan, SCMS School of Engineering and Technology, India
Nisha S. Raj, SCMS School of Engineering and Technology, India
Vinod P., SCMS School of Engineering and Technology, India

Sentiment analysis is an emerging field, concerned with the analysis and understanding of human emotions from sentences. Sentiment analysis is the process used to determine the attitude/opinion/emotions expressed by a person about a specific topic based on natural language processing. Proliferation of social media such as blogs, Twitter, Facebook and Linkedin has fuelled interest in sentiment analysis. As the real time data is dynamic, the main focus of the chapter is to extract different categories of features and to analyze which category of attribute performs better. Moreover, classifying the document into positive and negative category with fewer misclassification rate is the primary investigation performed. The various approaches employed for feature selection involves TF-IDF, WET, Chi-Square and mRMR on benchmark dataset pertaining diverse domains.

Section 2
Collaborative Filtering: An Introduction

Chapter 4

History and Overview of the Recommender Systems 74
Venkatesan M., Government Arts College (Autonomous), India
Thangadurai K., Government Arts College (Autonomous), India

This Chapter analyzes the recommender systems, their history and its framework in brief. The current generation of filtering techniques in recommendation methods can be broadly classified into the following five categories. Techniques used in these categories are discussed in detail. Data mining algorithms techniques are implemented in recommender systems to filters user data ratings. Area of application of Recommender Systems gives broad idea and such as how it gives impact and why it is used in the e-commerce, Online Social Networks (OSN), and so on. It has shifted the core of Internet applications from devices to users. In this chapter, issues and recent research in recommender system are also discussed.

Chapter 5

A Classification Framework Towards Application of Data Mining in Collaborative Filtering 100
Neeti Sangwan, Maharaja Surajmal Institute of Technology, India
Naveen Dahiya, Maharaja Surajmal Institute of Technology, India

Recommendation making is an important part of the information and e-commerce ecosystem. Recommendation represent a powerful method that filter large amount of information to provide relevant choice to end users. To provide recommendations to the users, efficient and cost effective methods needs to be introduced. Collaborative filtering is an emerging technique used in making recommendations which makes use of filtering by data mining. This chapter presents a classification framework on the use of data mining techniques in collaborative filtering to extract the best recommendations to the users on the basis of their interests.

Chapter 6
Collaborative Filtering Based Data Mining for Large Data.. 115
Amrit Pal, Indian Institute of Information Technology Allahabad, India
Manish Kumar, Indian Institute of Information Technology Allahabad, India

Size of data is increasing, it is creating challenges for its processing and storage. There are cluster based techniques available for storage and processing of this huge amount of data. Map Reduce provides an effective programming framework for developing distributed program for performing tasks which results in terms of key value pair. Collaborative filtering is the process of performing recommendation based on the previous rating of the user for a particular item or service. There are challenges while implementing collaborative filtering techniques using these distributed models. Some techniques are available for implementing collaborative filtering techniques using these models. Cluster based collaborative filtering, map reduce based collaborative filtering are some of these techniques. Chapter addresses these techniques and some basics of collaborative filtering.

Chapter 7
Big Data Mining Using Collaborative Filtering 128
Anu Saini, G.B. Pant Engineering College, India

Today every big company, like Google, Flipkart, Yahoo, Amazon etc., is dealing with the Big Data. This big data can be used to predict the recommendation for the user on the basis of their past behavior. Recommendation systems are used to provide the recommendation to the users. The author presents an overview of various types of recommendation systems and how these systems give recommendation by using various approaches of Collaborative Filtering. Various research works that employ collaborative filtering for recommendations systems are reviewed and classified by the authors. Finally, this chapter focuses on the framework of recommendation system of big data along with the detailed survey on the use of the Big Data mining in collaborative filtering.

Section 3
Applications of Data Mining Techniques and Data Analysis in Collaborative Filtering

Chapter 8
Collaborative and Clustering Based Strategy in Big Data.. 140
Arushi Jain, Ambedkar Institute of Advanced Communication Technologies and Research, India
Vishal Bhatnagar, Ambedkar Institute of Advanced Communication Technologies and Research, India
Pulkit Sharma, Ambedkar Institute of Advanced Communication Technologies and Research, India

There is a proliferation in the amount of data generated and its volume, which is going to persevere for many coming years. Big data clustering is the exercise of taking a set of objects and dividing them into groups in such a way that the objects in the same groups are more similar to each other according to a certain set of parameters than to those in other groups. These groups are known as clusters. Cluster analysis is one of the main tasks in the field of data mining and is a commonly used technique for statistical analysis of data. While big data collaborative filtering defined as a technique that filters the information sought by the user and patterns by collaborating multiple data sets such as viewpoints, multiple agents and pre-existing data about the users' behavior stored in matrices. Collaborative filtering is especially required when a huge data set is present.

Chapter 9

Association Rule Mining in Collaborative Filtering.. 159

Carson K. Leung, University of Manitoba, Canada
Fan Jiang, University of Manitoba, Canada
Edson M. Dela Cruz, University of Manitoba, Canada
Vijay Sekar Elango, University of Manitoba, Canada

Collaborative filtering uses data mining and analysis to develop a system that helps users make appropriate decisions in real-life applications by removing redundant information and providing valuable to information users. Data mining aims to extract from data the implicit, previously unknown and potentially useful information such as association rules that reveals relationships between frequently co-occurring patterns in antecedent and consequent parts of association rules. This chapter presents an algorithm called CF-Miner for collaborative filtering with association rule miner. The CF-Miner algorithm first constructs bitwise data structures to capture important contents in the data. It then finds frequent patterns from the bitwise structures. Based on the mined frequent patterns, the algorithm forms association rules. Finally, the algorithm ranks the mined association rules to recommend appropriate merchandise products, goods or services to users. Evaluation results show the effectiveness of CF-Miner in using association rule mining in collaborative filtering.

Chapter 10

A Classification Framework on Opinion Mining for Effective Recommendation Systems 180

Mahima Goyal, Ambedkar Institute of Advanced Communication Technologies and
Research, India
Vishal Bhatnagar, Ambedkar Institute of Advanced Communication Technologies and
Research, India

With the recent trend of expressing opinions on the social media platforms like Twitter, Blogs, Reviews etc., a large amount of data is available for the analysis in the form of opinion mining. This analysis plays pivotal role in providing recommendation for ecommerce products, services and social networks, forecasting market movements and competition among businesses, etc. The authors present a literature review about the different techniques and applications of this field. The primary techniques can be classified into Data Mining methods, Natural Language Processing (NLP) and Machine learning algorithms. A classification framework is designed to depict the three levels of opinion mining –document level, Sentence Level and Aspect Level along with the methods involved in it. A system can be recommended on the basis of content based and collaborative filtering

Chapter 11
Combining User Co-Ratings and Social Trust for Collaborative Recommendation: A Data
Analytics Approach... 195
Sheng-Jhe Ke, National Sun Yat-Sen University, Taiwan
Wei-Po Lee, National Sun Yat-Sen University, Taiwan

Traditional collaborative filtering recommendation methods calculate similarity between users to find the most similar neighbors for a particular user and take into account their opinions to predict item ratings. Though these methods have some advantages, however, they encounter difficulties in dealing with the problems of cold start users and data sparsity. To overcome these difficulties, researchers have proposed to consider social context information in the process of determining similar neighbors. In this chapter, we present a data analytics approach that combines user preference and social trust for making better collaborative recommendation. The proposed approach regards the collaborative recommendation as a classification task. It includes a data analysis procedure to explore the target dataset in terms of user similarity and trust relationship, and a data classification procedure to extract data features and build up a model accordingly. A series of experiments are conducted for performance evaluation. The results show that this approach can be used to enhance the recommendation performance in an adaptive way for different datasets without an iterative parameter-tuning process.

Chapter 12
Visual Data Mining for Collaborative Filtering: A State-of-the-Art Survey 217
Marenglen Biba, University of New York Tirana, Albania
Narasimha Rao Vajjhala, University of New York Tirana, Albania
Lediona Nishani, University of New York Tirana, Albania

This book chapter provides a state-of-the-art survey of visual data mining techniques used for collaborative filtering. The chapter begins with a discussion on various visual data mining techniques along with an analysis of the state-of-the-art visual data mining techniques used by researchers as well as in the industry. Collaborative filtering approaches are presented along with an analysis of the state-of-the-art collaborative filtering approaches currently in use in the industry. Visual data mining can provide benefit to existing data mining techniques by providing the users with visual exploration and interpretation of data. The users can use these visual interpretations for further data mining. This chapter dealt with state-of-the-art visual data mining technologies that are currently in use apart. The chapter also includes the key section of the discussion on the latest trends in visual data mining for collaborative filtering.

Chapter 13
Data Stream Mining Using Ensemble Classifier: A Collaborative Approach of Classifiers 236
Snehlata Sewakdas Dongre, Ghrce Nagpur, India
Latesh G. Malik, Ghrce Nagpur, India

A data stream is giant amount of data which is generated uncontrollably at a rapid rate from many applications like call detail records, log records, sensors applications etc. Data stream mining has grasped the attention of so many researchers. A rising problem in Data Streams is the handling of concept drift. To be a good algorithm it should adapt the changes and handle the concept drift properly.

Ensemble classification method is the group of classifiers which works in collaborative manner. Overall this chapter will cover all the aspects of the data stream classification. The mission of this chapter is to discuss various techniques which use collaborative filtering for the data stream mining. The main concern of this chapter is to make reader familiar with the data stream domain and data stream mining. Instead of single classifier the group of classifiers is used to enhance the accuracy of classification. The collaborative filtering will play important role here how the different classifiers work collaborative within the ensemble to achieve a goal.

Chapter 14
Statistical Relational Learning for Collaborative Filtering a State-of-the-Art Review 250
    Lediona Nishani, University of New York Tirana, Albania
    Marenglen Biba, University of New York in Tirana, Albania

People nowadays base their behavior by making choices through word of mouth, media, public opinion, surveys, etc. One of the most prominent techniques of recommender systems is Collaborative filtering (CF), which utilizes the known preferences of several users to develop recommendation for other users. CF can introduce limitations like new-item problem, new-user problem or data sparsity, which can be mitigated by employing Statistical Relational Learning (SRLs). This review chapter presents a comprehensive scientific survey from the basic and traditional techniques to the-state-of-the-art of SRL algorithms implemented for collaborative filtering issues. Authors provide a comprehensive review of SRL for CF tasks and demonstrate strong evidence that SRL can be successfully implemented in the recommender systems domain. Finally, the chapter is concluded with a summarization of the key issues that SRLs tackle in the collaborative filtering area and suggest further open issues in order to advance in this field of research.

Compilation of References 270

About the Contributors 302

Index 307

Foreword

The book entitled *Collaborative Filtering Using Data Mining and Analysis* comes as a timely and badly needed volume covering the most recent developments in this rapidly growing area. Even a quick query on Google Scholar when searching for "recommender system" shows a highly convincing pattern: the number of hits in 2000 was 489, in 2005 went up to 2,310 and in 2015 reached 9,900. The area is growing rapidly and calls for new methodologies, innovative ways of thinking and efficient solutions, especially when coping with new areas of applications. Recommender systems grow not only in their number but also in the level of sophistication and engagement of advanced information processing technologies including active involvement of Computational Intelligence, sentiment analysis, and text analysis, in general.

The book is organized in the three main parts being focused on data mining, collaborative filtering, and applications in collaborative filtering. The first part covers some review material on data mining, clustering, and dimensionality reduction. Definitely, this type of material is highly pertinent to the volume, given the evolution of the area of recommender systems where we have been witnessing a well-motivated quest for advanced techniques of data analysis, especially those falling under the rubric of data mining and becoming indispensable when coping with heterogeneous sources of data including textual ones. The second part of the book is aimed at the presentation of material on collaborative filtering. Collaborating filtering is inherently linked with recommender systems and constitutes an area of numerous and intensive research endeavors. The four chapters forming this part are a good reflection of the current tendencies. In addition to some historical exposure of the topic, discussed is a certain classification framework showing a role of data mining in collaborative filtering. The challenge posed by the emergence of big data is elaborated in the two last chapters of this part. The third part of the volume looks at various application facets, including studies on association rules, clustering, big data, data streams, all present in the setting of collaborative filtering.

The volume delivers a coherent, logically arranged, and up-to-date material addressing various facets of collaborative filtering and recommender systems.

The Editor and the authors deserve thanks for producing a timely, well-structured, and insightful volume, which will appeal to a broad readership. Not only those interested in recommender systems could find this book useful but the material could be of tangible value to researchers in data mining, sentiment analysis, and decision-making.

Witold Pedrycz
University of Alberta, Canada

Preface

Recommender systems have developed in parallel with the web. With the development of web, the information available online increased at an exponential rate. This information overload required a system which could remove redundant information and provide the most valuable information to a user in minimum time. Collaborative Filtering is one the most accurate and widely adopted approaches for providing such information. It has found its application in domains ranging from e-commerce and e-learning to social networks and web search. Owing to its vast field, techniques, and challenges pertaining to collaborative filtering requires it to be conglomerated at one place to understand its underlying principle, working and application in its entirety. Collaborative filtering finds its roots in data-mining.

Data mining is finding hidden and unknown information from inside large databases. Data mining tools and techniques are finding its immense applications in the modern day. Collaborative filtering using data mining will widen the application area and more interest will be created in budding researchers to pursue their research in the same. The implications of data mining can be understood by the fact that whether it's a public or private sector organization, all are taking the advantage of the data mining tools and techniques to reveal the hidden and unknown information from the available data. This has been widened primarily because of the large or can we say terabyte of data which is collected by all the organizations over the year and they are confused as how to use such a bulk of data. The new and emerging areas of data mining techniques have surprised many researchers and business persons who are gaining a lot of hidden and unknown information for increasing their ROI. Collaborative Filtering is one the most accurate and widely-adopted approaches for providing such information. It has found its application in domains ranging from e-commerce and e-learning to social networks and web search. The primarily techniques of data mining are:

1. **Classification:** A supervised learning-based technique in which different items are classified into target classes. This technique is used in the cases where the exact prediction is required. In this, a training set is prepared that finds the association between the values of predictors and the target. The target is the value assigned to the class and the predictor is the value associated with the domain whose target class needs to be found. The major classification techniques employed are Naïve Bayes Algorithm, Decision Tree and Support Vector Machines (SVM). This technique finds the significant application in the detection of credit card fraud, and suspicious emails.
2. **Clustering:** Cluster analysis, or clustering, is the exercise of taking a set of objects and dividing them into groups in such a way that the objects in the same groups are more similar to each other according to a set of parameters than to those in other groups. These groups are known as clusters. Cluster analysis is one of the main tasks in the field of data mining and is a commonly used

technique for the statistical analysis of data. Cluster analysis does not refer to an algorithm but an exercise that has to be undertaken on the given data set. Various algorithms can be used for cluster analysis. The algorithms are divided into various categories and they differ significantly in their idea of what a cluster is constituted of and how the clusters are identified. The most popular ideas on the basis of which clusters are defined and identified include groups with small distances among the constituent members, areas of the data space which are highly dense, intervals or particular distributions. Clustering is a multi-objective problem that it is a mathematical optimization problem. A clustering algorithm consists of parameter settings such as a distance function, a density threshold (the number of clusters expected to be formed). Based on the available data set and the use of result as intended by the user, apt clustering algorithm may be used.

3. **Association Rule Mining:** In association rule mining, the association between item sets are considered or found with the help of Support and Confidence. The Rule are framed according to the data values and corresponding relationship between them.

4. **Neural Network:** A Neural Network (NN) is used to recognize patterns in data. The data can be specified according to the different domains like Financial Fraud including Credit Card Fraud detection and phishing, etc. NNs are used for those problems where the exact solution is not required, such that this technique is not sensitive to errors. Some common types of NNs are Artificial Neural Networks (ANNs) and Multilayer Artificial Neural Networks (MNNs).

5. **Genetic Algorithms:** Genetic Algorithms (GAs) predict using generated logic rules and fitness functions in order to detect financial fraud and suspicious e-mails. The major steps used are Mutation, Inheritance, Selection and Crossover. GAs and NNs can be used in combination to solve a complex problem. Every model inherits traits from previous models and compares it with the other models to more accurately model remains. It is based on the theory of the survival of the fittest, which means that the model which is fit will survive to the next generation and the others will not be applied to the next level.

These techniques are able to classify the given data on the basis of whether it is supervised or unsupervised learning methodologies. In case of supervised learning, the dependent and independent variables are considered. There are a set of independent variables based on which the value of the dependent variable is predicted, while in the case of unsupervised learning, the useful information is searched by forming clusters or groups. The variables in both cases can be nominal, ordinal, categorical or continuous variables depending upon the available data which enables us to apply the various algorithms of the different techniques discussed above. Collaborative filtering finds its roots in data-mining. Data mining is finding hidden and unknown information from large databases. The data mining tools and techniques are finding its immense applications in the modern day. Such an application is being proposed by the editor of this book which aims to find the data mining applications in emerging areas. These areas are already hot topics in the research. By including data mining in such areas, the application and usability of all said areas will be widened. The researchers are already working in the area of Collaborative filtering using the traditional methodologies. The editors are finding the data mining applications in this field with a motive of developing an effective recommendation system with accurate and precise information at the disposal of the users.

Collaborative filtering is defined as a technique that filters the information sought by the user and patterns by collaborating multiple data sets, such as viewpoints, multiple agents and pre-existing data about the users' behavior stored in matrices. Collaborative filtering is required when a huge data set is present. The collaborative filtering methods are used to create recommender systems for a wide variety of fields with lots of data having varied formats, such as sensing and monitoring of data in battlefields, line of controls and mineral exploration; financial data of institutions that provide financial services, such as banks and stock markets; sensing of large geographical areas from which data is received from all kinds of sensors and activities; ecommerce and websites where the focus is to recommend products to users to increase sales, to name a few.

A definition of collaborative filtering, which is somewhat newer and a bit narrow in sense states that it is a way of automating the process of making predictions, a process which is known as filtering, about the preferences and dislikes of a user by collecting data from as big a number of users as possible, a process which is known as collaborating, hence the name collaborative filtering. The underlying assumption of the collaborative filtering approach is that if a person A has the same opinion of an issue as a person B, then A is more likely to have an opinion similar to B's opinion on a related but different issue. It is noteworthy that such predictions are specific to the user, but they are formed by using data from a number of users. The personal information of the user such as age, gender and location are generally not used in collaborative filtering (CF) but a partially observed matrix of ratings is used. The rating matrix may be binary or ordinal. The binary matrix contains the ratings by the users in columns in the form of likes or dislikes while the user' name or id is in the rows. The ordinal matrix contains ratings in form of a number of responses from the user such as excellent, very good, good, average, poor or simply in form of stars out of five or ten, a system that is used frequently in this day and age. The rating matrix can easily be gathered implicitly by the website's server, for example using click stream logging. Clicks on links to pages of goods or services provided can be considered to be a positive review of the user. While the rating matrices can prove to be useful, one major drawback is that they are extremely sparse, so it is very difficult to clump similar users together into classes. This is due to each and every user does not give reviews about each and every product. Thus, collaborative filtering consists of storing this sparse data and analyzing it to create a recommendation system.

The objective of the proposed publication was to make aware researchers and other prospective readers with latest trends and patterns in the inclusion of the data mining tools and techniques in the areas of Collaborative filtering which helps to develop a system with precise knowledge and accuracy for helping the users of the system. The inclusion of improved and proven algorithms of the data mining helps to extract the nuggets of hidden and unknown information which helps to frame an effective recommendation system using Collaborative filtering. The mission of the proposed publication was to come up with an edited book which aims at being the latest and most advanced topic inclusion and simultaneously acts as a discussion of the contributions of renowned researchers whose work has created a revolution in this area. The contributions by eminent researchers in fields of data mining, opinion mining, sentiment analysis and Collaborative filtering will be part of book in emerging e-areas like retail, financial institutions and social networks. The objective would be to cover each and every aspect of Collaborative filtering, such as memory-based, model-based and Hybrid methodologies. The unique characteristics of the publication were:

1. The proposed work of eminent researchers in the aspect of Collaborative filtering—like memory-based, model-based and Hybrid methodologies—in areas such as retail, financial institutions and social networks which are current focuses of research will be part of the proposed publication.

2. The proposed publication will be targeted towards providing the highest quality, most accurate and latest research by eminent researchers considering the facts of how such research affects and influences common people in their everyday lives with effective and precise recommendation systems.
3. The area which will be part of published work will have a significant influence on business users, common people and have a great impact on society.

In August 2015, in the call for chapters, I urged and sought contributions to this book from researchers, IT savvy's, and young Engineers across the globe with an aim to extract and accumulate the modern day research in the field of Collaborative Filtering Using Data Mining and Analysis, and gradually I started receiving quality and very conceptual, basic and advanced contributions from different contributors from across the globe. Initially, I thought as whether I will be getting any chapters on this topic as it is very new and emerging area, but surprisingly I saw a great response with authors started to respond, which encouraged me and motivated me by showing that this area is gaining importance. After screening through them, my objective was clear, this aimed and concentrated on getting chapters which focused on elementary issues, needs, and the demand for Collaborative Filtering.

The book is a collection of the fourteen chapters which have been written by eminent professors, researchers, and industry people from different countries. These chapters were initially peer-reviewed by the Editorial board members, reviewers, and industry people who themselves span over many countries. The book is divided into three sections: Section 1, Data Mining techniques and analysis: An Overview; Section 2, Collaborative filtering: An Introduction; and Section 3, Applications of data mining techniques and data analysis in collaborative filtering.

SECTION 1: DATA MINING TECHNIQUES AND ANALYSIS: AN OVERVIEW

Chapter 1 by Dr. Renuka Mahajan, revolves around the synthesis of three research areas- data mining, personalization, recommendation systems and adaptive e-Learning systems. It also introduces a comprehensive list of parameters, extricated by reviewing the existing research intensity during the period of 2000 to October 2014, for understanding what should be essential parameters for adapting an e-learning. In general, we can consider and answer few questions to answer this body of literature 'what' can be adapted? What can we adapt to? How do we adapt? This review tries to answer on 'what' can be adapted. Thus, it advances earlier personalization studies. The gaps in the previous studies in building adaptive e-learning systems were also reviewed. It can help in designing new models for adaptation and formulating novel recommender system techniques. This will provide a foundation to industry experts and scientists for future research in adaptive e-learning.

Chapter 2 by Mamta Mittal, Dr. R.K. Sharma, Dr. V.P. Singh and Lalit Mohan Goyal enlightened that Clustering is one of the data mining techniques that investigates these data resources for hidden patterns. Many clustering algorithms are available in literature. This chapter emphasizes on partitioning based methods and is an attempt towards developing clustering algorithms that can efficiently detect clusters. In partitioning based methods, k-means and single pass clustering are popular clustering algorithms but they have several limitations. To overcome the limitations of these algorithms, a Modified Single Pass Clustering (MSPC) algorithm has been proposed in this work. It revolves around the proposition of a threshold similarity value. This is not a user defined parameter; instead, it is a function of data objects left to be clustered. In our experiments, this threshold similarity value is taken as median of the paired distance of all data objects left to be clustered. To assess the performance of MSPC algorithm, five experiments for k-means, SPC and MSPC algorithms have been carried out on artificial and real datasets.

In Chapter 3 by Neethu Akkarapatty, Anjaly Muralidharan, Nisha S. Raj and Dr. Vinod P underlined that Sentiment analysis is an emerging field, concerned with the analysis and understanding of human emotions from sentences. Sentiment analysis is the process used to determine the attitude/opinion/emotions expressed by a person about a specific topic based on Natural Language Processing (NLP). Proliferation of social media such as blogs, Twitter, Facebook and LinkedIn has fuelled interest in Sentiment analysis. As the real time data is dynamic, the main focus of the chapter is to extract different categories of features and to analyze which category of attribute performs better. Moreover, classifying the document into positive and negative category with fewer misclassifications is the primary investigation performed. The various approaches employed for feature selection involves TF-IDF, WET, Chi-Square and mRMR on benchmark dataset pertaining diverse domains.

SECTION 2: COLLABORATIVE FILTERING: AN INTRODUCTION

Chapter 4 by Venkatesan M and Dr. Thangadurai K analyzes the recommender systems, their history and its framework in brief. The current generation of filtering techniques in recommendation methods can be broadly classified into the following five categories. Techniques used in these categories are discussed in detail. Data mining algorithms techniques are implemented in recommender systems to filters user data ratings. Area of application of Recommender Systems gives broad idea and such as how it gives impact and why it is used in the e-commerce, Online Social Networks (OSN), and so on. It has shifted the core of Internet applications from devices to users. In this chapter, issues and recent research in recommender system are also discussed.

In Chapter 5 by Neeti Sangwan and Naveen Dahiya urged that Recommendation making is an important part of the information and e-commerce ecosystem. Recommendation represent a powerful method that filter large amount of information to provide relevant choice to end users. To provide recommendations to the users, efficient and cost effective methods needs to be introduced. Collaborative filtering is an emerging technique used in making recommendations which makes use of filtering by data mining. This chapter presents a classification framework on the use of data mining techniques in collaborative filtering to extract the best recommendations to the users on the basis of their interests.

Chapter 6 by Amrit Pal and Dr. Manish Kumar describes that Size of data is increasing; it is creating challenges for its processing and storage. There are cluster based techniques available for storage and processing of this huge amount of data. Map Reduce provides an effective programming framework for developing distributed program for performing tasks which results in terms of key value pair. Collaborative filtering is the process of performing recommendation based on the previous rating of the user for a particular item or service. There are challenges while implementing collaborative filtering techniques using these distributed models. Some techniques are available for implementing collaborative filtering techniques using these models. Cluster based collaborative filtering, map reduce based collaborative filtering are some of these techniques. Chapter addresses these techniques and some basics of collaborative filtering

In Chapter 7 by Anu Saini focused that today every big company, like Google, Flipkart, Yahoo, Amazon etc., is dealing with the Big Data. This big data can be used to predict the recommendation for the user on the basis of their past behaviour. Recommendation systems are used to provide the recommendation to the users. The author presents an overview of various types of recommendation systems and how these systems give recommendation by using various approaches of Collaborative Filtering. Various research works that employ collaborative filtering for recommendations systems are reviewed and classified by the authors. Finally this chapter focuses on the framework of recommendation system of big data along with the detailed survey on the use of the Big Data mining in collaborative filtering.

SECTION 3: APPLICATIONS OF DATA MINING TECHNIQUES AND DATA ANALYSIS IN COLLABORATIVE FILTERING

Arushi Jain, Dr. Vishal Bhatnagar and Pulkit Sharma in Chapter 8 canvass that there is a proliferation in the amount of data generated and its volume, which is going to persevere for many coming years. Big data clustering is the exercise of taking a set of objects and dividing them into groups in such a way that the objects in the same groups are more similar to each other according to a certain set of parameters than to those in other groups. These groups are known as clusters. Cluster analysis is one of the main tasks in the field of data mining and is a commonly used technique for statistical analysis of data. While big data collaborative filtering defined as a technique that filters the information sought by the user and patterns by collaborating multiple data sets such as viewpoints, multiple agents and pre-existing data about the users' behaviour stored in matrices. Collaborative filtering is especially required when a huge data set is present.

In chapter 9 Prof. Carson K. Leung, Fan Jiang, Edson M. Dela Cruz and Vijay Sekar Elango presents that Collaborative filtering uses data mining and analysis to develop a system that helps users make appropriate decisions in real-life applications by removing redundant information and providing valuable to information users. Data mining aims to extract from data the implicit, previously unknown and potentially useful information such as association rules that reveals relationships between frequently co-occurring patterns in antecedent and consequent parts of association rules. This chapter presents an algorithm called CF-Miner for collaborative filtering with association rule miner. The CF-Miner algorithm first constructs bitwise data structures to capture important contents in the data. It then finds frequent patterns from the bitwise structures. Based on the mined frequent patterns, the algorithm forms association rules. Finally, the algorithm ranks the mined association rules to recommend appropriate merchandise products, goods or services to users. Evaluation results show the effectiveness of CF-Miner in using association rule mining in collaborative filtering.

Chapter 10 by Mahima Goyal and Dr. Vishal Bhatnagar discusses that the recent trend of expressing opinions on the social media platforms like Twitter, Blogs, Reviews etc., a large amount of data is available for the analysis in the form of opinion mining. This analysis plays pivotal role in providing recommendation for ecommerce products, services and social networks, forecasting market movements and competition among businesses, etc. The authors present a literature review about the different techniques and applications of this field. The primary techniques can be classified into Data Mining methods, Natural Language Processing (NLP) and Machine learning algorithms. A classification framework is designed to depict the three levels of opinion mining –document level, Sentence Level and Aspect Level along with the methods involved in it. A system can be recommended on the basis of content based and collaborative filtering.

Sheng-Jhe Ke and Wei-Po Lee in Chapter 11 emphasise that Traditional collaborative filtering recommendation methods calculate similarity between users to find the most similar neighbours and take into account their opinions to predict item ratings. Though these methods have some advantages, however, they encounter difficulties in dealing with the problems of cold start users and data sparsity. To overcome these difficulties, researchers have proposed to consider social context information in the process of determining similar neighbours. In this chapter, we present a data analytics approach that combines user preference and social trust. This approach regards the collaborative recommendation as a classification task. It includes a data analysis procedure to explore the target dataset in terms of user similarity and trust relationship, and a data classification procedure to extract data features and build up a model accordingly. A series of experiments are conducted for performance evaluation. The results show that this approach can enhance the recommendation performance in an adaptive way without an iterative parameter-tuning process.

In Chapter 12 Dr. Marenglen Biba, Dr. Narasimha Rao Rao Vajjhala and Lediona Nishani provides a state-of-the-art survey of visual data mining techniques used for collaborative filtering. The chapter will begin with a discussion on various visual data mining techniques along with an analysis of the state-of-the-art visual data mining techniques used by researchers as well as in the industry. Collaborative filtering approaches will be presented along with an analysis of the state-of-the-art collaborative filtering approaches currently in use in the industry. The chapter will also include the key section of the discussion on the latest trends in visual data mining for collaborative mining.

Chapter 13 by Snehalata Sewakdas Dongre and Dr. Latesh Malik explored that A data stream is giant amount of data which is generated uncontrollably at a rapid rate from many applications like call detail records, log records, sensors applications etc. Data stream mining has grasped the attention of so many researchers. A rising problem in Data Streams is the handling of concept drift. To be a good algorithm it should adapt the changes and handle the concept drift properly. Ensemble classification method is the group of classifiers which works in collaborative manner. Overall this chapter will cover all the aspects of the data stream classification. The mission of this chapter is to discuss various techniques which use collaborative filtering for the data stream mining. The main concern of this chapter is to make reader familiar with the data stream domain and data stream mining. Instead of single classifier the group of classifiers is used to enhance the accuracy of classification. The collaborative filtering will play important role here how the different classifiers work collaborative within the ensemble to achieve a goal.

Lediona Nishani and Prof. Marenglen Biba in Chapter 14 presents that people nowadays base their behaviour by making choices through word of mouth, media, public opinion, surveys, etc. One of the most prominent techniques of recommender systems is Collaborative filtering (CF), which utilizes the known preferences of several users to develop recommendation for other users. CF can introduce limitations like new-item problem, new-user problem or data sparsity, which can be mitigated by employing Statistical Relational Learning (SRLs). This review chapter presents a comprehensive scientific survey from the basic and traditional techniques to the-state-of-the-art of SRL algorithms implemented for collaborative filtering issues. Authors provide a comprehensive review of SRL for CF tasks and demonstrate strong evidence that SRL can be successfully implemented in the recommender systems domain. Finally, the chapter is concluded with a summarization of the key issues that SRLs tackle in the collaborative filtering area and suggest further open issues in order to advance in this field of research.

The applications of Collaborative Filtering Using Data Mining and Analysis are so vast that it cannot be covered in single book. However with the encouraging research contribution by the researchers in this book, we (contributors) tried to sum the latest development and work in the area. This edited book will serve as the stepping stone and a factor of motivation for those young Researchers and Budding Engineers who are witnessing the every stopping growth in the field of Collaborative Filtering Using Data Mining and Analysis.

Vishal Bhatnagar
Ambedkar Institute of Advanced Communication Technologies and Research, India

Acknowledgment

No work big or small is an accomplishment of any individual but a consistent and coordinated effort of a clique. Another driving force is the encouragement and guidance provided by friends and family, their words of motivation prove to be the guiding light in times of distress. I would like to express my heartfelt gratitude to all those, whose unremitting efforts helped me realize this piece of literature.

First of all, I would like to thank my colleagues at the publishing team at Idea Group Publishing for their wonderful collaboration and timely reminder for the needful action at my end. You have supported me incredibly throughout. In particular, I would like to single out the contributions of Courtney Tychinski whose continuous suggestions and valuable information kept me motivated also served as a timely reminder for the completion of the work. A journey of thousand miles begins with a single step, I would like to Kayla Wolfe for helping me with the inception of this book, I would also like to extend my gratitude to Jan Travers for timely completion of the contract agreement and helping me to finally decide the title of the book which I feel is essential for attracting the prospective contributors. I would like to thank all other support staff of Idea Group for extending their full support. A special word of mention to Professors and researcher's across globe for agreeing to be part of the EAB and helping me to find a professor to write the Foreword. Thanks a ton Sir!

Secondly, the editor would like to thank each one of the authors for their contributions. My sincere gratitude goes to the chapter's authors who contributed their time and expertise to this book. I wish to thank the authors for their meticulous efforts and unparalleled perseverance that paved the way for the success of the project. I am also deeply indebted to all the reviewers, there deep insights regarding the improvement of quality, coherence, and content presentation of chapters were invaluable. Most of the authors also served as referees; I highly appreciate their double task their suggestions have contributed immensely to change the structure of the chapters and have transformed the book into its current form.

Any project cannot succeed without a conducive environment. I would like to take this opportunity to thank my colleagues at AIACT&R for being the fulcrum of guidance & motivation. I would like to thank Prof Ashok Mittal for his words of encouragement and invigoration. Also, I would like to thank my students Amit Kumar, Pulkit Sharma and Komal Mahajan for their help during the whole development process.

At last, I would like to thank my parents for their blessing and words of wisdom, the values of hard work, passion and perseverance they inculcated in me as a child, have helped me sail through all the challenges I faced during the completion of this book. No words are enough to thank my beloved wife for standing by me at all times, without her perpetual support and counsel this book would not be a reality. Thank you for your unrelenting love and affection. I would also like to openly admit that I draw a great amount of inspiration from my son whose zeal and gusto for life has always motivated me to work better and faster. Thank you, one and all.

Vishal Bhatnagar
Ambedkar Institute of Advanced Communication Technologies and Research, India
February, 2016

Section 1
Data Mining Techniques and Analysis:
An Overview

Chapter 1
Review of Data Mining Techniques and Parameters for Recommendation of Effective Adaptive E–Learning System

Renuka Mahajan
Amity University UP, India

ABSTRACT

This chapter revolves around the synthesis of three research areas- data mining, personalization, recommendation systems and adaptive e-Learning systems. It also introduces a comprehensive list of parameters, extricated by reviewing the existing research intensity during the period of 2000 to October 2014, for understanding what should be essential parameters for adapting an e-learning. In general, we can consider and answer few questions to answer this body of literature 'what' can be adapted? What can we adapt to? How do we adapt? This review tries to answer on 'what' can be adapted. Thus, it advances earlier personalization studies. The gaps in the previous studies in building adaptive e-learning systems were also reviewed. It can help in designing new models for adaptation and formulating novel recommender system techniques. This will provide a foundation to industry experts and scientists for future research in adaptive e-learning.

INTRODUCTION: DATA MINING, RECOMMENDATION SYSTEMS AND PERSONALIZED ADAPTIVE E-LEARNING SYSTEMS

In the recent years, e-learning has become very important in various educational settings. This is because the number of participants is not limited to the number of available seats and physical infrastructure. Moreover, the learners can use the internet for information retrieval and communication with teachers as well as peer group from any remote location, suiting their convenience. Thus, the application of e-learning has traversed the boundaries of school, corporate training, college education and the internet-based coaching for examinations, to permeate the entire learning spectrum.

DOI: 10.4018/978-1-5225-0489-4.ch001

Various schools, universities and corporate trainers have realized and exploited the benefits of e-learning as an important supplement to the traditional learning scenarios. The worldwide sector for e-learning has anticipated reaching $51.5 billion by 2016. This offers tremendous opportunity to both local and global players to nurture online learning market and make further advances. India is one of the biggest education frameworks in the entire world, with a spread of 18,000 higher education institutions and more than one million schools. With National Skill Development Corporation (NSDC), planning to train 12 million people by 2022 to impart the skills required by a growing economy, the potential of growth is exponential. The Government of India has been effectively backing the e-learning initiative to fortify accessibility. Specific schemes namely National Program on Technology Enhanced Learning (NPTEL) and National Mission on Education through Information and Communication Technology (NMEICT) are advanced to integrate the capability of Information and Communication Technology (ICT) in web-based course content. Moreover, with the recent launch of 'Digital India', there's seemingly great potential to digitally educate the masses, especially in the remote and rural parts of India. Hence, there's a need for better quality of learning content and support in e-learning environment, which will not happen with few unrelated changes here and there. Given the differences in the learning capabilities of learners, web-based learning programs should abstain from forcing a "same content fits all" approach. Hence, we need to supplement the traditional e-learning system with flexible technology to offer quality education to large sets of learners per their requirements.

A personalized system recommends items to its users. People use recommender systems to retrieve information on books, movies, news, smart phones, vacation trips, practically every product or service. For this, recommender systems should be able to forecast the needs of customers and afterwards, give them with suggestions of items, which they are liable to acknowledge, in light of the previous interactions with the customers. The personalization task is basically a prediction problem i.e. the system should be able to predict the area of interest of the users, specific content and then their ranking (Brusilovsky & Millán, 2007).

In personalized adaptive e-learning systems, 'adaptability' is the ability to modify existing course materials on the basis of different learner parameters. The main idea behind adaptive e-learning systems is that, based on the learner characteristics, an appropriate adaptation method should be used, to adapt the presentation of the course content to the individual learner.

Lately, data mining has become an important tool for extracting data by establishing patterns. These patterns are analyzed to generate useful information required for decision-making. In any sector, for example marketing, banking and finance, telecom, retail, sales, population study, human migration, health sector, production, science or education, there are many ways available to store the data being generated. But they do not have the right tools and insight to use the patterns obtained from this data to track the future uncertainties. The business environment is prone to change very frequently due to a fierce competition from rivals. Therefore, it is pertinent to keep the customer consistently satisfied. This will reduce the risk of losing customers to its rivals and to lure potential customers thereby reducing customer churn (Mahajan et al, 2015). This gigantic growth of data and the pressing needs of customer relationship management (CRM) together with customer churn management have spawned new set of tools and techniques that can automatically and wisely transform data into a valuable and need based learning.

The first and foremost task for a researcher is the review of the previous work done so far in the related field. Hence a comprehensive review of the relevant literature is organized and reported in this chapter. The exploratory studies are divided into following sections.

Brief History of Data Mining

The term "Data mining" was introduced in the 1990s, although data mining techniques have evolved over a long period of time. Companies initially used research-driven tools that focused on single tasks. As 90's progressed, advances in data processing, database storage and statistical analysis software helped companies in improving their accuracy of the analysis. Lately, data mining has emerged as one of the most significant technology for extracting and manipulating knowledge and for producing patterns to represent useful information for decision making.

Current Trends

Almost every field of human life has become data-intensive, thereby making data mining an ever growing field. Today's customer is well informed and has enormous amount of information readily available on his technological gadgets. Therefore to predict future trends and behaviors, data mining is helping businesses to become proactive by taking knowledge driven decisions. Data mining applications have been effectively applied in various domains like Customer Relationship Management (CRM), retail finance, health care, automobiles, fraud detection and risk analysis.

However, the growing complexities in various domains as well as advancements in technology continue to pose new challenges to data mining. Nowadays, Big data is a widely used term which involves large scale storage of large data sets. So, data mining done of big data is very challenging and is getting lot of attention currently (Xindong et al., 2014). However, all big data task are not necessarily data mining ones. Big data mining issues include volume, velocity, accuracy, and interactivity that are not handled by existing mining techniques. Research in data mining with integrations of many techniques and methods have shaped the present data mining applications (Venkatadri, 2011).

Data Mining Concepts

Data Mining (also called KDD i.e. knowledge discovery in databases) is the process of extracting knowledge hidden from large volumes of raw data, by analyzing it from different perspectives and summarizing it into useful information. This is accomplished through series of steps like data preparation, the running of various algorithms and the presentation of results. (Han & Kamber, 2006; Klosgen & Zytkow, 2002; Sayyed & Tuteja, 2014).

According to Barracosa (2011), data mining derives from searching valuable information in a large database, which requires either sifting through a huge amount of data or intelligently investigate it to find exactly where the value is.

Data mining is best explained as the union of developments in statistics, Artificial Intelligence (utilizing human-thought-like processing) and Machine Learning (where you allow the software learn about data they study e.g. neural networks and pattern recognition). These techniques are collectively used to analyze and discover previously hidden trends or patterns inside databases (Dunham, 2006).

Data Mining and Its Applications

Understanding the current and past market trends and forecasting for the future is imperative in business. Consequently, data mining applications assume critical role in providing prediction on future estimates and decision making.

It empowers management to establish relationships between internal factors for example price or product positioning and external factors such as financial indicators, competition and customer demographics. It likewise enables them to determine the impact on sales, consumer satisfaction, and corporate profits. Finally, it enables them to drill down into summary information to view detailed transactional data (Palace, 1996).

Data mining is primarily used today by industries such as retail, government, financial institutions, telecommunication, medical diagnosis, population study, marketing, e-commerce applications etc. with a strong consumer focus.

Researcher Ngai et al. (2009) classified Customer Relationship Management (CRM) dimensions into four sets i.e. customer identification, customer attraction, customer retention and customer development. He used popular data mining functionalities such as forecasting, association, sequence discovery, clustering, classification, regression analysis and visualization.

Nsofor (2006) explored nature of these different datasets in different domains and defined their unique input data with the objective of appropriately using the right prediction technique in making predictions as shown in the Table 1.

Table 1. How data mining affects different applications

Application	Input	Data Mining Techniques Used	Output
Business Intelligence	Customers' past purchase transactions, credit card information	Association mining: link analysis, market basket analysis, correlation analysis, prediction and clustering	Frequently bought together products by the customers and other usage patterns
Financial Data Mining	Consumer credit rating, Loan payment performance	Statistical analysis, Classification, Clustering, Outlier Analysis	Loan payment prediction, money laundering patterns, customer classification for target marketing
Telecommunication	Calling time, duration etc.	Association, Outlier, Visualization tools	Customer usage patterns, fraudulent usage patterns
Prediction	Previous users ratings for services or other products	Collaborative Filtering, Classification: Decision Tree, Neural Networks	Recommended services and other products e.g. movies, pages, other items
Web Mining	Query provided by user, Learner usage and interaction Data	Association mining, Clustering	Topics ranked based on their relevance to user input, Usability studies, Patterns for website improvement and Network Traffic Analysis
Medical Diagnosis	Patient history, physiological data and Demographic data.	Association mining, Classification, Clustering, Outlier, Visualization tools	Diagnosis of patient's disease and categorization of illness, effectiveness of treatment
Climate Research	Measurements from sensors board, NASA, Earth observing satellites	Prediction analysis	Relationship patterns among Earth Science events, trends in time series

Data Mining Techniques

Technically, data mining is the process of finding patterns or correlations among fields in large databases. Main data mining techniques can be classified as follows: clustering, classification, multivariate statistical analysis, relationship mining (frequent pattern mining algorithms), prediction and outlier detection (Han & Kamber, 2001).

Privacy and Ethics Issues in Data Mining

Data mining functionalities are used to uncover patterns from large data sets. These patterns offer business intelligence to web vendors. It has been acknowledged for many years that such patterns can reveal sensitive information and can have significant privacy implications (Kobsa et al., 2007).

In e-learning, mostly the patterns are used to make recommendations by mining students' learning needs; and hence they give rise to a number of privacy concerns. The inherent challenge of the 'big data mining' further demands a careful consideration of the ethical dimensions of learning analytics (Bollier, 2010).

Consumer surveys often reveal that although online users prefer personalized content; but they are also concerned about their privacy on the Internet (ChoiceStream, 2005). Hence, the trade-off between privacy versus personalization is quite difficult (Romero et al., 2007).

Educational data analysts should share their insights with all those stakeholders who can benefit from them (for example, students, teachers, and school districts). Moreover, what is shared must be framed in a way that benefits instead of causing harm.

E-Learning

With the proliferation of Internet technologies, various academic institutes and organizations found a way to appropriately organize and disseminate their learning materials on the internet using electronic media and information and communication technologies (ICT). This led to new approaches in learning and training collectively called the e-learning

Obviously, the main advantages of e-learning are flexibility and convenience. Learners can use e-learning environments at any place and at any time using an Internet connection.

The Evolution of E-Learning

The emergence of e-learning has been a dynamic process due to the growing need of education which pays emphasis on the content of the subject being taught, the audience involved and the dynamics of the entire e-learning environment.

The first similar system developed by Bitzer in 1962 at the University of Illinois was called the PLATO, to deliver computer-based education instruction from which e-learning has evolved. Since the 1960s, e-learning has made rapid advances. Researcher Suppes in 1964 conducted experiments on the use of technology within an educational agenda.

Further, the 70s and 80s saw rise of computer-based learning for many early e-learning (research work developed by Murray Turoff and Starr Roxanne Hiltz). Researcher Whyte Cassandra B. (1989) researched about the upcoming role that information technology would bring around in education.

With advent of the web (1994 to 1999), educationists began to explore that how this new technology would improve learning. Incorporating emails, Web browsers, HTML, audio/video streams and core Java began to change the face of Web-based teaching. Commonly, e-learning came to be defined as Internet-enabled learning or the convergence of learning and the Internet (including any use of computers and the Internet to facilitate education) (Downs, 1998).

Technological advances including Java and IP network applications, rich media streaming, high-bandwidth access and the advanced website designing are revolutionizing the e-learning industry.

Definitions of E-Learning

According to Yusuf and Al-Banawi (2013) "e-learning refers to the employment of information and communication technologies to support the development and delivery of learning in academic and professional development institutions".

Education delivered via the internet, intranet, extranet network, or a standalone computer is called e-learning. E-learning was initially called "Internet-Based training" and later "Web-Based Training". E-learning has many synonyms for example- multimedia based learning, technology-enhanced learning (TEL), computer-based training (CBT), online education environment, virtual education, virtual learning environments (VLE), m-learning and digital education. These alternative names simply emphasize a particular aspect, component or a delivery method. The e-learning environment can be accessed with the help of a Web browser over the internet and supports different ways of interaction, communication and collaboration. Content could be delivered via any medium e.g. internet/intranet, video or an audio tape, a CD-ROM or a satellite TV.

In subsequent years, the development of e-learning has progressed to include a wide range of alternative e-learning techniques, such as sharing knowledge or web links to different resources via social media sites, viewing online lectures etc.

While there are major benefits for all concerned, e-learning continues to pose challenges for providers, to constantly develop new strategies for learning process. With the better scope of e-learning in schools and universities, there is an increased demand for better interpretation and implementation of e-learning platforms.

According to Radenkovi et al. (2006), in e-learning, learners face several issues, for instance - inflexibility of the content, lack of adaptability towards learners' needs, lack of effective design of e- content etc. This lack of environment with adaptive features or the adaptive learning environments is due to their same content delivery and same medium for all registered learners. Hence, the problem is that e-learning websites cannot educate learners in accordance to their pace and aptitude and provide adaptive material.

E-learning frameworks usually generate incremental amount of data and this information has the potential to understand existing gaps to improve it. Using this knowledge, e-learning environment can be made to adapt to learners' characteristics. This is why more recent trends incorporate the development of data mining techniques, to deliver learning according to learners' requirements. The adaptation of e-learning systems to an individual or to a group of learners on their expectations, knowledge, characteristics and preferences is the next step in the evolution of the newly evolving e-learning systems.

Need of Adaptive E-Learning

E-learning is powerful, as it enables individuals to learn 'anywhere, anytime' and gives instant access to specific knowledge. Many sophisticated e-learning environments have been developed and are used around the world. However, in reality, different behaviors of individuals affect learning. Moreover, information on the site is not effectively organized. Hence, while navigating, learners often tend to lose their basic aim of inquiry. These e-learning systems are now critiqued by many researchers for their limited adaptability of delivery process as compared to rich strategies employed by human expert teachers (Felix, 2005).

Dorrofield and Bagnall (2007) expressed that "there is a perception of e-learning being confusing and difficult to use". An effective solution to the reasons for e-learning obstacles is therefore needed.

Benefits of Adaptive E-Learning Site

E-learning platform allows assessment of students in systematic and real-time ways (Mahajan, 2015). This application can be oriented towards different stakeholders including learners and site administrators with different perspectives and goals. Researchers have been experimenting with rich educational datasets from various course management systems like Blackboard, Moodle and WebCT. An adaptive e-learning environment can be built into a self-improving platform (Mahajan et al., 2012).

The goals of an adaptive e-Learning site from web site designers' view point is, he should be able to categorize a learner into three categories namely novice, intermediate or advanced. Then, he should be able to help new learners based on their category to recognize the previous learners' navigation traces. It will help the designers to design a course intelligently based on their personalized cognitive patterns and augment the effectiveness of their teaching practices.

Learners will be interested in how such an environment might enhance their outcomes or help in building their personalized learning environments. Similarly, the goal of an adaptive e-learning site from learner's point of view is that the website could intelligently recommend resources that would improvise grades based on the previous learner's activities. This will help learner to traverse less links and use reduced clicks to study the relevant topics/material.

For this, the web data of completed activities and sequence of events along with their evaluation result can be mined, to deliver tailored e- content, as required by the learner.

The goal of adaptive e-learning is thus aligned with exemplary instruction: delivering the *right* content, to the *right* person, at the *proper* time, in the *most appropriate* way—*any time, any place, any path, any pace* (according to National Association of State Boards of Education Study Group, 2001).

Origin of Adaptive E-Learning

Simple arrangement of lecture material on the web during e-learning does not train. This situation needs to be improved through the use of a training software called Intelligent Tutoring Systems (ITS) which incorporates built-in expert systems to make e-Learning systems to be versatile (Phobun & Vicheanpanya, 2010).

The first milestone was laid with a publication in 1996 where an initial overview of adaptation methods and techniques was given, followed by an updated survey in 2001 (Brusilovsky, 1996a, 2001). Researcher De Bra (2004) continued further milestones in the evolution of adaptive systems.

According to Brusilovsky (1996b), e-learning delivers education to a diverse learner population with diverse needs. Learners may be keen on different parts of information and accordingly prefer different links for navigation. Therefore, information and links which are irrelevant to these users, simple over-burden their working memories and screen. To overcome this problem, the information about a particular user must be used and represented in the user model, to adapt the information and links being presented to the given user. He researched various areas where adaptive hypermedia would be useful. He highlighted that the most popular area for adaptive hypermedia research is educational hypermedia.

According to Brusilovsky (2001), an adaptive system must be capable of automatically detecting learners' needs and finally adapting to them. The main benefit of the adaptive presentation is that it reduces the amount of presented information with convenient link structure to the most relevant information for a particular user, solving the information overload and lost in hyperspace problem.

According to Hammond (1989), the e-content can be confusing for a learner who is at the beginner level but trivial or boring for an advanced level learner. Also, beginners have almost no knowledge about the educational material available online. Hence they need navigational help to find their way through the website.

De Bra and Calvi (1998) suggested that in an adaptive educational system, a learner will be given a content that is adapted specifically to his or her knowledge of the subject and suggested most relevant links to proceed further. The idea of adaptive e-learning system comes from hypermedia systems and intelligent tutoring systems (Surjono, 2011.)

Adaptive e-learning is the ability to modify the e-learning lessons using different parameters and a set of predefined rules (Riad et al., 2009).

An e-learning system is considered to be adaptive, if it is capable of monitoring the activities of its users; inferring these preferences out of the interpreted activities, appropriately representing these in associated models; and finally acting upon the available knowledge of its learners to facilitate the learning process (Paramythis & Loidl-Reisinger, 2004; Popescu, 2008).

Parameters for Adaptation in E-Learning

Understanding what should be essential parameters for adapting an e-learning site is one of the important questions in education. Several literature reviews have been published on the topic. In general, we can consider and answer few questions to answer this body of literature (Knutov et al., 2009):

- What can be adapted?
- What can we adapt to?
- How do we adapt?

So, we can distinguish between different ways and levels of adaptation. In trying to adapt an e-learning site, research has been conducted on 'what' can be adapted.

According to Brusilovsky (1996b) two types of adaptations can be *adaptive presentation* (content) level and *adaptive navigation* (link) level. The content level adaptation is used to solve the problem of hypermedia systems which are used by different categories of learners, while link-level adaptation is used to provide some kind of navigation support to prevent learners from getting lost in hyperspace.

Research has been conducted in trying to answer 'adapting to what?' i.e. what aspects of the learner interacting with the system can be taken into account when providing adaptation? The answer includes several learner characteristics, like knowledge, goals, interest, background, learning style etc. (Triantafillou et al., 2006).

Past researches indicate that there exist a number of parameters on which individuals may differ. Shute and Towle (2003), focused on how individual differences in aptitudes played out in different educational settings. This influences the way in which they learn from and interact with e-learning site (Mitchell et al., 2005).

Research by Botsios (2008) seeks to connect various adaptability parameters and standards. Findings from previous research by Goyal et al. (2012); Fathi et al. (2010) suggests an analysis of 16 personalization parameters of e-learning scenarios, few of which are: learner's level of knowledge, information seeking task, learning goals, learning style, progress on task, waiting for feedback, motivation level, navigation preference, cognitive traits, pedagogical approach etc. However, most of the systems majorly use the personalization parameter i.e. learner's level of knowledge. This personalization parameter uses the linguistics set of values such as novice, intermediate and advanced. Authors Nguyen and Phung (2008); Kirkwood and Price (2006); Giridharan (2005); Kumaran and Sankar (2013) also propose recommendation process on the basis of knowledge level of the learner.

To adjust learning material for the learners, we have to understand how the e-content was previously accessed by different learners with different knowledge levels. Authors Sfenrianto et al. (2011); Botsios and Georgiou (2008), proposed the influence of knowledge level as major adaptation consideration. Vatcharaporn et al. (2009) assess learners' knowledge level, based on the test scores. Watson et al. (2007) proposed assessment marks as the assessment method for determining the knowledge of the user.

Hence, from the literature review of above mentioned papers, we find that the knowledge is often argued to be an important determinant in adaptive e-learning systems (Mahajan et al., 2014a).

Large numbers of organizations have adopted e-learning programs, while very few have addressed the usability of their learning applications. More attention should be devoted to ensuring the usability of e-learning application, if organizations are to fully benefit from their investments (Miller, 2005).

For the purpose of this study, the focus will be on the usability factors for e-learning by mining the web data containing the interactions of learner and e-learning web site.

Strategies for designing good adaptive e-learning site are one of the great challenges for the human mind. Moreover, as given by Fathi et al. (2010), "the rules that are used to describe the creation of such systems are not yet standardized, and the criteria that need to be used pedagogically effective rule-sets (i.e. adaptation parameters) are, as yet, poorly mentioned" (Brown et al., 2005).

Lately, many researchers have worked to exploit the potential of data mining in e-learning applications. The present study is a step forward in continuing this work.

Data Mining in Adaptive E-Learning Environment

To show what kinds of analyses are possible, we define data mining in the context of e-learning and then describe the data mining techniques which are used to answer questions relevant to teaching and learning. Figure 1 describes the different applications of employing data mining in e-learning (as given by Romero et al., 2007)

Romero et al. (2004) reported that educational data mining extracts knowledge from e-learning sites through the analysis of the data generated by their users to potentially improve some aspects of education and for a more effective learning process. Castro et al. (2007) suggested few examples of educational

Figure 1. Diagram on areas of e-learning, where data mining can be applied

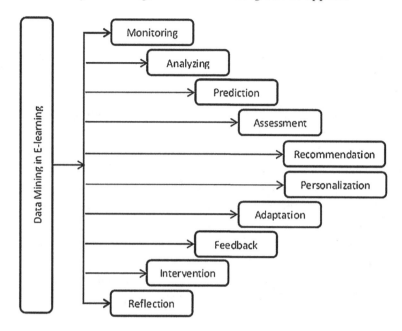

data mining tasks like identifying assessment of the student's learning performance, dealing with course adaptation and learning recommendations based on the student's learning behavior, approaches dealing with the evaluation of learning material and detection of atypical students' learning behaviors etc.

Web Mining

In general, web-based educational systems have a lot of information recorded in the log files, for example, interactions between students and the online learning systems, details of student successes and failures, student grades, and knowledge levels etc.

Web mining (according to Srivastava et al., 2000) is the use of data mining procedures to extract learning from the web data. Researcher Etzioni was the first to recommend this term of web mining in his research publication (Etzioni, 1996). Analyzing the web server logs and the history list helps to comprehend the web structure and the learner behavior, thereby improving the design of the website. Mining access log data reveals interesting access patterns that can be used to restructure sites, determine effective advertising locations, and planning specific selling strategies.

Web Mining is of three types:

- Web content mining, which is the process of extracting useful information from the contents of web documents.
- Web structure mining is the process of discovering structure information from the web.
- Web usage mining, which is the process of discovering meaningful patterns from data generated by client-server transactions stored in web logs. Hence, web usage mining is the process of finding out how user uses the Internet.

Web Mining for Adaptive E-Learning Domain

The web mining process using web log of an e-learning site is shown in Figure 2. Educational Data Mining (EDM) process allows discovering new knowledge based on learners' usage data in order to help validate educational systems. Data Mining in Educational systems can be seen as an iterative cycle of hypothesis formation, testing and refinement (Romero et. al., 2006). Dashboard software and warehouses are being developed for educators to scrutinize learning, performance, and behavioral issues for individual students. Dashboards compile key metrics in a simple and easy to interpret interface, so that the educators can quickly and visually see how useful the course framework is.

Educational data mining has started EDM workshops. It is concerned with innovative methods to explore the unique types of data that come from an educational context. It covers the use of these methods, to better understand both students and the settings in which the learners can learn (Romero and Ventura, 2006). EDM has led to organizing an annual International Conference on Educational Data Mining since the year 2008 along with the launch of the Journal of Educational Data Mining (JEDM). Specific books on EDM by Romero and Ventura (2010a) are very renowned and are guiding the research work. Researchers Baker and Yacef (2009) and Romero and Ventura (2010) also provide an excellent review of how EDM has developed in recent years as well as the major trends in EDM research up to the year 2009.

Various researchers have carried out usage pattern study in e-learning (Sheard et al., 2005; Peled & Rashty, 1999Gao & Lehman, 2003 McIsaac & Blocher 1999; Hellwege et al. 1996; Valsamidis & Democritus, 2011; Vanijja & Supattathum 2006) etc. The main objective becomes analyzing the patterns of system usage by teachers and learners and discovering the learners' learning behavior patterns (Castro et al., 2007). Romero et al., (2008) analyzed the sequences patterns of students' web usage after the analysis of log files data using data mining techniques. Chou et al. (2010) used e-learner's prior knowledge and proposes model to visualize the e-learner's click-stream data so that any interesting pattern can be detected. Romero and Ventura (2007) did a complete survey on pattern discovery methods used in e-learning from 1995 to year 2005 as shown in the Table 2.

Previous Researches

Previous researches done in usage patterns analysis using web mining techniques have been summarized in Table 2.

Figure 2. Web mining in e-learning domain

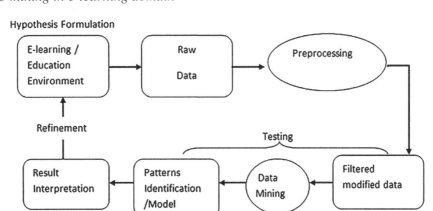

Table 2. Pattern discovery methods in e-learning and the patterns obtained

Pattern Discovery Method	Objective	Research Output	Author
Statistical analysis and Data visualization	statistical description (trend and periodicity) of pattern based on frequency table, mean, median, standard deviation, histogram, correlation analysis, regression analysis, hypothesis testing etc.	Patterns of use over time	(Ingram, 1999)
		Number of downloads of e-learning resources	(Grob, H.L, 2004)
		Total time for browsing the different web pages	(Hwang, 2008)
		Learners' behavior and time distribution (the distribution of network traffic over time)	(Zorrilla, 2005)
		Visualization of different educational data such as: patterns of annual, seasonal, daily and hourly user behavior on online forums	(Burr, 2004)
		Statistical graphs about assignments complement, questions admitted, exam score	(Shen et al., 2002)
		Navigational behavior and the performance of the learner	(Bellaachia, 2006)
Association rule mining	To find patterns of successful learner performance or to make better recommendation to learners having difficulty about how they can improve their performance	Explored how learners' behavior can be analyzed in web based learning system	(Zaiane, 2001)
Sequential pattern mining	To find out all frequent subsequences	Analyzed the sequences patterns of students' web usage from log file data	(Romero et al., 2007)
Relationship mining	To discover relationships between variables in a data set with a large number of variables	Educational Data Mining	(Baker and Yacef, 2009)
Classifications	To predict learner's performance	Predicting learner attrition, retention	(Lin 2012)
		Prediction of which learners could drop out of the school, and then return to the school later on	by Luan (2002)
Prediction	To develop a model which can infer a single aspect of the data	A methodology to improve the performance of developed courses through adaptation	(Romero et. al, 2004)
Clustering	To group together a set of data having similar characteristics	Clustering learners to give them differentiated guidance according to their aptitude	(Hamalainen et al., 2004)
		Clustering questions and tests into related groups based on the data in the score matrix	(Spacco et. al, 2006)
Causal data mining	To find whether one event was the cause of another event	To predict which factors will lead a student to perform poorly in a class	(Fancsali, 2012)
Social network analysis	models are developed from the relationships and interactions between individual actors and from the patterns that emerge from those relationships	How students' communication behaviors change over time	(Haythornthwaite, 2001)
		To study how students' situation in a social network relate to their perception of being part of a learning community	(Dawson, 2008)
		The patterns of interaction and connectivity indicate the prospects of academic success and learners' sense of engagement in a course	(Macfadyen and Dawson, 2010)

So far the primary work done in EDM is quantitative analyses of educational data using statistics, machine learning and artificial intelligence techniques. Frequent Pattern Mining (FPM) has emerged as another important area of research in educational data mining. Agarwal and Srikant (1994) presented two new algorithms namely Apriori and AprioriTid, for discovering significant association rules between items of large database. Pei et al. (2000) presented a novel data structure called Web Access Pattern Tree which is proposed for mining web log data and compares it with conventional methods. Ezeife and Lu (2005) proposed a new approach for using the preorder linked WAP-trees with binary position codes assigned to each node, to mine frequent sequences.

Han et al. (2007) gave brief overview of the current status of frequent pattern mining. Mabroukeh and Ezeife (2010) presented classification of pattern mining algorithms in literature into three categories with web mining application. It also gives comparative performance analysis of many of the key features of different categories. Madria et al. (1999) gave research issues in web data mining. Chand et al. (2012) gave classification of pattern mining algorithm, on the basis of algorithms which are designed to increase efficiency of mining and then on basis of various extensions of pattern mining designed for certain application.

Gaps in Adaptive E-Learning Systems

Lot of research effort is being made to enhance e-learning effectiveness through WUM. However, web usage mining process has various issues. The mining technique majorly used is association rule mining, which suffers from problems such as generation of irrelevant rules or generation of large number of rules affecting recommendation accuracy (García et al., 2007; Anitha & Krishnan, 2011). Moreover, handling multiple support and confidence levels in association rule mining as proposed by Mobasher et al. (2001) is cumbersome.

The studies done so far have catered to specific case studies. The results obtained are in the form of clusters, associations, classifications and predictions. However, these are not generalizable to other educational platforms. This clearly shows that the findings are highly associated to a particular e-learning site at a particular time. EDM should hence focus on results that are more generalizable.

Overcoming the challenges of big data mining will also help in reshaping the future of the data mining technology, bringing around many novel mining algorithms and techniques.

Previous Researches using Web Data for Recommendation of Adaptive E-Learning

There has been some work in using web data to build adaptive e-learning site which is given in Table 3.

Recommender System Approaches

Croft, W. B. (1993) proposed recommender system using contents from their profiles search. Walker et al., (2004) made a review on various filtering techniques. He proposed a new system called 'Altered Vista', using the collaborative information filtering approach, to evaluate the educational effectiveness and usefulness. A. A. Kardan (2009), proposed new architecture for a recommender system based on collaborative tagging and conceptual maps. Feng jang Liu (2007) examined a technical activity based recommendation system using collaborative filtering technique. This model was based on collecting and analyzing information about user activity. Later, researchers combined the collaborative and content-based filtering approaches and used a keyword map technique for extracting the content automatically. The selection of keywords from context-based documents therefore, helps to minimize the time required for providing those keywords. The commonly used filtering techniques are classified as following:

Table 3. Similar precedents (2004 to 2014)

Authors	Objective	Platform	Data Mining Task/ Adaptability Parameter
Cristóbal Romero, et. al. (2009)	Proposed a new architecture for a personalization system for Web mining.	AHA – open Source general Purpose adaptive hypermedia system.	Clustering
Wanga Feng-Hsu, et. al. (2004)	Proposed a new clustering method - HBM (Hierarchical Bisecting Medoids Algorithm) to cluster learners on the basis of Time Framed Navigation sessions	E-learning	Clustering, Association Mining
Cristóbal Romero et. al. (2013)	The usage of data mining techniques for predicting learners' final performance, based on participation indicators in Social Network Forums.	On-line discussion Forum	Classification and Clustering
Despotović Marijana et al. (Aug 2013)	Providing adaptability in Moodle LMS Course	Moodle-an Open Source Course Management System	Clustering on Learning style at the end of each PDCA cycle
Ghauth Khairil Imran et al. (2011)	An empirical Investigation of learner performance in e-learning	131 Power Point slides prepared by a course author for teaching XML	Good Learners' Rating by Prediction

Content Based Filtering (CBF)

It proposes items similar to the ones that each user liked in the past (Adomavicius et al., 2005). This type of filtering relies on the user or item profiles, that assign consequence to these characteristics e.g. Pendora.com. However, sometimes, there is not enough information available in the items' profile (Souali et al., 2011) or it may happen that the user did not access the item before and rate it, so the system is unable to conclude any recommendation for the new learners. This problem is known as cold-start in the context of recommender systems. The cold start problem occurs when the item (learning content) has not been rated by any learner. It may happen that there aren't enough keywords or tag information available in its profile. Since the learner has never rated any item (learning content) before, so it does not have sufficient information (item-ratings) regarding required interest. In this case, the domain system is unable to recommend any item (learning content) to user/learner. This is called user cold start problem.

Collaborative Filtering (CF)

The main motivation for collaborative filtering originates from the idea that people get the best recommendation from someone with comparative interests and preferences to themselves in adapting e-learning context. It works with numeric data based on multi-users network like their likes or dislikes; users-to-items profile ratings and the number of click of users on per item collaboration, etc. e.g. NewsWeeder. com. However, sparsity in cold-start is the main problems in collaborative filtering (Pan et al., 2010). Sparsity issue occurs when the learners "could not give high rating to the learning contents" and the domain system does not have relevant item (learning content) from past voting's/ratings or likes/dislikes history by significant number of learners. Recent work by Zapata (2014) proposes a collaborative methodology recommending learning objects in e-learning dataset.

Random Prediction Algorithm

It randomly selects the item from the available set of items. Hence, its accuracy is dependent on luck; greater the number of items, lesser is the chance of good item selection (Papagelis et al., 2005)

Issues in Adapting E-Learning Context

Originally personalized recommendation approaches that made use of data mining techniques were proposed and applied in e-commerce for purchase transactions. Raghavan (2005) suggested how to determine customers' preferences in order to increase online sales. There are also renowned research works about the use of various data mining techniques within recommender frameworks (Romero & Ventura, 2006). However, there has been comparatively less progress in e-learning domain, although the situation is improving (Romero & Ventura, 2010).

RESEARCH GAPS

Previous research in the field of Educational Data Mining and Learning Analytics, need detailed empirical analysis on the e-learning technology usage. Studies by Valsamidis et al. (2012) suggest that there exist problems with the exploitation of web log data, as the web usage reports generated, do not contribute in obtaining practical inferences about learning activity. Though, studies done by Ai and Laffey (2007) identified some meaningful patterns, but they further suggest conducting detailed research to build a context for understanding and drawing implications from the web data.

Many similar studies have been done and cited by Durairaj and Suresh (2014). Although many tools exist to record detailed navigational activities in web mining, they do not explore the impact of learners' usage patterns for constructing an adaptive e-learning site.

Most of the adaptive e-learning systems developed so far have few constraints. Firstly, there isn't a consensus about the best approach to be used. Secondly, if Sequential Pattern Mining is one of the few techniques that are mostly used, it still discovers large amounts of useless patterns in the real world problems (García et al., 2007; Barracosa, 2011). Hence, navigation and interaction optimization should be done to improve web usage mining process (particularly the frequent pattern mining) to provide systems' adaptability.

Most common problems of filtering techniques in context of the e-learning environment are the sparsity and the cold start problems. Another common limitation of overspecialization is caused when the recommended items are quite similar to each other and the recommended list of items is not diverse. The reason for this problem of overspecialization is the inadequate attribute information about users and items collected by server. Thus, an important challenge is to what detailed attribute data to collect and how to model the multi preferences of the learners. Such challenges serve are potential indicators to develop suitable recommendation techniques for the learners.

SUMMARY

This in-depth literature review facilitates in knowing the trends of thought and publications already done in this specific field, describing various methodologies used and several factors in the e-learning context, thereby providing a roadmap to new researchers to build upon new recommender systems. Thus, based on the review of the literature, there's need to conduct further research on how the learners use e-learning site, new tools, algorithms, methodologies to be used, how to apply them effectively, issues in big data mining and evaluate how well a recommender e-learning system works.

REFERENCES

Adomavicius, G., & Tuzhilin, A. (2005). Toward the next generation of recommender systems: A survey of the state-of-the-art and possible extensions. *IEEE Transactions on* Knowledge and Data Engineering, *17*(6), 734–749.

Agarwal, R., & Srikant, R. (1994), Fast algorithms for mining association rules. *Proc. 20th int. conf. very large data bases*, *VLDB* (Vol. 1215 pp. 487-499).

Anitha, A., & Krishnan, N. (2011). A Dynamic Web Mining Framework for E-Learning Recommendations using Rough Sets and Association Rule Mining. *International Journal of Computers and Applications*, *12*(11), 36–41. doi:10.5120/1724-2326

Baker, R. S., & Yacef, K. (2009). The State of Educational Data Mining in 2009: *A Review and Future Visions. Journal of Educational Data Mining*, *1*(1), 3–17.

Barracosa, J. I. M. S. (2011). *Mining Behaviors from Educational Data* [Doctoral Thesis].

Bellaachia, A., & Vommina, E. (2006), MINEL: A framework for mining e-learning logs. *Proceedings of theFifth IASTED International Conference on Web based Education*, Mexico (pp. 259-263).

Ben-Gal, I. (2005). Outlier detection. In *Data Mining and Knowledge Discovery Handbook: A Complete Guide for Practitioners and Researchers*. Kluwer Academic Publishers. doi:10.1007/0-387-25465-X_7

Bollier, D. (2010). The promise and peril of big data. Washington, DC: The Aspen Institute. Retrieved from http://www.aspeninstitute.org/sites/default/files/content/docs/pubs/The_Promise_and_Peril_of_Big_Data.pdf

Botsios, S., & Georgiou, D. (2008, July 22-25). Recent Adaptive E-Learning Contributions Towards A "Standard Ready" Architecture. *Proceedings of the IADIS International Conference e-Learning '08*, Amsterdam, The Netherlands.

Brown, E., Cristea, A., Stewart, C., & Brailsford, T. (2005). Patterns in authoring of adaptive educational hypermedia: A taxonomy of learning styles. *Journal of Educational Technology & Society*, *8*(3), 77–90.

Brusilovsky P. (1996a), Methods and techniques of adaptive hypermedia, *User Modeling and User Adapted Interaction* (Special issue on adaptive hypertext and hypermedia), 6(3), 87-129.

Brusilovsky, P. (1996b). *Adaptive Hypermedia: an Attempt to Analyze and Generalize Multimedia. In Hypermedia, and Virtual Reality,*LNCS (Vol. 1077, pp. 288–304). Berlin: Springer-Verlag.

Brusilovsky, P. (2001). Adaptive hypermedia. *Journal User Modeling and User Adapted Interaction, 11*(1-2), 87–110. doi:10.1023/A:1011143116306

Brusilovsky, P., & Millan, E. (2007). User Models for Adaptive Hypermedia and Adaptive Educational Systems. In The Adaptive Web, LNCS (Vol. 4321, pp. 3-53). Springer-Verlag Berlin Heidelberg. doi:10.1007/978-3-540-72079-9_1

Brusilovsky, P., & Peylo, C. (2003). Adaptive and intelligent web-based educational systems. *International Journal of Artificial Intelligence in Education, 13*, 156–169.

Burr, L., & Spennemann, D. H. (2004). Pattern of user behavior in university online forums. *International Journal of Instructional Technology and Distance Learning, 1*(10), 11–28.

Castro, F., Vellido, A., Nebot, A., & Mugica, F. (2007). Applying Data Mining Techniques to e-Learning. *Studies in Computational Intelligence, 62*, 183–221. doi:10.1007/978-3-540-71974-8_8

Chand, C., Thakkar, A., & Ganatra, A. (2012), Sequential Pattern Mining: Survey and Current Research Challenges. *International Journal of Soft Computing and Engineering, 2*(1), 185-193.

Cheng, S.-C., Huang, Y.-M., Chen, J.-N., & Lin, Y.-T. (2005). Automatic Leveling System for E-Learning Examination Pool Using Entropy-Based Decision Tree. In *Advances in Web-Based Learning, LNCS* (Vol. *3583*, pp. 273–278). Springer. doi:10.1007/11528043_27

ChoiceStream. (2005), ChoiceStream Personalization Survey: Consumer Trends and Perceptions. Retrieved from http://www.choicestream.com/pdf/ChoiceStream_PersonalizationSurveyResults2005.pdf

Chou, P.-H., Wu, M.-J., Li, P.-H., & Chen, K.-K. (2010). Integrating web mining and neural network for personalized e-commerce automatic service. *Journal Expert Systems with Applications: An International Journal, 37*(4), 2898–2910. doi:10.1016/j.eswa.2009.09.047

Dawson, S. (2008). A study of the relationship between student social networks and sense of community. *Journal of Educational Technology & Society, 11*(3), 224–238.

De Bra, P., & Calvi, L. (1998), AHA: a Generic Adaptive Hypermedia System. *Proceedings of the 2nd Workshop on Adaptive Hypertext and Hypermedia HYPERTEXT'98*, Pittsburgh, USA (pp. 20-24). Doi:10.1145/502932.502935

Despotović, M., Marković, A., Bogdanović, Z., Barać, D., & Krčo, S. (2013). Providing Adaptivity in Moodle LMS Courses. *Journal of Educational Technology & Society, 15*(1), 326–338. doi:10.1080/0952398990360206

Dorrofield & Bagnall. (2007), Education for all, Education for all, Thursday, 11 October 2007, Referred from URL: http://www.iweek.co.za/special-report/education-for-all

Downs, S. (1998): The future of online learning, Retrieved from URL: http://www.atl.ualberta.ca/downes/future/home.html

Dunham, M. H. (2002). Data Mining: Introductory and Advanced Topics. Upper Saddle River, NJ, USA: Prentice Hall PTR.

Durairaj. M. & Suresh C. (2014). A Study on Web Usage Mining For Web Based Adaptive Educational System. *International Journal of Innovative Science, Engineering and Technology,* 1(6).

Etzioni, O. (1996). The World Wide Web: Quagmire or gold mine. *Communications of the ACM, 39*(11), 65–68. doi:10.1145/240455.240473

Ezeife, C. I., & Lu, Y. (2005). Mining Web Log Sequential Patterns with Position Coded Pre-Order Linked WAP-Tree. *Data Mining and Knowledge Discovery, 10*(1), 5–38. doi:10.1007/s10618-005-0248-3

Fancsali, S. (2012). *Variable Construction and Causal Discovery for Cognitive Tutor Log data: Initial Results* (pp. 238–239). EDM.

Fathi, E. (2010). A fully personalization strategy of E-learning scenarios. *Computers in Human Behavior, 26*(4), 581–591. doi:10.1016/j.chb.2009.12.010

Felix, U. (2005). E-learning pedagogy in the third millennium: The need for combining social and cognitive constructivist approaches., J*ournal. ReCALL, 17*(1), 85–100. doi:10.1017/S0958344005000716

Feng-jung, L., & Bai-Jiun, S. (2007). Learning Activity- Based E-Learning Material Recommendation System. *Proceedings of the Ninth IEEE International Symposium on Multimedia Workshops ISMW '07.*

Gao, T., & Lehman, J. D. (2003). The effects of different levels of interaction on the achievement and motivational perceptions of college students in a web-based learning environment. *Journal of Interactive Learning Research, 14*(4), 367–386.

Ghauth, K. I., & Abdullah, N. A. (2010). An empirical evaluation of learner performance in e-learning recommender systems and an adaptive hypermedia system. *Malaysian Journal of Computer Science, 23*(3), 141–152.

Giridharan, A. (2005). Adaptive e-Learning Environment for Students with Divergent Knowledge Levels. *ELTECH INDIA*. Retrieved from www.elearn.cdac.in

Goyal, M., Yadav, D., & Choubey, A. (2012). E-learning: Current State of Art and Future Prospects. *IJCSI International Journal of Computer Science Issues, 9*(2), 490–499.

Grob, H. L., Bensberg, F., & Kaderali, F. (2004). Controlling Open Source Intermediaries – a Web Log Mining Approach. *Proceedings of theInternational Conference on Information Technology Interfaces,* Zagreb (pp. 233-242).

Hamalainen, W., Suhonen, J., Sutinen, E., & Toivonen, H. (2004). Data mining in personalizing distance education courses. *Proceedings of theWorld Conference on Open Learning and Distance Education,* Hong Kong (pp. 1-11).

Hammond, N. 1989, Hypermedia and learning: Who guides whom? In Computer Assisted Learning, LNCS (Vol. 360, pp. 167-181). Berlin: Springer-Verlag.

Han, J., Cheng, H., Xin, D., & Yan, X. (2007). Frequent pattern mining: Current status and future directions. *Journal of Data Mining and Knowledge Discovery, 15*(1), 55–86. doi:10.1007/s10618-006-0059-1

Han, J., & Kamber, M. (2006). *Data Mining, Concepts and Techniques* (2nd ed.). San Francisco, CA, USA: Morgan Kaufmann Publishers Inc.

Hanna, M. (2004). Data Mining in the e-Learning Domain. *Campus-Wide Information Systems, 21*(1), 29–34. doi:10.1108/10650740410512301

Haythornthwaite, C. (2001). Exploring Multiplexity: Social Network Structures in a Computer-Supported Distance Learning Class. *The Information Society International Journal (Toronto, Ont.), 17*(3), 211–226.

Hill, T., & Lewicki, P. (2006). *STATISTICS Methods and Applications*. StatSoft.

Hwang, G.J., Tsai, P.S., Tsai, C.C. & Tseng, J.C.R. (2008). A novel approach for assisting teachers in analyzing student web-searching behaviors. *Computer and Education Journal*, 51, 926-938.

Ingram, A. (1999). Using web server logs in evaluating instructional web sites. *Journal of Educational Technology Systems, 28*(2), 137–157. doi:10.2190/R3AE-UCRY-NJVR-LY6F

Jain, A. K., Murty, M. N., & Flynn, P. J. (1999). Data Clustering: A Review. *ACM Computing Surveys, 31*(3), 264–323. doi:10.1145/331499.331504

Kardan, A. A., Abbaspour, S., & Hendijanifard, F. (2009) A hybrid recommender system for e-learning environments based on concept maps and collaborative tagging. *Proceedings of the 4thInternational Conference on Virtual Learning ICVL.*

Kirkwood, A., & Price, L. (2006). Adaptation for a Changing Environment: Developing learning and teaching with information and communication technologies. *International Review of Research in Open and Distance Learning, 7*(2), 1–14.

Klosgen, W., & Zytkow, J. (2002). *Handbook of data mining and knowledge discovery*. New York: Oxford University Press.

Knutov, E., De Bra, P., & Pechenizkiy, M. (2009). AH 12 years later: A comprehensive survey of adaptive hypermedia methods and techniques. *New Review of Hypermedia and Multimedia, 15*(1), 5–38. doi:10.1080/13614560902801608

Kobsa, A., Chellappa, R. K., & Spiekermann, S. (2007). Privacy-Enhanced Personalization. *Communications of the ACM, 50*(8), 24–33. doi:10.1145/1278201.1278202

Kumaran, V. S., & Sankar, A. (2013). Recommendation System for Adaptive E-learning using Semantic Net. *International Journal of Computers and Applications, 63*(7), 19–24. doi:10.5120/10478-5210

Lin, S.-H. (2012). Data mining for student retention management. *Journal of Computing Sciences in Colleges, 27*(4), 92–99.

Luan, J. (2002). Data Mining and Knowledge Management in Higher Education-Potential Applications. *Paper presented at theAnnual Forum for the Association for Institutional Research*, Toronto, Ontario, Canada.

Mabroukeh, N. R. & Ezeife, C. I. (2010), Taxonomy of Sequential Pattern Mining Algorithms. *ACM Computing Surveys*, 43(1).

Macfadyen, L. P., & Dawson, S. (2010). Mining LMS data to develop an "early warning system" for educators: A proof of concept. *Computers & Education, 54*(2), 588–599. doi:10.1016/j.compedu.2009.09.008

Madria, S. K., Bhowmick, S. S., Ng, W. K., & Lim, E. P. (1999). *Research issues in web data mining* (pp. 303–312). Data Warehousing and Knowledge Discovery.

Mahajan, R. (2014). Real Time Analysis of Attributes Of An Indian E-Learning Site. *The International Journal of E-Learning and Educational Technologies in the Digital Media, 1*(2), 109–114. doi:10.17781/P001706

Mahajan, R., Sodhi, J. S., & Mahajan, V. (2012). Mining User Access Pattern for Adaptive e-learning environments. *International Journal of e-Education, e-Business, e-Management Learning, 2*(4), 277–279.

Mahajan, R., Sodhi, J. S., & Mahajan, V. (2014). Usage Patterns Discovery from a Web Log of an Indian e-learning site: A Case Study. *Education and Information Technologies, 19*, 1–26.

Mahajan, V., Misra, R., & Mahajan, R. (2015). Review of Data Mining Techniques for Churn Prediction in Telecom. *Journal of Information and Organizational Sciences, 39*(2), 183–197.

McIsaac, M. S., Blocher, J. M., Mahes, V., & Vrasidas, C. (1999). Student and Teacher Perceptions of Interaction in Online Computer Mediated Communication. *Journal Educational Media International, 36*(2), 121–131. doi:10.1080/0952398990360206

Miller, J. (2005). Usability in e-learning. Retrieved from www.learningcircuits.org

Mitchell, T. J. F., Chen, S. Y., & Macredie, R. D. (2005). Hypermedia learning and prior knowledge: Domain expertise vs. system expertise. *Journal of Computer Assisted Learning, 21*(1), 53–64. doi:10.1111/j.1365-2729.2005.00113.x

Mobasher, B., Dai, H., Luo, T., & Nakagawa, M. (2001). Effective Personalization based on Association Rule Discovery from web usage data. *Proceedings of the 3rd international workshop on Web information and data management* (pp. 9 – 15). doi:10.1145/502932.502935

Ngai, E. W. T., Xiu, L., & Chau, D. C. K. (2009). Application of data mining techniques in customer relationship management: A literature review and classification. *Expert Systems with Applications, 36*(2), 2592–2602. doi:10.1016/j.eswa.2008.02.021

Nguyen L., & Phung D. (2008). Learner Model in Adaptive Learning. *World Academy of Science, Engineering and Technology*, 45(70), 395-400.

Nsofor, G. C. (2006). *Comparative Analysis of Predictive Data-Mining Techniques* [Doctoral Thesis].

Palace, B. (1996). Data Mining. Retrieved from http://www.anderson.ucla.edu/faculty/jason.frand/teacher/technologies/palace/datamining.htm

Pan, P., Wang, C., Horng, G., & Cheng, S. (2010) The development of an Ontology-Based Adaptive Personalized Recommender System. *Proceedings of the 2010 International Conference On* Electronics and Information Engineering (ICEIE).

Papagelis, M., & Plexousakis, D. (2005). D. Qualitative analysis of user-based and item-based prediction algorithms for recommendation agents. *Engineering Applications of Artificial Intelligence, 18*(7), 781–789. doi:10.1016/j.engappai.2005.06.010

Paramythis A., Loidl-Reisinger S., (2004), Adaptive Learning Environments and e-Learning Standards, *Electronic Journal of eLearning, 2*(1), 181–194.

Pei, J., Han, J., Mortazavi-asl, B., & Zhu, H. (2000). Mining Access Patterns Efficiently from Web Logs. *Proc. of the 2000 Pacific-Asia Conf. on Knowledge Discovery and Data Mining (PAKDD'00)*, Kyoto, Japan.

Peled, A., & Rashty, D. (1999). Logging for success: Advancing the use of WWW logs to improve computer mediated distance learning. *Journal of Educational Computing Research, 21*(4), 413–431.

Phobun, P., & Vicheanpanya, J. (2010). Adaptive intelligent tutoring systems for e-learning systems, Innovation and Creativity in Education. *Procedia: Social and Behavioral Sciences, 2*(2), 4064–4069. doi:10.1016/j.sbspro.2010.03.641

Popescu, E. (2008). *Dynamic Adaptive Hypermedia Systems for E-Learning* [Doctoral Thesis]. University of Craiova, Romania.

Radenkovi, B., Despotovi, M., Bogdanovi, Z., & Bara, D. (2006). Creating Adaptive Environment for e-Learning Courses. *Journal of Information and Organizational Sciences, 33*(1), 179–189.

Raghavan N. R. S. (2005). Data mining in e-commerce: A survey. *Sadhna*, 30(Parts 2 & 3), 275–289.

Riad M., Hamdy K. El-Minir, Haitham A. El-Ghareeb, (2009), Review of e-Learning Systems Convergence from Traditional Systems to Services based Adaptive and Intelligent Systems. *Journal of Convergence Information Technology, 4*(2).

Romero, C., López, M.-I., Luna, J.-M., & Ventura, S. (2013). 'Predicting students' final performance from participation in on-line discussion forums'. *Computers & Education, 68*, 458–472. doi:10.1016/j.compedu.2013.06.009

Romero, C., & Ventura, S. (2006). *Data mining in e-learning*. USA: WIT Press. doi:10.2495/1-84564-152-3

Romero, C., & Ventura, S. (2010). Educational data mining: A review of the state of the art. *Journal of IEEE Transactions on Systems, Man, and Cybernetics, 40*(6), 601–618. doi:10.1109/TSMCC.2010.2053532

Romero, C., Ventura, S., & De Bra, P. (2004). Knowledge discovery with genetic programming for providing feedback to courseware author. *User Modeling and User-Adapted Interaction: The Journal of Personalization Research, 14*(5), 425–464. doi:10.1007/s11257-004-7961-2

Romero, C., Ventura, S., & García, E. (2008). Data mining in course management systems: Moodle case study and tutorial, *Elsevier. Computers & Education, 51*(1), 368–384. doi:10.1016/j.compedu.2007.05.016

Romero, C., Ventura, S., Pechenizkiy, M., & Baker, R. (2010a). *Handbook of Educational Data Mining*. Taylor & Francis. doi:10.1201/b10274

Romero, C., & Ventura, S.Romero & S. Ventura. (2007). Educational Data Mining: A Survey from 1995 to 2005. *Expert Systems with Applications, 33*(1), 135–146. doi:10.1016/j.eswa.2006.04.005

Romero, C., Ventura, S., Zafra, A., & De Bra, P. (2009). Applying Web usage mining for personalizing hyperlinks in Web-based adaptive educational systems. *Computers & Education*, *53*(3), 828–840. doi:10.1016/j.compedu.2009.05.003

Sayyed, M. Ali & Prof. Tuteja R.R. (2014). Data Mining Techniques. *International Journal of Computer Science and Mobile Computing*, *3*(4), 879–883. PMID:25509739

Sfenrianto, Hasibuan Z. A. & Suhartanto H. (2011). The Influence Factors of Inherent Structure in e-Learning Process, *International Journal of e-Education, e-Business, e-. Management Learning*, *1*(3), 217–222.

Sheard, J., Albrecht, D., & Butbul, E. (2005, July 2-6). ViSION: Visualizing student interactions online. *Proceedings of the 11th Australasian World Wide Web Conference (AusWeb05)*, Queensland, Australia (pp. 48–58).

Shen, R., Yang, F., & Han, P. (2002). Data analysis center based on eLearning platform. In *Workshop The Internet Challenge* (pp. 19–28). Berlin, Germany: Technology and Applications.

Shishehchi, S., Banihashem, S. Y., Zin, N. A. M., & Noah, S. A. M. (2011) Review of personalized recommendation techniques for learners in elearning systems. in Semantic Technology and Information Retrieval (STAIR). *Proceedings of the2011 International Conference*.

Shute, V., & Towle, B. (2003). Adaptive E-Learning. *Educational Psychologist*, *38*(2), 105–114. doi:10.1207/S15326985EP3802_5

Souali, K., Afia, A. E., Faizi, R., & Chiheb (2011) R. A new recommender system for e-learning environments. *Proceedings of the 2011 International Conference on Multimedia Computing and Systems (ICMCS)*.

Spacco, J., Winters, T., & Payne, T. (2006). Inferring use cases from unit testing. Proceedings of the AAAI Workshop on Educational Data Mining, New York (pp. 1-7).

Srivastava, J., Cooley, R., Deshpande, M., & Tan, P. (2000). Web usage mining: Discovery and applications of usage patterns from web data. *SIGKDD Explorations*, *1*(2), 12–23. doi:10.1145/846183.846188

Suppes. (n. d.). Addressing diversity in e-learning. Retrieved from http://suppes-corpus.stanford.edu/articles/comped/426.pdf

Surjono, H. D. (2011). The Design of Adaptive E-Learning System based on Student's Learning Styles. *International Journal of Computer Science and Information Technologies*, *2*(5), 2350–2353.

Valsamidis, S., Kontogiannis, S., Kazanidis, I., & Karakos, A. (2011). E-Learning Platform Usage Analysis. *Interdisciplinary Journal of E-Learning and Learning Objects*, *7*(1), 185-204.

Vanijja, V., & Supattathum, M. (2006). Statistical analysis of eLearning usage in a university. *Proceedings of the Third International Conference on eLearning for Knowledge-Based Society*, Bangkok, Thailand (pp. 22.1-22.5).

Vatcharaporn, E., Supaporn, L., & Clemens, B. (2009). Student Modelling in Adaptive E-Learning Systems, Knowledge Management and E-Learning. *International Journal (Toronto, Ont.)*, *3*(3), 342–355.

Venkatadri, M., & Reddy, L.C. (2011). A Review on Data mining from Past to the Future. *International Journal of Computer Applications*, 15(7), 19-22.

Walker, A., Recker, M., Lawless, K., & Wiley, D. (2004). Collaborative Information Filtering: A Review and an Educational Application. *International Journal of Artificial Intelligence in Education*, *14*(1), 3–24.

Wang, F.-H., & Shao, H.-M. (2004). Effective personalized recommendation based on time-framed navigation clustering and association mining. *Expert Systems with Applications*, *27*(3), 365–377. doi:10.1016/j.eswa.2004.05.005

Wang, L., Li, J., Ding, L., & Li, P. (2009), E-Learning Evaluation System Based on Data Mining. *Proceedings of the 2010 2nd International Symposium on Information Engineering and Electronic Commerce (IEEC)*.

Watson, S. F., Apostolou, B., Hassell, J. M., & Webber, S. A. (2007). Accounting education literature review (2003-2005). *Journal of Accounting Education*, *25*(1), 1–58. doi:10.1016/j.jaccedu.2007.01.001

Whyte, C. B., & Bolyard, C. (1989). Student Affairs-The Future. *Journal of College Student Development*, *30*, 86–89.

Xindong, W. (2014). Data Mining with Big data. *IEEE Transactions on Knowledge and Data Engineering*, *26*(1), 97–107. doi:10.1109/TKDE.2013.109

Yusuf, N., & Al-Banawi, N. (2013). The Impact of Changing Technology: The Case of E-Learning. *Contemporary Issues in Education Research*, *6*(2), 173–180. doi:10.19030/cier.v6i2.7726

Zaiane, O. R. (2001). Web Usage Mining for a Better Web-Based Learning Environment (Technical Report TR01-05). Department of Computing Science, University of Alberta.

Zorrilla, M. E., Menasalvas, E., Marin, D., Mora, E., & Segovia, J. (2005). Web usage mining project for improving web-based learning sites. *Proceedings of the International Conference on Computer Aided Systems Theory*, Las Palmas de Gran Canaria, Spain (pp. 205-210).

Chapter 2
Modified Single Pass Clustering Algorithm Based on Median as a Threshold Similarity Value

Mamta Mittal
G. B. Pant Govt. Engineering College, India

V.P. Singh
Thapar University, India

R. K. Sharma
Thapar University, India

Lalit Mohan Goyal
Bharati Vidyapeeth College of Enineering, India

ABSTRACT

Clustering is one of the data mining techniques that investigates these data resources for hidden patterns. Many clustering algorithms are available in literature. This chapter emphasizes on partitioning based methods and is an attempt towards developing clustering algorithms that can efficiently detect clusters. In partitioning based methods, k-means and single pass clustering are popular clustering algorithms but they have several limitations. To overcome the limitations of these algorithms, a Modified Single Pass Clustering (MSPC) algorithm has been proposed in this work. It revolves around the proposition of a threshold similarity value. This is not a user defined parameter; instead, it is a function of data objects left to be clustered. In our experiments, this threshold similarity value is taken as median of the paired distance of all data objects left to be clustered. To assess the performance of MSPC algorithm, five experiments for k-means, SPC and MSPC algorithms have been carried out on artificial and real datasets.

INTRODUCTION

Today, every organization is dealing with data repository systems like relational databases, data warehouses, temporal databases, transactional databases, spatial databases, multimedia databases or the World Wide Web, but a lot of them are not able to take advantage of their huge repositories. Data to be stored is often diverse in nature ranging from scientific to medical, geographic to demographic, financial to marketing as well as the volume of data is so high that human analyst cannot predict it without special tools. To automatically understand and analyze the data effectively and efficiently, the field of data min-

DOI: 10.4018/978-1-5225-0489-4.ch002

ing has emerged in recent years. One of the data mining tools that can be used to group the data objects into unknown classes is clustering. The goal of clustering is to discover the natural grouping among data objects such that the data objects in the same group are similar to one another and dissimilar to the data objects in other groups. Intensive research has been carried out in this field and many algorithms have been proposed. But, clustering is an NP-hard problem due to which the existing approaches have some limitations. To deal with the limitations of existing methods, research is continuously being done in this area. Beside this, collaborating Filtering which has its roots in data mining has now become recent research area for the researcher. It is a method of automatic filtering about the user's interest or likeness by collecting their preferences from many users (collaborating). Use of clustering helps a lot in the collaborating filtering as clustering gathers the information of similar liking users in one group and dissimilar liking users in others groups. When groups or clusters of same liking will be available then based on the user interest or user participation collaborating filtering further predict them.

Data Mining is so popular because it is used to mine interesting data from a large amount of data akin to the extraction of minerals from mineral ores. Most international organizations produce high amounts of information that could never be read by any person in a lifetime. The situation is even more alarming in the world wide networks. These days, gigabytes of data are distributed and exchanged over the world, the existing database management system allow retrieval of data but provide no tools to analyze it. Analysis is beneficial for unearthing the hidden relationships among the data. Data mining is one of the data analysis tools. It goes beyond the idea of conventional data analysis. It uses traditional analysis tools like statistics and graphics in conjunction with those associated with the field of artificial intelligence such as rule induction and artificial neural networks. It is an amalgam of all of these, but still somehow different.

Data mining is a distinctive approach towards the usual data analysis in the sense that the emphasis is not as much on extracting the facts as on generating the hypotheses. It is also capable of generating new business opportunities, the only condition being the provision of databases of sufficient size and acceptable quality. It is popular as it has the following capabilities:

- **Prediction of Trends and Behaviors**: It automates the tedious process of finding predictive behavior or information in huge databases. Before the emergence of data mining field, queries required excessive hands-on analysis, but now they can respond quickly and can be automated. Data mining analyzes past data to identify future trends. A common example is to know the future trends of the stock market.
- **Automated Discovery of Previously Unknown Patterns**: Data mining tools play a great role in identifying patterns which were previously hidden by sweeping through the database. A common example is to identify correlated products from the data of retail sales.

The field of data mining encompasses mainly three techniques: association rule mining, classification and clustering. These techniques are explained briefly as:

Association Rule Mining (ARM) generates an implication between two or more data objects of a database. In a transactional database for the given items, an association rule, $X \overset{m\_sup}{\Rightarrow} Y$, is an implication where X and Y are disjoint sets of items; m_sup is the value of minimum support. The meaning of such an implication is that $m\_sup\%$ transactions of a database which contain X also contain Y. For example, 90% ($m\_sup\%$) of the customers who purchase milk and eggs ($X = \{milk, eggs\}$) also purchase apples and onions ($Y = \{apples, onions\}$). In other words, the meaning of such rules is that *m_sup%* transactions of the given database have all the items of set X and all the items of set Y. The *m_sup* is a user defined parameter.

Classification is a supervised learning technique which classifies the data objects into pre-defined classes or categories. Its objective is to precisely classify each data object into a target class. For example, a new model of car can be put into one of the existing categories like hatchback, sedan. A classification model is derived based on the analysis of a set of training data. These models may be represented in various forms, like classification rules, decision trees or neural networks. A well-known classification problem is the binary classification, also known as IF-THEN rules. In this classification, the target attribute has only two possible values: low or high. In other type of classifications, target attribute has more than two values: very low, low, medium, high or very high. These types are represented by decision trees. Decision tree can easily be transformed to classification rules.

Clustering, unlike classification, analyzes data objects without considering class labels. It is an unsupervised learning technique which groups the data objects into unknown classes. The grouping of data objects is based on the principle of maximizing the intra-class similarity and minimizing the inter-class similarity. As clustering does not use pre-defined class labels, it is distinct from classification which seek to find rules for classifying data objects into pre-defined classes. A clustering algorithm should possess the following characteristics:

- **Scalability**: Scalability is the key issue in the implementation of clustering algorithm. These must be scalable for large as well as for high dimensional databases.
- **Dealing with Different Types of Attributes:** Although a major proportion of algorithms are developed in sync with numerical data as input, it is necessary for the algorithms to accommodate other formats too. These could be binary numbers, spatial data, ordinal data, or even a mixture of two or more of these data types according to the application that the algorithm serves.
- **Discovering Clusters with Arbitrary Shape**: A cluster's shape cannot be predetermined. Basic clustering algorithms based on the distance measure typically discover clusters to be of the same density and size with spherical boundaries. Though, this might not be true for every dataset. Hence, clustering algorithms should be designed in such a way that identify and work equally well with arbitrarily shaped clusters.
- **Minimal Requirements for Domain Knowledge to Determine Input Parameters:** In many algorithms there is a demand for the users to enter values of some predefined parameters for the algorithm to run and determine the clusters. These values supplied by the users can often be very crucial to how the end result of the clustering turns out. This brings a lot of pressure on the users as the values should be accurate. In addition, it also puts the quality of the algorithm in jeopardy.
- **Ability to Deal with Noise and Outliers**: Unlike ideal datasets that algorithms are designed to deal with, real world datasets are full of erroneous, missing, unknown data or outliers. Thus, algorithms should be resilient enough to handle such aberrations so that the quality of results generated is not compromised.
- **Insensitivity to the Order of Input Records**: The manner or the sequence in which the data is given to the algorithm should not have an impact on the clustering results. Hence, it is crucial that the algorithm's behavior remains independent of the order in which it receives the input.

- **High Dimensionality**: Algorithms, in general, work well with low dimensionality in the input datasets. Though, a database or a data warehouse in the real world is characterized by the presence of two or more attributes. Thus, the algorithms should be capable of successfully clustering multi-dimensional data.
- **Constraint Based Clustering**: Since real world models are implied by many constraints like domain knowledge, user given preferences. Clustering algorithms should also be adept to handle these constraints.
- **Interpretability and Usability**: The results of a clustering algorithm should be easily represented, understood and interpreted by its users. The results generated are of not very useful if they cannot be successfully comprehended by the concerned parties. Thus, it is imperative to study the ultimate goal of an application before a clustering method can be employed.

Many algorithms are available in literature to find the interesting patterns in a given dataset. Partitioning based methods, one of the popular clustering methods, is the major focus of this research work. There are many algorithms like k-means, k-medoid, k-mode and single pass clustering available in literature under the partitioning based methods. This chapter describes the detailed description of k-means and single pass clustering algorithms. A modified single pass clustering algorithm based on the median threshold similarity value has been proposed in this chapter. The proposed algorithm is compared with k-means and single pass clustering algorithms on the artificial and real datasets.

BACKGROUND

Development of algorithms for the automatic extraction of the relevant information from the datasets has been a dream of human beings since a long time. People had been working for the realization of this dream even before the emergence of data mining. In 1960s, statisticians used the terms like "Data Fishing" or "Data Dredging" to retrieve the information from the datasets. They proposed number of algorithms to partition the datasets into disjoint sets before the term "Data mining" emerged. Like in 1967, MacQueen has proposed k-means algorithm which is a multi-pass algorithm for obtaining disjoint sets. After that, Salton (1971) introduced single pass algorithm to partition the datasets. Duda and Hart (1973) described the importance of partitioning the datasets in the field of pattern recognition.

In 1982, Lloyd proposed k-means algorithm for partitioning the datasets into k disjoint sets. In these disjoint sets, distance between the data objects and their centroids is minimum. Alternately, Kaufman and Rousseeuw (1987) proposed k-medoid algorithm which is based on the search of k representatives called medoids in a given dataset. These medoids partition the dataset into k disjoint sets. In these sets, distance between data objects and their medoid is minimum. In 1993, Quinlan introduced the C4.5 algorithm that generates a classifier and expressed it in the form of decision tree. This decision tree is based on the attribute's information gain which splits the dataset into various classes.

In December 2008, top 10 algorithms are identified at the IEEE *I*nternational *C*onference on *D*ata *M*ining (*ICDM*) meeting (Wu *et al.*, 2008). These algorithms are being used by the research community in the field of classification, integration mining, rough sets, link mining, clustering, bagging and boosting, statistical learning, sequential patterns, *etc*. The identified algorithms are C4.5, *S*upport *V*ector *M*achine (*SVM*), EM, k-means, Apriori, kNN, PageRank, Naïve Bayes, AdaBoost and CART. These algorithms remain to be the most influential algorithms in the field of data mining that continue to engage researchers.

k-means algorithm is an active research area since researchers encountered the following problems in this algorithm.

- How to know the number of clusters present in the datasets?
- How to provide the initial centroids for clustering?
- How to overcome the effect of outliers on the quality of clustering?

Knowledge about the dataset is a major stimulant for finding the number of clusters that could exist in it. One such algorithm that determines the number of clusters has been proposed by Ray and Turi (1999). This algorithm is applied to the segments of color images and measured the compactness and separation for different values of k. They have inferred that the minimum ratio of compactness to the separation produces the actual number of clusters present in the image.

In order to determine the number of clusters, a gap statistic was introduced by Tibshirani *et al.* (2001). This gap statistic is a measure of difference between observed intra-cluster to the expected intra-cluster distance. This minimum difference determines the optimal value of k. The gap statistic measure has been replaced by a new function given by Pham *et al.* (2004). This function measures the ratio of the real distortion to the estimated distortion for a uniform distribution of the data objects. The minimum value of this function determines the number of cluster present in the dataset. The gap statistic measure compares the dispersion of the clustered data objects but it may overestimate the number of clusters. Inspired from the gap statistic method, weighted gap and data distribution weighted gap methods have been proposed by Yan (2005). In the weighted gap method, averaged pair wise distance among all the data objects of a cluster is considered. This method may also overestimate the number of clusters, yet gives better results than the gap statistic method. The data distribution weighted gap method searches for an optimal number of clusters so that the observed gap is sufficiently small under suitable reference distribution.

McCullagh and Yang (2008) have proposed an improved Dirichlet allocation model to determine the number of clusters. Wang *et al.* (2009) has determined the number of clusters by creating the *R*eordered *D*issimilarity *I*mage (*RDI*) of an image dataset. *RDI* analyzes the clustering tendency of the images. It is helpful in identifying the clusters in the form of dark blocks that lie along the diagonal of the image corresponding to the dense areas of the image. Thereafter, a black and white image is created followed by filtering, transforming and projecting the pixel values on to the diagonal axis of the image. The first order derivative is computed for the diagonal axis of the image and the major peaks and valleys are used to decide the number of clusters.

In k-means algorithm, the problem of initialization of centroids has been solved by Katsavounidis *et al.* (1994). They considered the very first centroid in one corner of the dataset having highest norm. Subsequently, other centroids are selected as farthest data objects from the data objects selected so far. In this process, the number of centroids selected is equal to the number of clusters required in the datasets. Bradley and Fayyad (1998a) proposed a sampling method to initialize the cluster centroids. Data samples are clustered using k-means algorithm for the given value of k. After that, centroids of all the samples are clustered again for the same value of k; and now, the obtained centroids act as the initial centroids for the entire dataset. Likas *et al.* (2003) presented a global k-means algorithm. In this algorithm, initial centroids are obtained dynamically one at a time until number of centroids is equal to the value of k. First initial centroid is obtained by executing the k-means algorithm for $k = 1$. In this case, the mean value of the dataset acts as the first initial centroid. Second initial centroid is obtained by executing the k-means algorithm for $k = 2$. In this case, each data object is considered a temporary initial centroid until better partition is acquired. Subsequently, k centroids are obtained by executing the k-means algorithm for required value of k.

Khan and Ahmad (2004) have proposed an algorithm for initialization of cluster centroids. This algorithm focused on the values of individual attributes. The mean and standard deviation of each attribute is computed to calculate importance of an attribute in terms of percentile. Then, attributes are partitioned by executing the k-means algorithm. Each data object is labeled according to the clustering results obtained from these partitions and a string of labels is generated corresponding to each attribute. Data objects with the same strings are merged into a single cluster. If the number of clusters generated is more than the required number of clusters, then density based data compression is used to get the required number of clusters. Finally, the mean value of k clusters is used as k initial centroids for clustering the data objects in full dimensional space. Yuan *et al.* (2004) proposed a method to form a group of similar data objects with the help of adjacency matrix. Each group consists of fixed number of data objects. Initially, in the first group, two closest objects are assigned. Other objects are added in the group that has closest distance to any member of the group till number of data objects is equal to the given fixed value. Afterwards, other k-1 groups of similar data objects are generated dynamically from the remaining data objects. Mean of each group is considered as the initial centroids.

Redmond and Heneghan (2007) proposed the initialization method for k-means clustering algorithm using k-d tree. The dataset is partitioned into smaller partitions till either k number of partitions are obtained or the partitions contain a predefined number of data objects. Centroids of the partitions are obtained according to the partition axis perpendicular to the highest variance derived by principal component analysis. These centroids act as initial centroids for the entire dataset. Arthur and Vassilvitskii (2007) extended the work of Katsavounidis *et al.* (1994). In this method, the centroids are selected probabilistically, except the first centroid. The probability of their selection is proportional to their distance from the selected data objects. Deelers and Auwatanamongkol (2007) considered all the data objects in a single cell. Then, a data object splits the cell into two cells. This data object minimizes the squared Euclidean distance of all data objects present in the cells. Subsequently, cells are partitioned until k cells are formed. Now, centroid of each cell acts as initial centroids for the entire dataset.

Chiang and Mirkin (2009) extracted anomalous centroids by considering origin as a reference point. These centroids are used to form clusters. Small sized clusters are removed and the remaining clusters are the true clusters present in the dataset. The centroids of the remaining clusters act as initial centroids. Cao *et al.* (2009) used the rough set model to measure the cohesion degree of the nearest object and coupling degree between the neighborhood objects. The k objects which have maximum cohesion degree but some fixed coupling degree are selected as initial centroids. Li (2011) proposed a centroid initialization method for the datasets having two clusters. In this method two nearest neighbor pairs are considered that are most dissimilar. These pairs should not be in the same cluster and moreover, should not be on the partitioning boundary of clusters. The mean of such selected pairs is considered as the initial centroids. Erisoglu *et al.* (2011) proposed a neighborhood model for initialization of cluster centroids. The mean object of the entire dataset is determined. Then, the data object farthest from the mean object is selected as the first initial centroid; second initial centroid is selected which is farthest from the first initial centroid; subsequently, the kth initial centroid is selected at the distance farthest from the $(k-1)^{th}$ initial centroid. Data objects once selected as the initial centroids are not considered again.

Reddy and Jana (2012) have given a novel method to select the initial centroids with the help of the Voronoi diagram. It is formed from the given set of data objects. The initial centroids will be those data objects which lie on the boundary of the Voronoi circles having highest radius. Zhang and Cheng (2013) proposed an initialization method based on the density. Density of all data objects is determined and the data objects with the same density are considered in the homogeneous group. Representative of each group acts as the initial centroid. Celebi *et al.* (2013) have given an exhaustive survey on various methods to initialize the centroids.

Fahim *et al.* (2006) proposed a variant of *k*-means algorithm. It improves the implementation of standard *k*-means algorithm by considering two data structures- first is used to store the index and the second is used to store the Euclidean distance. During iterations, previous distance of each data object is compared with the distance to its updated centroid. For an object, if previous distance is less than the new distance then the object is clustered with updated centroids.

Zalik (2008) has proposed an efficient *k*-means algorithm. It does not require the number of clusters to be generated. In this algorithm, a cluster membership function is defined which assigns data objects to the nearest centroid. The proposed algorithm consists of two phases: the first phase involves pre-processing procedures that carry out the initial clustering and the second phase adjusts the centroids in a way that minimizes the newly defined membership function.

Quality of clustering algorithms decreases when the dataset has spherical shaped cluster with large variance. A solution to this problem has been provided by Fahim *et al.* (2008a). In this solution, the centroid of the large clusters is shifted towards the small clusters. For this purpose, initially, radius of the large and its neighboring small clusters is determined. If the radius of large cluster overlaps with the radius of small cluster, the average mean value of their centroids is calculated. The data objects of small clusters are grouped again using *k*-means algorithm with two initial centroids. These initial centroids are: calculated average mean value and centroid of small cluster. The data objects close to the average mean value becomes the members of large cluster and the data objects close to the centroid of small cluster does not change their membership.

Lai *et al.* (2009) measured the displacement of cluster centers during iterations. If the center of cluster does not move, *i.e.*, displacement is zero, then it means that no new member is added in the cluster; otherwise cluster is active. In their method, computation time increases linearly when using *k-d* tree, otherwise, it increases exponentially. Cluster membership and geometrical information of the data objects is considered by Lai and Huang (2010). In addition to this, a set of inequalities are also incorporated to determine the centroid of first cluster. Multiple centroid selection method is employed to determine centroids of other clusters. Jain (2010) has provided a survey of last 50 years on the popularity of *k*-means algorithm and has elaborated some of the emerging and useful research directions. Cardot *et al.* (2012) proposed a recursive algorithm for clustering large datasets. This algorithm can easily handle large sample of high dimensional data.

Recently, Scitovski and Sabo (2014) proposed a technique to resolve the case when data object lies on the border of two or more clusters. In this technique, a unit weight is associated to all the data objects except the overlapped data objects. The weight of overlapped data object is uniformly divided in two or more clusters. For each participating cluster, the centroid and the objective function are calculated. The overlapped data objects become member of the cluster which gives better clustering with lower value of the objective function.

Salton (1971) introduced single pass clustering algorithm to cluster the data objects. First data object is randomly selected and assigned to the first cluster; second data object is again selected randomly and it is compared with the centroid of first cluster. If it is similar to first cluster, then it is assigned as member of first cluster; otherwise forms a new cluster. The level of similarity is defined by the given threshold value. Subsequently, other data objects are clustered. Salton and Wong developed a retrieval system for this algorithm in 1978.

Types of Partitioning Based Methods

There are two types of partitioning based methods: single pass clustering and multi-pass clustering. Single pass clustering, as the name implies, requires only one pass to cluster the given data objects; the time complexity of this method is of the order $O(nk)$. Multi-pass clustering is an iterative approach to cluster the given dataset; the time complexity of this method is of the order $O(nkl)$. Here, n is the number of data object, k is the number of clusters and l is the number of iterations.

k-Means Algorithm

k-means is a popular multi-pass partitioning based algorithm. It aims to find k number of clusters that have minimum sum of squared distance between the data objects and the centroids. In this algorithm, k is a user defined parameter and centroid is the mean value of data objects of a cluster. Distance between data objects d_i and d_j is calculated using Euclidean distance measure which is defined as:

$$dis\left(\boldsymbol{d}_i, \boldsymbol{d}_j\right) = \sqrt{(x_i^1 - x_j^1)^2 + (x_i^2 - x_j^2)^2 + \ldots + (x_i^d - x_j^d)^2} \tag{1}$$

where, $\boldsymbol{d}_i = \left(x_i^1, x_i^2, \ldots, x_i^d\right)$ and $\boldsymbol{d}_j = \left(x_j^1, x_j^2, \ldots, x_j^d\right)$ are d-dimensional data objects. Let $D = \left\{d_1, d_2, \ldots, d_n\right\}$ be the dataset of d-dimensional data objects that need to be partitioned into a set of k clusters $\left(K = \left\{k_1, k_2, \ldots, k_k\right\}\right)$. Each cluster has its own representative called centroid which is also a d-dimensional object. Centroids are represented by a centroid set $C = \left\{c_1, c_2, \ldots, c_k\right\}$. Centroid c_j is a d-dimensional object of cluster k_j, the value of ith dimension of centroid c_j is calculated as:

$$c_j^i = \frac{1}{m} \sum_{p=1}^{m} x_p^i \tag{2}$$

where, m is the number of data objects in cluster k_j and x_p^i is the value of ith dimension of pth data object belonging to cluster k_j. Similarly, other dimensions of centroid c_j are calculated. Initially, data objects are not the members of any cluster; k centroids are selected from the given dataset as the initial centroids of the k clusters; the distance of each data object from the k centroids is calculated using (1); data object is assigned as the member of cluster when the distance of this object is least from the centroid of that cluster. Now, centroid of each cluster is updated using (2). This process is repeated until a data object changes its cluster. This algorithm is simple to implement, so it is widely used for clustering. These steps of k-means algorithm are depicted in Figure 1.

Figure 1. Flow chart of k-means algorithm

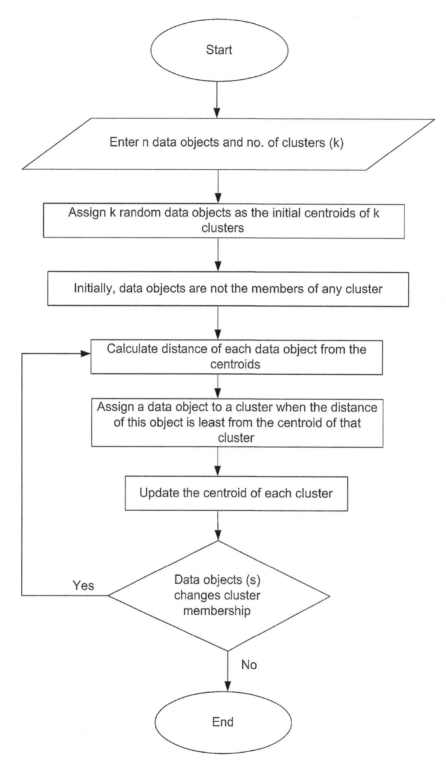

Single Pass Clustering Algorithm

Single Pass Clustering (*SPC*) is a popular one pass partitioning based algorithm. This algorithm is used to cluster the data objects based on the user defined threshold similarity value (T_{th}). Threshold similarity value is the maximum permissible distance between the data object and the centroid of a cluster. Initially, a random data object is assigned to the first cluster; this data object also serves as the initial centroid. Remaining data objects are iteratively merged into the existing clusters or form a new cluster based upon the given threshold similarity value. Unlike *k*-means algorithm, all the data objects need not to be in main memory during iterations; but like *k*-means algorithm, centroids are always present in the main memory. The steps involved in *SPC* algorithm are depicted in Figure 2.

Figure 2. Flow chart of SPC algorithm

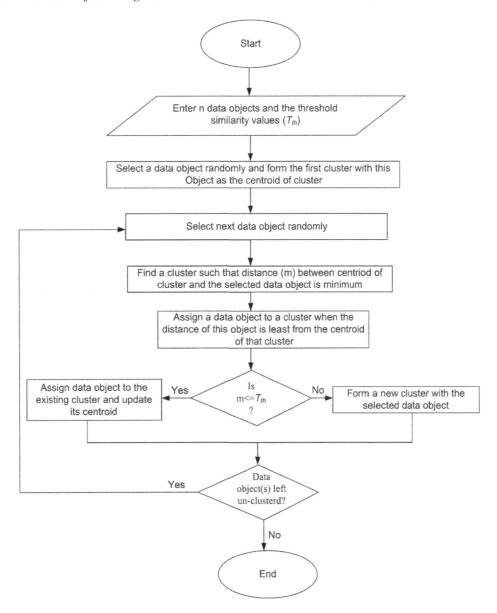

Limitations of *k*-Means and *SPC* Algorithms

A critical look at the *k*-means and *SPC* algorithms uncover the following shortcomings:

- In *k*-means clustering algorithm, the number of clusters (*k*) needs to be specified beforehand.
- *k*-means algorithm is dependent on the selection of initial centroids. Due to this, *k*-means is vulnerable to the local optima and may miss the global optima. Consequently, this suboptimal clustering requires multiple runs with updated initial centroids.
- *k*-means algorithm is sensitive to outliers. Their presence can affect the quality of clustering.
- *k*-means algorithm initializes cluster centroids randomly and iteratively updates them to have minimum sum of squared distance between the data objects and the centroids of clusters. Nevertheless, iterations are indefinite as *k*-means algorithm terminates only when stable clusters are formed.
- *SPC* algorithm depends on the order of selection of data objects.
- *SPC* algorithm requires threshold similarity value as a user defined parameter.
- *k*-means and *SPC* algorithms generate spherical clusters.

To overcome these limitations, a modified *SPC* algorithm has been proposed in this work.

MODIFIED SINGLE PASS CLUSTERING ALGORITHM

Modified Single Pass Clustering (*MSPC*) algorithm revolves around the proposition of a threshold similarity value. This is not a user defined parameter; instead, it is a function of data objects left to be clustered. In this algorithm, data objects are selected randomly and assigned to either one of the existing clusters or form a new cluster based on the threshold similarity value. Here, threshold similarity value is not a constant; rather, it is updated during the execution of proposed algorithm. In our experiments, this threshold similarity value is taken as median of the paired distance of all data objects left to be clustered. An adjacency matrix $\left(A \right)$ is used to store the paired distance between all the data objects.

Once a data object is clustered, its distance to other data objects is removed from the adjacency matrix; and threshold similarity value is updated to a new value.

The threshold similarity value as a median is calculated as when a_{ij}'s are sorted:

$$T_{th}\left(= f\left(A \right) \right) =$$

$$
\left[
\begin{array}{l}
Value\, of\, a_{ij}\, at\, postition \left(\dfrac{t\left(t-1\right)}{4} \right) when\, t\left(t-1\right)/2\, is\, odd \\[4mm]
Averge\, Value\, of\, a_{ij}\, at\, postition \left(\dfrac{t\left(t-1\right)}{4} \right) and \left(\dfrac{t\left(t-1\right)}{4}+1 \right) when\, t\left(t-1\right)/2\, is\, even
\end{array}
\right]
\tag{3}
$$

where, A $(= a_{ij})$ is the adjacency matrix, a_{ij} being the distance between data objects $\boldsymbol{d}_i$ and $\boldsymbol{d}_j$ and t is the number of data objects left to be clustered.

The proposed algorithm consists of the following steps:

1. Select Random data object from database D and consider it as the member and the centroid of first cluster.
2. Calculate Threshold similarity value (T_{th}) as defined in eq. (3).
3. Select the next data object randomly. Measure the distance between centroids of existing clusters and the selected random object and find minimum among them.
4. Compare this minimum distance with threshold similarity value (T_{th}), if it is less than T_{th} value then selected object will be part of one of the existing clusters whose centroid has minimum distance from the selected object.
5. Update the centroid of existing cluster when the selected object is added in the existing cluster.
6. Recalculate threshold similarity value (T_{th}) by removing distance of selected data objects to others left objects.
7. Go to step c and repeats d, e, f until objects left to cluster.

These steps are presented below in algorithm *MSPC* (*D*, *A*).
Algorithm MSPC (D, A).

//Input: Let $D = \{d_1, d_2, \ldots, d_n\}$ be a set of n data objects to cluster and a set $A = \{a_{ij} \mid a_{ij} = distance\,between\,data\,objects\,d_i\,and\,d_j\,for\,1 \leq i,j \leq n\,and\,j\rangle i\}$

//Output: A set $K = \{k_1, k_2, \ldots, k_k\}$ denotes k clusters and a set $C = \{c_1, c_2, \ldots, c_k\}$ denotes centroids of these clusters.

- $s = 1$;
- $k_s = \{d_p \mid \exists d_p \in D\}$; // $randomly\,select\,a\,\,data\,object\,d_p\,from\,D$
- $K = \{k_s\}$; $c_s = d_p$;
- $C = \{c_s\}$; // consider this object as centroid and first object
- $T_{th} = f\left(A\right)$ //defined in (3)

$while\left(n \geq 1\right)do$

$select\,next\,random\,data\,object\,d_q \in \{D\} - d_p$

$calculate\,T_{th} = f\left(A\right)by\,removing\,distance\,of\,selected\,object\,to\,others\,left\,objects.$

$do\,for\,each\,centroid\,c_r \in C$

- $do\,s_{c_r} = dis\left(d_q, c_r\right)$; // $dis\left(d_q, c_r\right)is\,\,the\,distance\,between\,d_q\,and\,c_r$
- $s_{c_j} = min\left(s_{c_1}, s_{c_2}, s_{c_3}, \ldots, s_{c_r}\right)$;

if $\left(s_{c_j} \leq T_{th}\right)$

- ***then*** $k_j = k_j \cup d_q$;

- ○　　*Update centroid c_j of cluster k_j*;
- ○　　***else*** $s = s + 1$;
- ○　　$k_s = \left\{ d_q \right\}$;
- ○　　$K = K \cup \left\{ k_s \right\}$;
- ○　　$c_s = d_q$;
- ○　　$n = n - 1$;

PERFORMANCE EVALUATION OF *MSPC* ALGORITHM BASED ON MEDIAN AS A THRESHOLD VALUE

In *k*-means algorithm, *k* random data objects are considered as the initial centroids; in the *SPC* algorithm, a constant threshold similarity value is given by the user; and in the proposed *MSPC* algorithm, median of paired distance of data objects has been considered as threshold similarity value. This section is divided into two sub-sections; in the first sub-section, the experiments have been performed on the artificial datasets; in the second sub-section, the experiments have been performed on the real datasets.

Artificial Datasets Experiments

To perform the experiments, fifteen artificial datasets each containing five hundred *2-D* data objects have been created. These data objects are generated randomly in the range of 100 to 499 in both dimensions. In *k*-means algorithm, the value of *k* is taken in the range of 4 to 10, in *SPC* algorithm, the value of threshold is taken in the range of 50 to 75 and in *MSPC* algorithm, threshold similarity value is calculated using (3) respectively. In these experiments, quality of clustering algorithms is assessed by means of separation and compactness validity measures and further, they are validated on Dunn and *DB* validity indices.

Figure 3 , Figure 4 and Figure 5 illustrate the single linkage, complete linkage and centroid linkage separation measures, respectively, for *k*-means, *SPC* and *MSPC* algorithms.

Figures 6 and Figure 7 show the centroid linkage and averaged paired compactness measures, respectively, for *k*-means, *SPC* and *MSPC* algorithms. From these figures, it can also be observed that clusters generated by *MSPC* algorithm are more separate and compact than the clusters generated by *k*-means and *SPC* algorithms.

It is not possible to draw conclusion about better clustering algorithm based upon compactness and separation alone. So, these algorithms are also evaluated on Dunn and *DB* index. Dunn index is used to measure the ratio of separation to compactness. Value of this index should be large for a good clustering algorithm. Figure 8 shows its value for *k*-means, *SPC* and *MSPC* algorithms. From this figure, it is evident that *MSPC* algorithm provides large value of Dunn index than the *k*-means and *SPC* algorithms.

DB index is used to measure the ratio of compactness to separation. Value of this index should be small for a good clustering algorithm. Figure 9 shows its value for *k*-means, *SPC* and *MSPC* algorithms. From this figure, it is evident that *MSPC* algorithm provides small value of *DB* index than the *k*-means and *SPC* algorithms.

Figure 3. Single linkage separation using median value as a threshold

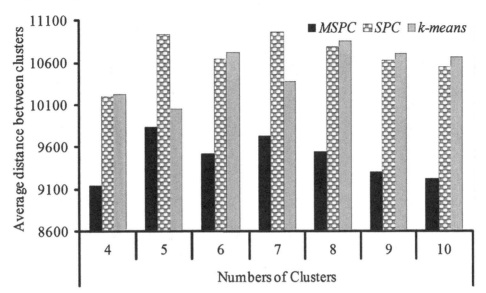

Figure 4. Complete linkage separation using median value as a threshold

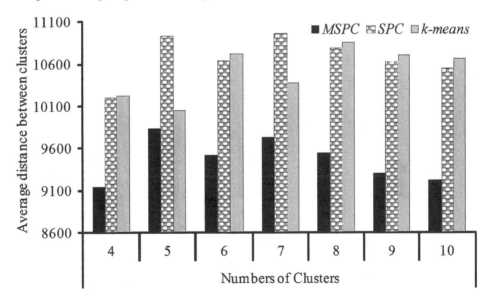

The experimental results obtained on artificial datasets confirm that *MSPC* algorithm is an efficient algorithm as it generates well separated and compact clusters. It also provides large Dunn index and small *DB* index values. Even though, these experiments are not the sole criteria to confirm its performance better than the *k*-means and *SPC* algorithms, it is evaluated on real datasets with threshold similarity value again taken as median of the data objects left to be clustered in the next section.

Figure 5. Centroid linkage separation using median value as a threshold

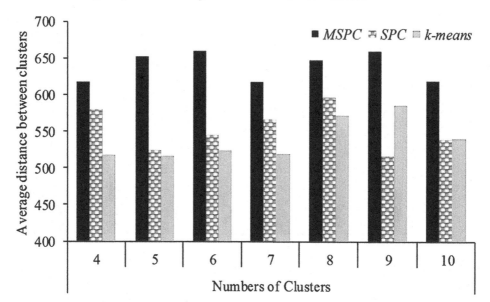

Figure 6. Centroid linkage compactness using median value as a threshold

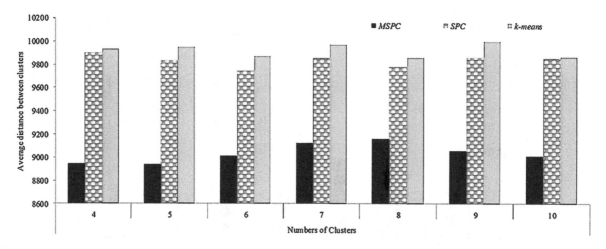

Real Datasets Experiments

Experiments have been carried out on real datasets in which threshold similarity value is taken as the median of paired distance of data objects. Four real datasets: Ecoli, Iris, Seeds and Wine have been considered. These datasets are taken from the UCI repository (http://archive.ics.uci.edu/ml/datasets. html). Table 1 shows the characteristics of these datasets.

The *MSPC* algorithm is executed 1000 times and a varying number of clusters are generated; and then the same number of clusters is generated by the *k*-means and *SPC* algorithms. Table 2 shows the frequency of number of clusters generated by *MSPC* algorithm.

Figure 7. Averaged paired compactness using median value as a threshold

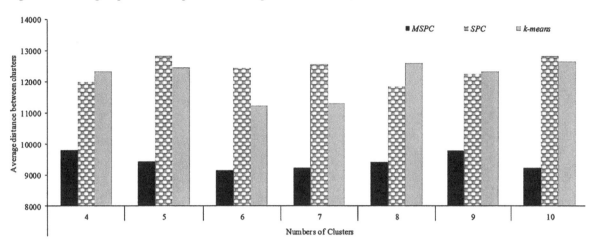

Figure 8. Dunn index using median value as a threshold

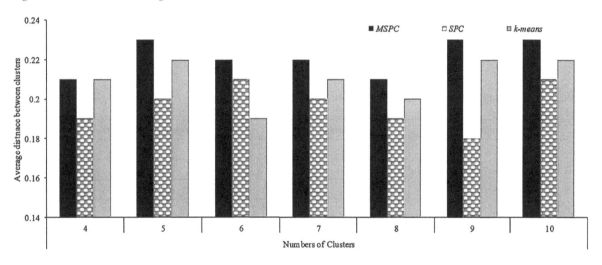

Table 1. Characteristics of real datasets

Dataset	# Data objects	# Attributes	# Clusters
Ecoli	336	7	8
Iris	150	4	3
Seeds	210	7	3
Wine	178	13	3

It can be observed that proposed algorithm generates mostly actual number of clusters present in the dataset as shown in the table by bold faces values. These values can be verified from the characteristics of datasets shown in the Table 1. A comparison of all validity measures for *k*-means, *SPC* and *MSPC* algorithms on Ecoli dataset is presented in Figure 10 and Figure 11. Table 3 presents the relative

Figure 9. DB index using median value as a threshold

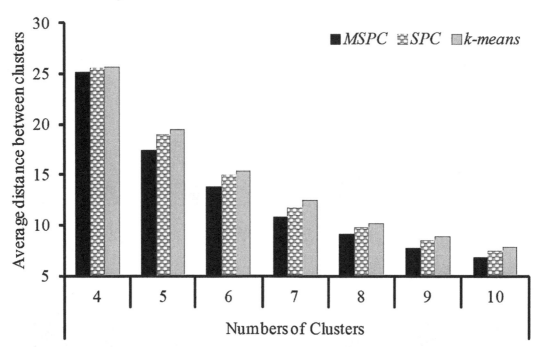

Table 2. Clusters generated using threshold similarity as a median value

Dataset	# Clusters	Frequency of Generation
Ecoli	5	3
	6	101
	7	278
	8	**429**
	9	134
	10	50
	11	5
Iris	2	306
	3	**674**
	4	20
Seeds	2	55
	3	**729**
	4	204
	5	12
Wine	**3**	**651**
	4	342
	5	7

Figure 10. Separation based comparison on Ecoli dataset using median as a threshold value

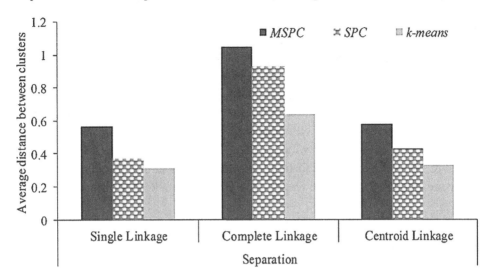

Figure 11. Compactness based comparison on Ecoli dataset using median as a threshold value

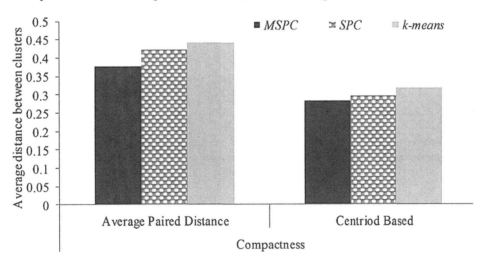

Table 3. Relative improvement of MSPC algorithm for validity measures on Ecoli dataset using median as a threshold value

Validity Measures		*SPC*	*k*-Means
Separation Methods	Single Linkage	35.2%	45.7%
	Complete Linkage	11.4%	39.1%
	Centroid Linkage	25.6%	42.9%
Compaction Methods	Averaged Paired Distance	11.6%	16.8%
	Centriod Based	5.2%	12.3%

improvement of *MSPC* algorithm for all validity measures on this dataset with respect to *k*-means and *SPC* algorithms.

A comparison of all validity measures for *k*-means, *SPC* and *MSPC* algorithms on Iris dataset is presented in Figure 12 and Figure 13. Table 4 presents the relative improvement of *MSPC* algorithm for all validity measures on this dataset with respect to *k*-means and *SPC* algorithms.

A comparison of all validity measures for *k*-means, *SPC* and *MSPC* algorithms on Seeds dataset is presented in Figures 14, Figure 15 and Table 5 presents the relative improvement of *MSPC* algorithm for all validity measures on this dataset with respect to *k*-means and *SPC* algorithms.

A comparison of all validity measures for *k*-means, *SPC* and *MSPC* algorithms on Wine dataset is presented in Figure 16 and Figure 17. Table 6 presents the relative improvement of *MSPC* algorithm for all validity measures on this dataset with respect to *k*-means and *SPC* algorithms.

Figure 12. Separation based comparison on Iris dataset using median as a threshold value

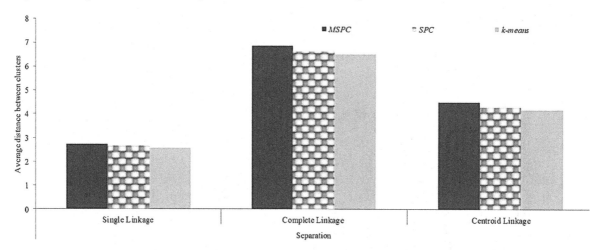

Figure 13. Compactness based comparison on Iris dataset using median as a threshold value

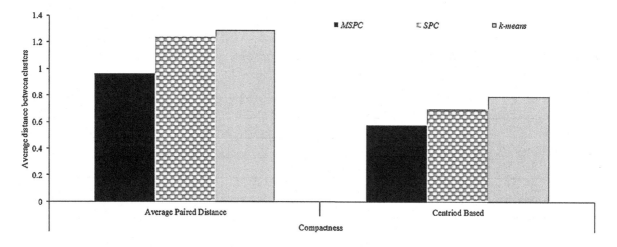

Table 4. Relative improvement of MSPC algorithm for validity measures on Iris dataset using median as a threshold value

Validity Measures		*SPC*	*k*-Means
Separation Methods	Single Linkage	2.8%	6.4%
	Complete Linkage	3.6%	5.1%
	Centroid Linkage	5.0%	7.2%
Compaction Methods	Averaged Paired Distance	28.5%	33.7%
	Centriod Based	20.8%	38.2%

Figure 14. Separation based comparison on Seeds dataset using median as a threshold value

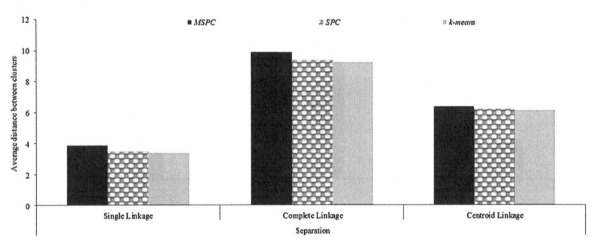

Figure 15. Compactness based comparison on Seeds dataset using median as a threshold value

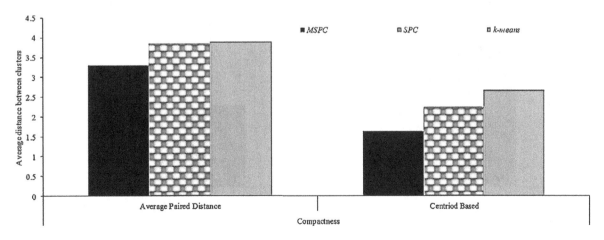

Table 5. Relative improvement of MSPC algorithm for validity measures on Seeds dataset using median as a threshold value

Validity Measures		SPC	k-Means
Separation Methods	Single Linkage	10.2%	12.5%
	Complete Linkage	5.1%	6.4%
	Centroid Linkage	2.7%	4.1%
Compaction Methods	Averaged Paired Distance	16.6%	18.1%
	Centriod Based	37.7%	64.2%

Figure 16. Separation based comparison on Wine dataset using median as a threshold value

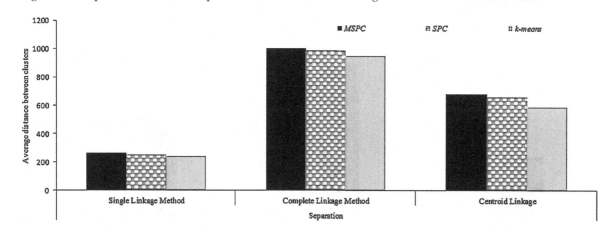

Figure 17. Compactness based comparison on Wine dataset using median as a threshold value

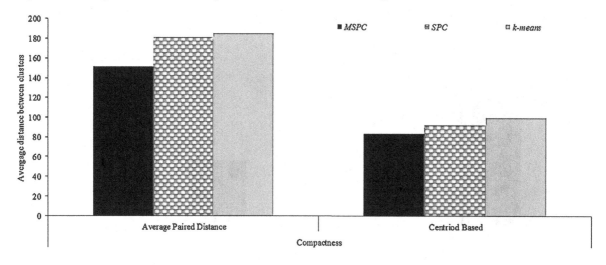

Table 6. Relative improvement of MSPC algorithm for validity measures on Wine dataset using median as a threshold value

Validity Measures		*SPC*	*k*-Means
Separation Methods	Single Linkage	6.3%	8.9%
	Complete Linkage	1.4%	5.2%
	Centroid Linkage	3.2%	13.5%
Compaction Methods	Averaged Paired Distance	19.4%	22.1%
	Centriod Based	11.2%	20.1%

From Figures 10 to 17 and Tables 3 to 6, it can be observed that *MSPC* algorithm performs better than *k*-means and *SPC* algorithms. Further, these algorithms are also evaluated on two validity indices: Dunn and *DB* index. Figure 18 depicts the graphical comparison of values of Dunn index and Figure 19 depicts the graphical comparison of values of *DB* index. From these figures, it is evident that *MSPC* algorithm provides large value of Dunn index and small value of *DB* index.

MSPC algorithm has been implemented median as the threshold similarity value. In this case, it gives better results than existing SPC and k-means algorithms. This is worth mentioning here that the proposed algorithm, MSPC, does not require user defined parameters. It, however, is sensitive to the order of selection of data objects. Due to this limitation, it generates variable number of clusters on successive runs.

CHAPTER SUMMARY

In this chapter, a modified single pass clustering algorithm has been proposed which is based on median threshold value. This similarity value is the paired distance of all data objects left to be clustered. Thus, it relinquishes the requirement of user specified parameters. Performance evaluation of clustering

Figure 18. Dunn index on real datasets using median as a threshold value

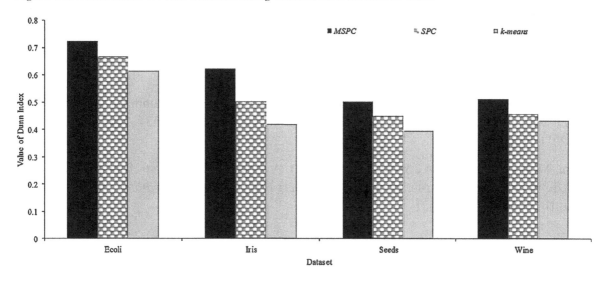

Figure 19. DB index on real datasets using median as a threshold value

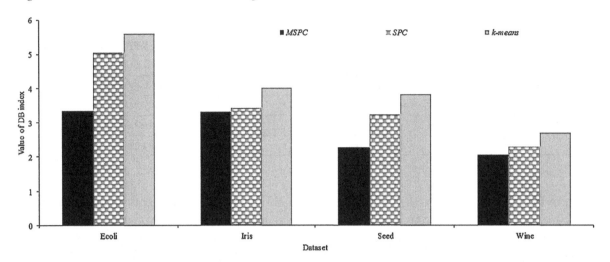

algorithms is one of the most important issues in cluster analysis to justify the selection of appropriate algorithm for clustering. The proposed algorithm has been compared with existing *k*-means and *SPC* algorithms on artificial and real datasets. Performance of these algorithms is validated for existing validity measures and indices. Collaborating filtering can utilize this algorithm to infer the user interest. From the experiments, it has been observed that proposed algorithm generates well separated and compact clusters. Moreover, it produces mostly the actual number of clusters present in the datasets.

REFERENCES

Arthur, D., & Vassilvitskii, S. (2007). *k*-means++: The advantage of careful seeding. *Proc. ofSymposium of Discrete Analysis* (pp. 1027-1035).

Bradley, P. S., Fayyad, U. M., & Reina, C. A. (1998b). Scaling clustering algorithms to large databases. *Proceedings of the4ᵗʰ International Conference on Knowledge Discovery and Data Mining* (pp. 9-15).

Cao, F., Liang, J., & Jiang, G. (2009). An initialization method for the *k*-means algorithm using neighborhood model. *Journal of Computers and Mathematics with Applications*, *58*, 474–483. doi:10.1016/j.camwa.2009.04.017

Cardot, H., Cenac, P., & Monnez, J.-M. (2012). A fast and recursive algorithm for clustering large datasets with *k*-medians. *Computational Statistics & Data Analysis*, *56*(6), 1434–1449. doi:10.1016/j.csda.2011.11.019

Celebi, M. E., Kingravi, H. A., & Vela, P. A. (2013). A comparative study of efficient initialization methods for the *k*-means clustering algorithm. *Expert Systems with Applications*, *40*(1), 200–210. doi:10.1016/j.eswa.2012.07.021

Chiang, M. M.-T., & Mirkin, B. (2009). Intelligent choice of the number of clusters in *k*-means clustering: An experimental study with different cluster spreads. *Journal of Classification, 27*(1), 3–40. doi:10.1007/s00357-010-9049-5

Deelers, S., & Auwatanamongkol, S. (2007). Enhancing *k*-means algorithm with initial cluster centers derived from data partitioning along the data axis with the highest variance. *International Journal of Computer Science, 2*(4), 323–328.

Duda, R. O., & Hart, P. E. (1973). *Pattern classification and scene analysis.* New York: John Wiley & Sons.

Erisoglu, M., Calis, N., & Sakallioglu, S. (2011). A new algorithm for initial cluster centers in *k*-means algorithm. *Pattern Recognition Letters, 32*(14), 1701–1705. doi:10.1016/j.patrec.2011.07.011

Fahim, A. M., Saake, G., Salem, A. M., Torkey, F. A., & Ramadan, M. A. (2008). K-means for Spherical Clusters with Large Variance in Sizes. Proc. of the World Academy Science, Engineering and Technology (Vol. 35, pp. 177-182).

Fahim, A. M., Salem, A. M., Torkey, F. A., & Ramadan, M. A. (2006). An efficient enhanced *k*-means clustering algorithm. *Journal of Zhejiang University Science A, 7*(10), 1626–1633. doi:10.1631/jzus.2006.A1626

Jain, A. K. (2010). Data clustering: 50 years beyond *k*-means. *Pattern Recognition Letters, 31*(8), 651–666. doi:10.1016/j.patrec.2009.09.011

Katsavounidis, I., Kuo, C.-C. J., & Zhang, Z. (1994). A new initialization technique for generalized Lloyd iteration. *IEEE Signal Processing Letters, 1*(10), 144–146. doi:10.1109/97.329844

Kaufman, L., & Rousseeuw, P. J. (1987). Clustering by means of medoids. In Statistical Data Analysis based on the L1 norm (pp. 405-416). Amsterdam.

Khan, S. S., & Ahmad, A. (2004). Cluster center initialization algorithm for *k*-means clustering. *Pattern Recognition Letters, 25*(11), 1293–1302. doi:10.1016/j.patrec.2004.04.007

Lai, J. Z. C., & Huang, T.-J. (2010). Fast global *k*-means clustering using cluster membership and inequality. *Pattern Recognition, 43*(5), 1954–1963. doi:10.1016/j.patcog.2009.11.021

Lai, J. Z. C., Huang, T.-J., & Liaw, Y.-C. (2009). A fast *k*-means clustering algorithm using cluster center displacement. *Pattern Recognition, 42*(11), 2551–2556. doi:10.1016/j.patcog.2009.02.014

Li, C. S. (2011). Cluster center initialization method for *k*-means algorithm over data sets with two clusters. Proc. *International Conference on Advances in Engineering* (*Vol. 24,* pp. 324-328). Elsevier.

Likas, A., Vlassis, N., & Verbeek, J. J. (2003). The global *k*-means clustering algorithm. *Pattern Recognition Letters, 36*, 451–461. doi:10.1016/S0031-3203(02)00060-2

Lloyd, S. P. (1982). Least squares quantization in PCM. *IEEE Transactions on Information Theory, 28*(2), 129–137. doi:10.1109/TIT.1982.1056489

MacQueen, J. (1967). Some methods for classification and analysis of multivariate observations. *Proc. 5th Symposium Mathematical Statistics and Probability,* Berkeley, CA (Vol. 1, pp. 281-297).

McCullagh, P., & Yang, J. (2008). How many clusters? *Bayesian Analysis*, *3*(1), 101–120.

Pham, D. T., Dimov, S. S., & Nguyen, C. D. (2004). Selection of k in k-means clustering. *Journal of Mechanical Engineering Science*, *219*(1), 103–119. doi:10.1243/095440605X8298

Quinlan, J. R. (1993). *C4.5: Programs for machine learning*. San Mateo: Morgan Kaufmann Publishers.

Ray, S., & Turi, R. (1999). Determination of number of clusters in k-means clustering and application in colour image segmentation.*Proc.4th International Conference on Advances in Pattern Recognition and Digital Techniques,*India (pp. 137-143).

Reddy, D., & Jana, P. K. (2012). Initialization for k-means clustering using voronoi diagram. *Procedia Technology*, *4*, 395–400. doi:10.1016/j.protcy.2012.05.061

Redmond, S. J., & Heneghan, C. (2007). A method for initializing the k-means clustering algorithm using k-d trees. *Pattern Recognition Letters*, *28*(8), 965–973. doi:10.1016/j.patrec.2007.01.001

Salton, G. (1971). *The SMART Retrieval System*. Upper Saddle River, NJ, USA: Prentice-Hall, Inc.

Salton, G., & Wong, A. (1978). Generation and search of clustered files. *ACM TODS*, *3*(4), 321–346. doi:10.1145/320289.320291

Scitovski, R., & Sabo, K. (2014). Analysis of the k-means algorithm in the case of data points occurring on the border of two or more clusters. *Knowledge-Based Systems*, *57*, 1–7. doi:10.1016/j.knosys.2013.11.010

Tibshirani, R., Walther, G., & Hastie, T. (2001). Estimating the number of clusters in a data set via the gap statistic. *Journal of the Royal Statistical Society. Series B. Methodological*, *63*(2), 411–423. doi:10.1111/1467-9868.00293

Wu, X., Kumar, V., Quinlan, J.-R., Ghosh, J., Yang, Q., Motoda, H., & Steinberg, D. et al. (2008). Top 10 algorithms in data mining. *Knowledge and Information Systems*, *14*, 1–37.

Yan, M. (2005). *Methods of Determining the Number of Clusters in a Data Set and a New Clustering Criterion* [Ph.D. Dissertation]. Faculty Virginia Polytechnic Institute and State University, Blacksburg, Virginia.

Yuan, F., Meng, Z.-H., Zhang, H.-X., & Dong, C.-R. (2004). A new algorithm to get the initial centroids. *Proc.International Conference on Machine Learning and Cybernetics* (Vol. 2, pp. 1191-1193).

Zalik, K. R. (2008). An efficient k-means clustering algorithm. *Pattern Recognition Letters*, *29*(9), 1385–1391. doi:10.1016/j.patrec.2008.02.014

Zhang, Y. J., & Cheng, E. (2013). An Optimized Method for Selection of the Initial Centers of k-means Clustering. *Integrated Uncertainty in Knowledge Modeling and Decision Making, LNCS* (Vol. 8032, pp. 149–156). doi:10.1007/978-3-642-39515-4_13

Chapter 3
Dimensionality Reduction Techniques for Text Mining

Neethu Akkarapatty
SCMS School of Engineering and Technology, India

Nisha S. Raj
SCMS School of Engineering and Technology, India

Anjaly Muralidharan
SCMS School of Engineering and Technology, India

Vinod P.
SCMS School of Engineering and Technology, India

ABSTRACT

Sentiment analysis is an emerging field, concerned with the analysis and understanding of human emotions from sentences. Sentiment analysis is the process used to determine the attitude/opinion/emotions expressed by a person about a specific topic based on natural language processing. Proliferation of social media such as blogs, Twitter, Facebook and Linkedin has fuelled interest in sentiment analysis. As the real time data is dynamic, the main focus of the chapter is to extract different categories of features and to analyze which category of attribute performs better. Moreover, classifying the document into positive and negative category with fewer misclassification rate is the primary investigation performed. The various approaches employed for feature selection involves TF-IDF, WET, Chi-Square and mRMR on benchmark dataset pertaining diverse domains.

INDRODUCTION

Mining is the process of extracting relevant information from large volume of data. The World Wide Web contains a huge volume of documents containing comments, feedback, critiques, reviews related to wide documents. Processing of natural language is a herculean task for humans to understand, analyze and to extract useful information from enormous amount of data. Thus the work helps to automatically determine the sentiment (positive or negative) of online texts is significant. Opinion mining or sentiment analysis (Liu, 2012), aim to extract the features upon which the reviewers express their opinions and help to determine whether the opinions are positive, negative or neutral.

DOI: 10.4018/978-1-5225-0489-4.ch003

In our day to day lives, analyzing the reviews/opinions has become an integral part for decision making. For example, if a person wishes to purchase a product online, he/she will refer to the prior reviews and comments posted by the experienced users in web. In order to enhance the product sales and to improve the customer's satisfaction, most of the on-line shopping sites provide facility for customers to write reviews/comments about the product they wish to purchase. But it seems to be a cumbersome task to read the entire reviews available in the web for purchasing a specific product. Hence, the user's interest is in determining if the reviews influences/ recommends in buying a product or not. If lot of reviews recommends buying the product, user will conclude to buy, otherwise not to buy (Feng, Zhang, & Deng, 2010).

Sentiment analysis has the wide spread applicative areas such as e-learning, automatic survey analysis, opinion extraction and recommender systems. In the past decade, opinion mining has been studied in fields like natural language processing, data mining, information retrieval, web mining etc.

SENTIMENT CLASSIFICATION

Sentiment classification is a part of opinion mining which refers to the task of extracting sentiment word from a given text and then classifying the content into positive or negative in its sentiment. Classification is usually performed at three levels namely:

1. Document.
2. Sentence.
3. Attribute level.

In the following section, each of them will be discussed in detail.

Document Level Sentiment Classification

Document level classification (Kumar, 2015; Bollegala, 2013; Singh, 2013; Mouthami, 2013; Wong, 2011) identifies the opinionated document (e.g product review) into classes such as positive, negative and neutral based on the overall sentiment expressed by the writer. The widely used dataset for document level sentiment classification is Cornell Movie review corpora (Mouthami, Devi & Bhaskaran, 2013) which were used in (Pang, 2004, 2002). Naïve Bayesian and Support Vector Machine are the supervised learning algorithms that are widely used to prepare model. The rating usually in the form of 1-5 stars is used by the reviewer for training as well as testing data. The features that are extracted can be any one/more combination of bag of words, adjectives from part of speech tagging, opinion words, phrases, negations, dependencies etc. Prior experiment results demonstrate that supervised learning is the most powerful method on preview of accuracy (Li & Liu, 2010). The unsupervised learning can also be performed by retrieving the opinion words inside a document. In order to find the semantics of the words that has been extracted, the point-wise mutual information can be used which in turn helps to improve the performance. The main challenge faced by the classification performed at the document level is that most of the sentences in a document seems to be irrelevant in expressing the opinion about an entity. As the comparative sentences appears in case of forums and blogs, customers compare one product with another that has similar type of characteristics. Hence the document level analysis is not preferable in forums and blogs.

The authors in (Kumar, Kansal & Ekbal, 2015) portrayed a method for document level classification of tweets, based on support vector machine and investigates the effectiveness of active learning techniques to improve the classification accuracy with minimal resources. Evaluation on benchmark dataset of tweets shows the highest classification accuracy of 83.95%. A new type of system architecture that can automatically extract the sentiments of micro-blog messages has been proposed by (Liang & Dai, 2013). In this architecture, machine learns to automatically extract group of messages containing opinions, filter out the messages that are non-opinionated and later to determine the direction of sentiment (i.e. positive or negative). In (Bollegala, Weir, & Carroll, 2013), authors proposed Cross-Domain Sentiment Classification method which outperforms different baselines and returns results that are comparable with prior works on Amazon user reviews (Mukherjee, Liu & Glance, 2012) for different types of products. In [19], performance evaluation of SentiWordNet approach for movie reviews and blog posts are conducted in document level sentiment classification. In (Wong, Pun, Kit, & Webster, 2011), authors studied the lexical cohesion, a quality attribute of Machine Translation evaluation at document level. A new algorithm called Sentiment Fuzzy Classification algorithm proposed in (Mouthami, Devi & Bhaskaran, 2013) helps to improve the accuracy of classification on benchmark movie review dataset.

Sentence Level Sentiment Classification

The sentiment classification at sentence level (Shahbaz, 2014; Karamibekr, 2013, 2012; Li, 2011; Baharudin, 2010) mainly applies to individual sentences in a document. Sentence level sentiment analysis has two tasks namely subjectivity classification and sentiment classification. Subjectivity classification identifies the sentence as subjective or objective. Sentiment classification further classifies the subjective information into positive or negative category. Usually, a simple sentence conveys single opinion about an entity. But in some cases, opinionated text may contain complex sentences. In such cases, sentiment classification at sentence level is not preferable.

In (Li, Zhu, & Zhang, 2011), sentence level sentiment classification is performed based on convolution tree kernel based approach. The authors in (Karamibekr & Ghorbani, 2012), proposed a verb oriented sentiment classification approach for social domains and this approach performs better than the bag of words attribute. In (Karamibek & Ghorbani, 2013), authors focus on sentence level subjectivity analysis of social issues and the proposed lexical-syntactic approach depicts the role of different opinion terms, especially verbs regarding social issues. The experimental results show that the proposed approach achieved improved performance on the subjectivity classification of sentences, especially on well built sentences that expresses opinions that are explicit. Authors in in (Shahbaz & Guergachi, 2014), describes a method to apply opinion mining on the texts that are usually unstructured, thereby extracting the polarity and finally performing the classification within a document at sentence level. The proposed solution was the development of a system called Sentiment Miner that provide features to process and then classify files (reviews and appraisals). A notable approach in (Baharudin, 2010) makes use of words as feature and classification is performed with Naïve Bayesian Classifier. Lexical contextual information and machine learning are used to classify and analyze the sentiment from reviews. The paper mainly focuses on sentence level to verify whether the sentences are objective or subjective and subsequently classify the polarity of the sentences.

Aspect/Feature Level Sentiment Classification

Although mining the opinions at the document and the sentence level is beneficial in many cases, it still seems to be inefficient. For example, while reviewing a product, the reviewer usually sketches out both negative and positive aspects of the product, although the general sentiment on the product may be negative or positive. To obtain more fine grained analysis of opinions, it seems to be a necessity to dive into the aspect level or feature level. This concept leads to aspect-based opinion mining (Chinsha, 2015; Marrese-Taylor, 2014; Zha, 2014; Zhang, 2013; Lu, 2011; Brody, 2010). It has been observed that while reviewing most of the websites, reviewers were asked to assign overall ratings (as stars) to express quality of the item reviewed (Marrese-Taylor, 2014; Moghaddam, 2011). But most of the readers seek to obtain detailed information rather a single rating so as to make the final decision (Kawamae, 2012). In the process of buying a digital camera, some may be interested in the quality of zoom and some may be interested in ease of use, while others may be interested in the brand name. Hence a fine grained opinion analysis is important for making decisions.

In (Chinsha & Joseph, 2015), authors proposed a novel syntactic approach for mining aspects which uses SentiWordNet, aggregate score of opinion words, aspect table, and syntactic dependency together for opinion mining. The authors in (Zha, Yu, Tang, Wang & Chua, 2014) proposed a product aspect ranking framework, which automatically identifies the relevant aspects of entity/product from online reviews and thereby aims to improve the usability of the reviews. In (Marrese-Taylor, Velásquez & Bravo-Marquez, 2014), a novel deterministic approach was proposed in order to apply on the tourism domain. A co-occurrence association-based method was proposed by (Zhang & Zhu, 2013) which aims to retrieve features that are implicit in customer reviews and provide fine grained and extensive mining results. The reviews are taken from two categories such as mobile phones and clothes. The authors in (Lu, 2011; Dang, 2010) proposed an optimization framework that focuses on the problem of building the sentiment lexicon which is domain specific and aspect dependent in the specific context.

BACKGROUND

Researchers in (Verbert et al.,2012) prepared a survey on context aware recommender systems in which the research contributions are developed as threefold. Firstly, a context aware recommender systems has been developed for TEL (Technology Enhanced Learning) applications that identifies the useful context dimensions. Secondly, context aware recommender system has been keenly analyzed for deploying in educational settings. Finally, they have figured out the future challenges for the validation and development of context aware recommender systems for learning.

In (Elahi, Ricci & Rubens, 2014), a precise review of the state-of-art in collaborative filtering recommendation systems on active learning has been presented. In this survey article, a comprehensive analysis has been performed and classified a wide range of active learning techniques, strategies, along two dimensions: (a) whether the ratings requested by the system are personalized or not and (b) whether the active learning is guided by heuristic criterion. As a future work, it is important to survey the works that have been done in active learning such as content-based and context-aware recommender systems. Future work focus to analyze active learning techniques based on their applicability to specific application domains. Moreover, an in depth stress must be given for the importance of conducting more live user studies, where active learning benefit can be better assessed.

In (Guo, Zhang & Yorke-Smith, 2015), multiview clustering method has been developed in which users are iteratively clustered from the views of both social trust relationships and rating patterns. Authors conducted experiments on three real world datasets namely Flixster, Filmtrust and Epinions. Clustering based methods implemented by the authors are KCF, KCFT, KTrust and MV. Moreover, 5-fold cross validation is used to evaluate the performance of each method. A support vector regression method was employed to determine an appropriate prediction in case where two predictions were generated for the users who were grouped in two different clusters due to the cluster combination. For this purpose, the authors have proposed and identified a number of user-item and prediction-related features in order to describe the characteristics of user-item predictions. In addition, to accommodate the cold users who cannot be clustered, a probabilistic method has been proposed to identify the likelihood of belonging to each possible cluster using both ratings and trust information. The proposed method enhances clustering based methods by virtue of the multiviews of trust and similarity, thereby improving the accuracy and coverage of recommendations.

In (Xu, Bu, Chen, & Cai, 2012), the authors formulate the multiclass Co-Clustering problem and proposed an effective solution to it. Later they proposed a unified framework to extent the existing CF (Collaborative Filtering) algorithms for improving their top-N recommendation performance. The experiments were conducted on three real datasets such as MovieLens-100K, MovieLens-1M and Lastfm. The authors in (Liu, Wu, Feng & Liu, 2015) proposed conditional preference in recommender systems. Conditional preference is taken into consideration in the recommender systems due to the high space complexity of already existing models representing conditional preference and the high computational complexity of the corresponding learning methods. Compared with the traditional conditional preference model, the proposed model can reduce learning complexity, save storage space, and can be used in rating based RSs (Recommender Systems) to actively process huge volume of data. The proposed method and the compared methods are tested on MovieLen (1M) dataset and Epinions dataset. The experimental results prove that the proposed method outperforms other methods based on matrix factorization.

In (Cantador & Cremonesi, 2014), cross domain recommender systems have been proposed. Cross-domain recommender systems aim to generate or enhance personalized recommendations in a target domain by exploiting knowledge (mainly user preferences) from other source domains. Future work deserves more attention in Cross-domain RS's due to the synergism between cross-domain and context-aware recommendations. Another important issue concerns with the evaluation metrics adopted. A third open research issue refers to the usage of cross-domain recommender systems for reducing the user model selection effort. A study of dynamic features of recommender systems has been depicted in (Rana & Jain, 2015). This paper presents problems related to the evolving trends of user requirements as well as transition in the systems contents. The RSs involving issues stated above are termed as DRSs or Dynamic Recommender Systems. The paper first defines the concept of DRS and researches the various guidelines that contribute in building/developing a Dynamic Recommender Systems. The paper also enlightens the scope of contributions in this field and concludes by citing in possible extensions that can improve the dynamic qualities of RSs (Recommender Systems) in future. The paper classifies the current RS research into a number of spheres based on various parameters namely diversity, temporal context, serendipity, novelty, temporal characteristic and dynamic environment. Dynamic recommender systems focus on the importance for inventive solutions that provides enhanced customer satisfaction as well as system performance.

A comparative study of reputation models that are collaboration based for the social recommender systems was discussed in (McNally, O'Mahony & Smyth, 2014). In this study, a generic approach for modeling user-item reputation in social recommender systems has been described. The study also aims to show how the various interactions between consumers and producers of content helps to create the graph called collaboration graphs, from which the reputation of items and users can be derived. The reputation models put forward in this article are based on that assertion, leveraging information gained from examining past user collaborations to positively influence interactions in the future. The main focus of the work was on the role of reputation during the recommendation process, in order to maximize the relevance of the community recommendations made by HeyStaks.

In (Chen, Chen & Wang, 2015), authors surveyed state-of-the-art research on review-based recommender systems. Generally, the systems are classified according to the two main types of profile building: review-based user profile building and review-based product profile building. In review-based user profile building, a detailed study on how existing studies have used reviews to create term-based user profile, enrich rating profile, and derive feature preference has been performed. Various types of review elements, such as review helpfulness, review topics, feature opinions, review contexts, and review emotions, have been used to enhance the standard content-based recommending method and rating-based collaborative filtering method. In the category of product profile building, feature opinions and comparative opinions have been exploited, which helps in increasing the product's ranking accuracy. Later, the practical implications of these studies in terms of solving the well-known rating sparsity and new user problems, proven ability to improve the currently used algorithms and practical uses in different types of product domains has been discussed. The authors expect this survey to encourage investigators to pursue the hidden values of reviews in future studies. The effects of reviews on enhancing multi-criteria recommenders, context-aware recommenders, and emotion-based recommenders could be investigated in more comprehensive studies.

The authors in (Yang, Guo, Liu & Steck, 2014), presented a survey of Collaborative Filtering-based social recommender systems. Initially, a short overview/summary of the role of recommender systems and the existing recommendation algorithms have been pointed out. Later they presented how social information on network can be adopted by recommender systems so as to improve accuracy. Further, they classified Collaborative Filtering-based social recommender systems into categories of two namely: neighborhood based and matrix factorization based social recommendation approaches. Later, both of these approaches are compared and surveyed. Preserving the privacy of social recommender systems is yet another interesting direction in future work area. The authors in (Satsiou & Tassiulas, 2014) examined an advanced collaborative filtering method that utilizes concepts of similarity transitivity. A recent study observed a strong interrelation between preference similarity and trust in rating systems that are online. In this paper, authors have proposed a novel similarity propagation algorithm that is based on similarity transitivity concepts. As a result, the proposed policy achieves better prediction accuracy and much higher coverage than most popular CF policy, even when cold start users are the majority in the system. The proposed method was validated on two datasets namely MovieLens and Jester. In this paper, the most popular similarity measure has been chosen, Pearson correlation, combined with a new metric in cases when Pearson correlation happens to be in vain. The experimental results prove that much higher recommendation coverage and better accuracy has been achieved than CF methods that were classical even under very scanty data conditions.

PROPOSED METHODOLOGY

Our proposed methodology (Refer *Figure 1&Figure 2*) involves collecting the relevant datasets, data pre-processing, extracting feature values, constructing feature vector table (FVT), applying feature selection method, generating reduced feature vector table and finally using WEKA tool (Hall et al., 2009) for classification.

Figure 1. Proposed framework for sentiment classification using cross validation

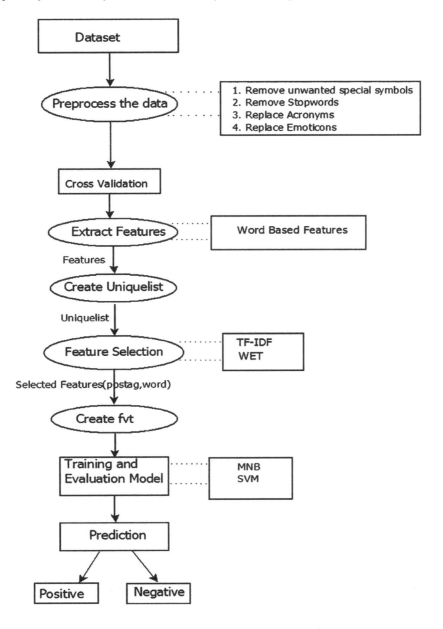

Figure 2. Proposed framework for sentiment classification using test and train

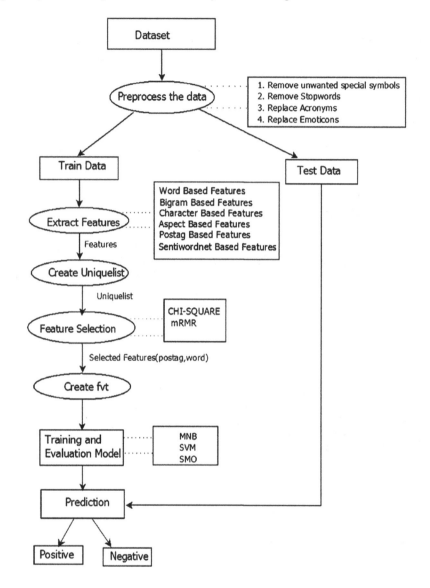

Dataset

The datasets that we have chosen for performing experiments and computations comprises of Cornell Movie Review (Li & Liu, 2010) TripAdvisor (Lu, Castellanos, Dayal & Zhai, 2011) as well as Multi domain sentiment dataset (Blitzer, Dredze & Pereira, 2007). The Cornell Movie review dataset is labeled and this helps the task of pre-processing easier to a certain extent. It consists of 1000 positive and 1000 negative text files comprising of movie reviews. TripAdvisor, Inc is an American travel website providing reviews/posts with respect to travel related content. It also includes collective travel forums. The original dataset includes 12,773 JSON (Java Script Object Notation) files comprising of hotel reviews from various hotels. The format of each JSON file is clumsy and it seems to be difficult to analyze and understand. Each JSON file consists of various hotel attributes such as ratings, service, cleanliness, overall, value, sleep quality, rooms, location etc. The hotel reviews written by the authors from different parts of the world is also included in each JSON file. Multidomain dataset consists of product reviews taken from various domains. In this study, we used Apparel, DVD and Grocery datasets from Amazon. com each comprising of 1000 files belonging to negative and positive polarity.

Pre-Process Data

Data pre-processing involves transforming raw data into an understandable format. The data pre-processing step involves tokenization, uppercase to lowercase conversion, removal of stop words, emoticons, unwanted punctuations, special characters, digits and symbols. *Figure 3* depicts the tokenization step.

Training and Testing

The dataset is divided into two subsets such as training and testing set in order to evaluate model performance accuracy. There is no predefined rule that has been set for the division of data in each dataset. In this study *random function* is used to divide the dataset in 60:40 proportions. The training data is used to build the model and this model is used to test with the new samples. It should be made sure that two models should have a similar fit otherwise it leads to a conclusion that the underlying patterns in the data have not uncovered. The train and test set is depicted in *Table 1*.

Figure 3. Tokenization

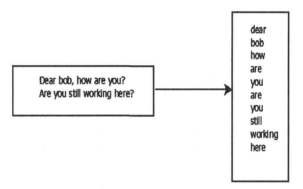

Table 1. Train and test set

Dataset		Positive Reviews		Negative Reviews	
		Training Data	**Testing Data**	**Training Data**	**Testing Data**
TripAdvisor		5987	3990	5556	3704
Cornell Movie Review		600	400	600	400
Multidomain Sentiment Dataset	Apparel	600	400	600	400
	DVD	600	400	600	400
	Grocery	600	400	600	400

Extract Features

The extracted features constitute Bag of Words (Lu, Castellanos, Dayal & Zhai, 2011), character-based (Cheng, Chandramouli, & Subbalakshmi, 2011), bigram-based, PoS tag based (Cheng, Chandramouli, & Subbalakshmi, 2011), SentiwordNet dictionary based (Bollegala, Weir & Carroll, 2013) and aspect-based features (Lu, Castellanos, Dayal & Zhai, 2011). Character-based features include 29 stylometric features including total number of digital characters, special characters, uppercase letters etc. A bigram is every sequence of two adjacent elements in a string of tokens, which are typically letters, syllables, or words; they are n-grams for n=2. Part of Speech tagging (Han, Du & Chen 2010) is the task of making every word in a sentence with part of speech. The most common part of speech in English includes nouns, verbs, adjectives, adverbs and much more. SentiWordNet is a wordnet or subjective lexicon knowledge base. It contains more than 117662 words. The objective of using SentiWordNet knowledge base is to improve the strength of opinions. Aspect-based features of a hotel domain include location, food, room quality, service etc.

Create Unique List

Initially term frequency is computed and later a unique list is created comprising of document frequency and overall term frequency. Document frequency refers to the number of documents in which a particular term appears. Term frequency in a given document is the number of times a given term appears in that document. Likewise, unique list is created for positive set and negative set. The combined unique list of PoS tag based features from TripAdvisor dataset is depicted in the *Table 2*.

Feature Selection

The algorithms in machine learning and pattern recognition are highly sensitive to dimensionality of feature vector space. It concerns about the degradation in performance of the learning of classification algorithm as the number of feature increases. Dimensionality reduction or feature selection is applied to handle this issue. It will find a low dimensional representation for a high dimensional vector space. Dimensionality reduction helps in understanding data, eliminating the irrelevant features thereby reducing processing overhead, reducing the effect of curse of dimensionality, improving the predictor performance and elevating the over fitting of the training data. The focus of feature selection (Chandrashekar, 2014; Koncz, 2011) is to select a subset of variables from the input which can efficiently describe the input data while reducing noise or irrelevant variables and still provide good prediction results. When two

Table 2. Combined uniquelist (PoS-tag)

Feature	Positive doc_count	Negative doc_count
CC	5971	5540
CD	5948	5467
DT	5970	5540
NN	5973	5544
....	....	....

features are perfectly correlated, only one feature is sufficient to describe the data. The dependant variables provide no extra information about the classes and thus serve as noise for the predictor. Hence by eliminating the dependent variables, the amount of data can be reduced which can lead to improvement in the classification performance.

In (Kohavi & John, 1997) the dimensionality reduction methods were broadly classified into filter wrapper methods and embedded methods. Filter methods uses ranking methods such as Correlation Criteria and Mutual Information (Chandrashekar & Sahin, 2014), which are applied before classification in order to filter out the less relevant variables. Filter methods act as preprocessing to rank the features wherein the highly ranked features are selected and applied to a predictor. In wrapper methods (Kohavi & John, 1997), the feature selection criterion is the performance of the predictor i.e. the predictor is wrapped on a search algorithm which will find a subset that result in highest predictor performance. Embedded methods reduce the computation time taken up for reclassifying different subsets which is done in wrapper methods. Embedded methods (Chandrashekar & Sahin, 2014) include variable selection as part of the training process without splitting the data into training and testing sets. Ensemble feature selection (Maimon, & Rockach, 2005) is a relatively new technique used to obtain a stable feature subset. A single feature selection algorithm is run on different subsets of data samples obtained from bootstrapping method. The results are aggregated to obtain a final feature set. In the following paragraphs we introduce feature selection techniques.

TF-IDF is a well known feature selection technique which is widely used as a weighting method in text categorization (Guyon, Gunn, Nikravesh & Zadeh, 2008*)*. TF-IDF means Term Frequency-Inverse Document Frequency. It is used to evaluate the importance of a term in a document in a corpus. Mathematically, the TF-IDF weight of a term *i* can be expressed as:

$$W_i = tf_i * \log\left(D \middle/ df_i \right) \tag{1}$$

where tf_i is the term frequency of term *i* in a document, *D* is the number of documents in the corpus, df_i is the document frequency and *log (D/df$_i$)* is the inverse document frequency. TF-IDF depicts the fact that if a term appears in more documents, then it becomes less important, and hence its weighting will also become less important in the given corpus.

The Weight of Evidence of Text (WET) (Guyon, 2008; Wang, 2003). feature selection method can be used to classify a new object against any user indicated attribute in the dataset. It is most effective in two-class classification task (Xu, 2012). Calculate the weight of evidence value using the following formula.

$$WET(f) = \sum p(C_i) \cdot p(f) \cdot \left| \log \left\{ \frac{p\left(C_i \middle/ f \right)\left(1 - p\left(C_i \right) \right)}{p\left(C_i \right)\left(1 - p\left(C_i / f \right) \right)} \right\} \right| \tag{2}$$

where *p(C$_i$)* is the marginal probability of class C_i *p(f)* is the probability of feature, and *p(C$_i$│f)* is the conditional probability of class for a given feature.

A weighting method named Pearson's Chi-Square (Guyon, Gunn, Nikravesh & Zadeh, 2008) is applied in this study. Chi-square is commonly used statistical test for comparing observed data with outcome that we would expect to obtain according to a hypothesis. Using Chi-square test we can determine whether there is a significant difference between the expected and the observed frequencies in one or more categories. The equation for Chi-Square is given as follows

$$\chi^2 = \sum_{k=1}^{n} \frac{\left(O_k - E_k\right)^2}{E_k} \tag{3}$$

where χ^2 is the Pearson's cumulative test statistic, O_k is the number of observations of type k, E_k is the expected (theoretical) frequency of type k and n is the number of cells in the table.

Minimum Redundancy and Maximum Relevance feature selection methods utilize correlation, mutual information, or distance/similarity scores for selecting the features. The aim of mRMR (Peng, Long & Ding, 2005). feature selection method is to classify the attributes that are strongly correlated to a class and subsequently retain those attributes that have minimum inter correlation between them. Equation 4 - Equation 7 depict mRMR feature selection approach.

The equation for Minimize Redundancy:

$$\max\left(W_1\right), W_1 = \frac{1}{\left|S^2\right|} \sum_{i,j \in S} I\left(i,j\right) \tag{4}$$

Where |S| is the no of features in S and I(i,j) is mutual information between features *i* and *j*.

The equation for Maximize Relevance:

$$\max\left(V_1\right), V_1 = \frac{1}{\left|S\right|} \sum_{i \in S} I\left(h,i\right) \tag{5}$$

I(h,i) denotes mutual information between targeted classes *h={h1,h2,......hk}*
The equation for Mutual Information Quotient:

$$mRMR = \max_{i \in \Omega_S} \left\{ I\left(i,h\right) \middle/ \left[\frac{1}{\left|S\right|} \sum_{j \in S} I\left(i,j\right) \right] \right\} \tag{6}$$

After the determination of significant attributes each sample is represented in the form of vectors. It is necessary to map features to Vector Space Model as only numerical vectors are understood by machine learning classifiers. Feature Vector Table (FVT) is constructed where rows represent both positive and negative reviews, columns designate features from unique list. Last column of FVT represents the class label (P:Positive and N:Negative). This labeled FVT is used to create a classification model.

TRAINING MODEL AND EVALUATION

Classification model is created using algorithms implemented in WEKA (Hall et al., 2009).

Algorithms such as Sequential Multinomial Optimization (SMO) Multinomial Naïve Bayes (MNB) and Support Vector Machine with kernels LibSVM K0, LibSVM K1, LibSVM K2, LibSVM K3 is used in this study. The Multinomial Naïve Bayes (MNB) model (Kibriya, Frank, Pfahringer & Holmes, 2004) has a number of attractive features for most text classification works. Multinomial Naïve Bayes is a preferred classifier for many text classification tasks, due to simplicity and trivial scaling to large scale tasks. Being a probabilistic model, it is easy to extend for structured modeling tasks, such as multi-label classes. Naïve Bayes classifiers are probabilistic classifiers applying Baye's theorem. Naive Bayes classifiers assume that the value of a particular feature is independent of the value of any other feature.

Support Vector Machine (SVM) (Joachims, 1998) analyzes the data and maps them into a multi-dimensional space. It is capable of effectively handling large dimensional input data. SVM identifies a hyper plane that separates the instances of classes in the multidimensional space. New instances are evaluated by mapping them to this region and observing to which side of the hyper plane it lies. The advantage of using SVM classifier is that it is suitable for high dimensional datasets and they provide better classification for binary features. The results are evaluated using evaluation metrics such as precision, recall, True positive rate, False positive rate and accuracy.

When a positive review is classified as positive, it is known as true positive (TP). A positive review misclassified as negative review, is known as false negative (FN). A negative review classified as negative, is known as true negative (TN). When a negative review is misclassified as positive review a false positive (FP) occurs. Sensitivity (also called the True Positive Rate) measures the ratio of actual positives that are identified correctly as positive and is complementary to the false negative rate. Specificity (sometimes called the True Negative Rate) measures the ratio of actual negatives which are identified accurately as negative and is complementary to the False Positive Rate (FPR). For any test, there is usually a trade-off between the measures. The equation for precision is as follows:

$$precision = \frac{TP}{TP + FP} \qquad (7)$$

Recall is the measure of the ability of a prediction model to select instances of a certain class from a data set.

$$recall = sensitivity = \frac{TP}{TP + FN} \qquad (8)$$

True Positive Rate is given by the equation:

$$TPR = \frac{TP}{TP + FN}$$

False Positive Rate is given by the equation:

$$FPR = \frac{FP}{FP + TN} \tag{10}$$

Accuracy is the overall correctness of the model and is calculated using equation 11.

$$Accuracy = \frac{TP + TN}{TP + TN + FP + FN} \tag{11}$$

The F-measure (F-score) can be interpreted as a weighted average of the recall and precision where an F1 score reaches the value at its best for 1 and worst score at 0. F-measure is calculated using equation 12.

$$F - measure = \frac{2TP}{2TP + FP + FN} \tag{12}$$

PREDICTION

Prediction refers to predict continuous valued function i.e. predicts unknown or missing values. In prediction, initially a model is constructed and later the constructed model is used to predict the future or unknown samples. The classification models are also evaluated using cross validation. It is a model validation technique for evaluating how the statistical analysis results will generalize to an independent set of data. It is mainly used in settings where the goal is prediction based, and one wants to estimate how accurately/precisely a predictive model will perform in practice. The approach evaluates classification performance and compares algorithms. The process is executed by dividing data into two parts. One is used to validate or test and one is used to train. The train and test data must pass through various successive rounds. The available data population is divided into k-folds. One part is used for testing and rest of the parts is used for training. The process is repeated k-times and their mean accuracy is calculated. In our experiments we have employed 10-fold cross validation; initially data is broken down into 10 sets of size n/10. Training is performed on 10 datasets whereas testing is performed on only 1 dataset at a time. The 10-fold cross validation technique is depicted in the Figure 4.

EXPERIMENTS AND RESULTS

Evaluation of Movie Review Dataset Using TF-IDF and WET

TF-IDF Method

From *Table 3*, it has been analyzed that in MNB classifier, the highest TPR of 94.10, lowest FPR of 6.50 and highest F-measure of 0.92 was obtained for feature length 12,400 in positive reviews (+) whereas the highest TPR of 93.70, lowest FPR of 5.80 and highest F-measure of 0.93 was obtained for feature set of length 10,900 in negative reviews (-).

Figure 4. Cross validation technique

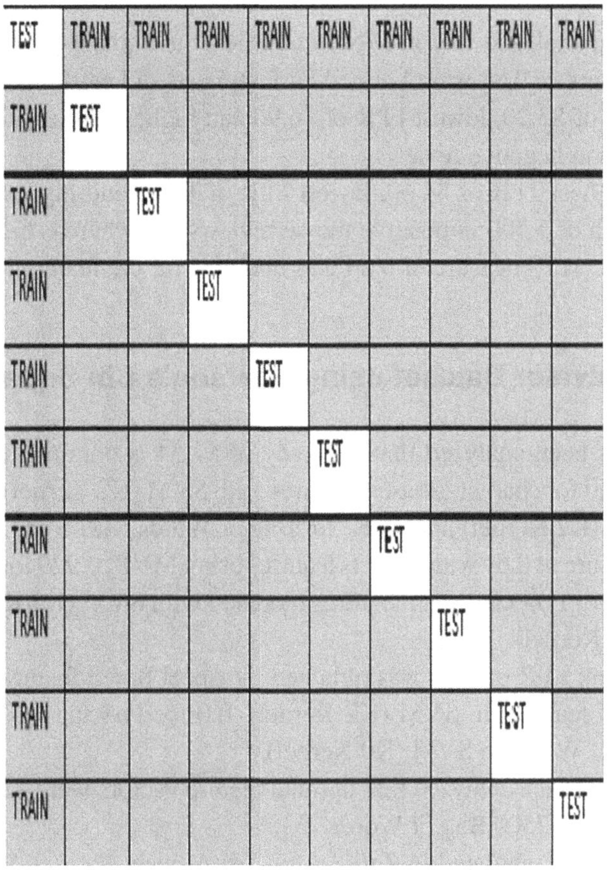

Table 3. Movie review classification using feature selection (TF-IDF,WET)

Feature Selection Method	Classifier	Feature Length	TPR	FPR	Accuracy	Precision	Recall	F1 Score	Time
TF-IDF	MNB(+)	12400	94.10	6.50	93.80	0.93	0.94	0.92	0.18
	MNB(-)	10900	93.70	5.80	93.95	0.94	0.93	0.93	0.16
	SMO(+)	15400	90.70	5.90	92.40	0.93	0.90	0.92	267.18
	SMO(-)	13900	93.40	8.60	92.40	0.91	0.93	0.92	206.57
WET	MNB(+)	6500	81.20	18.80	81.20	0.81	0.81	0.81	0.21
	MNB(-)	7500	83.20	16.90	83.15	0.83	0.83	0.83	0.20
	SMO(+)	5500	84.60	15.40	84.60	0.84	0.84	0.84	197.88
	SMO(-)	10000	84.80	15.20	84.80	0.84	0.84	0.84	452.86

In SMO classifier, highest TPR of 90.70, lowest FPR of 5.90 and highest F-measure of 0.92 was obtained for feature length of 15,400 in positive movie reviews (+) whereas highest TPR of 93.40, lowest FPR of 8.60 and highest F-measure of 0.92 was obtained for the feature length 13,900 in negative reviews (-).

WET Method

From *Table 3*, it has been analyzed that in MNB classifier, the highest TPR of 81.20, lowest FPR of 18.80 and highest F-measure of 0.81 was obtained for feature set of length 6,500 in positive reviews (+) whereas the highest TPR of 83.20, lowest FPR of 16.90 and highest F-measure of 0.83 is obtained for feature set of length 7500 in negative reviews (-).

In SMO classifier, highest TPR of 84.60, lowest FPR of 15.40 and highest F-measure of 0.84 was obtained for feature length of 5,500 in positive movie reviews (+) whereas highest TPR of 84.80, lowest FPR of 15.20 and highest F-measure of 0.84 was obtained for the feature length 10,000 in negative reviews (-).

Evaluation of TripAdvisor Dataset using Pearson's Chi Square

From the *Figure 5*, it has been analyzed that accuracy of 57.54 is obtained for aspect based features with MNB classifier, 92.60 for character-based features with SVM (K2 Kernel), 99.96 for PoS tag based features again with SVM (K2 Kernel) and 99.87 for Bag of Words with SVM (K0 Kernel).

Figure 6 depict F-measure of 0.69 with aspects features using MNB, 0.929 for character-based features (SVM, K2 Kernel), 0.99 for PoS tag based features modeled with SVM (K2 Kernel) and 0.998 for Bag of Words with SVM (K0 Kernel).

Figure 7 , shows that an FPR of 0.80 was obtained in aspect based features under MNB classifier, 0.089 for character-based features in SVM (K2 Kernel), 0.0 for PoS tag based features in SVM (K2 Kernel) and 0.0 for Bag of Words in SVM (K0 Kernel).

From the Figure 8, it has seen analyzed that optimal feature vectors were created using 180 Aspects, 5 characters, 20 PoS tags and 7500 Bag of Words.

The result of prediction is tabulated in *Table 4* for TripAdvisor dataset. Improved performance is obtained for Bag of Words and PoS tag based features.

Figure 5. Accuracy vs. classifier

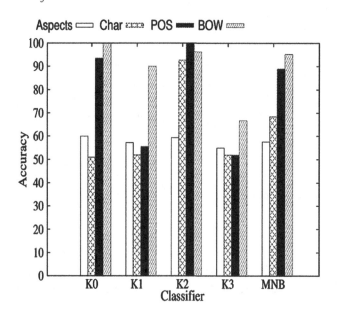

Figure 6. F-measure vs. classifier

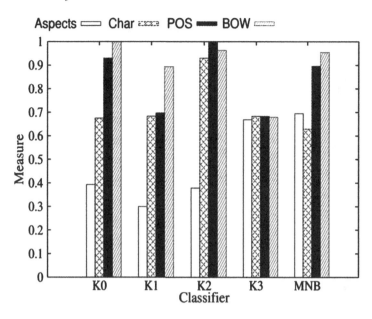

Figure 7. FPR vs. classifier

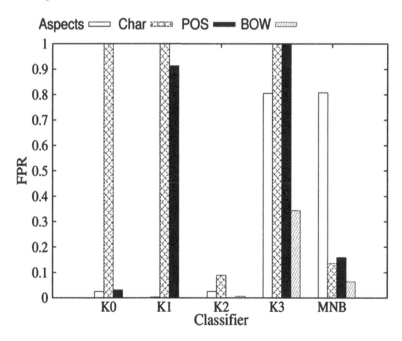

Evaluation of Multidomain Sentiment Dataset Using mRMR

Table 5 shows the performance of Apparel dataset. The better result is obtained for Bag of Words based features.

Table 6 depicts the performance of DVD dataset. The better result is obtained for bigram based features in SMO classifier with the highest F-measure of 1.0 and lowest FPR of 0.0.

Figure 8. F-Length vs. classifier

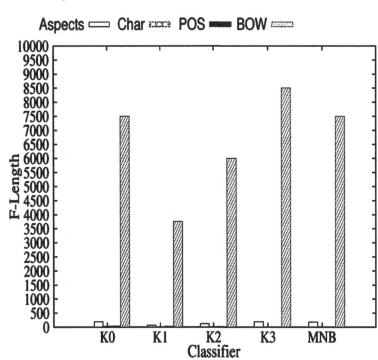

Table 4. Performance evaluation of TripAdvisor dataset using Pearson's Chi square

Feature	Classifier	Attributes	Time(sec)	FPR	TPR	ACC	F
BoW	K0	7500	123.62	0.0001	0.99	99.91	0.99
Aspects	MNB	180	0.060	0.8070	0.93	57.53	0.69
Character	K2	5	83.830	0.0941	0.91	91.18	0.91
PoS Tag	K2	20	115.73	0.0000	0.99	99.87	0.99

Table 5. Performance evaluation of apparel dataset using mRMR

Feature	Classifier	Attributes	Time(sec)	FPR	TPR	ACC	F
BoW	SMO	3750	54.84	0.0410	0.9599	95.6957	0.9568
Bigram	MNB	5000	0.19	0.9700	0.0400	72.5518	0.9769
SentiWordNet	SMO	3347	51.39	0.0360	0.959	96.1962	0.9218
PoS Tag	MNB	27	0.02	0.2793	0.5000	61.0486	0.5617

From *Table 7*, It has been analyzed that bag of words gives better result in SMO classifier attaining 100% accuracy with lowest FPR of 0.0 and highest F-measure of 1.0.

Table 8 evaluates Movie review dataset. It has been analyzed from the table that Bag of Words and Bigram gives 100% accuracy with lowest FPR of 0.0 and highest F-measure of 1.0.

Table 6. Performance evaluation of DVD dataset using mRMR

Feature	Classifier	Attributes	Time(sec)	FPR	TPR	ACC	F
BoW	SMO	3000	5.01	0.0000	1.0000	100.000	1.0000
Bigram	SMO	4750	4.68	0.0175	0.8295	90.6132	0.8982
SentiWordNet	SMO	5000	6.85	0.0050	0.9899	99.2490	0.9924
PoS Tag	K0	27	0.64	0.6084	0.7250	55.8052	0.6209

Table 7. Performance evaluation of Grocery Dataset using mRMR

Feature	Classifier	Attributes	Time(sec)	FPR	TPR	ACC	F
BoW	SMO	2250	3.53	0.0000	1.0000	100.000	1.0000
Bigram	SMO	4750	3.41	0.2960	0.9900	84.6633	0.9655
SentiWordNet	SMO	4500	6.12	0.0025	1.0000	99.8750	0.9987
PoS Tag	SMO	27	0.28	0.3566	0.7000	67.1660	0.6804

Table 8. Performance evaluation of movie review dataset using mRMR

Feature	Classifier	Attributes	Time(sec)	FPR	TPR	ACC	F
BoW	SMO	2000	3.63	0.0000	1.0000	100.000	1.0000
Bigram	SMO	3000	4.78	0.0000	1.0000	100.000	1.0000
SentiWordNet	SMO	1750	6.12	0.0025	0.0000	99.8750	0.9987
PoS Tag	SMO	29	0.35	0.2771	0.4500	58.6508	0.5209

CONCLUSION AND FUTURE SCOPE

Classifying the reviews as positive and negative with fewer misclassification is the major objective of this study. Different style markers are employed on various datasets. Character, PoS tag, Aspect and Bag of words (unigram only) are the style markers employed on Trip Advisor dataset whereas Unigram, Bigram, SentiWordNet and PoS tags are the various style markers applied on Apparel, DVD, Grocery and Movie Review Dataset. Dimensionality reduction (Guyon, Gunn, Nikravesh & Zadeh, 2008) is applied subsequently using TF-IDF, WET, Pearson's Chi-Square and mRMR to choose prominent features from the huge feature space. A vector space model for the relevant features was constructed and given to classifier through WEKA tool. The highest F-measure of 0.9998 was obtained in PoS tag based features using K2 classifier for TripAdvisor dataset. Among the Apparel, Grocery, DVD and Movie review datasets, the highest F-measure in the range 0.96 – 1.0 is obtained for unigram, bigram and SentiWordNet features using SMO classifier. Experimental results show that PoS tags and unigram of words provides excellent results in case of TripAdvisor and Multi domain sentiment datasets on the preview of accuracy and F-measure.

Future work focus to extract diverse features for performing a comparative analysis to evaluate the strength of feature for classification. Ensemble of features can also be taken into account for obtaining better results. Moreover, ensemble based feature selection methods can be employed on various domains for improved performance.

REFERENCES

Baharudin, B. (2010, December). Sentence based sentiment classification from online customer reviews. *Proceedings of the 8th International Conference on Frontiers of Information Technology* (p. 25). ACM.

Blitzer, J., Dredze, M., & Pereira, F. (2007, june). Biographies, Bollywood, Boom-boxes and Blenders: Domain Adaptation for Sentiment Classification. In ACL (Vol. 7, pp. 440-447).

Bollegala, D., Weir, D. J. & Carroll, J. A. (2013). Cross-Domain Sentiment Classification Using a Sentiment Sensitive Thesaurus. *IEEE transactions on Knowledge and Data Engineering*, 25(8), 1719-1731.

Brody, S., & Elhadad, N. (2010, June). An unsupervised aspect-sentiment model for online reviews. *Proceedings of Human Language Technologies: The 2010 Annual Conference of the North American Chapter of the Association for Computational Linguistics* (pp. 804-812). Association for Computational Linguistics.

Cantador, I., & Cremonesi, P. (2014, October). Tutorial on cross-domain recommender systems. *Proceedings of the 8th ACM Conference on Recommender systems* (pp. 401-402). ACM.

Chandrashekar, G., & Sahin, F. (2014). A survey on feature selection methods. *Computers & Electrical Engineering*, 40(1), 16–28. doi:10.1016/j.compeleceng.2013.11.024

Chen, L., Chen, G., & Wang, F. (2015). Recommender Systems Based on User Reviews: The State of the Art. *User Modeling and User-Adapted Interaction*, 25(2), 99–154. doi:10.1007/s11257-015-9155-5

Cheng, N., Chandramouli, R., & Subbalakshmi, K. P. (2011). Author gender identification from text. *Digital Investigation*, 8(1), 78–88. doi:10.1016/j.diin.2011.04.002

Chinsha, T. C., & Joseph, S. (2015, February). A syntactic approach for aspect based opinion mining. *Proceedings of the 2015 IEEE International Conference on Semantic Computing (ICSC)* (pp. 24-31). IEEE. doi:10.1109/COMSNETS.2015.7098727

Dang, Y., Zhang, Y., & Chen, H. (2010). A Lexicon-Enhanced Method for Sentiment Classification: An Experiment on Online Product Reviews. *IEEE Intelligent Systems*, 25(4), 46–53. doi:10.1109/MIS.2009.105

Elahi, M., Ricci, F., & Rubens, N. (2014). Active learning in collaborative filtering recommender systems. In *E-Commerce and Web Technologies* (pp. 113–124). Springer International Publishing. doi:10.1007/978-3-319-10491-1_12

Feng, S., Zhang, M., Zhang, Y., & Deng, Z. (2010, April). Recommended or not recommended? review classification through opinion extraction. *Proceedings of the2010 12th International Asia-PacificWeb Conference (APWEB)*, (pp. 350-352). IEEE. doi:10.1109/APWeb.2010.38

Guo, G., Zhang, J., & Yorke-Smith, N. (2015). Leveraging multiviews of trust and similarity to enhance clustering-based recommender systems. *Knowledge-Based Systems*, 74, 14–27. doi:10.1016/j.knosys.2014.10.016

Guyon, I., Gunn, S., Nikravesh, M., & Zadeh, L. A. (Eds.). (2008). *Feature Extraction: Foundations and Applications* (Vol. 207). Springer.

Hall, M., Frank, E., Holmes, G., Pfahringer, B., Reutemann, P. & Witten, I. H. (2009). The WEKA data mining software: an update. *ACM SIGKDD explorations newsletter*, 11(1), 10-18.

Han, P., Du, J., & Chen, L. (2010, September). Web opinion mining based on sentiment phrase classification vector. *Proceedings of the 2010 2nd IEEE International Conference on Network Infrastructure and Digital Content* (pp. 308-312). IEEE. doi:10.1109/ICNIDC.2010.5657968

Joachims, T. (1998). *Text categorization with support vector machines: Learning with many relevant features* (pp. 137–142). Springer Berlin Heidelberg.

Karamibekr, M., & Ghorbani, A. (2012, December). Verb oriented sentiment classification. *Proceedings of the 2012 IEEE/WIC/ACM International Conferences on Web Intelligence and Intelligent Agent Technology (WI-IAT)* (Vol. 1, pp. 327-331). IEEE doi:10.1109/WI-IAT.2012.122

Karamibekr, M., & Ghorbani, A. (2013, November). Sentence subjectivity analysis in social domains. *Proceedings of the 2013 IEEE/WIC/ACM International Joint Conferences on Web Intelligence (WI) and Intelligent Agent Technologies (IAT)* (Vol. 1, pp. 268-275). IEEE. doi:10.1109/WI-IAT.2013.39

Kawamae, N. (2012, September). Hierarchical Approach to Sentiment Analysis. *Proceedings of the 2012 IEEE Sixth International Conference on Semantic Computing (ICSC)* (pp. 138-145). IEEE. doi:10.1109/ICSC.2012.62

Kibriya, A. M., Frank, E., Pfahringer, B., & Holmes, G. (2004). Multinomial naive bayes for Text Categorization Revisited. Proceedings of AI 2004: Advances in Artificial intelligence (pp. 488–499). Springer Berlin Heidelberg. doi:10.1007/978-3-540-30549-1_43

Kohavi, R., & John, G. H. (1997). Wrappers for Feature Subset Selection. *Artificial Intelligence, 97*(1-2), 273–324. doi:10.1016/S0004-3702(97)00043-X

Koncz, P., & Paralic, J. (2011, June). An approach to feature selection for sentiment analysis. *Proceedings of the 2011 15th IEEE International Conference on Intelligent Engineering Systems (INES)* (pp. 357-362). IEEE.

Kumar, A., Kansal, C., & Ekbal, A. (2015, January). Investigating active learning techniques for document level sentiment classification of tweets.*Proceedings of the 2015 7th International Conference on Communication Systems and Networks (COMSNETS)* (pp. 1-6). IEEE.

Li, G., & Liu, F. (2010, November). A clustering-based approach on sentiment analysis. *Proceedings of the 2010 International Conference on Intelligent Systems and Knowledge Engineering (ISKE)* (pp. 331-337). IEEE.

Li, P., Zhu, Q., & Zhang, W. (2011, July). A dependency tree based approach for sentence-level sentiment classification. *Proceedings of the 2011 12th ACIS International Conference on Software Engineering, Artificial Intelligence, Networking and Parallel/Distributed Computing (SNPD)* (pp. 166-171). IEEE. doi:10.1109/SNPD.2011.20

Liang, P. W., & Dai, B.-R. (2013). Opinion Mining on Social Media Data. *Proceedings of the 2013 IEEE 14th international Conference on Mobile Data Management (MDM)* (Vol. 2, pp. 91-96). IEEE. doi:10.1109/MDM.2013.73

Liu, B. (2012). Sentiment Analysis and Opinion Mining. *Synthesis Lectures on Human Language Technologies*, *5*(1), 1–167. doi:10.2200/S00416ED1V01Y201204HLT016

Liu, W., Wu, C., Feng, B., & Liu, J. (2015). Conditional preference in recommender systems. *Expert Systems with Applications*, *42*(2), 774–788. doi:10.1016/j.eswa.2014.08.044

Lu, Y., Castellanos, M., Dayal, U., & Zhai, C. (2011, March). Automatic construction of a context-aware sentiment lexicon: an optimization approach.*Proceedings of the 20th international conference on World Wide Web* (pp. 347-356). ACM. doi:10.1145/1963405.1963456

Maimon, O., & Rockach, L. (Eds.). (2005). *Data mining and knowledge discovery handbook* (Vol. 2). New York: Springer. doi:10.1007/b107408

Marrese-Taylor, E., Velásquez, J. D., & Bravo-Marquez, F. (2014). A novel deterministic approach for aspect-based opinion mining in tourism products reviews. *Expert Systems with Applications*, *41*(17), 7764–7775. doi:10.1016/j.eswa.2014.05.045

McNally, K., O'Mahony, M. P., & Smyth, B. (2014). A comparative study of collaboration-based reputation models for social recommender systems. *User Modeling and User-Adapted Interaction*, *24*(3), 219–260. doi:10.1007/s11257-013-9143-6

Moghaddam, S., & Ester, M. (2011 December). AQA: Aspect-based Opinion Question Answering. *Proceedings of the2011IEEE 11*[th] *International Conference on Data Mining Workshops (ICDMW)* (pp. 89-96). IEEE.

Mouthami, K., Devi, K. N., & Bhaskaran, V. M. (2013, February). Sentiment analysis and classification based on textual reviews. *Proceedings of the 2013 International Conference on Information Communication and Embedded Systems (ICICES)* (pp. 271-276). IEEE. doi:10.1109/ICICES.2013.6508366

Mukherjee, A., Liu, B., & Glance, N. (2012, April). Spotting fake reviewer groups in consumer reviews.*Proceedings of the 21st international conference on World Wide Web* (pp. 191-200). ACM. doi:10.1145/2187836.2187863

Pang, B., & Lee, L. (2004, July), A sentimental education: Sentiment analysis using subjectivity summarization based on minimum cuts.*Proceedings of the 42nd annual meeting on Association for Computer Linguistics*, (p. 271). Association for Computational Linguistics. doi:10.3115/1218955.1218990

Pang, B., Lee, L., & Vaithyanathan, S. (2002, July). Thumbs up?: sentiment classification using machine learning techniques.*Proceedings of the ACL-02 conference on Empirical methods in natural language processing (Vol. 10,* pp. 79-86). Association for Computational Linguistics. doi:10.3115/1118693.1118704

Peng, H., Long, F., & Ding, C. (2005). Feature selection based on mutual information criteria of max-dependency, max-relevance, and min-redundancy. *IEEE Transactions on* Pattern Analysis and Machine Intelligence, *27*(8), 1226–1238.

Rana, C., & Jain, S. K. (2015). A study of the dynamic features of recommender systems. *Artificial Intelligence Review*, *43*(1), 141–153. doi:10.1007/s10462-012-9359-6

Satsiou, A., & Tassiulas, L. (2014, August). Propagating users' similarity towards improving recommender systems. *Proceedings of the 2014 IEEE/WIC/ACM International Joint Conferences on Web Intelligence (WI) and Intelligent Agent Technologies (IAT)* (Vol. 1, pp. 221-228). IEEE Computer Society.

Shahbaz, M., & Guergachi, A. (2014, May). Sentiment miner: A prototype for sentiment analysis of unstructured data and text. *Proceedings of the 2014 IEEE 27th Canadian Conference on Electrical and Computer Engineering (CCECE,* (pp. 1-7). IEEE. doi:10.1109/CCECE.2014.6901087

Singh, V. K., Piryani, R., Uddin, A., & Waila, P. (2013, February). Sentiment analysis of Movie reviews and Blog posts. *Proceedings of the2013 IEEE 3rd InternationalAdvance Computing Conference (IACC),* (pp. 893-898). IEEE. doi:10.1109/IAdCC.2013.6514345

Verbert, K., Manouselis, N., Ochoa, X., Wolpers, M., Drachsler, H., Bosnic, I., & Duval, E. (2012). Context-aware recommender systems for learning: A survey and future challenges. *IEEE Transactions on* Learning Technologies, *5*(4), 318–335.

Wang, Y. & Wong, A. K. C. (2003). From Association to Classification: Inference Using weight of evidence. *Knowledge and Data Engineering., IEEE transactions on* 15(3), 764-767.

Wong, B., Pun, C. F., Kit, C., & Webster, J. J. (2011, November). Lexical cohesion for evaluation of machine translation at document level. *Proceedings of the 2011 7th International Conference on Natural Language Processing and Knowledge Engineering (NLP-KE)* (pp. 238-242). IEEE.

Xu, B., Bu, J., Chen, C., & Cai, D. (2012). An exploration of improving collaborative recommender systems via user-item subgroups.*Proceedings of the 21st international conference on World Wide Web* (pp. 21-30). ACM. doi:10.1145/2187836.2187840

Xu, Y. (2012, December). A Comparative Study on Feature Selection in Unbalance Text Classification. *Proceedings of the 2012 International Symposium on Information Science and Engineering (ISISE)* (pp. 44-47). IEEE. doi:10.1109/ISISE.2012.19

Yang, X., Guo, Y., Liu, Y., & Steck, H. (2014). A survey of collaborative filtering based social recommender systems. *Computer Communications*, *41*, 1–10. doi:10.1016/j.comcom.2013.06.009

Zha, Z. J., Yu, J., Tang, J., Wang, M., & Chua, T. S. (2014). Product aspect ranking and its applications. *IEEE Transactions on* Knowledge and Data Engineering, *26*(5), 1211–1224.

Zhang, Y., & Zhu, W. (2013). Extracting implicit features in online customer reviews for opinion mining.*Proceedings of the 22nd international conference on World Wide Web companion* (pp. 103-104). International World Wide Web Conferences Steering Committee. doi:10.1145/2487788.2487835

KEY TERMS AND DEFINITIONS

Collaborative Filtering: It is the technique used by recommender systems and the main characteristic of CF is that it predicts the utility of items for a user based on the items previously rated by other like-minded users.

Dimensionality Reduction: The process of dimensionality reduction helps easier to visualize the data when reduced to very low dimensions such as 2D or 3D. It reduces time and storage space required.

Recommender Systems: Recommender systems are widely used on the web for recommending products and services to users. Most e-commerce sites have such systems.

Sentiment Analysis: Sentiment analysis aims at retrieving sentiment-related information from documents on the web.

TF-IDF: Term Frequency-Inverse Document Frequency. It is a popular feature selection algorithm widely used in text categorization.

WET: Weight of Evidence of Text. One amongst the dimensionality reduction technique.

WEKA: Waikato Environment for Knowledge Analysis is abbreviated as WEKA. It is open source software and is issued under GNU general public license.

Section 2
Collaborative Filtering:
An Introduction

Chapter 4
History and Overview of the Recommender Systems

Venkatesan M.
Government Arts College (Autonomous), India

Thangadurai K.
Government Arts College (Autonomous), India

ABSTRACT

This Chapter analyzes the recommender systems, their history and its framework in brief. The current generation of filtering techniques in recommendation methods can be broadly classified into the following five categories. Techniques used in these categories are discussed in detail. Data mining algorithms techniques are implemented in recommender systems to filters user data ratings. Area of application of Recommender Systems gives broad idea and such as how it gives impact and why it is used in the e-commerce, Online Social Networks (OSN), and so on. It has shifted the core of Internet applications from devices to users. In this chapter, issues and recent research in recommender system are also discussed.

INTRODUCTION

It is the recommender system which is considered one among the most powerful tools in the present digital world. Explanations are usually provided by it to their recommendations so that web users are helped to find its products, people and also their friends who are missing in social communities. In the field of recommender system, there are various methods and approaches which have been implemented. There are two approaches which are most widely used. They are content-based and collaborative approaches. These personalized approaches should be studied so that the best recommendations are provided to the end users.

Originally, we define Recommender systems as ones where ''recommendations are provided by people as inputs, which are then aggregated and directed to appropriate recipients by the system''. The clear main purpose of the current recommender systems is to guide the user to useful/interesting objects. Due to this, evaluation of recommender systems shows to what extent this goal has been achieved.

DOI: 10.4018/978-1-5225-0489-4.ch004

Explanations of its recommendations are usually provided by Recommender system so that users are helped better to choose products, activities or even friends. It is the task of recommender systems to turn data on users and their preferences into predictions of possible future likes and interests of the users. When an explanation is received by a user, a recommendation can be accepted more easily since transparency is provided by the system to its recommendations (which follows most of recommender algorithms). The Human Style, Feature Style and Item Style approaches are followed by the most traditional approaches. Even this simple approach can be realized in various ways.

There was an emergence of the first analysis paper on collaborative filtering in the mid-1990s. Since then, Recommender systems have become an important research area basically, recommender systems directly help users to identify content, products or services (such as books, digital products, movies, web sites etc...) with the aggregation and analysis of suggestions from other users, which also means the reviews from a number of authorities and users (Figure 1).

Filtering Technique is said to be the backdrop of every recommender system approach. It gives a clear working nature of this recommender system. This inter disciplinary approach shown here facilitates item ontology and it contains the details of the item for user. The most wanted purchases are watched carefully by the users in order to recommend with clear observation and also to enrich their product promotion. The concentration of item ontology is on the diversified items for the want of the need. The characteristics of each item, along with all recommendation, are given in order to provide a clear vision on the products which are searched. All these data are sent to the recommender systems and they act as filter to the user so that they are able to meet with their needs and purpose. The user modeling data looks up for their likes and interests and they are interpreted with rating in the user rating. The recommender system is the filtering technique. It now filters the data as per the need and interest of the user. They guide users to select the correct content to the correct person. Besides helping to decide the buying products, the recommended item also provides the list of availability to the need of the customer.

CLASSIFICATION METHOD

Our classification framework comprises of recommendation field and data mining techniques. In this research, we segregate the research papers that were analyzed into eight groups of application fields and

Figure 1. Recommender systems

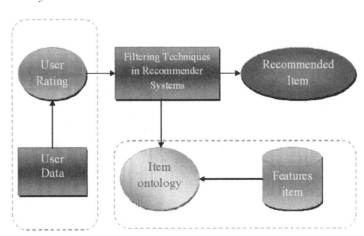

eight groups of data mining techniques. The general graphical classification framework for recommender systems research papers is shown in Figure 2.

Classification Framework for Application Fields

There are many recommender systems that have been utilized so that users are provided with information to guide them decide which products they could purchase (Schafer, Joseph, & Riedl, 2001). But, it is very difficult to find papers that segregate research papers systematically, in spite of applying recommender systems to different business areas. Consequently, it is momentous to explore application fields. Our research assumes the fundamental classification system of Schafer et al., 2001, where recommendation applications have been classified by real world such as books, movies, music, shopping and others. Research papers are classified by us using application fields such as books, documents, images, movies, music, shopping, TV programs and others. By means of in-depth analysis of research papers, classifying shopping fields include online, offline, and mobile shopping product, classifying document fields include papers, blogs and web pages. Apart from this, other fields include a marginal number of recommendation fields like hotel, travel, and food.

Classification Framework for Data Mining Techniques

Usually we define data mining techniques as drawing out or taking out knowledge from data. We use these techniques for exploration and analysis of large amount of data so that meaningful patterns and rules are discovered (Berry & Linoff, 2004). We can use them to escort decision making and to envisage the result of decisions. Considerably, many researchers have employed data mining techniques so that the performance of recommender systems is improved. As a result, it becomes significant to categorize the research papers as per data mining techniques. Data mining techniques are broadly classified into the following eight categories: association rule, clustering, decision tree, k-nearest neighbor, link analysis, neural network, regression, and other heuristic methods.

Figure 2. Recommender systems framework

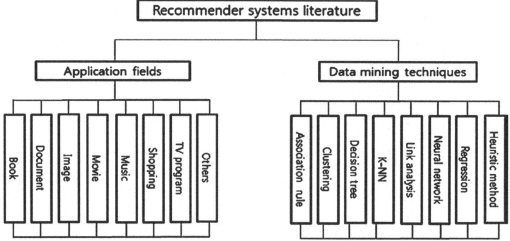

Association Rule

Association rule mining indicates the detection of all association rules which are more than user-specified minimum support and minimum confidence levels. When a set of transactions are given where each transaction consists of a set of items, an association rule pertains the form X) Y, in which X and Y are two sets of items (Cho, Kim, & Kim, 2002).

Clustering

The clustering method is used to identify a finite set of categories or clusters in order to depict data. Amongst the many clustering methods, the most famous are K-means and self-organizing map (SOM). K-means draws the input parameter, K and also divides a group of n objects into K clusters (Berry & Linoff, 2004). SOM method is used for an unconfirmed learning on the basis of a non-natural neurons clustering technique (Lihua, Lu, Jing, & Zongyong, 2005).

Decision Tree

Decision tree induction techniques are the most famous classification methods. Decision trees are built by them to mark or classify cases into a set of known classes. The top node in a tree is termed a root node. In a decision tree, every internal (non-leaf) node stands for a test on a quality and every branch constitutes a result of the test, and each terminal (leaf) node constitutes a class forecast (Kim, Cho, Kim, Kim, & Suh, 2002).

K-Nearest Neighbor

The k-NN (k-nearest neighbor) model is a usual traditional CF-based recommender system. It makes recommendations as said by the following three phases:

- A user profile is constructed by recommender systems with the help of the preference ratings of the user which are collected either straightly from precise ratings of items or obliquely from acquisition or usage information.
- Statistical or machine learning techniques are applied by recommender systems so that to k users who are known as neighbors or recommenders are discovered. They are those who have shown similar behaviors in the past. On the basis of the degree of similarity between a mark user and other users, a neighborhood is formed.
- As soon as a neighborhood is formed for a target user, a top-n item set which the target user is most likely to purchase is made by recommender systems. This is done by examining the items where more interest is exhibited by the neighbors (Kim, Kim, & Ryu, 2009).

Neural Network

A parallel distributed information processing system which can learn and self-organize is called a neural network. There are a large number of simple processing operations. They are interconnected in order to form a network which performs computational tasks which are complicated (Ibnkahla, 2000). It is the neural network which constructs a class of very flexible model that is used for a variety of different applications like prediction, non-linear regression, or classification (Anders & Korn, 1999).

Link Analysis

Link analysis is used to discover relations between domains in large databases. Social network analysis refers to the sociological approach that is used to analyze patterns, relationships and interactions between social actors so that a fundamental social structure is formed. Link analysis has also exhibited great prospective in enhancing the exactness of web searches. Link analysis comprises of Page Rank and HITS algorithms. Most link analysis algorithms are able to handle a web page as a single node in the web graph (Cai, He, Wen, & Ma, 2004).

Regression

A powerful process for surveying associative relationships between dependent variables and one or more independent variables is termed Regression analysis. Its uses have been for curve fitting, foretelling and checking methodical hypotheses about relationships between variables (Malhotra, 2007).

A BRIEF HISTORY / OVERVIEW OF RECOMMENDER SYSTEMS

The roots of recommendation systems are in "Usenet,". It is a globally distributed discussion system which originated at Duke University in the late 1970s. Usenet which is employed in a client/server format allows user input that was classified into specific "newsgroups." In Usenet, users' posts are classified into these newsgroups. They are again divided into sub-groups, if needed. It is done on the basis of a trust mechanism.

History: Before 1992

- Content Filtering.
  - An architecture for large scale information systems [1985] (Gifford, D.K).
  - A rule-based message filtering system [1988] (Pollock, S.).
  - MAFIA: An active mail-filter agent for an intelligent document processing support [1990] (Lutz, E.).

History: 1992-1998

- Tapestry by Xerox Palo Alto [1992].
  - First system designed by collaborative filtering.
- Grouplens [1994].
  - First recommender system using rating data.
- Movielens [1997].
  - First movie recommender system.
  - Provide well-known dataset for researchers.

- Empirical Analysis of Predictive Algorithms for Collaborative Filtering [1998] (John S. Breese).
    - Systematically evaluate user-based collaborative filtering.

History: 1999-2005

- Pandora began music genome project [2000].
- Amazon proposed item-based collaborative filtering (Patent is filed in 1998 and issued in 2001).
- Thomas Hofmann proposed pLSA [1999] and apply similar method on collaborative filtering [2004].
- Evaluating collaborative filtering recommender systems [2004] (Jonathan L. Herlocker).

History: 2005-2009

- Toward the Next Generation of Recommender Systems: A Survey of the State-of-the-Art and Possible Extensions. [2005] (Alexander Tuzhilin).
- Netflix Prize.
    - Latent Factor Model (SVD, RSVD, NSVD, SVD++).
    - Temporal Dynamic Collaborative Filtering.
    - Yehuda Koren's team get prize.
- ACM Conference on Recommender System [2007] (Minneapolis, Minnesota, USA).
- Digg, Youtube try recommender system.

History: From 2010 Onwards

- Context-Aware Recommender Systems.
- Music Recommendation and Discovery.
- Recommender Systems and the Social Web.
- Information Heterogeneity and Fusion in Recommender Systems.
- Human Decision Making in Recommender Systems.
- Personalization in Mobile Applications.
- Novelty and Diversity in Recommender Systems.
- User-Centric Evaluation.
- Facebook launches instant personalization [2010].

Through the 1990s and beyond, collaborative filtering recommendation systems included:

- **Mosaic**: First graphical browser allowing users to publish comments to Web pages.
- **HOMR:** Helpful Online Music Recommendations; predecessor to Firefly.
- **Ringo:** Social Information filtering system for music recommendations.
- **Firefly:** Grew out of Ringo project, music and movies.
- **Yahoo!:** Started by Princeton students David Filo and Jerry Yang.
- **Point's Top 5%:** NYC-based qualitative website rating.
- **PHOAKS**: People Helping One Another Know Stuff.
- **Fab**: Allowed users to create content-based filters.

- **Webdoggie**: Helped people find websites according to their likes.
- **Alexa Internet**: When someone visits a website, Alexa displays other websites they might be interested in recommendation systems are now an integral part of Amazon.com's purchasing power!

CLASSIFICATION

The means of an automatic filtration of items that are interesting are provided by recommender systems. This is done usually based on the past user ratings similarities. Users are allowed to construct recommender network by earlier mode. Recommender connections are grown with the users expressing trust and obtaining transparency Recommender system are built by using different techniques are currently available recommendation methods are extensively classified into fire categories as below based upon the knowledge of sources used in making Recommendations:

- Content - based Recommendations.
- Collaborative - based Recommendations.
- Knowledge - based Recommendations.
- Demographic Recommendations.
- Hybrid Recommendations.

General Requirements for Recommendation Systems

The following three factors are required to make a viable recommendation:

- **Background Information**: The information available in the systems before the recommendation process commences.
- **Input Information:** The information to be entered to the system by a user to start recommendation.
- **An Algorithm:** The combination of input information and back ground information to arrive at the recommendation.

Content-Based Recommendation

Usually, items similar to the ones preferred by a user already are recommended in content-based systems. For instance, the content- based recommendation system will be in search of similarities rated high by the user in the part parameters such as specific writers, subject content, genres etc. This enables the recommendation application to recommend book that are highly rated with a good degree of similarities alone would be recommended to the users invariable to the user's preferences.

Generally, text-based items are recommended and duly designed by content based systems. The evaluated preferences are known as 'Keywords' content based recommendations are of two categories

- **Memory /Heuristic**: Works on inverse document frequency (TF-IDF) text retrieval method and frequency.
- **Model Based**: Works on during or vector based representations, neural networks, Decision trees and Bayesian classifications.

Content-Based Recommendation Works

The profile of preferences of the user in kept in store as a vector of key words. Making use of techniques of keyword analysis and retrieval information. User profiles are taken by content analysis of already seen items by the user and are thereby constructed. Various weights to keywords are given during retrieval of information. These weights are given using algorithms namely Winnow and Rocchio. While implementing content based RS, Baysian classifiers and other machine learning techniques such as clustering, decision trees and artificial neural networks are made use of.

Content-Based Recommendation Works

Items which group peoples with same taste that are preferred in the part are suggested by collaborative recommendation systems. Tapestry, who in one of the makers of the earliest recommendation systems, coined at first the term "collaborative Filtering" a number of e-commerce websites use collaborative Fittings. They provide the users with personalized recommendations based on the products previous ratings. It is assured that in CF when both users A and B rate in items similarly, their personal tastes are correlated.

To predict properly, ratings for an item are required in collaborative filtering irrespective of explicit rating or implicit rating. The user into rate on item in explicit rating. The user's preference is inferred in implicit rating from user's actions. The user may be interested to buy a product and same in inferred when he visits a product page. He buys the product, when he buys the product it is inferred that the user has a very strong desire in similar products.

Knowledge-Based Recommendation

Knowledge based recommendation makes use of the knowledge with reference to users and products. It also sorts out the products according to the requirements of users. The systems which are currently used help to locate the product taking the user through a discrimination tree of products. The other system follows a quantitative decision support tool for this purpose.

Demographic-Based Recommendation

This recommends based on demography i.e. demographic classes' ex. men women, teenagers, college boys etc. this is almost similar to the advantage and disadvantage of knowledge based recommendation systems.

Hybrid Recommendation Systems

The aforesaid systems have strength and weakness as well. A combination of two or many recommendation system, using the strength of each system, result in a Hybrid recommendation system. Weaknesses in a Hybrid recommendation system are limited. Content based and collaborative filtering are two popular Hybrids.

Methods/Strategies of Hybridization

Hybrids are promoted by the different hybridization methods. They are classified into seven strategies. They are as bellows:

- **Weighted:** By combining the predications of *collaborative* and *content-based methods.*
- **Switching:** Interchange between two recommendation systems which operate on a single object in effected by certain switching mode.
- **Feature Combination**: Features of different recommendation system combine to form a single recommendation algorithm.
- **Cascading:** In this hybridization method, the results given by a recommendation system are refined by other system.
- **Meta Level:** In this method, the model of one recommendation system is used as on input to the other recommendation system. In *Feature Augmentation System,* the entire model is taken as on input. But in Meta level, it is not so.
- **Feature Augmentation:** The total output of a system serves as an input of another system.
- **Mixed:** In this, two are more recommendation system are integrated together. For instance, when content-based and collaborative filtering are integrated together, it is called Mixed.

TECHNIQUES APPLIED IN RECOMMENDER SYSTEMS

Data mining is nothing but a process which computer based methodology is applied to discover knowledge from data. Data mining a natural and evaluating product of Information Technology. The version faces of data mining are as follows: *Data collection, Data base creation, Data management* (data storage, date retrieval, database tram action process, advance data analysis, Data ware housing, Data mining, Data collection and data base creation form basis for effective data storage, retrieval and data base transaction process). The most common methods used in RS are Data Processing, Classification, Clustering and association rule discovery (Haw, Kamber & Pei, 2006).

CLASSIFICATION TECHNIQUES

A classifier is a mapping between a feature space and a label space, where the features represent characteristics of the elements to categorize and the labels represent the classes (Ricci, Rokach, Shapira & Kantor, 2011). Classifiers are nothing but usual computation models and they assign a category to an input. The inputs act as vectors of features for the items which are being classified. Otherwise, they may be data about relationships in between the items. A recommender system is developed utilizing a classifier by using information with reference to a product and as customer which are the inputs. The output is how vehemently the product is recommended to the customer.

A variety of machine-learning strategies are used to implement classifies. A training set is one to which grand truth classification are present. The classifiers are trained using training sets in each case.

There are new items without grand truths. In order to classify such items, the classifier may be retrained over time (Ben Schafer). Supervised or unsupervised classifications are usually discussed, though there are many kinds of classifiers available. A set of categories or labels which are already familiar as for as supervised classification is concerned. A set of labeled examples make a training set in this type of classification.

Nearest Neighbors

Instance-based classifiers store training records. Such records are used to predict class label of unknown cases. *Rote-learner* is a typical example. Only when the attributes of the new record match the training examples, then the classifier memories the training set. A more elaborate, and for more popular, instance-based classifier is the is the *Nearest Neighbors classifier* (*k*NN) (Cover & Hart, 1967). The *k*NN classifier locates the *k* closest points. *Nearest neighbors* from the training records, when a point is to be classified. Accordingly, class labels to the fall the *nearest neighbors* class labels. The idea the idea behind this is that when a record is fallen in a neighborhood with a predominant class label, it is sure the record definitely belongs to the same class.

Decision Trees

Decision trees are classifiers on a target (or class) in the form of a tree structure (Quinlan, Rokach & Maimon). The items which are to be classified are synthesized of attributes along with their target value. The nodes of the tree are a) *decision nodes*, a single attribute-value is examined to decide as to which branch the sub tree belongs to, *leaf nodes* identify the value of the target attribute. Decision trees have numerous algorithms. To quote a few are: Hunts Algorithm, CART, ID3, C4.5, SLIQ, SPRINT etc.

Decision trees are made use of for an RS in approach that is model based. One possibility is to use content features to build a decision tree that models all the variables concerned in the user preferences (Bouza, Reif Bernstein & Gall, 2008). A decision tree is constructed by them using this idea semantic information available for the items was used for this. On rating only two item by the user, the tree is constructed. The salient features of each item are taken into account to construct a model which will explain the rating of the user. Each and every features is used the splitting criteria. From a theoretical point of view, this approach looks very interesting but the precision is not reliable. It is worse than the precision of the average rating.

Bayesian Classifiers

A probable framework to solve problems of classification is a Bayesian classifier (Bouza, Reif, Bernstein, & Gall, 2008). It works on the basis of the Bayes theorem and conditional probability. Uncertainties of relationships which are gathered from the date are represented by the Bayesian school of thought and statistics using probability. Each and every attribute and class label which are either continuous as random variables by Bayesian classifiers. The aim is to predict class Ck by finding the value of Ck which takes to the maximizes level the given data's the posterior probability of the class $P(Ck|A1, A2, ..., AN)$. Applying Bayes' theorem $(Ck|A1, A2, ..., AN) \propto P(A1, A2, ..., AN|Ck)P(Ck)$.

For instance, a model based on a training set in each node of a decision tree is created by Bayesiasn networks and every edges represents user information. In a time span of hours or days, the model can be constructed off-line. The resultant model thus built is very tiny, accurate and very fast as CF methods (Breese et al., 1998). Bayesian classifiers are very common for model-based RS. A model for content-based RS is derived most often by using Bayesian classifiers. They are used in CF setting (Ghani & Fano, 2002)

Artificial Neural Networks

An Artificial Neural Network (ANN) (Zurada, J.) is a combination of many inter-connected nodes and weight links. ANN is inspired in the design, fabric and construction of a biological brain. Nodes are termed as neurons in a biological brain and are called so in ANN also. Nodes the basic functional units are composed to form networks. These networks, on training with sufficient data, are able to learn a classification problem. ANN could be made use of in the same way as Bayesian Networks to build model- based RS. It is not yet confirmed whether any performance gain is introduced in ANN.

Pazzani and Billsus performed a deep and comprehensive study on the usage of many machine learning algorithms to recommend for website. The main objective of them was to compare Bayesian classifier which is very simple and strength with decision trees and neural networks which very costly alternatives computationally. According to their experiments, the performance of decision trees is comparably worse. They concluded that ANN and Bayesian classifiers are equal in terms of performance. They also concluded that these is no need for non-linear classifier such as ANN Berka et al. made use of ANN to construct an URL RS for web navigation.

CLUSTERING

Clustering techniques work on the principle of locating groups of consumers with similar preferences. The opinions of other consumers are averaged in a cluster. It is used to predict the choice of an individual. Each user who partially participates in many clusters is represented in some clustering techniques. Among the clusters which are weighted by various degrees of participation, the prediction is averaged. Personal recommendations made in clustering techniques are far less than that of made in other methods. More so in terms of accuracy also CF-based algorithms (Breese et al., 1998) possesses more accuracy than the clusters. However, as, the size of the groups is very tiny, the performance rate will be better, once the clustering task is over. Clustering techniques may be applied as the 'First step' for narrowing the consumer set in a CF-based algorithm. They also can be to applied to distribute neighbor computations among many recommender engines. The accuracy of recommendations may get hurt while forming the population into clusters. Pre-clustering may prove worthy between accuracy and output.

K-Means

K-mean is a partitioning method clustering. The item of time is partitioned so that they are very near to each other clustering happens around the centroid. Distance is minimized here. K-mean algorithm is very simple and efficient at the same time. However, it has some short coming also.

Alternatives to k-Means

- **Density Based Clustering Algorithm:** (DBSCAN)-DBSCAN works on the density of definition, since the points are within the particular radius. DBSCAN defines three kinds of points namely Core points, Border point, Noise points.
- **Message –Passing Clustering:** Message passing clustering algorithm are the latest. They are graph–base clustering methods. All points are considered as centres are called examples. They exchange manager effectively with better results.
- **Hierarchical Clustering**: It produces a set of rested clusters, which are informed of a hierarchical tree. (Dendogram). Clusters are made in any desired number by locating in the proper level in the tree.

Association Rule Mining

Association rule mining deals with developing rules during occurrences of item in a transaction i.e., Co-occurrences. A two-step approach:

1. Generate all itemsets whose support ≥ minsup (Frequent Itemset Generation);
2. Create high confidence rules from every frequent itemset (Rule Generation).

The most common approach though, is to decrease the number of candidates using the *Apriori principle*

FILTERING TECHNIQUES

The basic task for any data mining process is "Filtering technique." It is the objective of a recommender system to deliver a list of personalized recommendation to its users. Through this technique, we can predict evaluations or assign alternative recommendation scores to objects yet unknown to a given user. Objects whose ratings are predicted to be the highest constitute the recommendation list and this list is given to the target user. In order to evaluate the resulting recommendation lists, we may use an extensive set of performance metrics. Information filtering is nothing but a method of examining the very large quantity (Over-abundance) of data on the web. Due to the exponential growth of news groups, database administrators were competing (Scrambling) with one another, so that they might find a way to reduce e- clutter. Tapestry, Lotus Notes and Group Lens are a few early solutions for data overload. The typical classifications of recommender systems are shown in Figure 3.

Demographic-Based Filtering

Though Demographic techniques form "people - to- people" correlations just as collaborative filtering, the data used are different. A demographic approach has an important advantage. Unlike collaborative and content-based techniques, it may not require a history of user ratings. But demographic filtering recommenders have certain shortcoming because they classify users using stereotyped descriptors and create user profiles. Moreover, they recommend the same items to users with similar demographic profiles. The quality of these recommendations might be very poor because every user is not the same.

Figure 3. Filtering techniques

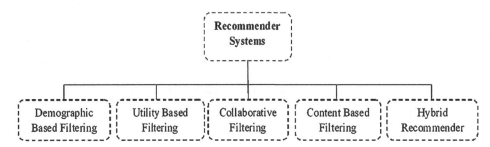

The users are categorized by Demographic filtering recommender systems. This categorization is based on their personal attributes like education, age, occupation and / or gender. It is done to learn the relationship between a single item and the kind of people who like it (Rich, 1979; Krulwich, 1997) so that recommendations are made on the basis of demographic class. A good example for demographic filtering recommender system is Grundy's system. Through this system personal information is gathered through an interactive dialogue and then books are recommended.

The responses of the users were matched against a library which contained manually assembled user stereotypes. A system where demographic groups are used from marketing research was proposed by Hill et al (1995) in order to suggest a range of products & services. They took a short survey so that the data for user categorization could be gathered. In Pazzani's (1999) proposed system, they use machine learning so that they may arrive at a classifier based on demographic data. But the interests of an individual user tend to change over time and hence there is a need for the user profile to adapt to change. This is usually available in collaborative filtering and content based recommenders because the input taken by them for recommendation making is user's preference data.

Utility-Based Filtering

Utility based recommender systems make recommendations on the basis of the computation of the utility of each item for the user. In utility-based recommendation techniques, features of items are used as background data, utility functions over items are extracted from users to describe used preferences and the function is applied to determine the rank of items for a user (Burke, 2002). Hence the user profile is the utility function derived by the system for the user and constraint satisfaction techniques are adopted to locate the best match. No attempts are taken by utility-based recommenders to build long- term generalizations about their users, instead their advice is based on an evaluation of the match between a user's need and the set of options available.

There are various techniques with the e–commerce site persona logic in order to arrive at a user–specific utility function and to apply it to the objects under consideration The utility–based recommendations do not face problems involving new users, new items and sparsity (Burke, 2002) and this is an added advantage for this. It can include non- product characteristics like reliability on vendor and availability of product into the utility computation, thereby it is made possible. We could describe all recommendation techniques as doing some kind of inference. How to create a utility function for each user is the main problem here. It is necessary for the user to build a complete preference function and weigh the importance of each attribute. This may often lead to a significant burden of interaction.

Collaborative Filtering

Collaborative filtering is one of the most famous recommender systems. It collects the opinions of customers in the form of ratings on items, services or service providers. People know it mostly for its use on popular e-commerce sites such as Amazon.com or NetFlix. Com (Linden et al., 2003). Most importantly, a collaborative filtering based recommender makes the process of the 'word -of- mouth' paradigm automatic. It consults the opinions or preferences of users with similar tastes to the target user (Breese et al., 1998; Schafer et al., 2001) and makes recommendations to a target user. Collaborative and content-based heuristic approaches were mostly utilized by early recommender systems. But for many years in the past, other broad range of techniques such as statistical, machine learning, information retrieval and other methods are used in recommender systems.

On the basis of information about similarities among the tastes of different users, collaborative filtering provides technology to recommend items of potential interest. Similarity measure takes the most prominent role in finding users with like mind, i.e. The target user's neighborhood. The standard collaborative filtering based recommenders use a user's item ratings as the data source so that they generate the user's neighborhood. Since different people have different tastes, rating is done differently according to their subjective taste. If a set of items is rated similarly by two people, they share similar tastes. In the recommender system, they use this information to recommend items which are liked by one participant to other persons in the same group.

Conventional collaborative filtering based recommenders usually suffer from problems like scalability and sparsity. So some researchers suggested a modified collaborative filtering paradigm to solve these problems. We refer to this adapted approach as item-based collaborative filtering. The basis on which the conventional collaborative filtering technique (or user-based collaborative filtering) operates is by utilizing the performance correlations among users. Different from the user-based collaborative filtering techniques, item- based collaborative filtering techniques examine the set of items the target user has rated and compute how much they are similar to the target items that are to be recommended. Content based filtering techniques compute item similarities on the basis of the content information of items whereas item- based collaborative filtering techniques check whether two items are commonly rated together with similar ratings and determine whether they are similar (Deshpande & Karypsis 2004)

The aim of a collaborative filtering system (CF) is to filter huge amount of information so that it can guide users of web applications towards items that may interest them. Such a system consists of recommending a set of personalized items for an active user, as per the preferences of other similar users (Salah, Rogovschi & Nadif, 2016).

Collaborative: "Tell Me What's Popular among My Peers"

Figure 4 shows that the collaborative filtering is the simplest and original implementation of this approach. The active user is recommended items which other users with similar tastes liked in the past. On the basis of the similarity in the rating history of the users, they calculate the similarity in the taste of two users. Collaborative filtering is called "People-to- people correlation". It is used by large, marketable e-commerce.

Figure 4. Collaborative filtering

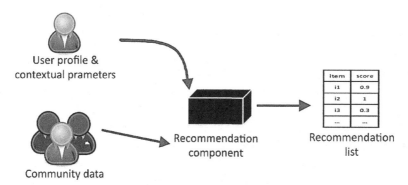

Benefits of Collaborative Filtering

- **Subjective View**: Usually subjective information about items (e.g., style, quality etc.) is incorporated into their recommendations. So in many cases, collaborative filtering based recommenders provide better recommendation quality than content-based recommenders because they have the ability to differentiate a badly written and a well written article if similar terms are used in both.
- **Broader Scope**: While collaborative filtering makes recommendations on the basis of the preferences of other users, content-based filtering solely uses the preference information of the target user. Thus, in turn, unanticipated recommendations are facilitated because other user's items which are interesting can extend the scope of interest of the target user beyond his or her already seen items.
- **Broader Applications**: Collaborative filtering based recommenders have the absolute liberty to represent the items that are recommended and so they can recommend any type of items including those items from which automatic extraction of semantic attributes is hard-for e.g. Video and audio files (Shardanand & Maes 1995, Terreen et al. 1997). Hence, CF based recommenders work well for complicated items like music and movies, where variations in preference are due to the responsibility of variations in taste (Burke 2002).

Limitations of Collaborative Filtering

- **Cold–Start**: The cold–start problem is one challenge which is commonly faced by collaborative filtering based recommenders. On the basis of different situations, we can classify the cold start problem into two types, namely 'new- system-cold-start problem' and 'new–user–cold–start–problem.' The circumstance in which a new system has inadequate profiles of users is referred to as new–system-cold–start problem. In this circumstance, Collaborative filtering based recommenders do not have any basis upon which they can recommend and so they perform poorly (Middleton et al. 2002). In the new–user–cold–start problem, quality recommendations are not able to be made by recommenders to new target users with no or limited rating information. This problem still happens for systems which have a certain number of user profiles (Middleton et al. 2002). When there is an appearance of a brand–new item in the system, without any way, we can recommend it to a user until we obtain more information through another user rating it. We commonly refer to this situation as the "early–rater problem" (Towle & Quinn 2000., Coster et al.2002)

- **Sparsity**: When the number of users is small compared to the number of items in the system, the coverage of user ratings can be sparse. In other words, when the system has too many items, many users might be there with no or few common items shared with others. We commonly refer to this problem as the "sparsity problem." A real computational challenge is posed by the sparsity problem because it is hard for collaborative filtering-based recommenders to find neighbours and it is also harder for them to recommend items because very few people have given ratings.

- **Scalability**: Another main challenge for collaborative filtering based recommenders is "Scalability." Before being effective, collaborative filtering based recommenders have need of data from a large number of users. They also require a large amount of data from each user when they limit their recommendations to the exact items which those users have specified. There might be a dynamic increase in the number of users and items in e–commerce sites. As a result, severe performance and scaling issues will inevitably be faced by the recommenders (Sarwar et al. 2000; Gui–Rong et al. 2005).

Content-Based Filtering

Content–based filtering techniques are used by conventional techniques which deal with overloaded information. They analyse whether items are similar on the basis of their contents and recommend similar items based on the previous preferences of the users. (Jian et al. 2005; Pazzani & Billsus 2007; Malone et al. 1987). Usually, content- based filtering techniques match items to users by using classifier–based approaches or nearest–neighbours methods. Classifier–based approaches associate each user with a classifier as a profile. An item is taken as an input by the classifier and then it is concluded whether associated users prefer the item based on the item contents (Pazzani & Billsus 2007).

Contrary to this, content-based filtering techniques store all items which are rated by a user in their user profile and this is based on nearest–neighbours methods. To determine the user's interests in an unseen item, one or more items which are in the user profile whose contents are closest to the unseen item are allocated, and on the basis of the preferences of the user to these discovered neighbours items, we can induce the user's preference to the unseen item (Montaner et al.2003; Pazzani & Billsus 2007). One of the major weaknesses of the collaborative filtering based recommenders–the cold–start problem does not effect this technique.

Figure 5 depicts that we use content based system to recommend items that are similar to the ones liked by the user in the past. It is user profile (preference). It is not explicitly elicited but learned. The origin of most CB-recommendation methods is from Information Retrieval (IR)-based methods on the basis of key words and there is no involvement of expert recommendation knowledge.:

- **New User Problem**: When a new user, with very few preferences known, logs on to the system, how does the content-based recommendation work? The system cannot get adequate user preference and it would not recommend an accurate item to the user. By using only content–based filtering techniques, the only factor which influences the recommenders' Performance is user's own rating. So users with only a few ratings will not have recommendation quality which is very precise (Montaner et al., 2003)

Figure 5. Content based filtering

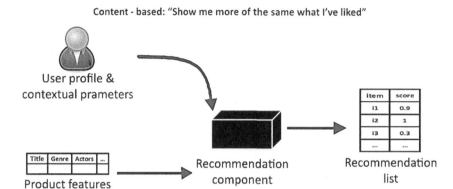

Content - based: "Show me more of the same what I've liked"

- **Undue Specialization**: The interests of people differ widely. For example, when three completely different areas like sport, health and finance are liked by a user, the major problem which occurs is that, it becomes very hard for the system to extract the commonalities from these completely different areas. Certainly, it is hard for a content-based recommendation to cope in this situation (Ma 2008). So, overspecialization problem is the regular suffering of this technique. No inherent method is there to generate unanticipated suggestions and so, the recommendation is more of what a user has already seen (Rasnick & Varian, 1997; Schafer et al., 2001)
- **Lack Of Subjective View**: The main basis of content-based filtering techniques is the objective information about the items like the text description of an item or the product's price (Montaner et al., 2003) while the selection of a user is usually based on the subjective information of the items like the style quality or point of-view of items (Goldberg et al., 1992) Besides, many content-based filtering techniques represent items content information as word vectors and there is no maintenance of context and semantic relations among the words. Ultimately, we obtain the resulting recommendations which are normally very content centric and of poor quality (Adomavicius & Tuzhilin, 2005; Surke, 2002; Ferman et al., 2002; Schafer et al., 2001).

Knowledge-Based Filtering

Knowledge-based recommender systems have knowledge about users and products. This is used to continue a knowledge-based approach so that they can generate a recommendation and reasoning about the products which meet the requirement of the users. The offering by the persona logic recommender system is the dialogue and it effectively brings the user down a discrimination tree which has product features. Quantitative decision support has been adapted by others for this task (Bhargava et al. 1999) There is no ramp-up-problem for a knowledge-based-recommender system because its recommendations are not dependent on a base of user ratings. There is no necessity for it to gather information about a particular user because its judgments have the freedom of individual tastes. Due to these characteristics, knowledge based recommenders are made a valuable system on their own and also complementary to other types of recommender systems.

There are distinctions among knowledge based approaches and other approaches. There is function knowledge with them, like how a particular item meets a particular user need. Because of this it can give an explanation about the association between a need and a possible recommendation. Any knowledge structure supporting this inference can become the user profile. In simple, like Google, it may be the user's simple formulated query. As far as other cases are concerned, it may represent the need of the user in a more detailed manner (Towel & Quinn 2000). Knowledge-based recommendation has been called the 'editor's choice" method by some researchers (Schafer et al. 2001; Konstan et al. 1997).

Figure 6 shows that many forms can also be taken by the knowledge used by a knowledge based recommender system. Information about the links between web pages is used by Google so that it can infer popularity and authoritative value (Brin & Page 1998). Users are able to explore and thereby understand an information space due to the help of the knowledge-based recommender systems. The intrinsic parts of the knowledge discovery process are the users and elaboration of their information needs also simultaneously happens during the interaction with the system. What one needs is just the general knowledge about the set of items and also an informal knowledge of one's needs; the tradeoffs, group boundaries and useful search strategies in the domain are known to the system. Utility-based approaches are able make a calculation of the utility value for objects to be recommended, and in general, such calculations are done on the basis of functional part.

Hybrid Recommender System

The recommendation techniques detailed in the previous sections vividly portray that there are strengths and limitations for different techniques and none can be considered the one and only best solution for all users in all circumstances Two or more diverse recommendation techniques comprise a hybrid recommender system and the fundamental principle is to gain better performance with fewer of the drawbacks of any individual technique and also to embody various datasets to produce recommendations which have higher accuracy and quality (Schafer et al.2001). It was in the mid-1990s that the first hybrid recommender system Fab was developed (Balabanovi and Shoham 1997). We can classify the combination approaches into three categories according to their method of combination: Combining separate recommenders, combining features and unification. (Adomavicicus & Tuzhilin 2005)

Figure 6. Knowledge based filtering

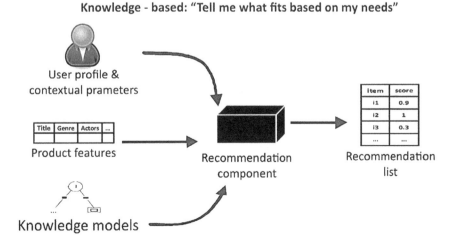

For example, we find a combination of both collaborative filtering and content-based filtering in the active Web museum so that recommendations can be produced with aesthetic quality and content relevancy proposed taxonomy, hybrid recommendation approaches are classified into seven categories which are 'weighted,' 'mixed,' 'switching,' 'feature combination,' 'cascade,' 'feature argumentation,' and 'meta–level.' Hybrid recommendation usually contains strengths from various recommendation techniques which is its central idea. But it also means that there might be a potential inclusion of the limitation from each technique. Besides, hybrid techniques are generally more resource intensive (in terms of computation competence and memory usage) than stand-alone techniques, because they accumulate their resource requirements from multiple recommendation techniques in the Figure 7.

SIMILARITY-BASED RECOMMENDER SYSTEMS

Similarity-based methods denote one of the most successful approaches to recommendation. Their various applications in e- commerce have been found through extensive study. We can further divide this class of algorithms into methods employing user and item similarity respectively. The basic assumption of a method on user similarity is that when people agree in their past evaluations, they are inclined to agree again in their future evaluations. Therefore, for a target user, we can estimate the potential evaluation of an object according to the ratings from users (taste mates) with similarities of the target user.

Unlike user similarity, an algorithm which is based on item similarity gives recommendation to a user about the objects that are similar to what this user has collected previously. What is to be noted is that, sometimes, the dissimilar user' opinions or the negative ratings can play an important (even positive) role in deciding the recommendation, particularly when the data set is very sparse and the information regarding relevance is more important than that regarding correlation and classification of Recommender systems research (Figure 8).

Figure 7. Hybrid recommender

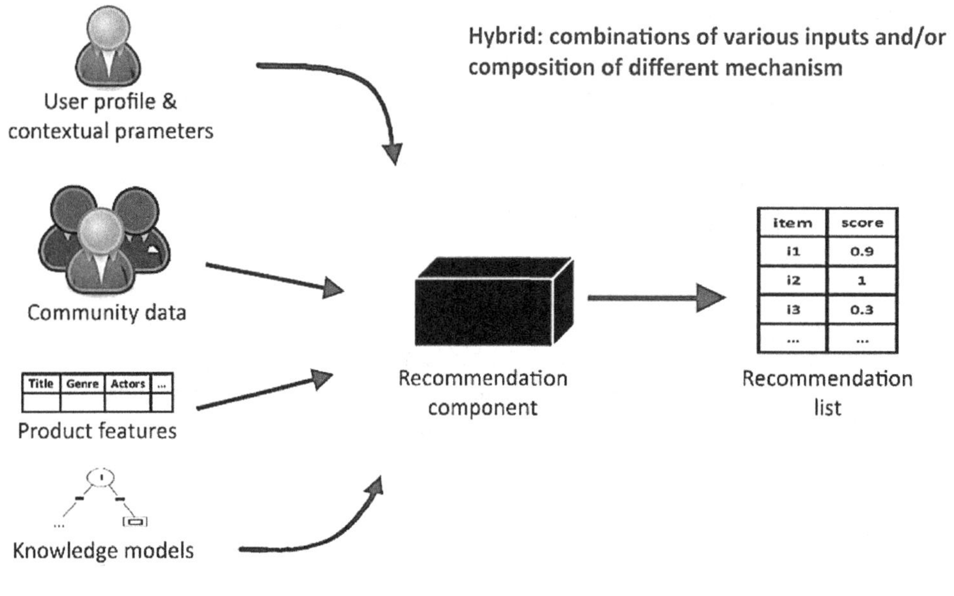

Figure 8. Similarity recommender systems

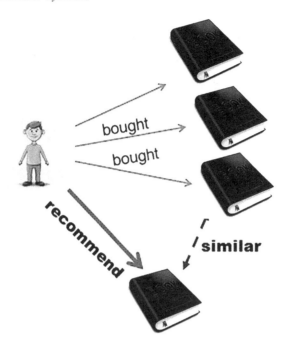

EVALUATING RECOMMENDER SYSTEMS

Offline Experiments

It is easy to conduct offline experiments. They are broadly used in the literature because there, it does not require interactions with real system users. By using a pre-collected data set of users choosing or rating items, we perform offline experiments. This data set can be used in order to try to simulate the behavior of users interacting with a recommendation system. Through offline experiments, we may compare a wide range of candidate algorithms at a low cost. A very narrow set of questions, usually questions about the prediction power of an algorithm alone can be answered by offline experiments. Offline experiments have the goal of filtering out inappropriate approaches and leaving a relatively small set of candidate algorithms which are to be tested by the costlier user studies or online experiments.

User Studies

A set of test subject is recruited and they are asked to perform several tasks which require an interaction with the recommendation system and then a user study is conducted. The subjects' behavior is observed and recorded while they perform the tasks. In the course of the observation, we collect any number of quantitative measurements like what portion of the task was completed, how much accurate the task results were or how much time was taken to perform the task. In many cases, qualitative questions can be asked before, during and after completing the task. Those questions will help in collecting data that are not directly observable, like "Did the subject enjoy the user interface?", "Did the user perceive the task as easy to complete?".

We require much more user effort and time for user studies. A frame work called ResQue (recommender systems' quality of user experience) is presented in user-centric measurement. ResQue comprises of evaluation constructs, ranging from perceived system qualities (the perception of the objective characteristics of the user such as recommendation quality) and belief (higher level perception of the system) to attitudes (The overall feeling of users towards a recommender) and behavioral intentions (the influence of recommendations on the decision making of the users).

Online Experiments

Experiments which are conducted on a running system with real system users so that new ideas can reliably be evaluated are called online experiments. They depict large scale highly interactive experiments, that is, experiments which involve a large number of users. Usually such online experiments are designed so that the behavior of users in real-world settings over a longer period of time can be understood. In many realistic recommendation applications, the system designer desires to influence the users' behavior.

Hence, our interest is to measure the change in user behavior while there is an interaction with different recommendation systems. An online evaluation refers to the experiment providing the strongest evidence as to the true value of the system. In this, the real users that perform real task use the system. It is most beneficial if a few systems are compared online by getting a ranking of alternatives instead of absolute numbers which have more difficulty in interpreting. They can be used to understand how system properties affect these overall goals such as recommendation accuracy and diversity of recommendations, and to understand the tradeoffs between these properties. But it is difficult to vary such properties independently and it is expensive to compare many algorithms through online trials and so gaining a complete understanding of these relationships can be difficult.

AREA OF APPLICATIONS

Social networking technologies and platforms: Social network profiles are created by most e- commerce companies on their own. Most of the people consider shopping a social experience and very often they wish to get the opinion of their friends before purchasing. Social commerce is helping people to buy where they connect. It integrates social media into e-retail sites and also includes e-commerce functionality to social networks. Online store owners, think about transacting business online, by using social commerce. In order to help one make better purchasing decisions, some e-commerce sites use the preferences of one's friends.

There is an increase in the acceptance of a Recommender system when the strengths and limitations of the recommendations in e–commerce can be understood by users. Improvement of customer attraction / retention and boosting sales are helped by justified recommendations because evaluation of the provided recommendations can be done more easily by customers and they accept them if they are satisfied. The following are the real applications which are used in e- commerce sites such as Amazon, E Bay, Snapdeal, flip kart, etc.

Tag method is being used by recommender systems in social web and it tolerates new innovations in online. More sharing between users of different networks has been encouraged by social networks. They make recommendations, on the basis of the common network that two users belong to. The most remarkable of these innovations is face book. The increasing famous location-based social networks are Foursquare.com, Facebook, Twitter, LinkedIn etc. Now there is an emergence of new geo-social systems that provide activity or location recommendation.

ISSUES IN RECOMMENDER SYSTEMS

The five most challenging issues faced by recommendation systems are:

1. **Changing Data:** Trying to keep pace with the tastes and changing opinions of people.
2. **Lack of Data:** Getting users to rate products and enter information about their likes and dislikes.
3. **Updating User Preferences:** Though Initial preferences are stored; users should update them.
4. **Unpredictable Results:** How would you ever guess that someone who listens to Barry Manilow is also a Depeche Mode fan?
5. **Lots of Work!:** Recommendation systems look simple, but they take lots and lots of computations.

CONCLUSION

In this digital era, seeking knowledge becomes more dependent on electronic data. Searching may lead to time consumption and tedious task for any user. Recommender systems give some assistance in finding some way. For like, search text in google, if trying to search something in google by typing its keywords. It provides some recommending suggestions. This suggestion is based on recommendations algorithms used by google. This book discusses the modern and current techniques to improve these recommender systems more effectively and the recent research related to this.

REFERENCES

Adomavicius, G., & Tuzhilin, A. (2005). Toward the next generation of recommender systems: A survey of the state-of-the-art and possible extensions. *IEEE Transactions on Knowledge and Data Engineering*, *17*(6), 734–749. doi:10.1109/TKDE.2005.99

Amatriain, X., Jaimes, A., Oliver, N. & Pujol, J.M. (2011). Data Mining Methods for Recommender Systems,, *by Springer*

Berry, M. J. A., & Linoff, J. S. (2004). *Data Mining Techniques for Marketing, Sales and customer Relationship Management* (2nd ed.). Wiley.

Bhargava, H. K., Sridhar, S., & Herrick, C. (1999). Beyond spreadsheets: Tools for building decision support systems. *IEEE Computer*, *32*(3), 31–39. doi:10.1109/2.751326

Bouza, A., Reif, G., Bernstein, A., & Gall, H. (2008). Semtree: ontology-based decision tree algorithm for recommender systems. *Proceedings of theInternational Semantic Web Conference*.

Breese, J., Heckerman, D., & Kadie, C. (1998). Empirical Analysis of Predictive Algorithms for Collaborative Filtering.*Proceedings of the 14th Conference on Uncertainty in Artificial Intelligence (UAI-98)*, (pp 43-52).

Burke, R. (2002). Hybrid recommender systems: Survey and experiments. *User Modeling and User-Adapted Interaction*, *12*(4), 331–370. doi:10.1023/A:1021240730564

Cai, D., He, X., Wen, J. R., & Ma, W. Y. (2004). Block-level link analysis. *Proceedings of the 27th annual international ACM SIGIR conference on Research and development in, information retrieval*, 440–447.

Cho, Y. H., Kim, J. K., & Kim, S. H. (2002). A personalized recommender system based on web usage mining and decision tree induction. *Expert Systems with Applications*, *23*(3), 329–342. doi:10.1016/S0957-4174(02)00052-0

Cover, T., & Hart, P. (1967). Nearest neighbor pattern classification. *IEEE Transactions on* Information Theory, *13*(1), 21–27.

Deshpande, M., & Karypis, G. (2004). Item-based top-N recommendation algorithms. *ACM Transactions on Information Systems*, *22*(1), 143–177. doi:10.1145/963770.963776

Frey, B. J., & Dueck, D. (2007). Clustering by passing messages between data points. *Science*, 2007, 307. PMID:17218491

Frias-Martinez, E., Chen, S. Y., & Liu, X. (2009). Evaluation of a personalized digital library based on cognitive styles: Adaptivity vs. adaptability. *International Journal of Information Management*, *29*(1), 48–56. doi:10.1016/j.ijinfomgt.2008.01.012

Frias-Martinez, E., Magoulas, G., Chen, S. Y., & Macredie, R. (2006). Automated user modeling for personalized digital libraries. *International Journal of Information Management*, *26*(3), 234–248. doi:10.1016/j.ijinfomgt.2006.02.006

Ghani, R., & Fano, A. (2002). Building recommender systems using a knowledge base of product semantics. *Proceedings of the2nd International Conference on Adaptive Hypermedia and Adaptive Web Based Systems*.

Goldberg, D., Nichols, D., Oki, B. M., & Terry, D. (1992). Using collaborative filtering to weave an information tapestry. *Communications of the ACM*, *35*(12), 61–70. doi:10.1145/138859.138867

Guha, R. V., Kumar, R., Raghavan, P., & Tomkins, A. (2004). Propagation of trust and distrust. *Proceedings of the 13th International World Wide Web Conference* (pp. 403–412).

Guttman, R. H., Moukas, A. G., & Maes, P. (1998). Agent-mediated electronic commerce: *A survey. The Knowledge Engineering Review*, *13*(2), 147–159. doi:10.1017/S0269888998002082

Han, J., Kamber, M., & Pei, J. (2006). *Data Mining: Concepts and Techniques* (2nd ed.). Elsevier Inc.

Ibnkahla, M. (2000). Applications of neural networks to digital communications-a survey. *Expert Systems with Applications*, *80*, 1185–1215.

Jian, C., Jian, Y., & Jin, H. (2005). Automatic content-based recommendation in e-commence. *Proceedings of the IEEE International Conference on e-Technology, e-Commerce and e-Service*, Washington, USA (pp. 748–753).

Kim, H. K., Kim, J. K., & Ryu, Y. U. (2009). Personalized recommendation over a customer network for ubiquitous shopping. *IEEE Transactions on Services Computing*, *2*(2), 140–151. doi:10.1109/TSC.2009.7

Kim, J. K., Cho, Y. H., Kim, W. J., Kim, J. R., & Suh, J. H. (2002). A personalized recommendation procedure for internet shopping support. *Electronic Commerce Research and Applications*, *1*(3-4), 301–313. doi:10.1016/S1567-4223(02)00022-4

Krulwich, B. (1997). Life style finder: Intelligent user profiling using large-scale demographic data. *AI Magazine*, *18*(2), 37–45.

Lihua, W., Lu, L., Jing, L., & Zongyong, L. (2005). Modeling user multiple interests by an improved GCS approach. *Expert Systems with Applications*, *29*(4), 757–767. doi:10.1016/j.eswa.2005.06.003

Linden, G., Smith, B., & York, J. (2003). Amazon.com recommendations: *Item-to-item collaborative filtering. IEEE Internet Computing*, *7*(1), 76–80. doi:10.1109/MIC.2003.1167344

Lu, L., Medo, M., Yeung, C. H., Zhang, Y. C., Zhang, Z. K., & Zhou, T. (2012). Recommender Systems. *Physics Reports*, *519*(1), 1–49. doi:10.1016/j.physrep.2012.02.006

Malhotra, N. K. (2007). *Marketing research: An applied orientation* (5th ed.). Pearson Education Inc. doi:10.1108/S1548-6435(2007)3

Manouselis, N., & Costopoulou, C. (2007). Experimental analysis of design choices in multiattribute utility collaborative filtering. *International Journal of Pattern Recognition and Artificial Intelligence*, *21*(2), 311–331. doi:10.1142/S021800140700548X

Middleton, S. E., Shadbolt, N. R., & Roure, D. C. D. (2004). Ontological user profiling in recommender systems. *ACM Transactions on Information Systems*, *22*(1), 54–88. doi:10.1145/963770.963773

Montaner, M., Lopez, B., & Rosa, J. L. (2003). A taxonomy of recommender agents on the Internet. *Artificial Intelligence Review*, *19*(4), 285–330. doi:10.1023/A:1022850703159

Montaner, M., Lopez, B., & Rosa, J. L. (2003). A taxonomy of recommender agents on the Internet. *Artificial Intelligence Review*, *19*(4), 285–330. doi:10.1023/A:1022850703159

Papadimitriou, A., Symeonidis, P. & Manolopoulos, Y. (2011). *A generalized taxonomy of explanations styles for traditional and social recommender systems.* Springer.

Park, D. H., Kim, H. K., Choi, Y., & Kim, J. K. (2012). A literature review and classification of recommender systems research. *Expert Systems with Applications*, *39*(11), 10059–10072. doi:10.1016/j.eswa.2012.02.038

Pazzani, M. J. (1999). A framework for collaborative, content-based and demographic filtering. *Artificial Intelligence Review*, *13*(5–6), 393–408. doi:10.1023/A:1006544522159

Pazzani, M. J., & Billsus, D. (1997). Learning and revising user profiles: The identification of interesting web sites. *Machine Learning*, *27*(3), 313–331. doi:10.1023/A:1007369909943

Pazzani, M. J., & Billsus, D. (2007). Content-based recommender systems. In P. Brusilovsky, A. Kobsa, & W. Nejdl (Eds.), *The Adaptive Web*. Berlin: Springer-Verlag. doi:10.1007/978-3-540-72079-9_10

Quinlan, J. R. (1986, March). Induction of decision trees. *Machine Learning*, *1*(1), 81–106. doi:10.1007/BF00116251

Recommender System. (n. d.). Retrieved from http://en.citizendium.org/wiki/Recommendation_system

Resnick, P., Iakovou, N., Sushak, M., Bergstrom, P., & Riedl, J. (1994). GroupLens: An open architecture for collaborative filtering of netnews. *Proceedings of theComputer Supported Cooperative Work Conf.* doi:10.1145/192844.192905

Ricci, F., Rokach, L., Shapira, B., & Kantor, P. N. (2011). *Recommender Systems Handbook*. USA: Springer. doi:10.1007/978-0-387-85820-3

Rich, E. (1979). User modeling via stereotypes. *Cognitive Science*, *3*(4), 329–354. doi:10.1207/s15516709cog0304_3

Rokach, L., & Maimon, O. (2008). *Data Mining with Decision Trees: Theory and Applications*. World Scientific Publishing.

Salah, A., Rogovschi, N., & Nadif, M. (2016). A dynamic collaborative filtering system via a weighted clustering approach. *Neurocomputing,* *175*(A), 206–215.

Sarwar, B., Karypis, G., Konstan, J., & Reidl, J. (2000, August). Application of Dimensionality Reduction in Recommender Systems. *Proceedings of theACM Workshop on Web Mining for E-Commerce Challenges and Opportunities, Boston, USA.*

Schafer, B. J. (n. d.). The Application of Data-Mining to Recommender Systems. University of Northern Illinois. Retrieved from http://www.cs.uni.edu/~schafer/publications/dmChapter.pdf

Schafer, J. B., Joseph, A., & Riedl, J. (2001). E-commerce recommendation applications. *Data Mining and Knowledge Discovery*, *5*(1/2), 115–153. doi:10.1023/A:1009804230409

Schafer, J. B., Konstan, J. A., & Riedl, J. (2001). E-Commerce Recommendation Applications. *Journal of Data Mining and Knowledge Discovery*, *5*(1–2), 115–153. doi:10.1023/A:1009804230409

Shani, G., & Gunawardana, A. (n. d.). *Evaluating Recommendation Systems.*http://research.microsoft.com/pubs/115396/evaluationmetrics.tr.pdf

Shardanand, U., & Maes, P. (1995). Social information filtering: Algorithms for automating 'Word of Mouth'. *Proceedings of the Human Factors in Computing Systems Conf.*

Stolze, M., & Stroebel, M. (2003). Dealing with learning in e-Commerce product navigation and decision support: the teaching salesman problem.*Proceedings of the 2nd Interdisciplinary World Congress on Mass Customization and Personalization*, Munich,Germany.

T. B. et al. (2002). A trail based internet-domain recommender system using artificial neural networks. *Proceedings of the Int. Conf. on Adaptive Hypermedia and Adaptive Web Based Systems.*

Towle, B., & Quinn, C. (2000). Knowledge Based Recommender Systems using Explicit User Models. *Proceedings of the AAAI Workshop on Knowledge-Based Electronic Markets*, Menlo Park, CA (pp. 74-77).

Wei, Y. Z., Moreau, L., & Jennings, N. R. (2005). A market-based approach to recommender systems. *ACM Transactions on Information Systems, 23*(3), 227–266. doi:10.1145/1080343.1080344

Wen Wu, Liang He, Jing Yang. (n. d.). *Evaluating Recommender Systems.*

Xiangliang, Recommender System Introduction (n. d.). Retrieved from http://www.slideshare.net/xlvector/recommender-system-introduction 12551956? from_action=save

Chapter 5
A Classification Framework Towards Application of Data Mining in Collaborative Filtering

Neeti Sangwan
Maharaja Surajmal Institute of Technology, India

Naveen Dahiya
Maharaja Surajmal Institute of Technology, India

ABSTRACT

Recommendation making is an important part of the information and e-commerce ecosystem. Recommendation represent a powerful method that filter large amount of information to provide relevant choice to end users. To provide recommendations to the users, efficient and cost effective methods needs to be introduced. Collaborative filtering is an emerging technique used in making recommendations which makes use of filtering by data mining. This chapter presents a classification framework on the use of data mining techniques in collaborative filtering to extract the best recommendations to the users on the basis of their interests.

INTRODUCTION

In everyday life, process of recommending choices to the user is very commonly used. Anyone who knows the likes and dislikes of other person can recommend the things which he likes and ignore the things which he dislikes. Recommendation system assists the process of making recommendations to help the people in different fields such as movies, books, restaurants etc. Recommender systems are either based on the content based recommendations or collaborative recommendations. Content based recommendation tends to recommend the items that lookalike to the user preferences. Collaborative filtering suggests recommendations on the basis of the preferences given by the other users with the

DOI: 10.4018/978-1-5225-0489-4.ch005

same interests or similar tastes. Collaborative filtering is more popular than content based filtering as in many domains it is very difficult to find out the useful features from the items which is the prerequisite for content based filtering.

This present work aims to provide a wide survey on the collaborative filtering. Various types of collaborative filtering are: Memory based collaborative filtering, Model based collaborative filtering and hybrid collaborative filtering. The chapter discusses the types of collaborative filtering approaches. The chapter provides a classification framework for the collaborative filtering approaches and the application of data mining in it. Authors have studied various techniques to make efficient recommendations in less time and cost. Data Mining is most emerging and useful technique in the filtering process for making recommendations to the users.

Data Mining is an approach to extract the significant, previously unseen information out of the data. Data mining finds application in model based collaborative filtering process to suggest the recommendations and to reduce the effort, cost and time spend on the recommendation process. Data Mining includes clustering, classification and association analysis which will be explained in detail later on in the chapter. This chapter focuses on the study of the various types of collaborative filtering and the role of data mining in order to improve the filtering process.

Organization of the chapter is as follows: firstly, the authors provide the research methodology used by them and various factors that motivated the authors to carry out this study. Then this chapter provides the introduction to collaborative filtering, different types of the collaborative filtering and their functionalities. Next the authors discussed the introduction to the data mining process and its various techniques. Afterwards chapter deals with the classification and describes the methods based on data mining to improve the collaborative filtering based recommendations. Subsequent section provides implications of our work to the research domain. Finally concludes the chapter and highlights some future enhancements that can be done in this field.

RESEARCH METHODOLOGY

In this chapter, various collaborative filtering techniques are studied for improving the quality of the recommendation process. The research starts with the study of recommender systems namely: Collaborative Filtering, Content Based filtering, Hybrid Recommender, Demographic based filtering and Utility Based Filtering. The features and properties of recommender system are overviewed. Then we identified collaborative filtering as the most promising approach towards recommender systems. Collaborative filtering is an approach to make the recommendations based on the user and other persons past behavior and predict the items on basis of their interest. Collaborative filtering is further classified as memory based filtering, model Based filtering and hybrid filtering. Various application areas of collaborative filtering include: Books, Social Networking Sites, Movies, Music, Images, and Shopping etc. (Figure 1).

Best recommender system used collaborative filtering based on Data Mining approach. Data mining is the process of discovering interesting knowledge from large amounts of data stored in databases, data warehouses, or other information repositories" (Han & Kamber, 2001). Finally, authors come up with a broad classification framework showing the use of data mining in collaborative filtering for effective recommendations to the users. Figure 1 shows the research roadmap that has been followed in the chapter.

Figure 1. Research roadmap

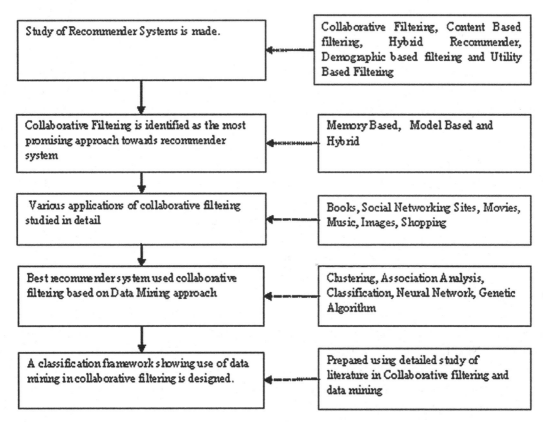

INTRODUCTION TO COLLABORATIVE FILTERING

Collaborative filtering is the most significant approach to make the recommendations for the users. Collaborative filtering does not use the actual content about the items as in content filtering which is used by the search engines. Collaborative filtering uses the relationship between the users and recommends the items to the users by collecting the feedbacks in the form of ratings from the users for various items as shown in Figure 2. Collaborative filtering is the process of filtering information and patterns using techniques involving collaboration among multiple agents, viewpoints, data sources etc. (Terveen & Hill 2001).

In 1990s, Collaborative filtering appeared as a solution to deal with overloading online information space. Most widely known application of this technology is Amazon.com. They recommend the items to the users for purchasing according to their purchasing history, browsing history and on the basis of the item a user is currently viewing. Many e-commerce and online systems have been using this technology. Prominent motivation behind using Collaborative filtering is to increase the sales. Information used for Collaborative filtering consists of users. Users give their preferences for various items. These preferences of items given by various users are known as rating. Rating matrix is formed on the basis of the ratings given by the users which are used for predictions in the coming future.

Figure 2. Process of collaborative filtering

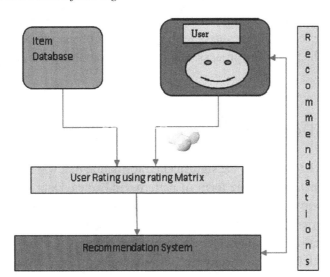

Collaborative filtering is usually applied on very large set of data. Collaborative filtering techniques find their applications on variable data including monitoring data after sensing as in exploring mineral, sensing related to large areas, financial data related to financial organization, in electronic commerce and various web applications etc.

Different collaborative filtering types are as follows:

- **Memory Based Collaborative Filtering**: In this method, similarity between the items or users is calculated by using the rating given by the users. This calculated resemblance is used to make recommendations (Xue et al, 2005). This earliest approach of collaborative filtering was used in many commercial organizations. This basic approach is easy to implement. Examples of this approach are neighbourhood-based Collaborative filtering and user-based/item-based top-N recommendations. The loophole of the approach is the problem of sparsity of data.
- **Model Based Collaborative Filtering**: In this type of collaborative filtering, real data is collected that works as training data. The data is then modeled using data mining or algorithms of machine learning. System learns according to the training data and finds patterns for future prediction of actual data. These useful patterns are extracted from the training data by using clustering, association analysis and classification techniques (Xue et al, 2005). Various model-based collaborative filtering algorithms includes Bayesian networks, clustering models, association analysis model, classification models and latent semantic models. This approach of collaborative filtering has advantages over memory based. It deals with sparse data better than memory based collaborative filtering. Model based collaborative filtering also provides scalability with large data sets. It improves the prediction process and makes more intuitive recommendations. The disadvantages of this approach is that building a model is an expensive process. There is a need to make a balanced scale between scalability and prediction performance. Information can be lost due to use of the reduction models.

- **Hybrid Collaborative Filtering**: This approach combines the features of model-based and memory-based Collaborative Filtering approaches. This approach finds the advantages of both the above mentioned approaches and overcome the drawbacks of sparsity and information loss. This approach improves the prediction process. But it is more complicated and expensive to implement (Xue et al 2005).

INTRODUCTION TO DATA MINING

Data Mining is an approach to fetch out the significant information that was not known previously from the data. Extracted information is in the form of patterns and rules. Data mining is defined as "The process of discovering interesting knowledge from large amounts of data stored either in databases, data warehouses, or other information repositories" (Han & Kamber 2001). Witten and Frank (2002) defines data mining as "The extraction of implicit, previously unknown, and potentially useful information from data". Hand et al. (2001) defines data mining as "The analysis of (often large) observational data sets to find unsuspected relationships and to summarize the data in novel ways that are both understandable and useful to the data owner". Data mining have its application in various fields. Some are: Healthcare, Retail, Marketing organizations, Banks and Insurance Company, Web Applications, Telecommunication Industry, Medical and many more.

There are three basic techniques of data mining which are as follows:

- **Clustering:** Clustering is the process in which similar data objects are grouped together and dissimilar data is grouped in different clusters. Similar data is grouped together on the basis of similar values for attributes (Han & Kamber 2001). There are various measures of similarity such as distance function, density-based, number of expected clusters. A major clustering method includes:
  - **Partition Clustering**: This method is implemented using K-mean algorithm. Initially K number of clusters is formed, and then iterative relocation takes place by shifting objects from one group to another based on the mean of the objects present in the cluster.
  - **Hierarchical Clustering**: In this clustering, data objects are grouped in the form of tree of the clusters. This clustering is categorized in two categories: Agglomerative clustering and Divisive Clustering. In Agglomerative clustering, atomic clusters merged into larger clusters. In Divisive clustering, data objects grouped in a single cluster and then further divided into sub clusters.
  - **Density Based Clustering**: It is used to discover clusters with arbitrary shape. It clusters objects on the basis of distance between the objects. Regions with sufficiently high density form the clusters.
- **Classification:** "Classification is the process of finding a model (or function) that describes and distinguishes data classes or concepts, for the purpose of being able to use the model to predict the class of objects whose class label is unknown" (Han & Kamber 2001). It makes analysis on a set of training data whose class to which it belongs is known. A model is prepared which is used for further classification of data based on the training data. Classification model consists of two steps. First step is learning step in which model is constructed using set of classes predetermined by training data. On the basis of these classes, classification rules are represented. A small data known as test data is used to conduct test against the rules constructed to check the accuracy of

the model generated. Model with appropriate accuracy is accepted, its rules are used to classify data whose class is unknown. Classification have various techniques such as decision tree, neural network, genetic algorithm, memory based reasoning etc.

- ◦ **Decision Tree**: A technique that classifies data using classification tree. Classification tree have internal nodes, external/leaf nodes and branching between them. Every internal node implies a test on an attribute. Each branch denotes the outcome of the test and leaf nodes represents the classes.
- ◦ **Neural Network**: The classification technique in which network is prepared on the basis of training data set and learning is applied to generalize the patterns for further classification. It also uses the outcome as feedback with inputs.
- • **Association Rules:** It is a technique of classification process in which relationship between various datasets forms the basis for the rules. Relationship between the datasets is established on the basis of the frequency of attribute occurring together. There are two components of the rules that signify the strength of the association. These are support and confidence. Support is defined as the probability of having the two attributes together and confidence is defined as the probability of having one attribute after having other one. A rule is strong if its support and confidence meets the threshold i.e. minimum support and minimum confidence on the basis of which frequent patterns is mined. General association analysis algorithms includes Apriori Algorithm, FP-growth algorithm etc.

CLASSIFICATION FRAMEWORK

The framework is classified on the basis of application of data mining techniques to the collaborative filtering. Data mining techniques improves the performance of making recommendations using collaborative filtering at less efforts, time and cost. The framework consists of the combination of various collaborative filtering approaches (memory Based, model Based and hybrid filtering) and different data mining techniques (clustering, association analysis and classification) as shown in Figure 3. This combination can be used to provide the better recommendations in comparison to the traditional systems. As in this chapter, we have focused on the model based approach which includes clustering, association analysis and classification. Applications of all these data mining approaches in collaborative filtering are discussed in detail in following section.

Use of Clustering in Collaborative Filtering

- • Kohrs and Merialdo (1999) deal with the sparse databases i.e. databases with few numbers of ratings. Recommendations made from sparse database provided few recommendations for new users. Authors described two types of sparse collaborative filtering databases namely: bootstrap case and new user case. Various parameters for simulation of the two cases are identified. Cost analysis is presented to select right algorithm in terms of cost and performance. A new algorithm is proposed by authors for collaborative filtering based on hierarchical clustering. Authors claim robust and accurate predictions by using this novel approach. It applies clustering to the collaborative filtering to perform better in sparse databases by clustering large dimensional sparse vectors

Figure 3. Classification framework

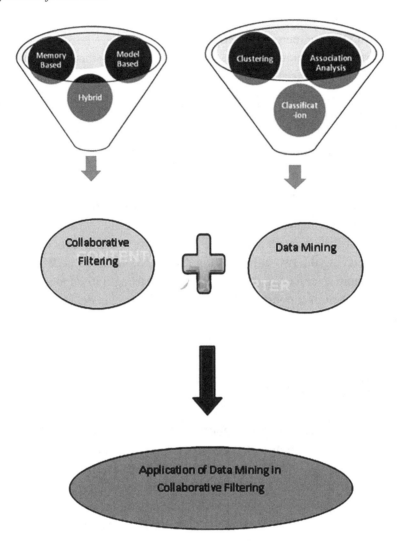

as the rating vector and predictions are made. Author also showed an experiment to prove the efficiency of the novel technique by comparing the performance of proposed algorithm with existing algorithms for sparse databases.

• Ungar and Foster (1998) proposed a statistical model of collaborative filtering and comparison of different algorithms is made for estimation of model parameters. These algorithms include variants of k-mean clustering (i.e. k-Nearest neighbors and repeated clustering) and Gibbs Sampling. K-mean clustering provides nearest neighbors in same clusters according to their mean. Repeated clustering performs reclustering i.e. clustering on clusters to provide generalization. Gibbs sampling reclassify the users and change the event in which they occur. These algorithms are compared on both the synthetic data (data with known correct answers) and real data. While working on synthetic data, all three algorithms gave equal rate of errors when classes are of equal size. Gibbs sampling gave better performance when class is not uniform. K-mean and repeated clustering perform almost equal. Real data is very sparse, therefore, K-mean and repeated clustering does not improve the performance and accuracy. Gibbs sampling works quite well and can be extended to more complex versions. But this modification is expensive.

- Pham et al (2011) introduced a clustering algorithm using social information of the users to identify their neighbors and to derive the recommendations for the users. A complex network clustering algorithm is implemented on the social network of the users to extract the similar user groups. Experimentation is done using real data of two application scenarios that are collaboration information based academic avenue recommendation and trust based recommendations.

- Gong (2010) described that traditional method for making recommendations consists of user based clustering and item based clustering methods. In these traditional methods, rating similarity is measured and neighbors are selected on the basis of rating similarity. Finally, predictions are made. But with increase in number of users and items, the searching of nearest neighbor and hence the collaborative filtering process become time consuming. User space failed in ensuring real time requirement of the system. When number of records of user increases, the source data becomes sparser and suffers from poor quality. To solve the problem of sparsity and scalability, author proposed a personalized recommendation approach that merges the user clustering based technologies and item clustering based technologies together. Recommendations from the proposed system on merging user clustering and item clustering are more accurate and scalable than traditional technology.

- O'connor and Herlocker (1999) provided the comparison of existing clustering algorithms to cluster set of items on the basis of user ratings. Experimentation on the four existing partitioning algorithms is provided. Four algorithms are: Average Link Hierarchical algorithm, ROCK (A robust clustering algorithm for categorical attributes) algorithm, kMetis algorithm and hMetis algorithm. Basic algorithm out of these four algorithms is the average link clustering. ROCK is a recent clustering algorithm developed at Bell Labs. It has improved performance on nominal data in comparison to the performance on the continuous data. kMetis and hMetis are two partitioning algorithms using high speed graph developed at the University of Minnesota. Comparison is made on these four algorithms. Random clustering provides base for the comparison against which all the clustering algorithm variants are compared. Comparison parameters includes Mean absolute error (MAE) which is the percentage of desired ratings that could be predicted by the algorithm i.e. the mean absolute error between the actual ratings and the predicted ratings of users in the test set. Finally, it is concluded that kMetis is the most promising algorithm.

- Xue et al (2005) suggested a new approach that merges the advantages of two approaches of collaborative filtering i.e. memory based and model based collaborative filtering to provide highly accurate and efficient recommendations. Two approaches are combined by introducing smoothing to recommendations from the similar users. Clusters are used for smoothing that allows to merge the advantages of both memory-based and model based collaborative filtering, hence, provide higher accuracy and efficiency in recommendations. Authors proposed the framework and provide experimentation for the same. Experimentation show that proposed framework can significantly improves the accuracy and solves the problem of scalability.

- Esslimani et al (2009) proposed PSN-CF (Pam clustering on similarities and navigational based collaboration filtering). This technique reduces the dimensions by clustering the users on the basis of users' similarity and these clustering results are further refined by using navigational patterns between the users based on the positive sequences in each cluster which produces recommendations. Then predictions are made on the basis of new generated neighbors. Comparison between PSN-CF and traditional clustering based collaborative filtering is provided. Experimentation is conducted to evaluate the proposed model performance with real data sets. Two metrics namely: Mean Absolute Error (MAE) and High Mean Absolute Error (HMAE) are used to evaluate the performance. MAE gives the error between predicted ratings and actual ratings given by the users on the items. HMAE also gives the error between predicted ratings and actual ratings, but it only considers the items that are predicted with value of 4 or 5. Experiment shows the high interest of using PSN-CF algorithm on the accuracy of the predictions. Experimentation shows that role of usage of navigational patterns and positive sequences from the actual users for accurate predictions are very significant.

- Narang et al (2012) presented a new design for soft real time distributed co-clustering based collaborative filtering algorithm. Theoretically high efficiency and scalability are proven. This algorithm provides best performance with highly accurate predictions. Authors explained a soft real time parallel collaborative filtering on multi core architecture using real datasets. It gives the best training time of 9.38s with best predictions of 2us per rating for 1.4M ratings with high prediction accuracy.

- George and Merugu (2005) designed a new approach that uses incremental and parallel versions of weighted co-clustering algorithm that involves the clustering of the users and items simultaneously to overcome the disadvantages of techniques like singular value decomposition (SVD) and Non Negative Matrix Factorization (NNMF). These approaches have a drawback of containing very expensive training components. The new proposed approach based on weighted co-clustering overcomes this drawback. Empirical evaluation indicates that the proposed algorithm can provide predictions of high quality at much lower expense as compared to the traditional approaches.

- Hu et al (2014) proposed a Clustering based Collaborative Filtering approach (ClubCF). This approach clusters the same services in same cluster that give recommendations of services collaboratively. This approach is implemented in two phases: first phase makes the clusters of available services for future processing and second phase implement the ClubCF Clustering-based Collaborative Filtering approach on one of the clusters. As the number of services in cluster is very less as compared to the number of services on web, hence online execution time of collaborative filtering is reduced.

Use of Association Analysis in Collaborative Filtering

Kumar and Thambidurai (2010) suggested a new algorithm i.e. Fuzzy Association Rule Mining Algorithm (FARM) which overcomes the disadvantages of the traditional algorithms. Traditional algorithms utilized the interests of the user and recommended the same to the users with similar interests with the help of association rules generated by Apriori algorithm. FARM algorithm have mainly four steps:

1. Firstly, database of ordinary web logs is filtered and transformed into average web system attributes logins.
2. Secondly, web system attributes logins are transformed into database containing fuzzy extensions. Then this transformed database is normalized in this step.
3. Thirdly, Candidate is generated and searching is done for all fuzzy frequent itemsets in candidate that are having fuzzy support higher than defined threshold.

4.   Finally, these frequent itemsets are used to calculate the confidence of fuzzy association rules to generate important websites desired by the users.

This proposed approach is more accurate and effective for making web recommendations than conventional method of association rule mining. Experimentation conducted in the paper also shows the good performance of proposed FARM algorithm in terms of quality and time taken.

Shyu et al (2005) proposed a new methodology for mining the patterns of web pages accessed by the users. Existing approaches worked on mining the patterns only for continuous sequential access of the web pages. But this novel approach can predict for the patterns accessing non sequential web pages. This approach follows two main steps: first step deals with shortest path algorithm to find the distance between various web pages. These distances are referred as minimum reaching distance information and second step applies the association rule mining to generate predictive rules which are further filtered using minimum reaching distance information. Experiment is also performed to prove the better performance of the proposed approach over the existing approaches in recommending the web pages within a website in reduced user access time.

Letham (2013) stated that association rules are used for making recommendations to form name recommender system. Author introduced a new attribute of confidence for association rule which associates user similarities. This confidence with similarity weightage is well suited for the dataset of name recommender system. In proposed approach, firstly Bayesian adjustment is done on sparse data to reduce variance for itemsets with low support and secondly similarity weighting based on users' interest and confidence measure are incorporated together for generating more intuitive, scalable recommender system. This system increases the ability of prediction for the users.

Veloso et al (2004) introduced a new technique for making groups or teams in an organization to do a particular task. This method is based on the association rules generated about the resources by using their real activity data. Experimentation is performed which shows positive impact of the proposed method on team making. This method provides the alternative choices for planning a team.

Leung et al (2005) proposed a collaborative filtering architecture based on Fuzzy Association Rules and Multiple-level Similarity (FARAMS). FARAMS extended existing techniques by using fuzzy association rule mining and make use of similarity between the items to find out sparseness of data and non-transitive associations. Sparseness of data and non-transitive associations are handled by using multiple levels of similarities of the products. Experimentation is conducted to evaluate the FARAMS against conventional approaches. Experimental results show that FARAMS improves prediction quality as compared to other traditional approaches

Use of Classification in Collaborative Filtering

Lee et al (2005) proposed a new recommendation approach for model based collaborative filtering by using logistic regression models applied on binary user-item data. Approach considers it as two-class classification problem. Learning model is provided for classification rule generation on the basis of which prediction are made. Approach also uses principal component analysis to create new variables. To generate new variables, large number of items is considered and correlation between these items is high which may cause inefficiency in model. Authors also conducted experimentation on proposed scheme and found it better than the existing approaches in terms of recommendation precision.

Hwang and Jun (2014) stated that if users or items are sparse in given training data then approach is called cold start problem. Authors deal with binary user item data in this paper. Application of binary logistic regression approach is appropriate where predictor variables are principal components. But the binary logistic regression approach may not work properly if principal components are inefficient for cold start. For this purpose, authors proposed three approaches based on supervised learning: random forest regression, random forest classification, and elastic net to handle the cold-start problem.

Kim et al (2010) described that there are various approaches for the location based advertising for the services. But some of them have only theoretical implications and others gave benefits only to the service providers. In this paper, authors introduced a new recommender system i.e. LARMU (Location-based Advertisement Recommender for Mobile Users) recommender system that can be used for recommendation for the advertisements of context-aware services to mobile users. In Proposed model, Classification rules are generated to know the needs of users with the help of decision tree algorithm. Data from mobile phone users is used to experiment on novel approach to evaluate its effectiveness. Experiment shows that the model performs better than existing models in terms of accuracy and quality of advertisements.

HYPOTHETICAL CASE STUDY

The authors provide a hypothetical case study to recommend books to certain users based on their interests and user ratings of books entered into the database as shown in Figure 4. Database contains the variety of books which are categorized using various data mining techniques. Using Clustering similar kind of books is clustered in same cluster and dissimilar books are organized into different clusters. All the books of technical background are organized in the cluster for technical books. Technical books cluster contains the small clusters for various domains in technical field such as computer, electronics etc. Classification technique is used to classify the data in the form of hierarchical structure using decision tree in which each node further divided the tree in sub-categories such as computer books are further sub-categorized as network related books and databases related books. Association analysis is used to find the association between the various books using association rules. For example, if a user searches for computer book and C++ book may also want to know about advanced languages like Java in computer sciences. So there is an association between the books for C++ and Java. Similarly, data mining is used to cluster the users in user database according to their interests. Users of same interest are put into same cluster. User rating database is generated on the basis of the preferences given by the users. Users in same cluster give almost same preferences. The user rating data is further used by recommender system based on collaborative filtering to recommend the books to the end users. Firstly, interest of end user is compared with the interest of the users present in database. Books are suggested to the end user according to the rating given by the users present in the database with similar interest.

IMPLICATIONS

The implications of the current research work find application in various domains. Few of the research implications are as follows:

Figure 4. Case study

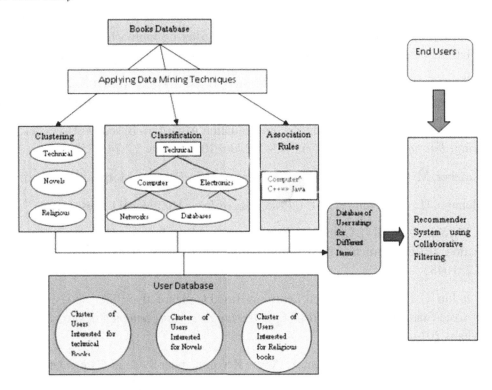

1. The current research work enriches researchers with knowledge of research work conducted in collaborative filtering.
2. The research work aims to provide detailed analysis of the various aspects related to the data mining techniques to the researchers working in the related domain.
3. The chapter discusses the use of data mining in the collaborative filtering and presents a classification framework for the same. The classification framework provides a base for the extension of collaborative filtering by inclusion of new aspects and dimensions.

CONCLUSION AND FUTURE SCOPE

In this chapter, the authors have presented a detailed literature on the use of data mining in collaborative filtering. Various types of collaborative filtering namely: Memory based collaborative filtering, Model based collaborative filtering and hybrid collaborative filtering in detail. Various collaborative filtering techniques have been discussed in detail in the chapter. On the basis of literature study, the authors have proposed a classification framework for effective use of data mining in collaborative filtering. The collaborative filtering can provide base for extension of application of data mining in collaborative filtering. The collaborative filtering can be extended by inclusion of new aspects to data mining and collaborative filtering to give new dimensions and shape for future researches.

REFERENCES

Esslimani, I., Brun, A., & Boyer, A. (2009). A collaborative filtering approach combining clustering and navigational based correlations. In *Web Information Systems and Technologies* (pp. 364-369).

George, T., & Merugu, S. (2005). A Scalable Collaborative Filtering Framework Based On Co-Clustering. *Proceedings of theData Mining Fifth IEEE International Conference*. doi:10.1109/ICDM.2005.14

Gong, S. (2010). A Collaborative Filtering Recommendation Algorithm Based On User Clustering And Item Clustering. *Journal Of Software*, *5*(7), 745–752. doi:10.4304/jsw.5.7.745-752

Han, J., & Kamber, M. (2001). *Data Mining: Concepts and Techniques*. Morgan Kaufmann.

Hand, D., Mannila, H., & Smyth, P. (2001). *Principles of Data Mining*. MIT Press.

Hu, R., Dou, W., & Liu, J. (2014). Clubcf: A Clustering Based Collaborative Filtering Approach For Big Data Application. *IEEE Transaction On Emerging Topics In Computing*, *2*(3), 302–313. doi:10.1109/TETC.2014.2310485

Hwang, W., & Jun, C. (2014). Supervised Learning-Based Collaborative Filtering Using Market Basket Data For Cold-Start Problem. *Industrial Engineering And Management Systems*, *13*(4), 421–431. doi:10.7232/iems.2014.13.4.421

Kim, K., Ahn, H., & Jeong, S. (2010). Context-Aware Recommender Systems Using Data Mining Techniques. *International Scholarly And Scientific Research And Innovation*, *4*(4), 276–281.

Kohrs, A., & Merialdo, B. (1999). Clustering For Collaborative Filtering Applications. *Intelligent Image Processing, Data Analysis & Information Retrieval*, *3*, 199.

Kumar, A., & Thambidurai, P. (2010). Collaborative Web Recommendation Systems Based On An Effective Fuzzy Association Rule Mining Algorithm (FARM). *Indian Journal Of Computer Science And Engineering*, *1*(3), 184–191.

Lee, J., Jun, C., Lee, J., & Kim, S. (2005). Classification-Based Collaborative Filtering Using Market-Basket Data. Expert Systems With Application, 29, 700-704.

Letham, B. (2013). Similarity-Weighted Association Rules For A Name Recommender System.*Proceedings of European Conference on Machine Learning and Principles and Practice of Knowledge Discovery in Databases Discovery Challenge*.

Leung, C. W., Chan, S. C., & Chung, F. (2005). A Collaborative Filtering Framework Based On Fuzzy Association Rules And Multiple-Level Similarity. *Knowledge and Information Systems*, *10*(3), 357–381. doi:10.1007/s10115-006-0002-1

Narang, A., Srivastava, A., & Kata, N. P. K. (2012). Distributed Hierarchical Co-Clustering And Collaborative Filtering Algorithm.*Proceedings of 19th International Conference on High Performance Computing (HiPC)*. IEEE. doi:10.1109/HiPC.2012.6507497

O'connor, M., & Herlocker, J. (1999). Clustering Items For Collaborative Filtering. *Proceedings of the ACM SIGIR workshop on recommender systems*, UC Berkeley.

Pham, M. C., Cao, Y., Klamma, R., & Jacke, M. (2011). A Clustering Approach For Collaborative Filtering Recommendation Using Social Network Analysis. *Journal of Universal Computer Science*, *17*(14), 583–604.

Shyu, M., Haruchaiyasak, C., Chen, S., & Zhao, N. (2005). Collaborative Filtering By Mining Association Rules From User Access Sequences.*Proceedings of International Workshop on Challenges in Web Information Retrieval and Integration, WIRI'05* (pp. 128-135). IEEE. doi:10.1109/WIRI.2005.14

Terveen, L., & Hill, W. (2001). Beyond Recommender Systems: Helping People Help Each Other. In Human Computer Interaction in the New Millennium (pp. 487-509).

Ungar, L. H., & Foster, D. P. (1998). Clustering Methods For Collaborative Filtering. Proceedings of the AAAI workshop on recommendation systems (pp. 114-129).

Veloso, M., Jorge, A., & Azevedo, P. (2004). Model-Based Collaborative Filtering For Team Building Support. *Proceedings International Conference on Enterprise Information Systems* (pp. 241-248).

Witten, I. H., & Frank, E. (2002). *Data Mining: Practical Machine Learning Tools and Techniques with Java Implementations*. San Francisco, CA: Morgan Kaufmann.

Xue, G., Lin, C., Yang, Q., Xi, W., Zueng, H., Yu, Y., & Chen, Z. (2005). Scalable Collaborative Filtering Using Cluster Based Smoothing.*Proceedings Of 2005 ACM SIGIR Conference*, Salvador, Brazil (pp. 114-121). doi:10.1145/1076034.1076056

ADDITIONAL READING

Ekstrand, M. D., Riedl, J. T., & Konstan, J. A. (2011). Collaborative filtering recommender systems. *Foundations and Trends in Human-Computer Interaction*, *4*(2), 81–173. doi:10.1561/1100000009

Hegde, A., & Shetty, S. K. (2015). Collaborative Filtering Recommender System. *International Journal of Emerging Trends in Science and Technology*, *2*(07).

Liu, F., & Lee, H. J. (2010). Use of social network information to enhance collaborative filtering performance. *Expert Systems with Applications*, *37*(7), 4772–4778. doi:10.1016/j.eswa.2009.12.061

Lops, P., De Gemmis, M., & Semeraro, G. (2011). Content-based recommender systems: State of the art and trends. In Recommender systems handbook (pp. 73-105). Springer US.

Maltz, D., & Ehrlich, K. (1995). Pointing the way: active collaborative filtering.*Proceedings of the SIGCHI conference on Human factors in computing systems* (pp. 202-209). ACM Press/Addison-Wesley Publishing Company.

Resnick, P., Iacovou, N., Suchak, M., Bergstrom, P., & Riedl, J. (1994). GroupLens: an open architecture for collaborative filtering of netnews.*Proceedings of the 1994 ACM conference on Computer supported cooperative work* (pp. 175-186). ACM. doi:10.1145/192844.192905

Ricci, F., Rokach, L., & Shapira, B. (2011). *Introduction to recommender systems handbook* (pp. 1–35). Springer, US. doi:10.1007/978-0-387-85820-3_1

Schafer, J. B., Frankowski, D., Herlocker, J., & Sen, S. (2007). Collaborative filtering recommender systems. In *The adaptive web* (pp. 291–324). Springer Berlin Heidelberg. doi:10.1007/978-3-540-72079-9_9

KEY TERMS AND DEFINITIONS

Association Analysis: Association analysis is a technique useful for discovering interesting patterns or relationships hidden in large amount of datasets in the form of association rules.

Classification: Classification is the process of finding a model (or function) that describes and distinguishes data classes or concepts, for the purpose of being able to use the model to predict the class of objects whose class label is unknown.

Clustering: Clustering is the process in which similar data objects are grouped together and dissimilar data is grouped in different clusters. Similar data is grouped together on the basis of similar values for attributes.

Recommender System: Recommender systems is an information filtering system that provide the predicted rating that a user would give to an item or social element they had not yet considered.

Chapter 6
Collaborative Filtering Based Data Mining for Large Data

Amrit Pal
Indian Institute of Information Technology Allahabad, India

Manish Kumar
Indian Institute of Information Technology Allahabad, India

ABSTRACT

Size of data is increasing, it is creating challenges for its processing and storage. There are cluster based techniques available for storage and processing of this huge amount of data. Map Reduce provides an effective programming framework for developing distributed program for performing tasks which results in terms of key value pair. Collaborative filtering is the process of performing recommendation based on the previous rating of the user for a particular item or service. There are challenges while implementing collaborative filtering techniques using these distributed models. Some techniques are available for implementing collaborative filtering techniques using these models. Cluster based collaborative filtering, map reduce based collaborative filtering are some of these techniques. Chapter addresses these techniques and some basics of collaborative filtering.

INTRODUCTION

In this big technological environment, the amount of data generated is increasing at a very high rate. Computer Engineers at European Council for Nuclear Research (CERN) announced that the amount of data recorded by them for CERN Data Centre has crossed 100 Petabytes of physics data in the last 20 years (CERN, 2015). Experiments in the Large Hadron Collider (LHC) generates huge amount of data, more than 75 Petabytes of this data is generated in last four years. Amazon has about 270 million accounts of active users worldwide (Amazon, 2015). Recommendation for this huge amount of users requires extra efforts. For finding information from this huge and distributed data parallel processing can be used, Google's Map Reduce provides an effective framework for finding information from this data. Hadoop distributed file system for storage of the data and the MapReduce for the retrieval of the relevant information from this data. It is known that the Hadoop framework works well on large file size.

DOI: 10.4018/978-1-5225-0489-4.ch006

Collaborative filtering (CF) is used in recommender system which involves a collection of agents, different viewpoints and data sources. CF main challenges (Su, 2009) are data sparsity, scalability, synonymy, gray sheep, shilling attacks, privacy protection etc. (Linden, 2003). There are three types of collaborative techniques available Memory-based CF, Model-based CF and Hybrid recommenders. Chapter will address, the scalability challenges in performing the collaborative filtering on large datasets, clustering based collaborative approach available for collaborative filtering on large datasets, Prediction algorithms which can be used for a parallel analysis of the datasets using collaborative filtering techniques, challenges in the algorithm design for collaborative filtering on large datasets, real time approach for collaborative filtering of data.

COLLABORATIVE FILTERING

It's a rating system where a user provides his/her response in a specific domain, these responded values by the user helps in recommending the next items to the similar users. There are two basic methods neighborhood and model-based for selecting the users and find similarity among them (Resnick, 1994).

There are two types of user information in system active users and passive users. The users which are currently using the system are active users and the information stored about the activity and their response for the items is stored in a database act as a passive user or passive user information. The process of neighborhood based filtering (Herlocker, 2002) starts with selection of a sample of users from the set of passive users based on their response to a particular item, basically similarity in their response for that item.

The prediction process for an item from item set to an active user can be described as:

- Select a set of passive users based on their similarity with the active user.
- Calculate the mean rating for the active and passive users.
- To measure the similarity Pearson correlation coefficient can be used.

$$w_{a,u} = \frac{\sum_{i \in I}\left(ur_{a,i} - \overline{ur_a}\right)\left(ur_{u,i} - \overline{ur_u}\right)}{\sqrt{\sum_{i \in I}\left(ur_{a,i} - \overline{ur_a}\right)^2 \sum_{i \in I}\left(ur_{u,i} - \overline{ur_u}\right)^2}}$$

- Select users which are having high similarity value corresponding to an active user.
- Use this weight for calculating the weighted average of the deviations from the neighbor's mean as:

$$p_{a,i} = \overline{ur_a} + \frac{\sum_{u \in K}\left(ur_{u,i} - \overline{ur_u}\right) \times w_{a,u}}{\sum_{u \in K} w_{a,u}}$$

here:

$w_{a,u}$ is weighed of similarity between the active user a and passive user u.

$p_{a,i}$, is prediction for active user a and for item i.

$ur_{a,i}$ is the user rating provided by the active user a to the item i.

$\overline{ur_a}$ is the average rating provided by the user a.

As the number of dimension can be very high while calculating the similarity between user and predicting items to the user, a vector space model can be used for calculating the similarity between the users.

$$w_{a,u} = \cos\left(\overrightarrow{ur_a} \bullet \overrightarrow{ur_u}\right) = \frac{\overrightarrow{ur_a} \bullet \overrightarrow{ur_u}}{\left\|\overrightarrow{ur_a}\right\|_2 \times \left\|\overrightarrow{ur_u}\right\|_2} = \frac{\sum_{i=1}^{m} ur_{a,i}\, ur_{u,i}}{\sqrt{\sum_{i=1}^{m} ur_{a,i}^{2}}\sqrt{\sum_{i=1}^{m} ur_{u,i}^{2}}}$$

ITEM-BASED COLLABORATIVE FILTERING

Instead of user based similarity to reduce complexity item to item based similarity can be used (). When user give there feedback for rating items these items are compared with the other items to find the similarity between them. This approach provides faster recommendation then the user based similarity. The Pearson correlation can be used to find the similarities between the items

Consider two items i and j whose similarity we need to find, U is a set of all users who have given their feedback for i and j. The Pearson similarity is given by:

$$w_{i,j} = \frac{\sum_{u \in U}\left(ur_{u,i} - \overline{ur_i}\right)\left(ur_{u,j} - \overline{ur_j}\right)}{\sqrt{\sum_{u \in U}\left(ur_{u,i} - \overline{ur_i}\right)^2}\sqrt{\sum_{u \in U}\left(ur_{u,j} - \overline{ur_j}\right)^2}}$$

where:

$ur_{u,I}$ is the feedback given by the user u for the item i.

$\overline{ur_i}$ is the average rating for the item i by different users.

Prediction for a particular user for a corresponding item i can be done using a simple weighted average:

$$p_{a,i} = \frac{\sum_{j \in K} ur_{a,j}\, w_{i,j}}{\sum_{j \in K}\left|w_{i,j}\right|}$$

MODEL BASED COLLABORATIVE FILTERING

Statistically modeling of the user feedback can result in better recommendation from the system. Some unknown factors can affect the user ratings; matrix factorization uses these factors. In this technique unknown factors are considered, these factors can be user or items and the similarity between these factors can be due to some hidden factors. In latent factor models these hidden factors are being considered. Matrix factorization is a class of techniques which come under latent factor model. Here a compound factor like the inner product of two feature vectors like $w_i, h_i \in R^k$ for k dimensions. The learning of these features can help in approximation of the rating $(r_{u,i})$ for user u for item i.

Big Data

There are three basic V of big data, velocity, volume and variety. Applying collaborative techniques on big data needs some further extension of the collaborative filtering technique while considering the distributed architecture. Creating a scalable collaborative filtering algorithm is main challenge while dealing with big data. There can be two main tasks while dealing with the data, processing of data and storage of data. There are technologies or specifically programming model like MapReduce available for processing this huge amount of data in distributed manner. Storage of this huge amount of data can be done in distributed manner, systems like Hadoop Distributed File System provides this type of storage.

MapReduce

MapReduce programming model is basically a combination of two functions, which are Map and Reduce. Map functions maps data on the distributed storage and process the data according to a given task (Hennessy (2011)). A pair of <Key, Value> combination is generated as an output. The main strategy in this model is to generates intermediate output <Key, Value> combination from mapper and then linearly combine these different pairs according to the value of key. The number of mappers and reducers can vary according to the requirement of the data. Figure 1 shows a simple visualization of MapReduce, data is divided shown as *split( )* and stored in a HDFS system. Mapper run independently and produce results in form of *<key,value>*combination then reducer combine their results and store that results on HDFS.

Hadoop Distributed File System

For storing data in a scalable distributed way Hadoop distributed file system can be used. The main components are Namenode, Datanode (Figure 2) and Secondary namenode. In this data is divided into blocks and each blocks are stored in distributed manner. Datanode is where the data is actually stored in form of blocks. Namenode has the information about each file and corresponding block information about that file. When a mapreduce task is initiated the mapping for the data blocks is done at Namenode. HDFS takes care of the functionalities that are required for a distributed system like the replication, synchronization etc.

Figure 1. Map Reduce basic functionality

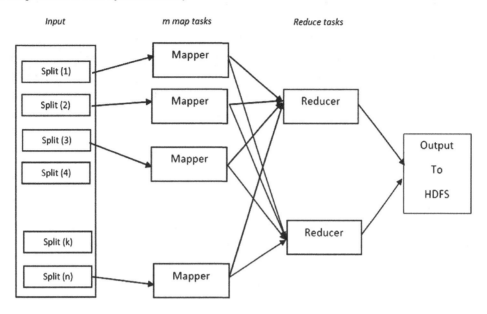

Figure 2. Basic HDFS architecture

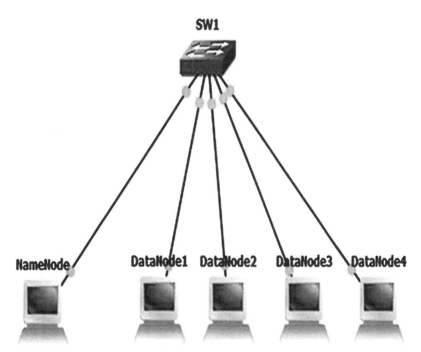

CLUSTER-BASED COLLABORATIVE FILTERING APPROACH

As per the requirement of the big data cluster computing suits best for storage and processing of the data. A cluster based collaborative filtering approach can be used to perform collaborative filtering tasks in this huge amount of data (Hu et al., 2014). It is a combination of different component as described in the diagram below. First the data will be stored in distributed on a cluster and then preprocessing of the data will be done. In this case preprocessing is stem words step. All these services will be provided as cluster services (Figure 3) for further processing.

Pearson Based Similarity

It is useful to find that the rating of the two items is found same on the basis of voting done by a number of users. Calculation of such similarities can be done by using the Pearson correlation coefficient. It has been observed that Pearson correlation coefficient give better performance than the cosine similarity calculation. Considering the PCC is given by:

$$R_{\_sim(s_t,s_j)} = \frac{\sum_{u_i \epsilon U_t \cap U_j} \left(r_{u_i,s_t} - \overline{r_{s_t}} \right) \left(r_{u_i,s_j} - \overline{r_{s_j}} \right)}{\sqrt{\sum_{u_i \epsilon U_t \cap U_j} \left(r_{u_i,s_t} - \overline{r_{s_t}} \right)^2} \sqrt{\sum_{u_i \epsilon U_t \cap U_j} \left(r_{u_i,s_j} - \overline{r_{s_j}} \right)^2}}.$$

where:

U_t and U_j are the set of users who has given their feedback for s_t and s_j.
u_i is a user who had rated both s_t and s_j.
r_{u_i,s_j} is the rating given to the item s_j by the user u_i.

Figure 3. Cluster-based Collaborative filtering approach

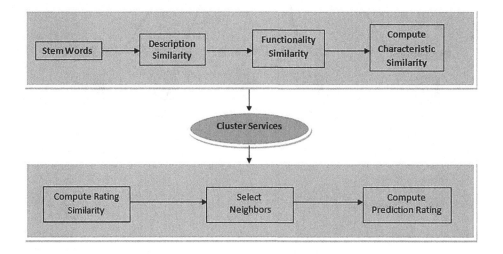

Enhanced Rating Similarity

When the sample size for the correlated services for the estimation of the similarity is small then there can be a chance of error which can affect the efficiency. Enhanced rating similarity for Pearson correlation coefficient considers these factors while calculating the similarity. The enhanced rating similarity for Pearson correlation coefficient is given by:

$$R_{\_sim'}\left(s_t, s_j\right) = \frac{2 \times \left|U_t \cap U_j\right|}{\left|U_t\right| + \left|U_j\right|} \times R_{\_sim\left(s_t, s_j\right)}$$

Selection of Neighbors

After the calculation of the enhanced similarity between the factors selection of the neighbors can be done using the constraint formula given below.

$$N\left(s_t\right) = \left\{ s_j \mid R_{\_sim'}\left(s_t, s_j\right)\right) \gamma, s_t \neq s_j \right\}$$

where: $R_{\_sim'}$ is the enhanced similarity for user rating, which is calculated for the s_j and s_t.

Calculating Predicted Rating

The final stage is that whether to recommend a service s_t to the active user or not. The decision of this factor can be done using the predicted rating given by the equation below. It uses the enhanced rating similarity for calculating the predicted rating.

$$P_{u_a, s_t} = \overline{r_{s_t}} + \frac{\sum_{s_j \in N\left(s_t\right)} \left(r_{u_a, s_j} - \overline{r_j}\right) \times R_{\_sim'}\left(s_t, s_j\right)}{\sum_{s_j \in N\left(s_t\right)} R_{\_sim'}\left(s_t, s_j\right)}$$

where:

$N(s_t)$ is the set of neighbor for s_t,

r_{s_t} is the average feedback for the service s_t.

$s_j \in N\left(s_t\right)$ means that service s_j is a neighbor of service s_t.

As per the process for cluster based collaborative filtering the preprocessing is done initially and then calculation for similarity and neighbors. Based on the value of predicted rating a service will be recommended to the user.

A FEATURE BASED MODEL

A feature based model (Chen et al., 2012) can be developed by the feature based settings for incorporating side information such as temporal dynamics, neighborhood relationship, and hierarchical information. Feature based collaborative filtering, an approach known as SVDFeature can be used. SVDFeature is also already implemented and available as a toolkit which is accessible on its project website. SVDFeature can be used for handling large datasets. It has been studied that SVDFeature can work on the problem related with the Matrix Factorization. It is a unique technique to sole such class of problems.

There are some basic aspects of a collaborative filtering algorithm or basic classes which are dependent on each other. Each class can have factors affecting the quantitative and qualitative values in that class. The number of these factors can vary based on the complexity of the entire system. Considering more factors would result in a very sophisticated but accurate filtering system.

The process starts with identification of main properties (Figure 4) about the system which can be used for applying collaborative filtering technique. These properties can be the logs of the system user history etc. Consider an example for factor summarization, let there are three properties like users' interest, items' property. Now the first thing is the mapping (Figure 5) of the available information for modeling the system and quantification of the factors.

Figure 4. Factors summarization process for CF System

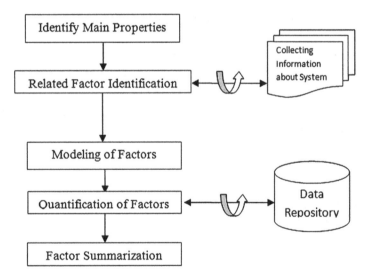

Figure 5. Mapping of factors

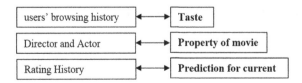

Three feature vectors can be considered as $a \ \varepsilon \ R^m$, $b \ \varepsilon \ R^n$, $c \ \varepsilon \ R^s$. The formulation of estimation for the preference score y is done by:

$$y\left(a,b,c\right) = \left(\sum_{j=1}^{s} c_j.bias_j^{(g)} + \sum_{j=1}^{n} a_j.bias_j^{(u)} + \sum_{j=1}^{m} b_j.bias_j^{(i)}\right) + \left(\sum_{j=1}^{n} a_j.p_j\right)^T \left(\sum_{j=1}^{m} b_j.q_j\right)$$

Parameter modeling is done by using set $\theta = \left\{bias^{(g)}, bias^{(u)}, bias^{(i)}, p, q\right\}$. $p_j \ \varepsilon \ R^d$ and $q_j \ \varepsilon \ R^d$ are d dimension latent factors associated with each feature. Directly effecting factor bias is used to influence the results.

Handling Big Data

There are some challenges while dealing with the large amount of data, like number of I/O requires. Using SVD Feature approach data can be stored into the buffers files for fast access from the hard disk. A storage process has been followed for storing the data into the disk while using the SVD Feature approach. Before the storage of the data on disk shuffling of the data is done. Training of model start with the shuffled data and iteration of the process is done. As long as the data fits into the memory the training part is done when there is requirement of more data then I/O is done. Number of I/O required for training will affect the performance of the overall system. To increase the performance of the overall system a pre-fetch method can be used to speed-up the I/O process. Multithreading can be used for fetching the data in parallel. An independent thread can be used which can parallelize the complete I/O process and a pipelining of the complete system can be done. Figure 6 below show shows the process of parallel pipeline training.

MAPREDUCE BASED COLLABORATIVE FILTERING

Map Reduce programming model is a disk based model, where each file whether it is intermediate data of output is stored on disk (Zhao & Shang, 2010). It increases the scalability of the complete system. Due to its linearity implementing collaborative filtering techniques creates challenges. There are basically two function in this programming model, map function and reduce function. This filtering technique uses user specific information for encapsulating the map function for each user. The recommendation process is combined with the mapper function.

There are three phases:

Figure 6. Pipeline training

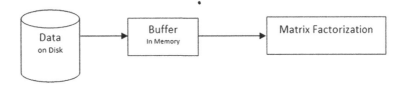

1. Data Partitioning phase.
2. Map phase.
3. Reduce phase.

Data Partitioning Phase

In data partitioning step, each user ID is saved as a row entry in file which will act as input for the map phase. There are two basic principles which needs to be taken care.

- The large chunk of time available should be spent in the processing instead of initialize the mapper.
- Each mapper task should end at the same time.

Map Phase

The numbers of mappers are initialized based on the requirements. First each mapper creates a matrix for the rating done by the users. The user ID stored in the data phase acts as input for this phase and mapper do reading of the user ID from the file. There are two parts of mapper, the <key, value > combination. Here in this phase line number in the file act as key and the user ID corresponding to the line number act as the value for that key. In such manner the key value combination is generated. The similarity between users rating is calculated by cosine similarity. Weighted average is used to calculate the nearest neighbor user on the basis of similarity. These two tasks are completed by each mapper. For checking the similarity cosine similarity can be calculated. Weighted average can be calculated as shown in the collaborative filtering section. Figure 7 shows the process of implementing collaborative filtering using MapReduce.

Figure 7. Pipeline training

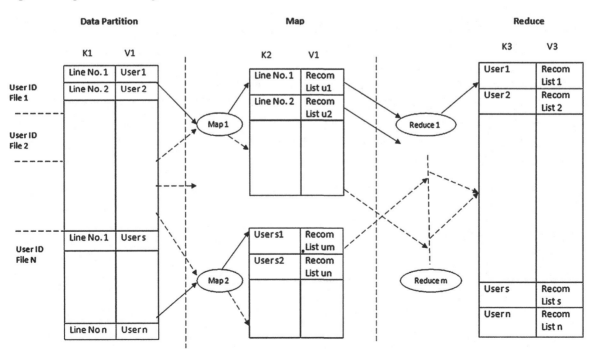

Reducer Phases

Reducer is basically a combiner which combines the <key, value> pairs based on the value of key. Each reducer run independently and merge the mappers output. The reducers are automatically generated by Hadoop environment according to the requirements. The sorting is done according to the user ID. The recommendation generated in the mapper phase are combined based on User ID. A final list of recommendation is written in Hadoop distributed file system as a result.

CONCLUSION

Collaborating filtering techniques are proven to be efficient for a recommendation system. Continuous increasing size of data and its heterogeneity is creating challenges while implementing these techniques. This huge amount of data requires a nonlinear system for its processing and storage. Mapping collaborating filtering techniques in these nonlinear approaches is a challenge. Chapter had covered some based techniques based on clustering for handling large datasets. Techniques which are scalable and size independent provides approaches to handle challenges of large datasets.

REFERENCES

Adomavicius, G. & Zhang, J. (2012). Stability of recommendation algorithms. *ACM Trans. Inf. Syst.*, 30(4), 23:1-23:31.

CERN. (2015). CERN data center passes 100 petabytes. Retrieved from http://home.web.cern.ch/about/updates/2013/02/cern-data-centre-passes-100-petabytes

Chen, T., Zhang, W., Lu, Q., Chen, K., Zheng, Z. & Yu, Y. (2012). SVDFeature: A Toolkit for Feature-based Collaborative Filtering. *Journal of Machine Learning Research*, 13, 3619-3622.

Hennessy, J. L., & Patterson, D. A. (2011). *MapReduce: Simplified Data Processing on Large Clusters Computer architecture: a quantitative approach*. Elsevier.

Herlocker, J., Konstan, J.A. & Riedl, J. (2002). An empirical analysis of design choices in neighborhood-based collaborative filtering algorithms. *Inf. Retr.*, 5(4), 287-310.

Hu, R., Dou, W. & Liu, J. (2014, September). ClubCF: A Clustering-Based collaborative Filtering Approach for Big Data Application. *IEEE transactions on emerging topics in computing*, 2(3).

Julie, D. & Kumar, K.A. (2012). Optimal web service selection scheme with dynamic QoS property assignment. *Int. J. Adv. Res. Technol.*, 2(2), 69-75.

Koren, Y., Bell, R., & Volinsky, C. (2009). Matrix factorization techniques for recommender systems. *Computer*, 42(8), 30–37. doi:10.1109/MC.2009.263

Linden, G., Smith, B., & York, J. (2003). Amazon. com recommendations: Item-to-item collaborative filtering. *IEEE Internet Computing, 7*(1), 76–80. doi:10.1109/MIC.2003.1167344

Melville, P., & Sindhwani, V. (2010). *Recommender Systems Encyclopedia of machine learning.*

Resnick, P., Iacovou, N., Suchak, M., Bergstrom, P., & Riedl, J. (1994, October). GroupLens: an open architecture for collaborative filtering of netnews.*Proceedings of the 1994 ACM conference on Computer supported cooperative work* (pp. 175-186). ACM.

Sarwar, B., Karypis, G., Konstan, J., & Riedl, J. (2001, April). Item-based collaborative filtering recommendation algorithms.*Proceedings of the 10th international conference on World Wide Web* (pp. 285-295). ACM.

Statista. (2015). Statistics and facts about Amazon. Retrieved from http://www.statista.com/topics/846/amazon/

Su, X., & Khoshgoftaar, T. M. (2009). A survey of collaborative filtering techniques. *Advances in Artificial Intelligence, 2009.* doi:10.1155/2009/421425

Yamashita, H. Kawamura, & K. Suzuki (2011). Adaptive fusion method for user-based and item-based collaborative filtering. *Adv. Complex Syst., 14*(2), 133-149.

Zhao, Z. D., & Shang, M. S. (2010) User-based Collaborative-Filtering Recommendation Algorithms on Hadoop. *Proceedings of the 2010 Third International Conference on Knowledge Discovery and Data Mining.*

ADDITIONAL READING

Dean, J. (2014). *Big Data, Data Mining, and Machine Learning: Value Creation for Business Leaders and Practitioners.* John Wiley & Sons.

Ekstrand, M. D., Riedl, J. T., & Konstan, J. A. (2011). Collaborative filtering recommender systems. *Foundations and Trends in Human-Computer Interaction, 4*(2), 81–173.

Rajaraman, A., & Ullman, J. D. (2012). *Mining of Massive Datasets.* Cambridge, U.K.: Cambridge Univ. Press.

Wu, X., Zhu, X., Wu, G. Q., & Ding, W. (2014, January). Data mining with big data. *IEEE Transactions on Knowledge and Data Engineering, 26*(1), 97–107.

KEY TERMS AND DEFINITIONS

HDFS: Hadoop distributed file system is a file system in which data is stored in form blocks in a distributed manner.

MapReduce: It is a programming model which can be executed on a cluster for processing of the data.

Rating: Rating is the feedback given by a user for a service. It can be quantitative or qualitative.

Similarity: It is amount that how much two users are similar in context of providing there rating for a particular service or item. It can be measured using techniques like Pearson based similarity.

Chapter 7
Big Data Mining Using Collaborative Filtering

Anu Saini
G.B. Pant Engineering College, India

ABSTRACT

Today every big company, like Google, Flipkart, Yahoo, Amazon etc., is dealing with the Big Data. This big data can be used to predict the recommendation for the user on the basis of their past behavior. Recommendation systems are used to provide the recommendation to the users. The author presents an overview of various types of recommendation systems and how these systems give recommendation by using various approaches of Collaborative Filtering. Various research works that employ collaborative filtering for recommendations systems are reviewed and classified by the authors. Finally, this chapter focuses on the framework of recommendation system of big data along with the detailed survey on the use of the Big Data mining in collaborative filtering.

INTRODUCTION

Nowadays maintaining and dealing with huge data is the main concern of the industries, government, academia, research, science etc. Data can be in structured or in unstructured format. Each company will try to access their huge volume of data with high velocity. But traditional processing tools are not capable to deal with large amount of data. The solution of this problem is Big Data. Big Data can be defined as the huge volume of data which can be structured or unstructured and it cannot be processed on the traditional databases. Major users of Big Data are Amazon, YouTube, Facebook, Twitter, Flipkart etc.

In this chapter, main concern of the author is to provide a Big Data mining through which recommendation can be made according to the user preferences. Since Big Data is very big. So, choosing data according to their choice from the Big Data is the very tedious task for the consumer. The solution of this problem is the Recommendation Systems. Recommendation systems, recommends the products or data that fits to the user choice. There are various techniques are used by many researchers for recommendation system named as Collaborative Filtering Systems, Content Based Filtering System, Hydrid Filtering and Item based Filtering.

DOI: 10.4018/978-1-5225-0489-4.ch007

The organization of chapter is as follows: chapter starts with the introduction to Recommendation System along with the associated technologies. Then author will discuss the Recommendation system based on the Collaborative filtering systems and its classification. Afterward section contains the description of user based and item based collaborative filtering. Next section gives the introduction of Big Data Mining along with various characteristics i.e. V's of big data. After that author explains the framework of the recommendation system by using Big data. Subsequently, describes the implications of our work to research domain. Finally, the author concludes the research work and highlights some future enhancements.

Research Methodology

Handling of data is the basic and most important aspect in every field like industry, research, academics etc. Several approaches have been proposed to handling and maintaining the huge data but the management is still tedious. The continuous and rigours efforts of industry as well as researchers in the filed of huge data tempted the author to come across for new emerging techniques for organizing the large volume of data. The most efficient and up coming technique, to the best of author knowledge, for handling, maintaining and organizing the data is Big Data. Big Data is used to handle the complex and huge data. Big Data mining is the other aspect which is handling in this chapter. Recommendations system are used for Big Data mining, which can be classified as collaborative filtering, content based filtering and hybrid filtering. The relevant material was found in various journals and conferences. The database of various journals and conferences has been searched regarding the literature of Big Data.

1. Inderscience Journals.
2. ACM publications.
3. Big Data Journals.
4. KDD.
5. IEEE publication.
6. IGI Global Publication.

The research roadmap leading to the study of various recommendation systems for Big Data Mining as shown in Figure 1. The research roadmap shows the path followed by author that led them to carry out the wide study and literature review.

Recommendation Systems

In today's world everyone is experienced the recommendation system on the internet. When we log in to the YouTube, Amazon, Flipkart etc. the list of recommendations is provided to us based on our previously searched items. Recommendation systems are the systems that predict the user responses on the basis of their past behavior.

Let's say author is made a website to recommend books. By using the past history of the user who have visited the particular website or surf and purchase the books, author can group those users based on their behavior.

Figure 1. Research roadmap

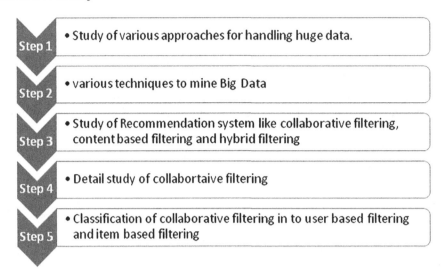

Verma et al (2015) discussed the Recommendation system that are worked for the large amount of data which is available on the web like ratings, reviews, opinions, complain, remarks, feedback, and comments about any item. To do so, Hadoop framework has been used. Here recommendations are provided in terms of numerical data like ratings.

Yang et al. (2014) described the Recommendation systems for the online social networks is also propose by the authors here they divide the Recommendation system in two categories Matrix Factorization (MF) based social recommendation approaches and Neighborhood based social recommendation approaches.

Raju (2014) explains the Recommendation system that basically contains the three fields named as User, Item and Rating Recommendation system uses various algorithms namely Collaborative filtering system, Content based filtering system and hybrid filtering system as shown in Figure 2.

Collaborative filtering is used to provide the recommendations to user on the basis of the user and similar taste of the users past behavior. In Content based filtering, recommendation is given only on the basis of the user past behavior. For example, if the user reads only Java and C++ blogs and articles

Figure 2. Techniques of recommendation systems

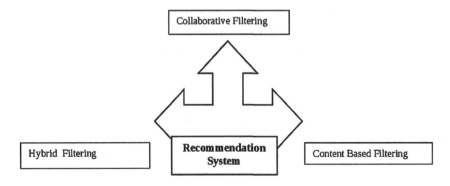

then content based filtering save this behavior of the user as a history and suggest the similar kind of articles in the future. Hybrid filtering is the combination of collaborative and content based filtering. In hybrid filtering the weighted average of collaborative and content based filtering is find out. On the basis of this weighted average recommendations have been made. In this chapter, author main focus is on Collaborative Filtering

Collaborative Filtering

Collaborative Filtering (CF) model is mainly based on the user behavior or the behavior of other users who are having same taste. The Classification of CF is shown in Figure 3.

Hu et al (2008) describe the CF that uses a dataset of implicit feedbacks given by the user. Here the implicit feedback is divided into two pairs; preferences and confidence levels. They have proposed a latent factor algorithm that addresses the preferences and confidence.

Darvishi et al. (2013) and Rong et al. (2014) propose the Cluster based CF which is also used for recommendation system of Big Data. Author proposed a new approach named as "Clustering-based Collaborative Filtering approach (ClubCF)". This approach is the two-step process first, divide the services in the cluster for further processing and secondly apply the collaborative filtering algorithm on every cluster. Here services are merged by using AHC algorithm.

Figure 3. Classification of collaborative filtering

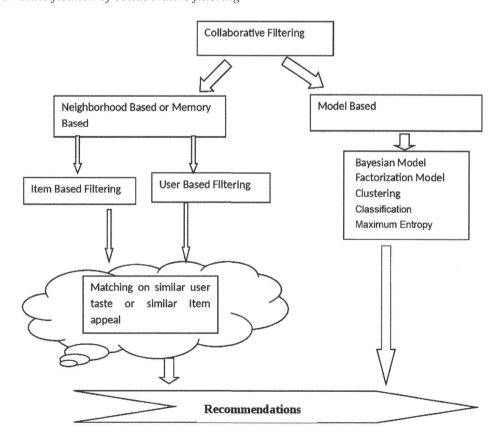

In Zheng et al. (2011), the authors have made the recommendation systems for QoS of Web Service by using CF. They follow the two step process; firstly QoS information from the history of different type of users who have used the service have been collected by using user collaborative method. Secondly, collaborative filtering approach is implemented to predict the QoS of web service. For this they implemented a prototype WSRec for conducting real world experiments.

Yang et al. (2014) describe the Collaborative filtering which is further categorizes in Memory based filtering and Model Based filtering. In Memory Based filtering, similarities between the users or items are calculated by using the rating or preferences given by the users. Memory based CF is further classifying in User based CF and Item Based CF. Various algorithms used for Memory Based CF are K-nearest neighbor, Pearson correlation coefficient, Cosine distance Whereas in model based filtering data is collected and this data works as training data. Then the data is modeled using data mining, machine learning algorithms. Various Model based collaborative filtering algorithms includes Bayesian networks, clustering models, latent semantic models such as singular value decomposition, etc.

User Based Collaborative Filtering

User-based collaborative filtering predicts a user's interest in an item which is based on the similar user profiles. Thokal and Bhusari (2014) has the believes that the excellent way to find the user's interest is to find the interest of other users who are having same interest. This type of technique first tries to find the user's neighbors based on user similarities and then combine the neighbor users' rating scores. The rating matrix has been formed to represent the user's history. The example of rating matrix is shown in the Table 1.

In Table 1, each row represents the users and each column represents the item. Each column represents the books of various computer subjects. Each cell contains the ratings between 1-5, where 1 represent the lowest rating and 5 represent the higher rating that book is least recommend. Here user 1 is more interest in the computer language books. Whereas user 3 is more interested in Database and cutwork book. Now suppose author wants to recommend books for the user 5, so here similarity matrices have been used like dot product, cosine similarity.

Here in a given table, user 1 and user 5 have read similar kinds of book. Both like C++ and Java books and dislike database book. So we conclude that the interest of User 1 and user 5 are same. So the network books will be recommended to the User 5.

Table 1. Rating matrix

	C++	Java	Linux	Database	Network
1	4	5	1		4
2	1	1		5	
3				5	5
4	1	1	5		
5	5	4			

User based CF is two-step process. In first step finds the neighbor of the user's based on their similar interest and in second step the combine the neighbor user's rating score.

Wang et al. (2006) presents a generative probabilistic framework which is set up to utilize more of the data available in the user-item matrix. To do so authors combine all the ratings with predictive value for a recommendation to be made. Here predictions are made on the basis of the average of all the individual ratings. This paper the hybrid approach of user –based and item based is used to take advantage for making user item matrix.

Zhao and Shang (2010) discussed the User Based CF the can also be used for cloud computing platform. This paper is divided into two phases. First the user based CF algorithm has been designed for MaprReduce framework and implement it on Hadoop. In Second phase, authors test the implementation of CF which is done on Eclipse platform. Here recommendations have made for every user and these recommendations have encapsulated in map reduce functions.

Item Based Collaborative Filtering

Item based collaborative filtering technique is used to predict the users interest on the basis of the similarity between the items. In Table 1, item is represents by the computer books. Here the item i.e. books of network is liked by the user1 and user3. Here user3 also liked the database books. This suggests that user who liked the database books also like the network books. So on this basis database books will be recommending to user 1.

Hengsong and Hong (2009) have made the recommendation system based on the item classification prediction by using collaborative filtering. Here firstly items are classify using the item attribute content then make the item matrix accordingly by using collaborative filtering. Later on they have used the item based filtering to produce the predictions.

Tan and Ye (2009) have discussed the item based CF to predict the rating of the item where vacant values are required and then produce the recommendations. To fill the vacant ratings authors have used the user based CF. This paper is divided into two phases. In first phase, the authors have used item classification to pre produce prediction and sub matrix has been made to fill the vacant values. In second phase item based CF is used to produce recommendations.

Big Data Mining with Collaborative Filtering

Researchers have proposed many definitions of Big Data. In simple term, Big Data is used to describe the huge and complex data which cannot be handling by the conventional data processing applications. The major sources of big data are web logs, social media, internet text and documents, internet pages etc. Various charteristics of Big Data is known as the "V's of Big Data". Traditional there are 3 V's of Big Data i.e. Volume, Velocity and Variety. Manulty (2014) have discussed more V's such as Variability, Veracity, Visualization, Value as shown in Figure 4.

We have selected four contributions that together shows very significant state-of-the-art research in Big Data Mining. The major journals and conferences of big data mining are KDD, ICDM, Data Mining and Knowledge Discovery Journal.

Figure 4. Seven V's of big data

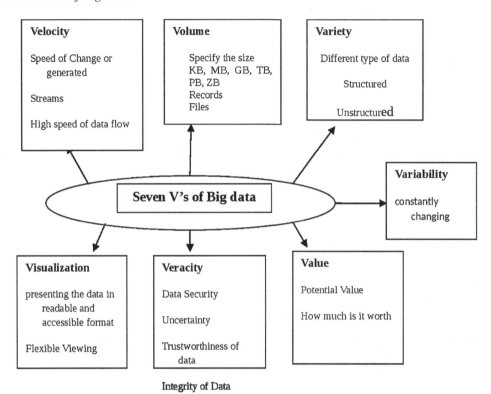

One of the major challenges of big data is processing of large volumes of data and extracts useful information or knowledge for future actions. This challenge can be handling by the Big Data Mining. Big data mining refers to technique to find out the useful information from the huge amount of available data due to its volume, velocity, variety. With the help of Big Data mining we discover knowledge that no one has discovered before. Many researchers are working on this.

Lin and Ryaboy (2013) have taken the example of Twitter's huge data as Big Data. To perform analytics, it is not easy to perform with the help of traditional data mining tools. The largest part of the time of the preprocessing is taken by the introductory work of data mining methods, and turning preliminary models into robust solutions.

Sun and Han (2013) are worked with semi-structured heterogeneous information network. For this type of data, they are structuring the objects and various type of interactions. Here authors have proposed new approach named as "Meta-Path-Based Similarity Search and Mining". This systematic approach deals with the heterogeneous data. They are addressing the similarity search and interesting mining tasks, such as relationship prediction.

Kang and Faloutsos (2013) s are working on mining the Big Graph. To mine Big Graphs authors have used Peagus, which is a big graph mining sys-tem built on over and above of MapReduce, a modern distributed data processing platform.

Amatriain (2013) proposed an approach a large stream data to provide recommendations. For this they have used Netflix Prize. The Netflix Prize abstracted the recommendation problem to a proxy and simply question of predicting ratings.

Recommendation System Framework

The proposed framework provides the 3-layer architecture where first layer is the user, second layer represent the recommendation engine and the third layer tell us about the various sources of big data as shown in Figure 5. Each layer is describing below.

First layer is the user interaction layer. Basic use of this layer is to search for the service by the user. This layer is used by the user to provide the ratings and preferences. On basis of which recommendations is predicted and given to user. This layer is worked a frond end in the given architecture.

Second layer is divided into two parts first is the recommendation engine and second is recommendation models. Recommendation Engine uses the MapReduce framework for consuming data sources from big data and for saving recommendation into the database. Whereas recommendation model consists of various type of algorithms used to provide recommendation like user based, item based, content based etc.

Third layer provide the data storage in form of Big Data. Since the data are from various source like web logs, sensor data, social network data, media data etc. Also there are data of recommendations,

Figure 5. Recommendation system framework for big data

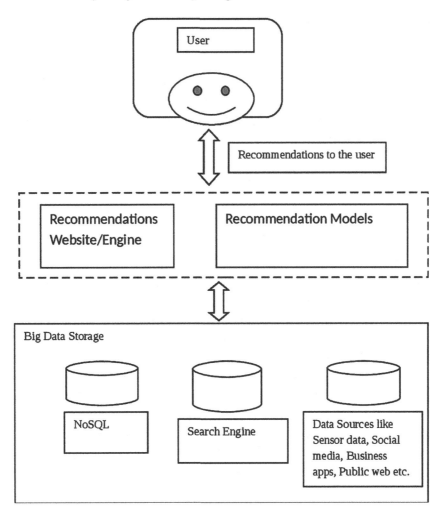

ratings and preferences. So we have to store these data into the databases. There I use NoSQL database to store the data because NoSQL is more flexible as compare to the RDBMS. In NoSQL data is not stored in terms of relations. It is used to store the recommendations and ratings of the user which may be in unstructured format.

Research Implications

This chapter has presented a literature survey on the application of Big Data Mining in Collaborative Filtering. The implication of the research is as follows:

1. The overall picture of the Big Data has been studied along with various V's of Big Data as discussed in Figure 4.
2. The literature review will help the researchers to gain knowledge of the ways and methods for efficient recommendations system using various collaborative filtering techniques. The classification of collaborative filtering is presented through various approaches used by researchers.
3. The author has presented the survey of the collaborative filtering technique for the big data by detailed study of various conference, journals and articles.
4. The current research will form the basis for identification of new approaches and techniques towards building efficient recommendation systems.
5. The classification of collaborative filtering will enable the researchers to carry on further research.
6. Several collaborative filtering techniques have been identified from various research journals. The classification at a glance is capable enough to give research insights to researchers pursuing work in the recommendation systems domain regarding existing research work and covers the way for future work related to the domain.
7. The overall working of the recommendation system for big data has been shown in a form of recommendation framework in Figure 5.

CONCLUSION

In this chapter the author has given the survey of the collaborative filtering for big data mining. The author has also discussed Big Data along with the various characteristics of it. The classification of recommendation systems using Collaborative Filtering approach is also discussed in this chapter. The author provides the depth in collaborative filtering which could be used by researchers to further explore knowledge from big data. Author has also discussed the types of collaborative filtering: user based filtering and item based filtering. The recommendation system framework is proposed by the user for Big Data. The framework will provide a foundation for researchers in understanding the role of recommendation system in Big Data mining and create platform towards the identification of newer techniques in building efficient software. The author have tried to include most of the possible information from various research journals and conferences, still there are possibility of extension of literature review.

In future work, author tries to study more aspects of the architectural proposal. In addition, I would also like to try proposing effective algorithms on the collaborative filtering for Big Data by using MapReduce framework.

REFERENCES

Amatriain, X. (2013). Mining large streams of user data for personalized recommendations. *ACM SIG-KDD Explorations Newsletter, 14*(2), 37–48. doi:10.1145/2481244.2481250

Darvishi-mirshekarlou, F., Akbarpour, S. H., & Feizi-Derakhshi, M. (2013). Reviewing Cluster Based Collaborative Filtering Approaches. *International Journal of Computer Applications Technology and Research, 2*(6), 650–659. doi:10.7753/IJCATR0206.1004

Hengsong, T., & Hong Wu Ye. (2009, May 16-17). A Collaborative Filtering Recommendation Algorithm Based on Item Classification. *Proceedings of the Pacific-Asia Conference on Circuits, Communications and Systems* (pp. 694-697).

Hu, Y., Koren, Y., & Volinsky, C. (2008). Collaborative Filtering for Implicit Feedback Datasets. *Proceedings of the2008Eighth IEEE International Conference on Data Mining.*

Kang, U., & Faloutsos, C. (2013). Big graph mining: Algorithms and discoveries. *ACM SIGKDD Explorations Newsletter, 14*(2), 29–36. doi:10.1145/2481244.2481249

Lin, J., & Ryaboy, D. (2013). Scaling big data mining infrastructure: The twitter experience. *ACM SIG-KDD Explorations Newsletter, 14*(2), 6–19. doi:10.1145/2481244.2481247

Mcnulty, E. (2014). Understanding Big Data: The Seven V's. *DataEconomy.com.* Retrieved from http://dataconomy.com/seven-vs-big-data/

Raju, R. (2014). Big Data Recommendation Systems. *Whishworks.com.* Retrieved from www.whishworks.com/blog/recommendation-systems/

Rong Hu. Wanchun Dou & Jianxun Liu, (2014, September). ClubCF: A Clustering-Based Collaborative Filtering Approach for Big Data Application. IEEE Transactions on Emerging Topics in Computing, 2(3), 302-313.

Sun, Y., & Han, J. (2013). Mining heterogeneous information networks: A structural analysis approach. *ACM SIGKDD Explorations Newsletter, 14*(2), 20–28. doi:10.1145/2481244.2481248

Tan, H., & Ye, H. (2009, May). A collaborative filtering recommendation algorithm based on item classification. *Proceedings of the Pacific-Asia Conference on Circuits, Communications and Systems, 2009* (pp. 694-697). IEEE. doi:10.1109/PACCS.2009.68

Thokal, S., & Bhusari, V. (2014). Review Paper on Clustering Based Collaborative Filtering. *International Journal of Advance Research in Computer Science and Management Studies, 2*(11), 558–561.

Verma, J. P., Patel, B., & Patel, A. (2015, February). Big Data Analysis: Recommendation System with Hadoop Framework. *Proceedings of the 2015 IEEE International Conference onComputational Intelligence & Communication Technology (CICT)* (pp. 92-97). IEEE.

Wang, J., De Vries, A. P., & Reinders, M. J. (2006, August). Unifying user-based and item-based collaborative filtering approaches by similarity fusion.*Proceedings of the 29th annual international ACM SIGIR conference on Research and development in information retrieval* (pp. 501-508). ACM. doi:10.1145/1148170.1148257

Yang, X., Guo, Y., Liu, Y., & Steck, H. (2014). A survey of collaborative filtering based social recommender systems. *Computer Communications*, *41*, 1–10. doi:10.1016/j.comcom.2013.06.009

Zhao, Z. D., & Shang, M. S. (2010, January). User-based collaborative-filtering recommendation algorithms on hadoop. *Proceedings of the Third International Conference on Knowledge Discovery and Data Mining WKDD '10* (pp. 478-481). IEEE.

Zheng, Z., Ma, H., Lyu, M. R., & King, I. (2011). Qos-aware web service recommendation by collaborative filtering. *IEEE Transactions on* Services Computing, *4*(2), 140–152.

ADDITIONAL READING

Chen, M., Mao, S., Zhang, Y., & Leung, V. C. (2014). *Big data: related technologies, challenges and future prospects*. Springer; doi:10.1007/978-3-540-72079-9_9

Li, G. (2015). Big data related technologies, challenges and future prospects. *Information Technology & Tourism*, *15*(3), 283–285. doi:10.1007/s40558-015-0027-y

Ricci, F., Rokach, L., & Shapira, B. (2011). *Introduction to recommender systems handbook*. Springer, US.

Schafer, J. B., Frankowski, D., Herlocker, J., & Sen, S. (2007). Collaborative filtering recommender systems. In *The adaptive web* (pp. 291–324). Springer Berlin Heidelberg.

KEY TERMS AND DEFINITIONS

Big Data: Big Data is defined as the huge, complex, structured and unstructured data that cannot be processed by traditional methods.

Collaborative Filtering: Approach for recommendation system based on the user and other persons past behavior.

Item Based Collaborative Filtering: Systems where items have same ratings or preferences.

Recommendations System: System that provide recommendation to the user for item and products on the basis of their past behavior.

User Based Collaborative Filtering: System where users' same ratings or preferences.

Applications of Data Mining Techniques and Data Analysis in Collaborative Filtering

Chapter 8
Collaborative and Clustering Based Strategy in Big Data

Arushi Jain
Ambedkar Institute of Advanced Communication Technologies and Research, India

Vishal Bhatnagar
Ambedkar Institute of Advanced Communication Technologies and Research, India

Pulkit Sharma
Ambedkar Institute of Advanced Communication Technologies and Research, India

ABSTRACT

There is a proliferation in the amount of data generated and its volume, which is going to persevere for many coming years. Big data clustering is the exercise of taking a set of objects and dividing them into groups in such a way that the objects in the same groups are more similar to each other according to a certain set of parameters than to those in other groups. These groups are known as clusters. Cluster analysis is one of the main tasks in the field of data mining and is a commonly used technique for statistical analysis of data. While big data collaborative filtering defined as a technique that filters the information sought by the user and patterns by collaborating multiple data sets such as viewpoints, multiple agents and pre-existing data about the users' behavior stored in matrices. Collaborative filtering is especially required when a huge data set is present.

INTRODUCTION

A huge surge in the amount of data being generated that needs to be stored and analyzed quickly has been witnessed in the recent years. Walmart handles millions of transactions per hour while Facebook handles 40 billion photos uploaded by its users each day. Big data has become important part of data analytics market. Big Data can be defined using five v's. These are:

1. **Volume**: This refers to the amount of data. While volume is indicatory of more data, it is the particulate nature of the data that is exclusive. For example data logs from twitter, click streams

DOI: 10.4018/978-1-5225-0489-4.ch008

of web pages and mobile apps, sensor-enabled equipment capturing data, etc. It is the task of big data for converting data into useful information so that valuable action could be taken.

2. **Velocity**: This refers to the rate at which data is generated, captured and received. For example, to make lucrative offers ecommerce applications combines mobile location and personal choices of the buyer.

3. **Variety**: This refers to various types of structured, unstructured and semi- structured data types. Unstructured data consist of files such as audio and video. Unstructured data has many of the requirements similar to that of structured data, such as summarization, audit ability, and privacy. This data is generated from varied sources such as satellites, sensors, social networks, etc.

4. **Value**: This refers to the intrinsic value that the data may possess, and must be discovered. There is wide variety of techniques to derive value from data. The advancement in the recent years have led to exponential decrease in the cost of storage and processing of data, thus providing statistical analysis on the entire data possible, unlike the past where random samples were analyzed to draw inferences.

5. **Veracity**: This refers to the abnormality in data. Veracity in data analysis is one of the biggest challenges. This is dealt with by properly defining the problem statement before analysis, finding relevant data and using proven techniques for analysis so that the result is trustworthy and useful. There are various tools and techniques in the market for big data analytics.

Some of the challenges of big data are:

1. The biggest challenge in big data is to aggregate data from heterogeneous sources and analyzes it to get useful information out of it to improve various aspects of functioning and business process of organizations. The data may come from various social networks, with each having a different format.

2. One of the main characteristics of big data is Autonomous where data source works independently without being dependent on centralized control. For example World Wide Web generates function correctly without involving other servers.

3. Another challenge is complexity. The complexity of Big Data is due to multiple data; the data is collected in very different contexts (multi-source, multi-view, multi-tables, sequential, etc.).

4. Big data is always evolving, thus evolution of complex data which poses a big challenge. The typical example is when a customer posts a review on a page of social networking, it has to be extracted over specific periods of time so that the algorithm can operate and provide relevant information to the users.

LITERATURE SURVEY

To manage the growing demands, there is a need to increase the capacity and performance of tools and methods employed for analysis of data. Chen et al. (2014), in their work "Big data: A survey" focused on big data and reviewed related technologies and examined the application of big data in various fields. Al-Jarrah et al. (2015), in their work "Efficient Machine Learning for Big Data: A Review" reviewed the data modeling in large scale data intensive field relating to model efficiency and new algorithm approaches. Hoffmann and Birnbrich (2012) to protect their customer from third party fraud proposed a conceptual link between retail bank activities in "The impact of fraud prevention on bank-customer relationships: An empirical investigation in retail banking". Srivastava and Gopalkrishnan (2015) revealed some of the best techniques which are used by the banks across the globe and can be used by the Indian banks to enhance their services offerings to the customers in "Impact of Big Data Analytics on Banking Sector: Learning for Indian Banks". Azar and Hassanien (2014) for dimensionality reduction presented a linguistic hedges neuro-fuzzy classifier with selected features (LHNFCSF). In this paper author compared the new classifier with the other classifiers for various classification problems in "Dimensionality reduction of medical big data using neural-fuzzy classifier". Hassanien et al. (2015) focused on application, challenges and opportunities of big data in "Big Data in Complex Systems: Challenges and Opportunities". Wahi et al. (2014) proposed a social media and its implication on customer relationship management in "Social Media: The core of enterprise 2.0.". Shabeera and Madhu Kumar (2015), in their work "Optimizing virtual machine allocation in MapReduce cloud for improved data locality" focused on improving data locality by allocating virtual machines for executing map reduce jobs. Aloui and Touzi (2015) proposed a methodology for designing ontology on a new platform called "FO-FQ Tab plug-in" and then querying them smartly based on conceptual clustering and fuzzy logic in "A Fuzzy Ontology-Based Platform for Flexible Querying". Ghallab et al. (2014), in their work "Strictness petroleum prediction system based on fussy model" predicted the status of crude oil and then compared it with other petroleum values. Huang et al. (2015) summarized the latest application of big data in health science. The authors also reviewed the latest technologies of big data and discussed the future perspective of health sciences in "Promises and challenges of big data computing in health science". Jagadish (2015) in "Big Data and Science: Myths and Reality" explored myths about big data and exposed the underlying truth. Jin et al. (2015) introduced the concept of big data and described the challenges as well as solution to these challenges in "Significance and challenges of big data research". Ryan and Lee (2015) presented a Multi-tier resource allocation as resource management technique for distributed systems in "Multi-tier resource allocation for data-intensive computing". Tiwari and Joshi (2015) in "Data security for software as a service" discussed security vulnerabilities of software as a service (SaaS) and its solution. Wahi et al. (2015) focused on whether the organization could able to address challenges posed by big data successfully or not. It also focused on the reasons why it is necessary to transit from the enterprise 1.0 stage to enterprise 2.0 stage in "Big Data: Enabler or Challenge for Enterprise 2.0. Deepak and John (2016) illustrated that information system is one of the most significant problem in fuzzy domain. Authors illustrated a case where hesitant membership value arrived from attribute value whose membership values are a family of set and also discusses the homomorphism between hesitant information systems in "Information Systems on Hesitant Fuzzy Sets". Bhanu and Tripathy (2016) in "Rough Set Based Similarity Measures for Data Analytics in Spatial Epidemiology" carried out epidemiological studies to understand a pattern and transmission of disease instances.

AN INTRODUCTION TO COLLABORATIVE AND CLUSTERING BASED STRATEGY IN BIG DATA

To manage the growing demands of this day and age, there is a need to increase the capacity and performance of tools and methods employed for analysis of data. but it can be very costly and time taking for development of hardware which can handle such loads. The hardware thus developed may become insufficient in a matter of months, given the rate at which the data is increasing and evolving. In order

Figure 1. Euclidean distance

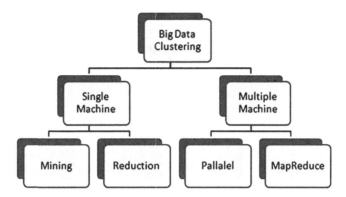

to exploit this voluminous data without much financial and time overhead, efficient processing model with a reasonable computational cost of this huge, complex, highly dynamic and heterogeneous data set is needed.

Cluster analysis or clustering is the exercise of taking a set of objects and dividing them into groups in such a way that the objects in the same groups are more similar to each other according to a certain set of parameters than to those in other groups. These groups are known as clusters. Cluster analysis is one of the main tasks in the field of data mining and is a commonly used technique for statistical analysis of data.

Cluster analysis does not refer to an algorithm but an exercise that has to be undertaken on the given data set. Various algorithms can be used for cluster analysis. The algorithms are divided into various categories and they differ significantly in their idea of what a cluster is constituted of and how the clusters are identified. The most popular ideas on the basis of which clusters are defined and identified include groups with small distances among the constituent members, areas of the data space which are highly dense, intervals or particular distributions. Clustering is a multi-objective problem that it is a mathematical optimization problem. A clustering algorithm consists of parameter settings such as a distance function, a density threshold (the number of clusters expected to be formed). Based on the available data set and the use of result as intended by the user, apt clustering algorithm may be used.

Similarity measures can be chosen on the basis of following:

Euclidean Distance

Figure 1 presents the equation for Euclidean Distance where n= number of dimensions in the data vector.

Pearson Linear Correlation

The value of Pearson Linear Correlation (PLC) lies between -1 and + 1 which implies anti correlated or perfectly correlated. It is a measure that is invariant to scaling and shifting. Pearson Linear correlation can be calculated using equation presented in Figure 2

Cluster analysis cannot be considered to be an automatic task, but an iterative process of discovery of knowledge from data or an interactive multi-objective optimization that involves a probabilistic model having trial and failure. Therefore, it is sometimes necessary to preprocess data set before implementation

Figure 2. Pearson linear correlation

$$d = \sqrt{\sum_{i=1}^{n} (x_i - y_i)^2}$$

of clustering and sometimes even the preprocessing task may have to be modified to obtain the desired results. Cluster analysis has been used in a variety of fields.

BIG DATA CLUSTERING

Big Data clustering techniques can be broadly classified into two categories as shown in Figure 3:

1. Single machine clustering techniques.
2. Multiple machine clustering techniques.

In recent the latter have drawn more attention because they are faster and more adapt to the new challenges of Big Data.

Single-Machine Clustering

Mining

The unsupervised classification, called clustering, is an essential data mining based tool for analyzing Big Data. Clustering aims to reinforce the significant class data objects, called clusters, so that the objects aggregated in the same cluster are similar and consistent when weighed against certain parameters. It is a bit tricky to apply data mining based clustering techniques in Big Data because of the new challenges it brings with itself. With the great mass of data that needs to be analyzed and the complexity of clustering algorithms which can lead to really high costs, dealing with this problem and deploying clustering techniques Big Data to obtain results in a decent time is a huge challenge. There are many different methods in the literature which can be used to generate clusters. These methods can be classified into five broad categories:

Figure 3. Big data clustering techniques

$$r = \frac{\sum_{i=1}^{n} \left((x_i - \bar{x})(y_i - \bar{y}) \right)}{\sqrt{\sum_{i=1}^{n} (x_i - \bar{x})^2 \sum_{i=1}^{n} (y_i - \bar{y})^2}}$$

1. Partitioning methods.
2. Hierarchical methods.
3. Method based.
4. Density-based methods.
5. Methods based on a model.

- **Partitioning Based Clustering Algorithms**: These methods divide a data set in a single partition using distance for classification of points based on their similarities. The drawback of the partitioning methods is that these methods generally require the user to use a predefined K parameter for a clustering the data which is often non-deterministic. There are many partitioning algorithms such as K-means, K-modes, PAM, CLARA, CLARANS and FCM.
- **Hierarchical Based Clustering Algorithms:** These methods partition data into different levels that look like a hierarchy, thus providing a classification that gives clear data visualization. The aim of these methods is to group objects into classes which are increasingly wide, using mathematical measures of similarity or distance. The results of the classification are usually represented as a hierarchy. The hierarchical method has a major drawback that is once a stage is completed the algorithm moves to a subsequent stage and there can be no backtracking. Some of the hierarchical algorithm are BIRCH, CURE, ROCK and Chameleon.
- **Density Based Clustering Algorithms:** These methods are able to find clusters in an capricious manner. The clusters are simply defined as dense regions separated by low density areas. The clustering algorithms based on density are not suitable for large data sets as the output distribution can be too much to handle with this approach. DBSCAN, OPTICAL DBCLASD and DENCLUE are the algorithms using density to filter noise (outliers).
- **Model Based Clustering Algorithms**: These clustering algorithms can measure the uncertainty of the classification by a law of multivariate probability distributions based on a mixture model, where each mixture represents a different cluster. The classification problem using model based algorithms is that the processing time is very slow in case of large data sets. Examples of this type of classification algorithms are EM, COBWEB, CLASSIT and SOM.
- **Grid Based Clustering Algorithms:** These algorithms consist of three stages: first is dividing the space into rectangular cells to obtain a grid with each cell having equal size, second is deleting the low density cells from the grid, and third is combining adjacent cells having a high density to complete formation of clusters. The great plus point of grid based classification is the significant reduction in time complexity. Some examples of algorithms in this class are GRIDCLUS, STING, CLICK and Wave Cluster.

While evaluating the different methods of classification in terms of Big Data using specific criteria to assess the strengths and weaknesses of each algorithm with respect to Big Data such as size of input data, scalability, stability and cluster quality, it is found that there is no completely efficient algorithm which scores on all criteria and can be entrusted the responsibility of analyzing big data. Although some algorithms such as the EM and FCM shows better performance in terms of quality than the other algorithms. But as mentioned earlier, for large amount of data the calculated time is exploding. Therefore, an efficient programming language which provides users with better speeds or advanced technical equipment with high processing ability can overcome time complexity issues to a great extent. The major limitation that is there with clustering algorithms is the instability, which leads to a situation where implementing the same algorithm can provide different results from one run to another on the very same data set. The EM algorithm offers the highest stability compared to other algorithms, whereas FCM algorithm is the worst when it comes to stability. The algorithm BIRCH, DENCLUE and OptiGrid are more adept to large amounts of data but they have low stabilities.

Dimension Reduction

The size of the data set can be measured using two dimensions, the number of variables and the number of examples. These two dimensions can have very high values, which may lead to problems during the exploration and analysis of the data set. So, to implement clustering it is essential to implement data processing tools and preprocess the dataset before applying clustering algorithms for a better understanding the inherent value contained in the data. The Dimension reduction technique is one of the oldest and most used to help cope with this problem. The purpose of using dimension reduction is to select or extract an optimal subset of relevant features that can be used for clustering. The selection of the subset of features can eliminate irrelevant and redundant information such as personal information from a dataset having customer reviews, according to the criteria used. For large sets of data, dimension reduction is usually performed before applying the clustering algorithm on the following bases:

1. **Feature Selection**: This method aims at selecting an optimal subset of variables from a set of original variables, according to certain specified criteria. The main objective of this selection is to reduce the number of required actions. Big data can be easily classified using feature in two steps; first, the feature selection algorithm is designed to reduce the size of the dataset. Then, a parallel k-means algorithm is applied to the data subsets selected in the first step. Experimental results show that the proposed algorithm provides better classification accuracy than existing algorithms and takes much less time than other classification algorithms for Big Data.
2. **Feature Extraction**: This method aims at selecting features in a transformed space which is created by the extraction methods which use all the information to compress and produce a vector of smaller dimension.

Multiple-Machine Clustering

1. **Parallel Clustering**: The processing of large amounts of data imposes a parallel computing to achieve results in reasonable time. Parallel algorithms and distributed clustering can be used to treat Big Data; the parallel classification divides the data partitions that will be distributed on different machines. This makes an individual classification to speed up the calculation and increases scalability.
2. **MapReduce Based Clustering:** MapReduce is a programming paradigm which can run parallel processing tasks on nodes in a cluster simultaneously and is able to both process and generate really large data sets with ease. It takes input and gives the output in form of key-value pairs. MapReduce is able to achieve all this by simply dividing each problem into two broad phases, the map phase and the reduce phase. The Map phase processes each record sequentially and independently on each node and generates intermediate key-value pairs. The Reduce phase takes the output of the Map phase. It processes and merges all the intermediate values to give the final output, again in form of key-value pairs. The output gets sorted after each phase, thus providing the user with the

aggregated output from all nodes in an orderly fashion. This can be easily used for clustering large data sets. MapReduce programs have to be written for the query and the classification takes place on a cluster of interconnected computers, whose numbers may run into thousands.

Table 1 presents various clustering techniques, their advantages and its limitation.

Since the birth of the computers, improving the computing performance and the processing speed of the computers has been an omnipresent topic. Ever since the advent of big data, it has gained even more voice. Because of the limitation of physical devices, parallel computing was conceptualized and brought to life. It has gained a lot of fame since its advent and has now become a comprehensive field in computer science. The discipline includes the hardware concurrent designing and software concurrent designing. According to the hardware concurrent design for a computer, the different types of hardware architectures can be divided into single instruction stream and data stream (SISD); single instruction multiple data (SIMD) flows; multiple instruction stream data flow (MISD); the instruction stream and data stream (MIMD). The software concurrent design on the other hand includes the algorithms of concurrent design, high-speed internet clustering framework, and high-efficiency concurrent calculation model. Hardware concurrent design is skilled in numerical analysis and the floating point precision but it faces a technical bottleneck in case of big data, especially when the data is unstructured, while the software concurrent design, which includes parallel computing model and cluster system design, has been very successful in making up for the defects above.

For example, cluster system is constituted with the workstation or PC, which is linked via a high-speed network with a certain optimizing structure, and a unified dispatching visual human-computer interface, thus it is an efficient parallel processing system. These cluster systems have the good scalability and the system development cycle is little short. With a good programming model, the system can be very successful in coping with Big data. Hadoop is one of the most popular cluster systems, which includes the high-performance calculation model Map Reduce and Spark. Hadoop is an excellent and robust analytics platform for Big Data which can process huge data sets at a really quick speed by providing scalability. It can manage all aspects of Big Data such as volume, velocity and variety by storing and processing the data over a cluster of nodes whose numbers can run into thousands. The best thing about it is that the nodes in the cluster need not possess complex and costly hardware but simply commodity hardware which neither costly nor difficult to procure. Hadoop has a proper architecture

Table 1. comparison of clustering techniques of big data

S.No.	Clustering Techniques	Advantages	Limitations
1	Data Mining clustering algorithms	Easy to implement	Do not have the ability to work with huge amounts of data
2	Dimension reduction	Reduces the dataset, optimized complexity, high speed and scales algorithm	Do not offer an efficient solution for datasets with high dimensions, has to be performed before applying the clustering algorithm
4	Parallel classification	Minimize the time of execution and are highly scalable	Implementing the algorithms are a bit more difficult
5	MapReduce	Offer impressive scalability and generate instant responses, which are inherently parallel	Need more resources, each query has to be implemented as an MR program

which consists of two components, MapReduce and the Hadoop Distributed File System (HDFS). With the introduction of YARN (Yet Another Resource Negotiator) in later releases, Hadoop was integrated with a number of wonderful projects which can be used for storing, processing and analyzing data a lot more efficiently, thus aiding in exploration of data for undiscovered facts at a smooth pace. Hadoop is an open source project written in Java and is currently under the Apache Software Foundation and is free to use. The initial design idea is mainly used to deploy on the cheap hardware. The framework implements a distributed file system, referred to as "HDFS," which has high fault tolerance and high speed and scalability to store large amounts of data and implements a computation model of parallel processing large data sets; this model is of high speed computing in big data processing field. In addition to these advantages, the distributed system framework is open source software. With the advent of big data, it has become a good and reliable solution, which can store and process big data with ease. While in this day and year it has become a famous big data processing framework in the field of the big data analytics, at the same time, Hadoop ecosystem, with continuous improvement and optimization, has become better. With the advent of second generation, a lot more projects have been introduced into the hadoop ecosystem. Hive helps in querying and managing large dataset. Pig Latin is the scripting language to construct MapReduce programs for an Apache project which runs on Hadoop. The benefit of using this is that there is a need to write much fewer lines of code which reduces overall development and testing time. However, in order to improve the performance of the distributed system framework, many companies and supporters provide their first-class good components and high performance code for Hadoop, such as YARN, Hcatalog, Oozie, and Cassandra, which make the performance of Hadoop become more and more strong, and the application field of Hadoop is becoming more and more wide.

R language, as a data analysis and visualization tool, is widely used for statistical analysis, drawing, data mining, machine learning, and visualization analysis. Particularly, R tool has been built in a variety of statistical, digital analysis functions and drawing functions. R language is an open source software, and very useful third-party packages which are written by the developers in it's community around the world can be downloaded and used for free. Therefore, its application field is wide, from statistical analysis, to applied mathematics, econometrics, financial analysis, financial analysis, human science, data mining, artificial intelligence, bioinformatics, biomedical, data visualization and many more.

BIG DATA CLUSTERING EXAMPLES

Clustering Algorithms and Identification of Cancerous Tissue

For identification of cancerous tissue, clustering algorithms can prove to be really handy. This is done by using cancerous and non-cancerous data set samples. These data sets are labeled as samples data sets. Then, both samples are randomly mixed. Then these are applied with different clustering algorithms and accordingly the results are checked for the correct results (since these are known samples and results are known beforehand) and hence the percentage of correct results obtained is calculated. This is the learning phase of clustering mechanism. Now, if for some arbitrary sample data, the same algorithm is applied, the result received after analysis of the data set can be expected by the user to have same percentage of accuracy in diagnosing the data set as the accuracy the algorithm achieved in the learning phase on the samples data sets. This approach can be used to find the most suitable algorithm for this analysis. The suspicious data sets from patients can now be analyzed by computers to identify if the disease is present or not. Experimentation has revealed that data sets for cancerous tissue can be most accurately analyzed using non-linear clustering algorithms. This can be used to infer that these kinds of data sets are non-linear in nature.

Clustering Algorithms and Search Engines

It is a perpetual task in search engine to group similar objects into distinct clusters and dissimilar object away from the clusters. Thus, clustering algorithms are an essential constituent for making a well performing search engine. The clustering is used to provide data to the users of the search engine as they post queries to search on various topics. The results are given to the user by the engine according to the similar objects in the particular user's cluster using previously gathered data about preferences of similar users. The better the performance of the clustering algorithm is for the users, the more the chances are that the users are able to find the thing they are looking for on the very first page itself and they don't have to spend time looking up further results. Therefore the definition based on which the algorithm forms clusters and defines objects has to be spot on to get the best results. The better this performance is; the more users are attracted to the search engine.

Clustering Algorithms and Academics

Clustering algorithms can be used to monitor the academic performances of individual students in a university. This is a really important task that needs to be accomplished by universities and can prove to be very tedious for the ones with thousands of students enrolled under various courses in one of the colleges enrolled to them. Based on the students' scores in examination, clustering algorithms can be used to form clusters of students with similar performances; clusters would therefore signify level of performance. This could be used by the university to identify the top performers, average performances and the poor performers. This data can prove to be invaluable to the university.

Clustering Algorithm and Wireless Sensor Network

Clustering algorithms can be vital in analyzing data from wireless sensor networks. One such application can be detection of landmines hidden beneath the soil, especially in civilian regions the algorithms can find clusters of electromagnetic activity in areas where such spikes in radiations are not expected by analyzing satellite images which contain electromagnetic field sensing data. This can be useful in saving scores of civilian lives by identifying hidden explosives before they can cause any harm.

FUTURE CASES OF BIG DATA CLUSTERING

There are several potential future directions which can be explored when it comes to collaborative filtering, particularly in relation to information filtering in the case of highly dynamic big data.

Better Learning Algorithms for Online Collaborative Filtering

Collaborative filtering based recommendation systems have been very successful in creating a great experience for users on social networking websites in recent years. The major task in building these systems is capturing the behavior of the users, translating it into a data set and analyzing it to build an accurate cost function. The top-N recommendations method is the most useful, widely used and important approach of collaborative filtering and it has to be taken as a ranking task. There have been lots of studies and a lot of work in the field of optimizing recommendations by personalized ranking and there is still a lot of scope for further improvement.

Prediction of Individual and Collective Behavior in Real-Time

An active and critical area in machine learning techniques and recommendation systems is modeling of complex and non-linear dynamics along with data sets having high dimensions. There a number of models existing which are used in practice a lot. Some of these are matrix factorization, non-linear clustering and neighborhood based algorithms, but, these have a wide scope. Building a generic behavior prediction model can have huge implications for consumer based industries, governments and political parties.

Real-Time Experimentation

Today in the IT industry, evaluation of a project's features against the previous versions of the project is a common approach to support decision making process and A/B testing is the most widely used technique to accomplish this. The problem with such evaluations is that they take up a lot of valuable testing and are time consuming. Exploring new and cost effective techniques for aligning long term goals with the current essential requirements of the industry is a necessary and really interesting research area and can have wonderful implications in not just IT but various other industries as well in the future.

Integrating Heterogeneous Information Sources

To improve recommendation quality, the first and the most obvious directions in which efforts need to be made are integration of information sources. Organizations can use any number of information sources for this such as data from various sensors, friendship graphs and the user's demographic information. There are a lot of approaches that use all kinds of specific side information for generating recommendations. However, a generic framework that can incorporate any number of side information sources into the system is an essential research topic.

BIG DATA COLLABORATION

A recommender system is a software system which suggests a user an item to purchase, subscribe, invest, or any other venture that the user may need suggestions for. Such systems may be personalized for the user to base recommendations based on data specific to the user. A great way of building a reliable recommender system for the users is collaborative filtering. Collaborative filtering is defined as a technique that filters the information sought by the user and patterns by collaborating multiple data sets such as viewpoints, multiple agents and pre-existing data about the users' behavior stored in matrices. Collaborative filtering is especially required when a huge data set is present. The collaborative filtering methods are used to create recommender systems for a wide variety of fields with lots of data having varied formats such as sensing and monitoring of data in battlefields, line of controls and mineral exploration; financial data of institutions that provide financial services such as banks and stock markets; sensing of large geographical areas from which data is received from all kinds of sensors and activities; ecommerce and websites where the focus is to recommend products to users to increase sales, to name a few.

A definition of collaborative filtering which is somewhat newer and a bit narrow in sense states that it is a way of automating the process of making predictions, a process which is known as filtering, about the preferences and dislikes of a user by collecting data from as big a number of users as possible, a process which is known as collaborating, hence it is given the name collaborative filtering. The underlying assumption of the collaborative filtering approach is that if a person has the same opinion of an issue as a person B, A is more likely to have an opinion similar to B's opinion on a related but different issue. It is noteworthy that such predictions are specific to the user, but they are formed by using data from a number of users. The personal information of the user such as age, gender and location are generally not used in collaborative filtering (CF) but a partially observed matrix of ratings is used. The rating matrix may be binary or ordinal. The binary matrix contains the ratings by the users in columns in the form of likes or dislikes while the user' name or id is in the rows. The ordinal matrix contains ratings in form of a number of responses from the user such as excellent, very good, good, average, poor or simply in form of stars out of five or ten, a system that is used a lot in this day and age. The rating matrix can easily be gathered implicitly by the website's server, for example using click stream logging. Clicks on links to pages of goods or services being provided can be considered to be positive review of the user. While rating matrices can prove to be really handy, one major drawback they have is that they are extremely sparse, so it is very difficult of club similar users together in classes. This is so because each and every user does not give the reviews about each and every product. Thus collaborative filtering consists of storing this sparse data and analyzing it to create a recommendation system.

Collaborative filtering generally requires:

1. Active participation from users.
2. A simple way of representing users' interests to the software system.
3. An algorithm to match people with similar interests.

A key challenge of collaborative filtering is to combine and weigh the preferences of users with similar interests. This is coped with by providing users with means to give feedback in the form of ratings or simply likes-dislikes along with reviews.

Collaborative filtering systems have many forms, but many common systems can be reduced to two steps:

1. Users with similar rating patterns are identified are clubbed together into classes, so that when one of them is in need of a recommendation, it can be provided using the data of the users in the class.
2. The products matching the preferences of the user are then recommended, based on the data in the ratings matrix.

This approach is used by algorithms which use user-based collaborative filtering for building the recommendation system. A specific application of this is the user-based Nearest Neighbor algorithm.

Alternatively, there is item-based collaborative filtering which identifies like-minded people from the list of costumers who avail a certain product. It uses an item-centric approach for collaborative filtering using the following basic steps:

1. An item-item matrix is built to determine the relationships between products on the basis of user buying patterns.
2. When a product is searched by the user, the preferences are identified by using the previously built matrix and relevant recommendations are provided.

Relying on scoring or rating systems is not exactly ideal in tasks where there is a large variations in interests and a lot of users' interests may be idiosyncratic. This is so because rating which is averaged across all users ignores demands specific to a particular. This is particularly common in the music and movie industries. However, the developers may use alternative methods to combat information explosion, such as data clustering.

Therefore, there is another form of collaborative filtering that does not rely on imposition of artificial behavior by a rating or binary system but uses implicit observations of the behavior of common user for filtering. Such systems log the user's behavior based on previous purchases to identify a pattern which can be used to group that user with a class of users with similar behavior. This can then be used to provide recommendation, predict future purchases and can even be used to predict a user's behavior in a hypothetical situation which can be essential for decision support systems. These predictions are then filtered by analyzing each one on the basis of business logic which helps to determine how a prediction might affect the business system. For example, it is not useful to recommend a user a particular piece of art if they already have demonstrated that they own that artwork or a similar artwork.

Types of Big Data Collaboration Filtering (CF):

1. **Memory Based CF:** This is an approach of collaborative filtering that uses the users' rating data to find the similarity amongst particular users or items. This similarity is then used for making a recommendations system for the users by collaborating similar users or items. This approach for collaborative filtering is the oldest, the easiest to implement and very effective. Some of the techniques that use memory based CF to provide recommendations to the users are the top-N recommendations based on users or items and the Neighborhood-based CF.
2. **Model Based CF:** There are a number of model-based CF algorithms that are commonly used. These CF techniques based on a model include probabilistic latent semantic analysis, Bayesian networks, latent semantic models, Markov decision process based models and clustering models. Model based CF uses models which are developed using machine learning algorithms and data mining to find patterns in the data sets after training. These models are then used to make predictions for actual data sets.
3. **Hybrid CF:** Hybrid CF technique contains a number of CF applications that combine both the memory-based and the model-based CF algorithms to provide solutions to the limitations of these collaborative filtering techniques. Most importantly, these overpower the common problems such

as loss of information and sparsity in the data set. But, hybrid CF techniques have higher complexity compared to native CF techniques and are financially expensive to implement. Usually most of the commercial recommender systems that are used nowadays are hybrid.

Advantages and limitations of various CF techniques are discussed in Table 2.
Challenges in CF:

1. **Data Sparsity:** A number of recommender systems that are commercially used are required to process large datasets regularly. A result of this is that the matrix containing the ratings data by the users which is essential for collaborative filtering is, more often than not really big in size and even sparse. This leads to some really serious challenges to the performances of the recommender system. One of the problems caused by the sparse data is the cold-start problem. As collaborative filtering methods recommend items based on users' past preferences new users are not able to get recommendations from the system as their historic data is not there in the system. The new users will only start receiving recommendations after they have rated a number of items based on their preferences to enable the system to capture the data and thus provide reliable recommendations. Unless this is done, the system will not be able to give reliable recommendations for the user.
2. **Synonyms:** Synonyms refer to a number of situations where the similar or different items may have different names or entries. The recommender system is not able to identify such associations amongst the products and thus ends up treating them differently.
3. **Gray Sheep:** Gray sheep is a term used to refer to the users whose opinions do not match with any group of people consistently or altogether and thus recommender system is not able to provide them with useful recommendations. Black sheep are another opposite set of users whose choice and preference patters idiosyncratic to them which makes recommending products for them nearly impossible. This is a short-coming of collaborative filtering but is acceptable as an automatic system to identify and predict such behavior is next to impossible.

Table 2. CF comparison

S. No.	CF Category	Representative Techniques	Advantages	Shortcomings
1.	Memory-based CF	It gives recommendations based on items or users or Neighbor-based CF	It is easy to implement and it scales well with the items which are co-rated and it doesn't need to take the contents of the products being recommended into consideration	It is highly dependent on user ratings so the data is sparse which decreases the performance, has limited scalability in case data set is large and has cold start problem
2.	Model-based CF	It uses models for recommendations such as MDP-based latent semantic CF'S; gives good scalability and performance; has sparse factor analysis	It has an improved performance because it better addresses issues such as the sparsity of data and scalability; gives a reasoned logic for recommendations it makes.	It requires building an expensive model, has trade-off between performance and scalability and it loses useful information for dimensionality reduction
3.	Hybrid CF	It is a CF based on content, combines memory-based and model-based algorithms to overcome their issues	Overcomes CF problems in native approaches such as gray sheep and sparsity thus providing an improve prediction performance	It has higher complexity and its implementation is expensive, sometimes requires external information for predictions that is not always available

4. **Attacking of Products by Users:** In a recommendation system everyone can give the ratings to all sorts of products. But some users use it to give positive ratings for their own products to make sure they are recommended to lots of people even though the products are not that good or match their preferences. In some cases, users start giving negative ratings for their competitors' products so that they don't get recommended over their product to customers. It is therefore a huge challenge for the collaborative filtering systems to prevent such kind of manipulations and a necessity to identify such actions and rectify them.

5. **Newly Introduced Products' Recommendations:** Collaborative filters are expected to help the user in discovering newer products that are similar to their tastes and thus promoting diversity. However, some of the collaborative filtering algorithms end up doing absolutely the opposite. This happens because collaborative filters recommend products based on sales or ratings that are the historic data of the product. Therefore, they are not able to recommend the products which have limited data on sales. More often than not, new products are not recommended to users because of this shortcoming of recommender systems. This can lead to new products not getting recommended to the users, thus making it impossible for new sellers to pitch their product to the customers and for the customers to discover these products even though they might like it.

EXAMPLE OF COLLABORATIVE FILTERING AND CLUSTERING FILTERING IN BIG DATA

To predict the user's behavior in the future, or to predict how a user will likely to behave in a given situation. Following frame work in figure 4 is used for such analysis.

Figure 4. Workflow

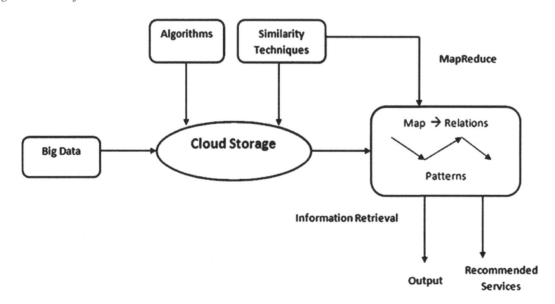

Role of MapReduce and Hadoop in Collaborative Filtering and Clustering Filtering in Big Data

MapReduce is a programming paradigm which can do parallel processing on nodes in a cluster. It takes input and gives the output in form of key-value pairs. MapReduce is able to achieve all this by simply dividing each problem into two broad phases, the map phase and the reduce phase. The Mapper processes each record sequentially and independently in parallel and generates intermediate key-value pairs.

- **Map(k1, v1) → list(k2, v2)**

The Reduce phase takes the output of the Map phase. It processes and merges all the intermediate values to give the final output, again in form of key-value pairs.

- **Reduce(k2, list (v2)) → list(k3, v3)**

The output gets sorted after each phase, thus providing the user with the aggregated output from all nodes in an orderly fashion.

Hadoop is an excellent and robust analytics platform for Big Data which can process huge data sets at a really quick speed by providing scalability. It can manage all aspects of Big Data such as volume, velocity and variety by storing and processing the data over a cluster of nodes whose numbers can run into thousands. The best thing about it is that the nodes in the cluster need not possess complex and costly hardware but simply commodity hardware which neither costly nor difficult to procure. Hadoop has a proper architecture which consists of two components, MapReduce and the Hadoop Distributed File System (HDFS). With the introduction of YARN (Yet Another Resource Negotiator) in later releases, Hadoop was integrated with a number of wonderful projects which can be used for storing, processing and analyzing data a lot more efficiently, thus aiding in exploration of data for undiscovered facts at a smooth pace Hadoop is an open source project written in Java and is currently under the Apache Software Foundation and is free to use. The initial design idea is mainly used to deploy on the cheap hardware. The framework implements a distributed file system, referred to as "HDFS," which has high fault tolerance and high speed and scalability to store large amounts of data and implements a computation model of parallel processing large data sets; this model is of high speed computing in big data processing field. In addition to these advantages, the distributed system framework is open source software. With the advent of big data, it has become a good and reliable solution, which can store and process big data with ease. While in this day and year it has become a famous big data processing framework in the field of the big data analytics, at the same time, Hadoop ecosystem, with continuous improvement and optimization, has become better. With the advent of second generation, a lot more projects have been introduced into the Hadoop ecosystem.

Typically, workflow is as follows:

- An item-item matrix is built to determine the relationships between products on the basis of user buying patterns.
- When a product is searched by the user, the preferences are identified by using the previously built matrix and relevant recommendations are provided.

CONCLUSION

To manage the growing demands of this day and age, there is a need to increase the capacity and performance of tools and methods employed for analysis of data. Collaborative filtering is defined as a technique that filters the information sought by the user and patterns by collaborating multiple data sets such as viewpoints, multiple agents and pre-existing data about the users' behavior stored in matrices. Collaborative filtering is especially required when a huge data set is present. The collaborative filtering methods are used to create recommender systems for a wide variety of fields with lots of data having varied formats such as sensing and monitoring of data in battlefields, line of controls and mineral exploration; financial data of institutions that provide financial services such as banks and stock markets; sensing of large geographical areas from which data is received from all kinds of sensors and activities; ecommerce and websites where the focus is to recommend products to users to increase sales, to name a few. . Clustering aims to reinforce the significant class data objects, called clusters, so that the objects aggregated in the same cluster are similar and consistent when weighed against certain parameters. It is a bit tricky to apply data mining based clustering techniques in Big Data because of the new challenges it brings with itself. With the great mass of data that needs to be analyzed and the complexity of clustering algorithms which can lead to really high costs, dealing with this problem and deploying clustering techniques Big Data to obtain results in a decent time is a huge challenge.

REFERENCES

Al-Jarrah, O. Y., Yoo, P. D., Muhaidat, S., Karagiannidis, G. K., & Taha, K. (2015). Efficient Machine Learning for Big Data: A Review. *Big Data Research*, *2*(3), 87–93. doi:10.1016/j.bdr.2015.04.001

Aloui, A., & Touzi, A. G. (2015). A Fuzzy Ontology-Based Platform for Flexible Querying. *International Journal of Service Science, Management, Engineering, and Technology*, *6*(3), 12–26.

Aye, K. N., & Thein, T. (2015). A platform for big data analytics on distributed scale-out storage system. *International Journal of Big Data Intelligence.*, *2*(2), 127–141. doi:10.1504/IJBDI.2015.069088

Azar, A.T. & Hassanien, A.E. (2014). Dimensionality reduction of medical big data using neural-fuzzy classifier. *Soft computing.* 19(4), 1115-1127. DOI:.10.1007/s00500-014-1327-4

Barker, K. J., Amato, J., & Sheridon, J. (2008). Credit card fraud: Awareness and prevention. *Journal of Financial Crime*, *15*(4), 398–410. doi:10.1108/13590790810907236

Bhanu, S. K., & Tripathy, B. K. (2016). Rough Set Based Similarity Measures for Data Analytics in Spatial Epidemiology. *International Journal of Rough Sets and Data Analysis*, *3*(1), 114–123. doi:10.4018/IJRSDA.2016010107

Chen, M., Mao, S., & Liu, Y. (2009). Big Data: A Survey. *Springer-*. *Mobile Networks and Applications*, *19*(2), 171–209. doi:10.1007/s11036-013-0489-0

Deepak, D., & John, S. J. (2016). Information Systems on Hesitant Fuzzy Sets. *International Journal of Rough Sets and Data Analysis*, *3*(1), 55–70.

Fedoryszak, M., Tkaczyk, D., & Bolikowski, L. (2013). Large Scale Citation Matching Using Apache Hadoop. In Research and Advanced Technology for Digital Libraries, LNCS (Vol. 8092, pp. 362-365). Springer.

Ghallab, S. A., Badr, N. L., Salem, A. B., & Tolba, M. F. (2014). Strictness petroleum prediction system based on fussy model. *International Journal of Service Science, Management, Engineering, and Technology*, 5(4), 44–65. doi:10.4018/ijssmet.2014100104

Hashem, I. A. T., Yaqoob, I., Anuar, N. B., Mokhtar, S., Gani, A., & Khan, S. U. (2015). The rise of "big data" on cloud computing: Review and open research issues. *Information Systems*, 47, 98–115. doi:10.1016/j.is.2014.07.006

Hassanien, A. E., Azar, A. T., Snasel, V., Kacprzyk, J., & Abawajy, J. H. (2015). *Big Data in Complex Systems: Challenges and Opportunities. In Studies in Big Data* (Vol. 9). Springer.

Hoffmann, A. O. I., & Birnbrich, C. (2012). The impact of fraud prevention on bank-customer relationships. *International Journal of Bank Marketing*, 30(5), 390–407. doi:10.1108/02652321211247435

Huang, T., Lan, L., Fang, X., An, P., Min, J., & Wang, F. (2015). Promises and challenges of big data computing in health science. *Big Data Research*, 2(1), 2–11. doi:10.1016/j.bdr.2015.02.002

Ibrahim, S., Jin, H., Lu, L., Qi, L., Wu, S., & Shi, X. (2009). Evaluating MapReduce on Virtual Machines: The Hadoop Case. In Cloud Computing, LNCS (Vol. 5931, pp. 519-528). Springer.

Jacobs, A. (2009). The pathologies of big data. *Communications of the ACM - A Blind Person's Interaction with Technology.* 52(8), 36-44.

Jagadish, H. V. (2015). Big Data and Science: Myths and Reality. *Big Data Research*, 2(2), 49–52. doi:10.1016/j.bdr.2015.01.005

Jin, X., Wah, B. W., Cheng, X., & Wang, Y. (2015). Significance and challenges of big data research. *Big Data Research*, 2(2), 59–64.

Kolomvatsos, K., Anagnostopoulos, C., & Hadjiefthymiades, S. (2015). An Efficient Time Optimized Scheme for Progressive Analytics in Big Data. *Big Data Research*, 2(4), 155–165. doi:10.1016/j.bdr.2015.02.001

Labrinidis, A., & Jagadish, H. V. (2012). Challenges and opportunities with big data. *Proceedings of the VLDB Endowment*, 5(12), 2032-2033.

Lee, Y., & Lee, Y. (2013). Toward scalable internet traffic measurement and analysis with Hadoop. *ACM SIGCOMM Computer Communication*, 43(1), 5–13. doi:10.1145/2427036.2427038

Ryan, T., & Lee, Y. C. (2015). Multi-tier resource allocation for data-intensive computing. *Big Data Research*, 2(3), 110–116. doi:10.1016/j.bdr.2015.03.001

Shabeera, T. P., & Madhu Kumar, S. D. (2015). Optimizing virtual machine allocation in MapReduce cloud for improved data locality. *International Journal of Big Data Intelligence.*, 2(1), 2–8. doi:10.1504/IJBDI.2015.067563

Srivastava, U., & Gopalkrishnan, S. (2015). Impact of Big Data Analytics on Banking Sector: Learning for Indian Bank. *Big Data, Cloud and Computing Challenges*, *50*, 643–652.

Tiwari, P. K., & Joshi, S. (2015). Data security for software as a service. *International Journal of Service Science, Management, Engineering, and Technology*, *6*(3), 47–63. doi:10.4018/IJSSMET.2015070104

Wahi, A. K., Medury, Y., & Misra, R. K. (2014). Social Media: The core of enterprise 2.0. *International Journal of Service Science, Management, Engineering, and Technology*, *5*(3), 1–15. doi:10.4018/ijssmet.2014070101

Wahi, A. K., Medury, Y., & Misra, R. K. (2015). Big Data: Enabler or Challenge for Enterprise 2.0. *International Journal of Service Science, Management, Engineering, and Technology*, *6*(2), 1–17.

KEY TERMS AND DEFINITIONS

Big Data: The voluminous and complex collection of data that comes from different sources such as sensors, content posted on social media website, sale purchase transaction etc. Such voluminous data becomes tough to process using ancient processing applications.

Clustering: It is the exercise of taking a set of objects and dividing them into groups in such a way that the objects in the same groups are more similar to each other according to a certain set of parameters than to those in other groups. These groups are known as clusters.

Collaborative Filtering: It is defined as the process of filtering for information or patterns, by the use of techniques which collaborate multiple agents, viewpoints, data sources, etc. Collaborative filtering is typically used to process very large data sets.

Hadoop: It is an excellent and robust analytics platform for Big Data which can process huge data sets at a really quick speed by providing scalability. It can manage all aspects of Big Data such as volume, velocity and variety by storing and processing the data over a cluster of nodes whose numbers can run into thousands.

MapReduce: It is a programming paradigm which can do parallel processing on nodes in a cluster. It takes input and gives the output in form of key-value pairs.

Chapter 9
Association Rule Mining in Collaborative Filtering

Carson K. Leung
University of Manitoba, Canada

Edson M. Dela Cruz
University of Manitoba, Canada

Fan Jiang
University of Manitoba, Canada

Vijay Sekar Elango
University of Manitoba, Canada

ABSTRACT

Collaborative filtering uses data mining and analysis to develop a system that helps users make appropriate decisions in real-life applications by removing redundant information and providing valuable to information users. Data mining aims to extract from data the implicit, previously unknown and potentially useful information such as association rules that reveals relationships between frequently co-occurring patterns in antecedent and consequent parts of association rules. This chapter presents an algorithm called CF-Miner for collaborative filtering with association rule miner. The CF-Miner algorithm first constructs bitwise data structures to capture important contents in the data. It then finds frequent patterns from the bitwise structures. Based on the mined frequent patterns, the algorithm forms association rules. Finally, the algorithm ranks the mined association rules to recommend appropriate merchandise products, goods or services to users. Evaluation results show the effectiveness of CF-Miner in using association rule mining in collaborative filtering.

INTRODUCTION

With the advances in technology, high volumes of high-veracity and valuable data can be easily generated or collected at a high velocity from large varieties of data sources in various real-life applications for both public services and private sectors. Embedded in these data—such as the financial data, retail data, social network data, and web data—are rich sets of useful information and knowledge. Hence, with rich sets of information, it is desirable to be able to remove redundant information and to be provided with valuable information in short periods of time. To this end, having a recommendation system would be helpful because such a *recommendation system* helps users make appropriate decisions in various real-life applications—such as e-commerce, e-learning, social networks, and web search—by remov-

DOI: 10.4018/978-1-5225-0489-4.ch009

ing redundant information and providing users with valuable information in short periods of time. For instance, a recommendation system helps business owners make business decisions by revealing their customers' shopping behavior. Similarly, a recommendation system helps consumers by recommending goods, products, or services. As a third example, a recommendation system helps social network users connect to appropriate person or organizations by recommending friends or social communities (Lu & Lakshmanan, 2012; Maserrat & Pei, 2012; Leung, Medina & Tanbeer, 2013; Jiang & Leung, 2014; Leung, Tanbeer & Cameron, 2014).

With the exponential growth rate of data, collaborative filtering is commonly used to make recommendations. *Collaborative filtering*—which usually applies data mining techniques to develop a system with precise knowledge and accuracy for helping users—is a popular technique used for recommendation system. Here, *data mining* aims to search data for rich sets of implicit, previously unknown and useful information and knowledge embedded in the data. Common data mining tasks including classification, clustering, and association rule mining. Classification focuses on performing supervised learning from the historical/training data and categorizing future/test data with class labels describing the data. Clustering focuses on performing unsupervised learning and grouping similar data together. Association rule mining focuses on mining frequent patterns as well as forming rules in the form of A➜C (where both A and C are frequent patterns) for revealing the associations or relationships between frequent patterns A and C. *Frequent pattern mining* (Aggarwal & Srikant, 1994; Leung et al., 2013; Leung, 2014b) focuses on discovering knowledge and useful information—in the form of patterns revealing frequently co-occurring items, events, or objects (e.g., frequently purchased merchandise items in shopper market basket, frequently co-located events)—from the data.

Since the introduction of the research problem of frequent pattern mining (Aggarwal & Srikant, 1994), numerous algorithms (Leung, 2013; Négrevergne et al., 2013; Cuzzocrea et al., 2014; Leung, MacKinnon & Jiang, 2014). Among them, the Apriori algorithm (Aggarwal & Srikant, 1994) is a notable one. However, as a breadth-first, level-wise bottom-up mining algorithm, Apriori requires many database scans—one scan for each level/cardinality of frequent patterns. The FP-growth algorithm (Han, Pei & Yin, 2000) improves efficiency by using a depth-first, tree-based approach. However, FP-growth improves efficiency at a price of requiring memory space to keep the following:

1. **The Global Frequent Pattern Tree (FP-Tree):** Captures the content of the original database.
2. **All Subsequent Sub-Trees**: Each captures the contents of subsequent projected databases.

Both the TD-FP-Growth algorithm (Wang et al., 2002) and the H-mine algorithm (Pei et al., 2001) avoid building and simultaneously keeping multiple FP-trees during the mining process. However, during the mining process, TD-FP-Growth keeps updating the global FP-tree by adjusting tree pointers, whereas H-mine keeps updating pointers/hyperlinks in the corresponding H-struct. As alternatives to the aforementioned "horizontal" frequent pattern mining algorithms (which use a transaction-centric approach to find which pattern is supported by or contained in a transaction), both the Eclat algorithm (Zaki, 2000) and the VIPER algorithm (Shenoy et al., 2000) mine frequent patterns "vertically" by using an item-centric approach to count the number of transactions supporting or containing the patterns. Take into account the advantages and disadvantages of the above algorithms, we present an algorithm that performs association rule mining for collaborative filtering. The objective of this chapter is to show how association rule mining can be applicable in collaborative filtering.

BACKGROUND

Recall that association rule mining consists of the following two key steps:

1. Mining of frequent patterns, and
2. Formation of association rules from the mined frequent patterns.

Between these two key steps, the former is more computational intensive. This explains why numerous algorithms have been proposed for frequent pattern mining over the past two decades.

As a classical frequent pattern mining algorithm, the Apriori algorithm (Aggarwal & Srikant, 1994) applies a generate-and-test paradigm in mining frequent patterns in a level-wise bottom-up fashion: It first generates candidate patterns of cardinality k (i.e., candidate k-itemsets) and tests if each of them is frequent (i.e., tests if its support or frequency meets or exceeds a user-specified *minsup* threshold). Based on these frequent patterns of cardinality k (i.e., frequent k-itemsets), Apriori then generates candidate patterns of cardinality $k+1$ (i.e., candidate $(k+1)$-itemsets). This process is applied repeatedly to discover frequent patterns of all cardinalities. Hence, it requires k database scans to find a frequent pattern of cardinality k.

To improve algorithmic efficiency, the FP-growth algorithm (Han, Pei & Yin, 2000) uses a Frequent Pattern tree (FP-tree) to capture the content of the transaction database. Unlike Apriori (which scans the database K times, where K is the maximum cardinality of the discovered frequent patterns), FP-growth scans the database twice. To mine frequent patterns, FP-growth recursively extracts relevant paths from the FP-tree to form projected databases (i.e., collections of transactions containing some items), from which sub-trees (i.e., smaller FP-trees) capturing the content of relevant transactions are built. While FP-growth avoids the generate-and-test paradigm of Apriori (because FP-growth uses the divide-and-conquer paradigm), FP-growth requires lots of memory space to build many smaller FP-trees (e.g., for $\{a\}$-projected database, $\{a,b\}$-projected database, $\{a,b,c\}$-projected database, ..., for items a, b & c) during the mining process.

To avoid building and keeping multiple FP-trees at the same time during the mining process, the TD-FP-Growth algorithm (Wang et al., 2002) builds and keeps only a single global FP-tree during the mining process. Unlike FP-growth (which mines frequent patterns by traversing the global FP-tree and sub-trees in a bottom-up fashion), the TD-FP-Growth algorithm traverses only the global FP-tree and in a top-down fashion. During the mining process, instead of recursively building sub-trees, TD-FP-Growth keeps updating a single global FP-tree by adjusting tree pointers.

As a second alternative that avoids building and keeping multiple FP-trees at the same time during the mining process, the H-mine algorithm (Pei et al., 2001) uses a hyperlinked-array structure called H-struct, which captures the content of the transaction database. During the mining process, H-mine also recursively updates many pointers/hyperlinks in the H-struct.

In addition to these four algorithms (i.e., Apriori, FP-growth, TD-FP-Growth, and H-mine algorithms) that mine frequent patterns "horizontally" (i.e., using a transaction-centric approach to find which pattern is supported by or contained in a transaction), the Eclat algorithm (Zaki, 2000) mines frequent patterns "vertically" (i.e., using an item-centric approach to count the number of transactions supporting or containing the patterns), in a level-wise, bottom-up fashion. The Eclat algorithm treats the database as a collection of item lists. A list is created for each domain item. The list for an item x captures IDs of transactions containing the item x. The length of the list for x gives the support of a pattern $\{x\}$ of cardinality 1. If its support is not less than the user-specified *minsup* threshold, $\{x\}$ is considered frequent. By taking the intersection of the lists for the two frequent patterns Y and Z, the Eclat algorithm returns the IDs of those transactions containing (Y∪Z), i.e., a list of IDs of those transactions containing items in the both frequent patterns Y as well as Z. Again, the length of the resulting (intersected) list gives the support of the pattern (Y∪Z). Eclat works well when the database is sparse. However, when the database is dense, these item lists can be long.

As another algorithm that mines frequent pattern "vertically", the VIPER algorithm (Shenoy et al., 2000) represents the item lists in the form of bit vectors. A vector is created for each domain item. Each bit in a vector for a domain item x indicates the presence (bit "1") or absence (bit "0") of a transaction containing x. The number of "1" bits for x gives the support of a pattern $\{x\}$ of cardinality 1. If its support is not less than the user-specified *minsup* threshold, $\{x\}$ is considered frequent. By computing the dot product of vectors for two frequent patterns Y and Z, the VIPER algorithm returns the vector indicating the presence of transactions containing (Y∪Z), i.e., a bit vector in which each bit represents the presence (by a "1" bit) or the absence (by a "0" bit) of (Y∪Z) in the transaction corresponding to that bit. Again, the number of "1" bits of this vector gives the support of the resulting pattern (Y∪Z). Consequently, VIPER works well when the database is dense. However, when the database is sparse, lots of space may be wasted because the vector contains lots of 0s. Hence, between the aforementioned vertical frequent pattern mining algorithms (i.e., Eclat and VIPER algorithms), Eclat is recommended when the database is sparse, whereas VIPER is recommended when the database is dense.

CF-MINER: ASSOCIATION RULE MINING FOR COLLABORATIVE FILTERING

Taking in account the advantages and disadvantages of the existing algorithms mentioned above, we present an algorithm—called *CF-Miner*—for *collaborative filtering with association rule miner*. The CF-Miner algorithm first (1) builds a data structure to capture important contents in the data to facilitate mining, then (2) finds frequent patterns, (3) forms association rules from the discovered frequent patterns, and finally (4) applies collaborative filtering to select useful rules for making recommendations to users.

Step 1: Construction of a Bitwise Table, Column Indices, and Column Sums

To capture important contents in the data, the CF-Miner algorithm builds the following data structure. Specifically, for each transaction in the data, the data structure captures a list of items in that transaction. For example, in a shopper market database, the data structure captures a list of merchandise items purchased by consumers. As another example, for a service provider, the data structure captures a list of services requested by customers. As a third example, for a social network, the data structure captures a list of friends or fans.

For N transactions in the database, the data structure consists of N lists. Each list captures a transaction and represents it in a bitwise tabular form. Such a data structure contains the following three key portions:

- **A Bitwise Table**: The main bitmap-based structure, in which each row contains information about a list of items in a transaction;
- **A Column Index** (to the right of the bitwise table): Initially indicates the location of first relevant bit; and

- **Column Sum** (below the bitwise table): Counts the number of users associated with that items (e.g., the number of consumers who purchased that merchandise item, the number of customers who requested that particular service, or the number of friends/fans who like/follow that particular social network user).

In more details, to capture important contents of data, a bitwise table and its associated column index and column sum are constructed by using the following three steps:

- For each transaction t_j, a bitmap row with size M is created, where M is the total number of distinct domain items (e.g., M distinct merchandise items, products, goods, services, events, social network users). Each column (represented by a bit) in the bitmap row represents the item in each transaction. In other words, a "1" in the ith bit (where $1 \leq i \leq M$) indicates that the ith item is present in t_j; a "0" in the ith bit (where $1 \leq i \leq M$) indicates that the ith item is absent from t_j. By repeating this step N times (one for each bitmap rows), a bitwise table containing information about items in the N transactions in the data (where N is the number of transactions in the data) is constructed. As there are N bitmap rows and each bitmap row consists of M bits, there are a total M * N bits in the resulting bitwise table.
- For each row r in the bitwise table, a column index is created for the first occurrence of the "1" bit in row r. Such a column index is kept on the right side of the bitwise table. Each column index takes a value in the range [1, M]. As there are N rows in the bitwise table, there are a total of N values in the column index.
- For each column c of the table, a column sum is computed by counting the number of 1s in column c. Such a column sum is kept on the bottom side of the bitwise table. Each column sum takes a value in the range [0, N], where N is the number of transactions in the data. Moreover, as there are M columns in the bitwise table, there are a total of M values in the column sum.

Note that all the above three steps can be completed in only one scan of the database. In other words, only one database scan is required to build the bitwise table (cf. two database scan required by the H-Mine algorithm). Moreover, the bitwise table does not contain a high number of hyperlinks (cf. a high number of hyperlinks is kept in the H-struct used by H-Mine). Furthermore, each cell/entry in the bitwise table takes only 1 bit of memory (cf. each tree node in the FP-tree used by either the FP-growth or TD-FP-Growth algorithm requires more than 1 bit because the tree node captures an item ID, frequency, and/or a pointer; each cell/entry in the H-struct used by H-Mine also requires more than 1 bit because the cell captures an item ID, frequency, and/or a hyperlink).

Step 2: Mining of Frequent Patterns

Once the bitwise table and its associated column index and column sum are constructed, CF-Miner mines frequent patterns from the bitwise table as follows. The CF-Miner algorithm first finds those frequent patterns of cardinality 1 (which are also known as frequent singletons or frequent 1-itemsets) by checking the column sum. Recall that the column sum for a column c representing an item is computed by counting the number of 1s in that column c. Items with column sum values $\geq$ the user-specified *minsup* threshold are considered to be frequent.

Once the CF-Miner algorithm found the frequent patterns of cardinality 1 from the bitwise table based on the column sum, it then mines frequent patterns of higher cardinalities (which are also known as frequent non-singletons or frequent k-itemsets where $k \geq 2$) from the bitwise table based on the contents of the column index. More specifically, CF-Miner considers only those rows having the column index value x—where $\{x\}$ is the first frequent singleton found earlier by CF-Miner (i.e., the column sum of $\{x\} \geq$ the user-specified *minsup* threshold)—to obtain the projected database for $\{x\}$. The column sum for the $\{x\}$-projected database can then be computed and appended below the bitwise table. Again, if the value for any item y in this new column sum for the $\{x\}$-projected database $\geq$ *minsup*, then $\{x, y\}$ is considered as a frequent pattern of cardinality 2 (which is also known as a frequent pair or a frequent 2-itemset).

After finding these frequent patterns $\{x, y\}$ of cardinality 2—where $\{x\}$ is the first frequent singleton, the CF-Miner algorithm mines frequent patterns of cardinality 3 (which are also known as frequent triplets or frequent 3-itemsets) in a similar fashion as described above. For instance, CF-Miner considers only those rows having the column index value y_1 to obtain the projected database for the first frequent pair $\{x, y_1\}$. The column sum for the $\{x, y_1\}$-projected database can then be computed and appended below the bitwise table. If the value for any item z in this column sum for the $\{x, y_1\}$-projected database $\geq$ *minsup*, then $\{x, y_1, z\}$ is considered as a frequent triplet.

The aforementioned mining process is recursively applied to mine frequent extensions of $\{x, y_1, z_1\}$ (i.e., frequent supersets of $\{x, y_1, z_1\}$ having $\{x, y_1, z_1\}$ as a prefix) in a depth-first manner. In other words, the CF-Miner algorithm obtains the projected database for the first frequent pattern of cardinality k (i.e., frequent k-itemset). The column sum for its projected database can then be computed and appended below the bitwise table. If the value for every item in this new column sum for the projected database $\geq$ the user-specified *minsup* threshold, then the resulting patterns of cardinality $k+1$ (i.e., $(k+1)$-itemsets) are considered frequent.

The CF-Miner algorithm backtracks when no more frequent extensions can be mined from a particular frequent pattern. Recall that a column index is created for the first occurrence of the "1" bit in a row. So, when backtracking after processing a row, CF-Miner updates the column index by capture the next "1" bit in that row. As a concrete example, with the updated column index after processing frequent triplet $\{x, y_1, z_1\}$, the CF-Miner algorithm obtains the projected database for the second frequent triplet $\{x, y_1, z_2\}$. Then, the aforementioned depth-first mining process can then be recursively applied to mine frequent extensions of $\{x, y_1, z_2\}$. This backtracking and updating of the column index is repeated for other frequent triplets such as the third frequent triplet $\{x, y_1, z_3\}$, the fourth frequent triplet $\{x, y_1, z_4\}$, and so on.

Once it is done, the backtracking moves to the previous level (i.e., lower cardinality). Specifically, the CF-Miner algorithm then mines for frequent extensions of the second frequent pair $\{x, y_2\}$, of the third frequent pair $\{x, y_3\}$, and so on until no more column index values can be computed—which means that all relevant transactions in the database have been examined and all frequent patterns have been discovered from the database.

Step 3: Formation of Association Rules

Next, based on the frequent patterns mined from the bitwise table and its associated column indices and column sums, the CF-Miner algorithm forms association rules of the form A➔C that reveal interesting associations or relationships among items in these frequent patterns in various real-life applications including the following:

1. An association rule A➜ C expresses that consumers who purchase a bag A of merchandise items also purchase another bag C of merchandise items;
2. An association rule A➜ C expresses that customers who request a bundle A of services also request another bundle C of services; or
3. An association rule A➜ C expresses that social network users who follow a group A of friends also follow another group C of friends.

To form an association rule of the form A➜C, the CF-Miner algorithm picks a pair of two related frequent patterns—namely, A and (A∪C)—such that the following conditions hold:

1. Frequent pattern A is put as an antecedent.
2. Subset C in a related frequent pattern (A∪C) is put as a consequent of the rule.

Note that, if (A∪C) is a frequent pattern, then the subset C of (A∪C) is guaranteed to be frequent. The reason is that, if C was not frequent, then any superset including (A∪C) cannot be frequent due to the Apriori property—which states that any subsets of a frequent pattern must also be frequent. Equivalently, any supersets of an infrequent pattern must also be infrequent. Hence, if (A∪C) is frequent, then C must be frequent. So, both the antecedent A and consequent C of any association rule of form A➜C formed by CF-Miner are frequent patterns.

Once an association rule A➜C is formed, the CF-Miner algorithm then computes the confidence of the rule, which measures the fraction of frequent pattern containing A also contains C. In other words, the confidence measures that, among all the frequent patterns containing A, how many of them also contain C (i.e., how many of these frequent patterns contain both A and C)? More formally, the confidence of a rule A➜C is defined as the fraction or ratio of the frequency or occurrence of (A∪C) among that of A as follows:

$$\text{confidence}(A➜C) = \text{frequency}(A∪C) / \text{frequency}(A).$$

If the confidence of a rule A➜C (i.e., fraction of frequent pattern containing A also contains C) meets or exceeds the user-specified *minconf* threshold, i.e.,

$$\text{frequency}(A∪C) / \text{frequency}(A) \geq \textit{minconf},$$

then such a rule is considered interesting or high-confident.

After finding an interesting or high-confident association rule, the CF-Miner algorithm then applies a similar procedure to perform the following:

1. Pick another pair of two related frequent patterns to form another association rule,
2. Compute the confidence of the resulting association rule, and
3. Determine whether or not such an association rule is interesting or high-confident.

The procedure is repeated until no more association rules can be formed by using pairs of the mined frequent patterns.

Step 4: Recommendation via Collaborative Filtering

Once the CF-Miner algorithm formed all interesting high-confident association rules association rules based on the frequent patterns mined from the bitwise table and its associated column indices and column sums, when a user interests in patterns appearing in the antecedent A of an association rule A➜C, the CF-Miner algorithm makes recommendation via collaborative filtering by providing the user with the consequent C of such an association rule.

Recall that the CF-Miner algorithm considers all association rules with their confidence values ≥ the user-specified *minconf* threshold. So, it is not uncommon that, for a query antecedent A, multiple association rules can be found with different consequents associated with the same antecedent A. For completeness, CF-Miner returns all association rules with different frequent patterns in the consequent.

When the number of interesting high-confident association rules is high, the CF-Miner algorithm sorts these rules in non-ascending order of their confidence values. By doing so, CF-Miner would be able to recommend the user with higher-confident association rules.

An Illustrative Example

For this illustrative example, let us consider a small database, which consists of N=6 transactions. Each of these transactions is following some of the M=4 items with IDs 1, 2, 3 and 4 as described below:

- Transaction t_1 contains Items 2 and 4;
- Transaction t_2 contains Items 1 and 3;
- Transaction t_3 contains Items 1 and 4;
- Transaction t_4 contains Items 2, 3 and 4;
- Transaction t_5 contains Items 1, 2 and 3; and
- Transaction t_6 contains Items 1, 2, 3 and 4.

The resulting bitwise table and its associated column index and column sum (which gives the frequency of each item) are shown in Table 1.

Here, as transaction t_1 contains Items 2 and 4, the CF-Miner algorithm puts 1s in both the 2nd & 4th bits and puts 0s in both the 1st & 3rd bits in the bitwise table. Similarly, as transaction t_2 contains Items 1 and 3, CF-Miner puts 1s in both the 1st & 3rd bits and puts 0s in both the 2nd & 4th bits in the bitwise

Table 1. Bitwise table with its associated column index and column sum

Illustrative database	Item 1	Item 2	Item 3	Item 4	Column index
t_1	0	1	0	1	2
t_2	1	0	1	0	1
t_3	1	0	0	1	1
t_4	0	1	1	1	2
t_5	1	1	1	0	1
t_6	1	1	1	1	1
Column sum (Frequency of item)	4	4	4	4	

table. As transaction t_3 contains Items 1 and 4, CF-Miner puts 1s in both the 1st & 4th bits and puts 0s in both the 2nd & 3rd bits in the bitwise table. As transaction t_4 contains Items 2, 3 and 4, CF-Miner puts 1s in the 2nd, 3rd & 4th bits puts a 0 in the 1st bit in the bitwise table. As transaction t_5 contains Items 1, 2 and 3, CF-Miner puts 1s in the 1st, 2nd & 3rd bits and puts a 0 in the 4th bit in the bitwise table. Finally, as transaction t_6 contains all items (i.e., Items 1, 2, 3 and 4), CF-Miner puts 1s in all bits (i.e., 1st, 2nd, 3rd & 4th bits) in the bitwise table.

For transaction t_1, the CF-Miner algorithm creates a column index "2" indicating the first occurrence of a "1" bit is in column 2 (for Item 2). Among all column indices, two rows (namely, rows for transactions t_1 and t_4) contain lists that start with Item 2, and four rows (namely, rows for transactions t_2, t_3, t_5 and t_6) contain transactions that start with Item 1. Note that the value in each column index is at most M=4 (where M is the total number of distinct items).

For each column c of the bitwise table, the CF-Miner algorithm computes a column sum by counting the number of 1s in column c. For instance, Item 1 appears in transactions t_2, t_3, t_5 and t_6 as indicated by the four 1s in column 1. So, the column sum for column 1 becomes 4. Similarly, as Item 2 appears in transactions t_1, t_4, t_5 and t_6 as indicated by the four 1s in column 2, the column sum for column 2 becomes 4. As Item 3 appears in transactions t_2, t_4, t_5 and t_6 as indicated by the four 1s in column 3, the corresponding column sum also becomes 4. Finally, as Item 4 appears in transactions t_1, t_3, t_4 and t_6 as indicated by the four 1s in column 4, the corresponding column sum becomes 4 as well. Note that each sum is at most 6 (because there are only N=6 transactions).

Next, let us explain the frequent pattern mining process. Let the user-specified *minsup* threshold be set to 2 indicating any pattern needs to appear in at least 2 transactions in order to be considered *frequent*. The mining process starts from the bitwise table and its associated column index and column sum. Based on the column sum, Item 1 is observed to appear in 4 transactions (namely, transactions t_2, t_3, t_5 and t_6) $\geq$ *minsup*. So, {Item 1} is considered as a frequent singleton, which is a frequent pattern. Similarly, Item 2 also appears in 4 transactions (namely, transactions t_1, t_4, t_5 and t_6). Item 3 appears in 4 transactions (namely, transactions t_2, t_4, t_5 and t_6), and item 4 also appears in 4 transactions (namely, transactions t_1, t_3, t_4 and t_6). In other words, the CF-Miner algorithm found four frequent singletons {Item 1}, {Item 2}, {Item 3} and {Item 4}.

The CF-Miner algorithm then uses the column index (e.g., with value 1 representing Item 1) to "extract" (or consider) all relevant rows (i.e., rows for transactions t_2, t_3, t_5 and t_6) to form the {Item 1}-projected database as shown Table 2.

Afterwards, the CF-Miner algorithm appends a column index (for the {Item 1}-projected database) to the right of the bitwise table. In addition, the algorithm also appends the column sums for the {Item

Table 2. Bitwise table with its associated column index and column sum for {1}-projected DB

{1}-projected database	*Item 1*	Item 2	Item 3	Item 4	{1}-column index
t_2	*1*	0	1	0	3
t_3	*1*	0	0	1	4
t_5	*1*	1	1	0	2
t_6	*1*	1	1	1	2
{1}-column sum (Frequency of item appears with Item 1)		2	3	2	

1}-projected database below the bitwise table. For readability, irrelevant portions of this bitwise table were not shown. However, it is important to note that their contents remind unchanged throughout the entire mining process.

Based on this new {1}-column sum, Items 1 and 2 are observed to appear together in 2 transactions (namely, transactions t_5 and t_6) ≥ *minsup*. So, {Items 1, 2} is considered as a frequent pair. Similarly, Items 1 and 3 appear together in 3 transactions (namely, transactions t_2, t_5 and t_6); Items 1 and 4 appear together in 2 transactions (namely, transactions t_3 and t_6). In other words, the CF-Miner algorithm found three frequent pairs {Items 1, 2}, {Items 1, 3} and {Items 1, 4} as frequent patterns of cardinality 2.

The CF-Miner algorithm then uses the new {1}-column index to "extract" all relevant rows (i.e., rows for transactions t_5 and t_6) with value 2 to form the {items 1, 2}-projected database as shown in Table 3.

Based on this new {1,2}-column sum, Items 1, 2 and 3 are observed to appear together in 2 transactions (namely, transactions t_5 and t_6) ≥ *minsup*. So, {items 1, 2, 3} is considered as a frequent triplet. However, Items 1, 2 and 4 appear together in only 1 transaction (namely, transaction t_6) < *minsup*, and thus is infrequent. In other words, the CF-Miner algorithm found one frequent triplet {Items 1, 2, 3} as a frequent pattern of cardinality 3.

The CF-Miner algorithm then uses the new {1,2}-column index to "extract" all relevant rows (i.e., rows for transactions t_5 and t_6) with value 3 to form the {Items 1, 2, 3}-projected database as shown in Table 4.

Based on this new {1,2,3}-column sum, Items 1, 2, 3 and 4 are observed to appear together in only 1 transaction (namely, transaction t_6) < *minsup*. Then, the CF-Miner algorithm backtracks to form the {Items 1, 2, 4}-projected database based on the updated {1, 2}-column index values as shown in Table 5.

Table 3. Bitwise table with its associated column index and column sum for {1, 2}-projected DB

{1, 2}-projected database	Item 1	Item 2	Item 3	Item 4	{1, 2}-column index
t_5	1	1	1	0	3
t_6	1	1	1	1	3
{1, 2}-column sum (Frequency of item appears with Items 1 & 2)			2	1	

Table 4. Bitwise table with its associated column index & column sum for {1, 2, 3}-projected DB

{1, 2, 3}-projected database	Item 1	Item 2	Item 3	Item 4	{1, 2, 3}-column index
t_5	1	1	1	0	-
t_6	1	1	1	1	4
{1, 2, 3}-column sum (Frequency of item appears with Items 1, 2 & 3)				1	

Table 5. Updated bitwise table with its associated column index and column sum for {1, 2}-projected DB

{1, 2}-projected database	Item 1	Item 2		Item 4	Updated {1, 2}-column index
t_5	1	1		0	-
t_6	1	1		1	4
Updated {1, 2}-column sum **(Frequency of item appears with Items 1 & 2)**				1	

Again, no frequent patterns can be found from this projected database. Hence, the CF-Miner algorithm backtracks and updates {1}-column index values as shown in Table 6.

Based on this updated {1}-column index values, the CF-Miner algorithm forms the {Items 1, 3}-projected database as shown in Table 7.

At this point, the CF-Miner algorithm has found all frequent patterns containing Item 1. Then, the algorithm updates the original column index values to get a new column index as shown in Table 8.

Afterwards, the CF-Miner algorithm applies similar steps to find the remaining frequent patterns {Items 2, 3}, {Items 2, 4}, {Items 2, 3, 4} and {Items 3, 4}. More specifically, CF-Miner uses this updated column index (e.g., with value 2 representing Item 2) to "extract" all relevant rows (i.e., rows for transactions t_1, t_4, t_5 and t_6) to form the {Item 2}-projected database as shown Table 9.

Table 6. Updated bitwise table with its associated column index and column sum for {1}-projected DB

{1}-projected database	Item 1		Item 3	Item 4	Updated {1}-column index
t_2	1		1	0	3
t_3	1		0	1	4
t_5	1		1	0	3
t_6	1		1	1	3
Updated {1}-column sum **(Frequency of item appears with Item 1)**			3	2	

Table 7. Bitwise table with its associated column index and column sum for {1, 3}-projected DB

{1, 3}-projected database	Item 1		Item 3	Item 4	{1, 3}-column index
t_2	1		1	0	-
t_5	1		1	0	-
t_6	1		1	1	4
{1, 3}-column sum **(Frequency of item appears with Items 1 & 2)**				1	

Table 8. Updated bitwise table with its associated column index and column sum

Illustrative database	Item 1	Item 2	Item 3	Item 4	Updated column index
t_1	0	1	0	1	2
t_2		0	1	0	3
t_3		0	0	1	4
t_4	0	1	1	1	2
t_5		1	1	0	2
t_6		1	1	1	2
Updated column sum (Frequency of item)		4	4	4	

Table 9. Bitwise table with its associated column index and column sum for {2}-projected DB

{2}-projected database	Item 1	Item 2	Item 3	Item 4	{2}-column index
t_1	0	1	0	1	4
t_2	1	0	1	0	
t_3	1	0	0	1	
t_4	0	1	1	1	3
t_5	1	1	1	0	3
t_6	1	1	1	1	3
{2}-column sum (Frequency of item appears with Item 2)			3	3	

Based on this new {2}-column sum, Items 2 and 3 are observed to appear together in 3 transactions (namely, transactions t_4, t_5 and t_6) $\geq$ *minsup*. So, {Items 2, 3} is considered as a frequent pair. Similarly, Items 2 and 4 also appear together in 3 transactions (namely, transactions t_1, t_4 and t_6). In other words, the CF-Miner algorithm found two frequent pairs {Items 2, 3} and {Items 2, 4} as frequent patterns of cardinality 2.

The CF-Miner algorithm then uses the new {2}-column index to "extract" all relevant rows (i.e., rows for transactions t_4, t_5 and t_6) with value 3 to form the {items 2, 3}-projected database as shown in Table 10.

Based on this new {2,3}-column sum, Items 2, 3 and 4 are observed to appear together in 2 transactions (namely, transactions t_4 and t_6) $\geq$ *minsup*. So, {items 2, 3, 4} is considered as a frequent triplet. In other words, the CF-Miner algorithm found one frequent triplet {Items 2, 3, 4} as a frequent pattern of cardinality 3.

Table 10. Bitwise table with its associated column index and column sum for {2, 3}-projected DB

{2, 3}-projected database	Item 1	Item 2	Item 3	Item 4	{2, 3}-column index
t_1	0	1	0	1	
t_2	1	0	1	0	
t_3	1	0	0	1	
t_4	0	1	1	1	4
t_5	1	1	1	0	-
t_6	1	1	1	1	4
{2, 3}-column sum (Frequency of item appears with Items 2 & 3)				2	

At this point, the CF-Miner algorithm has found all frequent patterns containing Item 2. Then, the algorithm updates the column index values again to get a new column index as shown in Table 11.

The CF-Miner algorithm then uses this updated column index (e.g., with value 3 representing Item 3) to "extract" all relevant rows (i.e., rows for transactions t_1, t_4, t_5 and t_6) to form the {Item 3}-projected database as shown Table 12.

Based on this new {3}-column sum, Items 3 and 4 are observed to appear together in 2 transactions (namely, transactions t_4 and t_6) $\geq$ *minsup*. So, {Items 3, 4} is considered as a frequent pair. In other words, the CF-Miner algorithm found one frequent pair {Items 3, 4} as a frequent pattern of cardinality 2. At this point, CF-Miner has found all frequent patterns containing Item 3, as well as all frequent patterns that can be mined from the database.

To recap, with the above frequent pattern mining, the CF-Miner algorithm found the following 12 frequent patterns (with their frequency values):

- {Item 1}:4, {Item 2}:4, {Item 3}:4, {Item 4}:4,
- {Items 1, 2}:2, {Items 1, 3}:3, {Items 1, 4}:2, {Items 2, 3}:3, {Items 2, 4}:3, {Items 3, 4}:2,
- {Items 1, 2, 3}:2, and {Items 2, 3, 4}:2.

Afterwards, the CF-Miner algorithm uses these mined frequent patterns to obtain the following 24 related pairs of frequent patterns $\langle A, (A \cup C) \rangle$ to be put as antecedents A and consequents (A $\cup$ C) of association rules of the form A➔C:

Table 11. Updated bitwise table with its associated column index and column sum

Illustrative database	Item 1	Item 2	Item 3	Item 4	Updated column index
t_1			0	1	4
t_2			1	0	3
t_3			0	1	4
t_4			1	1	3
t_5			1	0	3
t_6			1	1	3
Updated column sum (Frequency of item)			4	4	

Table 12. Bitwise table with its associated column index and column sum for {3}-projected DB

{3}-projected database	Item 1	Item 2	Item 3	Item 4	{3}-column index
t_2			1	0	-
t_4			1	1	4
t_5			1	0	-
t_6			1	1	4
{3}-column sum (Frequency of item appears with Item 3)				2	

- ⟨{Item 1}, {Items 1, 2}⟩,
- ⟨{Item 1}, {Items 1, 2, 3}⟩,
- ⟨{Item 1}, {Items 1, 3}⟩,
- ⟨{Item 1}, {Items 1, 4}⟩;
- ⟨{Item 2}, {Items 1, 2}⟩,
- ⟨{Item 2}, {Items 1, 2, 3}⟩,
- ⟨{Item 2}, {Items 2, 3}⟩,
- ⟨{Item 2}, {Items 2, 3, 4}⟩,
- ⟨{Item 2}, {Items 2, 4}⟩;
- ⟨{Item 3}, {Items 1, 2, 3}⟩,
- ⟨{Item 3}, {Items 1, 3}⟩,
- ⟨{Item 3}, {Items 2, 3}⟩,
- ⟨{Item 3}, {Items 2, 3, 4}⟩,
- ⟨{Item 3}, {Items 3, 4}⟩;
- ⟨{Item 4}, {Items 1, 4}⟩,
- ⟨{Item 4}, {Items 2, 3, 4}⟩,
- ⟨{Item 4}, {Items 2, 4}⟩,
- ⟨{Item 4}, {Items 3, 4}⟩;
- ⟨{Items 1, 2}, {Items 1, 2, 3}⟩;
- ⟨{Items 1, 3}, {Items 1, 2, 3}⟩;
- ⟨{Items 2, 3}, {Items 1, 2, 3}⟩,
- ⟨{Items 2, 3}, {Items 2, 3, 4}⟩;
- ⟨{Items 2, 4}, {Items 2, 3, 4}⟩; and
- ⟨{Items 3, 4}, {Items 2, 3, 4}⟩.

Based on these 24 pairs of frequent patterns, the CF-Miner algorithm forms 24 association rules, which are then grouped according to nine distinct antecedents. Within each group (having a distinct antecedent), association rules are sorted in descending order of their confidence values as shown below:

- Group 1:
  - {Items 1 & 2} ➜ {Item 3} with a confidence value of 100% indicating that 100% of consumers who purchased Items 1 & 2 also purchase Item 3 (or all customers who requested Services 1 & 2 also request Service 3, or all social network users who followed social networking pages 1 & 2 also follow social networking page 3);
- Group 2:
  - {Items 1 & 3} ➜ {Item 2} with a confidence value of 67%;
- Group 3:
  - {Item 1} ➜ {Item 3} with a confidence value of 75%;
  - {Item 1} ➜ {Items 2 & 3},
  - {Item 1} ➜ {Item 2}, and
  - {Item 1} ➜ {Item 4} all three with confidence values of 50%;
- Group 4:
  - {Items 2 & 3} ➜ {Item 1}, and
  - {Items 2 & 3} ➜ {Item 4} both with confidence values of 50%;

- Group 5:
  ○ {Items 2 & 4} ➔ {Item 3} with a confidence value of 50%;
- Group 6:
  ○ {Item 2} ➔ {Item 3}, and
  ○ {Item 2} ➔ {Item 4} both with confidence values of 75%;
  ○ {Item 2} ➔ {Items 1 & 3},
  ○ {Item 2} ➔ {Item 1}, and
  ○ {Item 2} ➔ {Items 3 & 4} all three with confidence values of 50%;
- Group 7:
  ○ {Items 3 & 4} ➔ {Item 2} with a confidence value of 50%;
- Group 8:
  ○ {Item 3} ➔ {Item 1},
  ○ {Item 3} ➔ {Item 2} both with confidence values of 75%;
  ○ {Item 3} ➔ {Items 1 & 2},
  ○ {Item 3} ➔ {Items 2 & 4}, and
  ○ {Item 3} ➔ {Item 4} all three with confidence values of 50%;
- Group 9:
  ○ {Item 4} ➔ {Item 2} with a confidence value of 75%;
  ○ {Item 4} ➔ {Items 2 & 3} with a confidence value of 67%;
  ○ {Item 4} ➔ {Item 1}, and
  ○ {Item 4} ➔ {Item 3} both with confidence values of 50%.

If a new future query matches an antecedent of any association rule, the CF-Miner algorithm recommend the corresponding consequent of the rule. For instance, for a consumer who is purchasing Item 1, CF-Miner recommends the consumer to purchase Item 3 to see if the consumer would like to bundle the two items and purchase them together to save shipment and handling fee. This is because, among the four association rules with Item 1 as the antecedent, the rule having Item 3 as the consequent leads to higher confidence value of 75% than confidence values of 50% in the other three rules.

Depends on the real-life applications, CF-Miner is flexible that it can give a top-k list of recommendation from the most relevant recommendation on the top of the list. For instance, for a customer who is requesting Service 2, CF-Miner first recommends the customer to order Service 3 or 4, then recommends the customer to order the following services:

1. Service 1,
2. Both Services 1 & 3, or
3. Both Services 3 & 4, to see if the customer would like to bundle the two services and order the bundle at a discounted rate.

Similarly, for a social network user who followed social networking page 3, CF-Miner recommends the user to follow social networking page 1 or social networking page 2.

EVALUATION

This section presents the analytical and experimental evaluation results—especially on (i) the memory usage of the presented bitwise table and (ii) runtime comparisons of the CF-Miner algorithm with its related ones such as the Eclat (Zaki, 2000), FP-growth (Han, Pei & Yin, 2000), VIPER (Shenoy et al., 2000), H-mine (Pei et al., 2001), and TD-FP-Growth (Wang et al., 2002) algorithms.

First, the memory space consumption of the CF-Miner algorithm is compared with that of a related work—namely the FP-growth algorithm (Han, Pei & Yin, 2000). Recall that FP-growth is the tree-based divide-and-conquer approach to mine frequent patterns from shopper market basket datasets. FP-growth first builds a global FP-tree to capture important contents of the dataset in the tree. The number of tree nodes is theoretically bounded above by the number of occurrences of all items (say, $O(N_{occurrence})$) in the dataset. Practically, due to tree path sharing, the number of tree nodes (say, $O(N_{tree}) < O(N_{occurrence})$) is usually smaller than the upper bound. However, during the mining process, multiple smaller sub-trees need to be constructed. Specifically, for a global FP-tree with depth k, it is not unusual for $O(k)$ sub-trees to coexist with the global tree, for a total of $O(k * N_{tree})$ nodes. In contrast, on the surface, the bitwise table may appear to take up more space (due to the lack of tree path sharing). The bitwise table contains $O(N_{occurrence})$ entries. However, it is important to note that each entry in the bitwise table is just a single bit, instead of an integer for an item ID. In other words, the bitwise table requires $O(N_{occurrence})/8$ bytes of space. Moreover, unlike FP-growth, the CF-Miner algorithm does not need to build additional copies of bitwise tables. Thus, the bitwise table requires $O(N_{occurrence})/8$ bytes, which is much less than $O(k * N_{tree})$ bytes in FP-growth.

The above analysis focused on the bitwise table. Next, the focus is on the column indices and column sums. For any interesting frequent patterns of cardinality k, the CF-Miner algorithm needs to keep k column indices and k column sums. Note that the FP-growth algorithm also creates $O(k)$ header tables for the $O(k)$ sub-trees. In other words, the amount of space required by these column indices and column sums is similar to that by sub-trees. However, the bitwise table (used by CF-Miner) requires much less space than all the FP-trees (used by FP-growth). Moreover, CF-Miner requires less space (for the bitwise table, column indices, and column sums) than FP-growth (which stores global FP-tree, multiple sub-trees, and multiple header tables).

Then, the performance of the CF-Miner algorithm is compared with related works by using the following datasets:

1. Synthetic datasets, which are generally sparse and are generated by the IBM Quest synthetic data generator (Aggarwal & Srikant, 1994),
2. Several real life datasets from the Frequent Itemset Mining Dataset Repository (http://fimi.ua.ac.be/data/), as well as
3. Several Facebook and Twitter datasets from Stanford Network Analysis Project (SNAP) (http://snap.stanford.edu/data/).

Five frequent pattern mining algorithms were compared with the CF-Miner algorithm: Eclat (Zaki, 2000), FP-growth (Han, Pei & Yin, 2000), VIPER (Shenoy et al., 2000), H-mine (Pei et al., 2001), and TD-FP-Growth (Wang et al., 2002). All experiments were run multiple times using the dense real-life retail dataset and sparse IBM synthetic datasets in a time-sharing environment in a 1 GHz machine. Evaluation results on the dense dataset show that CF-Miner gave the best performance over the other five algorithms because CF-Miner takes advantage of using the bitwise table to capture the information in a bitwise manner (especially, for dense dataset). The results on the sparse datasets show that, when the user-specified *minsup* threshold is low, algorithms such as H-mine and VIPER did not perform very well. Eclat showed its advantages when handling sparse datasets. Moreover, CF-Miner performed better than the other five.

In terms of recommendation quality, evaluation results show that recommendations made by the CF-Miner algorithm led to high true positive rate. Occasionally, CF-Miner missed a few products or services that the users like (i.e., CF-Miner led to low false negative rate). More importantly, users like most, if not all, the products and services recommended by CF-Miner (i.e., CF-Miner led to very low false positive rate). This is encouraging because false positives are less desirable than false negatives as recommending false positives can annoy or anger users when compared with the failure to recommend false negatives.

As for real-life applications, the CF-Miner algorithm was applied to social network datasets to recommend relevant popular social networking pages for social network users to follow. Note that many social networks are made not only of individual users but also corporations or organizations. As there are more than 1 billion people in different social network media (e.g., Facebook, Twitter, Weibo), many corporations or organizations create and use their business or corporate accounts on these social network media to either reach the right audience for their business and turn them into customers or build a closer relationship with their customers (Lauschke & Ntoutsi, 2012; Schaal, O'Donovan & Smyth, 2012; Yuan et al., 2013). Consequently, their customers can follow the products or services provided by these corporations or organizations as followers or fans. They can also write online reviews, comments, or tweets about the positive or negative aspects of some products or services provided by these organizations. Such feedback is useful for improving their organizational design, operations, and performance. However, with limited resources, the management teams of these organizations may not be able to listen to all customers, fans, or followers. So, it is desirable to find those who follow collections of popular social networking pages (i.e., who care more about the products or services) among many customers, fans, and followers. As such, the application of association rule mining in collaborative filtering helps reveal which merchandise items, goods, services, or social networking pages are supported by users or fans. This reveals the popularity of recommended products or services (or products or services promoted on the recommended social networking pages). This helps organizations enhance their organizational design and production of these strongly supported products, as well as their organizational operations and performance of these strongly supported services. Such a collaborative filtering result is beneficial (e.g., increases profits) to organizations and their business applications.

FUTURE RESEARCH DIRECTIONS

This chapter has presented how the CF-Miner algorithm uses association rule mining in collaborative filtering for traditional datasets. Nowadays, big data (Leung, 2014a) are everywhere. High volumes of high-veracity and valuable data can be generated or collected at a high velocity from large varieties of data sources in various real-life applications for both public services and private sectors. Embedded in these big data are richer sets of useful information and knowledge. Having a recommendation system would be more beneficial. Hence, a future research direction is to use association rules in collaborative filtering on big data.

Moreover, "a picture is worth a thousand words". The use of visual representation (Leung, 2013) can enhance user understanding of the inherent relations among the frequent patterns and association rules. Hence, another future research direction is visual analytics of association rule mining in collaborative filtering.

CONCLUSION

Collaborative filtering usually applies data mining techniques—such as association rule mining—to develop a system with precise knowledge and accuracy for helping users is a popular technique used for recommendation system, which helps users make appropriate decisions in various real-life applications—such as e-commerce, e-learning, social networks, and web search—by removing redundant information and providing users with valuable information in short periods of time. This chapter presents the CF-Miner algorithm for collaborative filtering with association rule miner. The algorithm first builds a bitwise table, together its associated column indices and column sums to capture important contents in the data to facilitate mining. Then, CF-Miner recursively finds frequent patterns by traversing relevant portions of the same bitwise table to construct column indices and column sums. Based on the mined frequent patterns, CF-Miner forms association rules using these frequent patterns as antecedent A and consequent C of association rules of the form A➔C. Finally, CF-Miner applies collaborative filtering to rank the mined association for making recommendations to users in various applications. Consequently, CF-Miner algorithm recommends appropriate merchandise products, goods or services to users. Evaluation results show the effectiveness of the CF-Miner algorithm in using association rule mining in collaborative filtering.

REFERENCES

Aggarwal, R., & Srikant, R. (1994). Fast algorithms for mining association rules. In J. B. Bocca, M. Jarke, & C. Zaniolo (Eds.), *Proceedings of the 20th International Conference on Very Large Data Bases (VLDB 1994)* (pp. 487-399). San Francisco, CA: Morgan Kaufmann.

Cuzzocrea, A., Jiang, F., Lee, W., & Leung, C. K.-S. (2014). Efficient frequent itemset mining from dense data streams. In L. Chen, Y. Jia, T. K. Sellis, & G. Liu (Eds.), *Proceedings of the 16th Asia-Pacific Web Conference (APWeb 2014)* (pp. 593-601). Heidelberg, Germany: Springer. doi:10.1007/978-3-319-11116-2_56

Han, J., Pei, J., & Yin, Y. (2000) Mining frequent patterns without candidate generation. In W. Chen, J. F. Naughton, & P. A. Bernstein (Eds.), *Proceedings of the 2000 ACM SIGMOD International Conference on Management of Data* (pp. 1-12). New York, NY: ACM. doi:10.1145/342009.335372

Jiang, F., & Leung, C. K.-S. (2014). Mining interesting "following" patterns from social networks. In L. Bellatreche, & M. K. Mohania (Eds.), *Proceedings of the 16th International Conference on Data Warehousing and Knowledge Discovery (DaWaK 2014)* (pp. 308-319). Heidelberg, Germany: Springer. doi:10.1007/978-3-319-10160-6_28

Lauschke, C., & Ntoutsi, E. (2012). Monitoring user evolution in Twitter. In *Proceedings of the 2012 IEEE/ACM International Conference on Advances in Social Networks Analysis and Mining (ASONAM)*, (pp. 972-977). Los Alamitos, CA: IEEE Computer Society. doi:10.1109/ASONAM.2012.171

Leung, C. K.-S. (2013). Mining frequent itemsets from probabilistic datasets. *Proceedings of the Fifth International Conference on Emerging Databases (EDB 2013)* (pp. 137-148).

Leung, C. K.-S. (2014a). Big data mining and analytics. In J. Wang (Ed.), *Encyclopedia of business analytics and optimization* (pp. 328–337). Hershey, PA: IGI Global. doi:10.4018/978-1-4666-5202-6.ch030

Leung, C. K.-S. (2014b). Uncertain frequent pattern mining. In C. C. Aggarwal & J. Han (Eds.), Frequent pattern mining (pp. 417–453). Heidelberg, Germany: Springer. doi:10.1007/978-3-319-07821-2_14

Leung, C. K.-S., Carmichael, C. L., Johnstone, P., & Yuen, D. S. H.-C. (2013). Interactive visual analytics of databases and frequent sets. *International Journal of Information Retrieval Research*, *3*(4), 120–140. doi:10.4018/ijirr.2013100107

Leung, C. K.-S., MacKinnon, R. K., & Jiang, F. (2014). Reducing the search space for big data mining for interesting patterns from uncertain data. *Proceedings of the 2014 IEEE International Congress on Big Data (BigData Congress)*, (pp. 315-322). Los Alamitos, CA: IEEE Computer Society. doi:10.1109/BigData.Congress.2014.53

Leung, C. K.-S., Medina, I. J. M., & Tanbeer, S. K. (2013). Analyzing social networks to mine important friends. In G. Xu & L. Li (Eds.), Social media mining and social network analysis: emerging research (pp. 90–104). Hershey, PA: IGI Global. doi:10.4018/978-1-4666-2806-9.ch006

Leung, C. K.-S., Tanbeer, S. K., & Cameron, J. J. (2014). Interactive discovery of influential friends from social networks. *Social Network Analysis and Mining, 4*(1). doi:10.1007/s13278-014-0154-z

Lu, W., & Lakshmanan, L. V. S. (2012). Profit maximization over social networks. In M. J. Zaki, A. Siebes, J. X. Yu, B. Goethals, G. I. Webb, & X. Wu (Eds.), *Proceedings of the 12th IEEE International Conference on Data Mining (ICDM 2012)* (pp. 479-488). Los Alamitos, CA: IEEE Computer Society. doi:10.1109/ICDM.2012.145

Maserrat, H., & Pei, J. (2012). Community preserving lossy compression of social networks. In M. J. Zaki, A. Siebes, J. X. Yu, B. Goethals, G. I. Webb, & X. Wu (Eds.), *Proceedings of the 12th IEEE International Conference on Data Mining (ICDM 2012)* (pp. 509-518). Los Alamitos, CA: IEEE Computer Society. doi:10.1109/ICDM.2012.14

Négrevergne, B., Dries, A., Guns, T., & Nijssen, S. (2013). Dominance programming for itemset mining. In H. Xiong, G. Karypis, B. M. Thuraisingham, D. J. Cook, & X. Wu (Eds.), *Proceedings of the 13th IEEE International Conference on Data Mining (ICDM 2013)* (pp. 557-566). Los Alamitos, CA: IEEE Computer Society. doi:10.1109/ICDM.2013.92

Pei, J., Han, J., Lu, H., Nishio, S., Tang, S., & Yang, D. (2001). H-Mine: hyper-structure mining of frequent patterns in large databases. In N. Cercone, T. Y. Lin, & X. Wu (Eds.), *Proceedings of the First IEEE International Conference on Data Mining (ICDM 2001)* (pp. 441-448). Los Alamitos, CA: IEEE Computer Society. doi:10.1109/ICDM.2001.989550

Schaal, M., O'Donovan, J., & Smyth, B. (2012). An analysis of topical proximity in the Twitter social graph. In K. Aberer, A. Flache, W. Jager, L. Liu, J. Tang, & C. Guéret (Eds.), *Proceedings of the Fourth International Conference on Social Informatics* (*SocInfo 2012*) (pp. 232-245). Heidelberg, Germany: Springer. doi:10.1007/978-3-642-35386-4_18

Shenoy, P., Haritsa, J. R., Sudarshan, S., Bhalotia, G., Bawa, M., & Shah, D. (2000). Turbo-charging vertical mining of large databases. In W. Chen, J. F. Naughton, & P. A. Bernstein (Eds.), *Proceedings of the 2000 ACM SIGMOD International Conference on Management of Data* (pp. 22-33). New York, NY: ACM. doi:10.1145/342009.335376

Wang, K., Tang, L., Han, J., & Liu, J. (2002). Top down FP-growth for association rule mining, In M.-S. Cheng, P. S. Yu, & B. Liu (Eds.), *Proceedings of the Sixth Pacific-Asia Conference on Knowledge Discovery and Data Mining* (*PAKDD 2002*) (pp. 334-340). Heidelberg, Germany: Springer. doi:10.1007/3-540-47887-6_34

Yuan, Q., Cong, G., Ma, Z., Sun, A., & Magnenat-Thalmann, N. (2013). Who, where, when and what: discover spatio-temporal topics for Twitter users. *Proceedings of the 19th ACM SIGKDD International Conference on Knowledge Discovery and Data Mining* (*KDD 2013*) (pp. 605-613). New York, NY: ACM. doi:10.1145/2487575.2487576

Zaki, M. J. (2000). Scalable algorithms for association mining. *IEEE Transactions on Knowledge and Data Engineering*, *12*(3), 372–390. doi:10.1109/69.846291

ADDITIONAL READING

Barbieri, N., Manco, G., & Ritacco, E. (2011). A probabilistic hierarchical approach for pattern discovery in collaborative filtering data. *Proceedings of the 11th SIAM International Conference on Data Mining* (*SDM2011*) (pp. 630-641). Philadelphia, PA: SIAM. doi:10.1137/1.9781611972818.54

Cai, Y., Leung, H., Li, Q., Min, H., Tang, J., & Li, J. (2014). Typicality-based collaborative filtering recommendation. *IEEE Transactions on Knowledge and Data Engineering*, *26*(3), 766–779. doi:10.1109/TKDE.2013.7

Cao, L., Zhang, C., Joachims, T., Webb, G. I., Margineantu, D. D., & Williams, G. (Eds.), (2015). *Proceedings of the 21st ACM SIGKDD International Conference on Knowledge Discovery and Data Mining* (*KDD 2015*). New York, NY: ACM.

Cao, T., Lim, E.-P., Zhou, Z.-H., Ho, T.-B., Cheung, D. W.-L., & Motoda, H. (Eds.), (2015). *Proceedings of 19th Pacific-Asia Conference on Knowledge Discovery and Data Mining* (*PAKDD 2015*). Heidelberg, Germany: Springer.

Jannach, D., Zanker, M., Felfernig, A., & Friedrich, G. (2010). *Recommender systems: an introduction*. Cambridge, UK: Cambridge University Press. doi:10.1017/CBO9780511763113

Kobsa, A., Zhou, M. X., Ester, M., & Koren, Y. (Eds.). (2014). *Proceedings of the Eighth ACM Conference on Recommender Systems* (*RecSys 2014*). New York, NY: ACM.

Kumar, R., Toivonen, H., Pei, J., Huang, J. Z., & Wu, X. (Eds.). (2014). *Proceedings of the 14th IEEE International Conference on Data Mining* (*ICDM 2014*). Los Alamitos, CA: IEEE Computer Society.

Leung, C. K.-S., Jiang, F., Pazdor, A. G. M., & Peddle, A. M. (2016). Parallel social network mining for interesting "following" patterns. *Concurrency and Computation: Practice and Experience*. doi:10.1002/cpe.3773

Liu, T.-Y., Scollon, C. N., & Zhu, W. (Eds.), (2015). *Proceedings of Seventh International Conference on Social Informatics* (*SocInfo 2015*). Heidelberg, Germany: Springer.

Pei, J., Silvestri, F., & Tang, J. (Eds.), (2015). *Proceedings of the 2015 IEEE/ACM International Conference on Advances in Social Networks Analysis and Mining* (*ASONAM*). New York, NY: ACM.

Ricci, F., Rokach, L., Shapira, B., & Kantor, P. B. (Eds.), (2011). *Recommender systems handbook*. New York, NY: Springer US. doi:10.1007/978-0-387-85820-3

Salehi, M., Kamalabadi, I. N., & Ghoushchi, M. B. G. (2014). Personalized recommendation of learning material using sequential pattern mining and attribute based collaborative filtering. *Education and Information Technologies*, *19*(4), 713–735. doi:10.1007/s10639-012-9245-5

Werthner, H., Zanker, M., Golbeck, J., & Semeraro, G. (Eds.). (2015). *Proceedings of the Ninth ACM Conference on Recommender Systems* (*RecSys 2015*). New York, NY: ACM.

KEY TERMS AND DEFINITIONS

Association Rule Mining: A data mining task that discovers association rules of the from A➔C (where both A and C are frequent patterns) revealing the associations or relationships between both frequent patterns A and C. Association rule mining usually consists of two key steps: 1) Mining of frequent patterns and 2) Formation of association rules based on the mined frequent patterns.

Big Data: Interesting high-velocity, high-value, and/or high-variety data with volumes beyond the ability of commonly-used software to capture, manage, and process within a tolerable elapsed time. These big data necessitate new forms of processing to deliver high veracity (& low vulnerability) and enable enhanced decision making, insight, knowledge discovery, and process optimization.

Collaborative Filtering: A technique that filters information collaboratively collected from multiple users and makes "prediction" about user interests, preference or rating. As collaborative filtering usually applies data mining techniques to develop a system with precise knowledge and accuracy for helping users, it is a popular technique used for recommendation system.

Data Mining: A non-trivial extraction of implicit, previously unknown, and potentially useful information from data.

Frequent Pattern Mining: A data mining task that discovers frequently co-occurring items, events, or objects, products from data.

Itemset: A set of items.

Recommendation System: A system that helps users: 1) Remove redundant information, 2) "Predict" the user interest, preference or rating, and 3) Give valuable information in short periods of time. Hence, such a recommendation system helps users make appropriate decisions in various real-life applications.

Chapter 10
A Classification Framework on Opinion Mining for Effective Recommendation Systems

Mahima Goyal
Ambedkar Institute of Advanced Communication Technologies and Research, India

Vishal Bhatnagar
Ambedkar Institute of Advanced Communication Technologies and Research, India

ABSTRACT

With the recent trend of expressing opinions on the social media platforms like Twitter, Blogs, Reviews etc., a large amount of data is available for the analysis in the form of opinion mining. This analysis plays pivotal role in providing recommendation for ecommerce products, services and social networks, forecasting market movements and competition among businesses, etc. The authors present a literature review about the different techniques and applications of this field. The primary techniques can be classified into Data Mining methods, Natural Language Processing (NLP) and Machine learning algorithms. A classification framework is designed to depict the three levels of opinion mining –document level, Sentence Level and Aspect Level along with the methods involved in it. A system can be recommended on the basis of content based and collaborative filtering

INTRODUCTION

People's opinions and sentiments of different entities can be analyzed using opinion mining. These entities can be classified into products, services, issues and different topics (Liu, 2012). It is an important research field of Natural Language Processing (NLP) and text classification. It involves both NLP and machine learning algorithms to extract the opinions from different available sources.

Some researchers stated that Opinion Mining and Sentiment Analysis (SA) have different notions (Tsytsarau, 2012). Opinion Mining is being derived from Information Retrieval (IR) field. It analyzes people's opinion about an entity. SA, on the other hand, falls under NLP that identifies the sentiment expressed in a text by analyzing it. However, we will use both the terms interchangeably because they both have mutual meanings.

DOI: 10.4018/978-1-5225-0489-4.ch010

Opinion forms the basis for people, organizations and social communities to take accurate and effective decisions. People mostly ask their friends, peers and knowledgeable persons about their opinion on an entity while taking the decision, since, they believe the experiences, observations, concepts and beliefs of other individuals will help them in boosting the decisiveness of that entity. The inception of expressing the opinions and views on these portals has become a huge trend due to the growth of social platforms in the form of reviews, blogs, twitter, etc. Due to this large volume of opinionated data is being loaded for analysis. Thus, opinion mining plays a pivotal role in extracting the positive or negative sentiments.

Document level, sentence level and Aspect or feature level are the three classification levels in opinion mining. (Medhat et al., 2014). SA has various applications in different fields of products and services and political elections. Apart from the popular applications, many other applications like twitter analysis and sales performance evaluation are also flourishing.

Recommender systems are designed to help the user in finding the most interesting and valuable information for them (Resnick & Varian, 1993). Content based filtering and collaborative filtering (CF) are the two types of recommendation systems. In content based filtering the Recommendation System(RS) maintains a user profile pertaining to the items user has liked before. A separate metadata pertaining to the all the items is separately maintained. The RS tries to find item having similar attributes to the user profile and predicts the likeable items for the user using the same. On the other hand, collaborative filtering selects items for users based on the similarity between the user and other users, eliminating the problem of overspecialization.

This paper presents a rigorous literature survey that contains a comprehensive overview of recent research trends, advances, and challenges in the field of opinion mining and Collaborative Filtering(CF). The goal of the study is to make students and researchers access to the latest works in this field by providing them ample of knowledge. In this survey, we have reviewed some fifty papers on opinion mining and Collaborative filtering in different applications and domains.

This paper has been classified into different sections. The research design of this paper will be elucidated in the section 2. The classification framework is presented in section 3. The classification of papers along different specifications is discussed in section 4. The analysis based on the classification of articles is discussed in section 5. The implication of research is shown in section 6 and in the final section, the conclusion is drawn by mentioning its immense possibility for further research.

LITERATURE REVIEW

A lot of authors have written about opinion mining in different papers. Some of the authors have used machine learning algorithms while some have incorporated Natural Language Processing (NLP) techniques. Turney (2002) performed the classification at document level using unsupervised machine learning technique. Liu (2012) implemented the classification of reviews at document level.

Zhang et al. (2011) classified reviews of restaurants using supervised machine learning techniques like Naïve Bayes and SVM (Support Vector Machines). Kang et al. (2011) classified the reviews based on traditional machine learning techniques. Tsytsarau et al. (2011) focused on the subjectivity by classifying the sentence into objective and subjective.

(Hu and Liu, 2004) first described about the aspect or feature level opinion mining. In this, the opinions are mined according to the features of the product or services. Decker and Trusov (2010) have also focused on aspect based opinion mining in different domains. Pang et al. (2002) identifies the opinion words to find the orientation of the sentence on a feature.

A statistical approach for opinion mining has been discussed in Coling (2010). Miller (1995) elucidated a dictionary based approach while a semantic based approach has been discussed in Ding et al. (2008). Hannon et al., (2010) gave architecture for giving recommendation to Twitter users based on CF techniques

RESEARCH DESIGN

Sentiment analysis is the field of study which has enormously gained huge popularity in a few years. It is a diverse discipline on which extensive research work is being done. This field is being tempted by a lot of researchers because of its wide applications in different domains. This rigorous work comprises different research journals, conference proceedings and case studies. Different papers in the publication limit from 2008 to 2015 were reviewed manually by the authors. The various online publishers which were selected for an extensive catalogue of the research on opinion mining and recommendation systems are IEEE/IEEE Electronic Library, Science Direct, ACM Digital, IGI Global and Inderscience.

The linguistics 'Sentiment Analysis' or 'opinion mining' was searched in choosing the articles. Every paper was comprehensively reviewed and then classified according to the Sentiment Analysis and the Opinion mining. The articles were segregated individually by the authors. The article was decided whether to include in the final set if any disagreement in the selection of the papers was demarcated.

Classification Framework of Opinion Mining in Recommendation System

The framework is classified into different levels of Sentiment analysis. The framework is shown in Figure 1. It shows the tasks involved in these levels and the approaches or techniques required in the respective levels. The framework proposes meaningful research questions by comprehending the past research. The potential of SA in different applications is moderately being unmasked. The main approaches that have been inquested in this paper are namely:

1. Sentiment Classification
2. Subjectivity Analysis
3. Lexicon based
4. Statistical based
5. Dictionary based
6. Semantic based

These are the approaches used in different levels of OM. The techniques which are examined in this study are:

1. Naïve Bayesian (NB) Classification
2. Support Vector Machine (SVM)
3. Natural Language Processing (NLP)

Figure 1. Classification framework based on the OM for recommendation

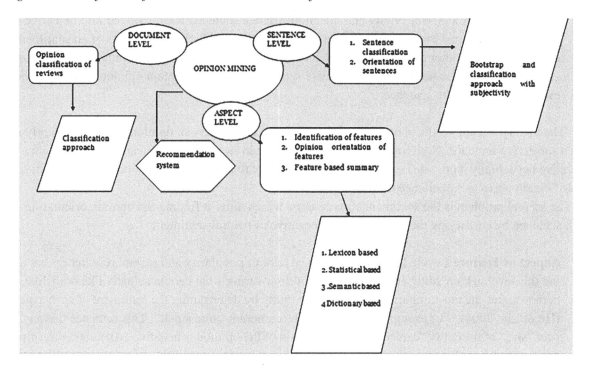

4.   Point Wise Mutual Information (PMI)
5.   Multiclass SVM

The framework shown in Figure 1 mainly presents the different tasks involved in OM. The framework mentions the remarkable achievements of this diverse. This framework is then comprehensively discussed in different approaches mentioned in the framework. The Recommendation system comes into play after the task of opinion mining is completed.

CF is a technique which recommends items to the user based on the users' ratings.Conventional CF techniques depend on numerical ratings which can be sometimes missing. Therefore, opinion is extracted from the user reviews by opinion mining . This opinion is used for recommendation using a CF technique.

Levels of Opinion Mining

Opinion mining can be broadly divided into three levels-Document, sentence and Aspect or Feature level.The further explanation of these topics is given below stating the use of these in different ways:

- **Document Level:** In this level, the whole document is classified either into positive or negative orientation (Liu, 2002). The assumption considered in this level is that it is being assumed that the whole document consists of an opinion about the same or single entity. For example-a review about a particular product whether it is a camera, phone etc.. In such types, opinion about the particular product is calculated in terms of either positive or negative as a whole . However, it will not be applying for a blog post because in such posts the opinion holder compares different products with each other.

- **Sentence Level:** This level is closely related to Subjectivity Analysis by Tsytsarau et al. (2011). In this the first task is subjectivity classification where a sentence is categorized into objective or subjective sentence. Objective sentences are those sentences which contain facts or no sentiments explicitly. On the other hand, subjective sentences are those which contain opinion or sentiments . However, it must be noted that the objective sentences may also contain opinions implicitly. For example- consider the sentence

"The battery backup of the phone is very nice". This sentence has an opinion defined explicitly so it is a subjective sentence. Now consider "The screen broke in two days". It appears that the sentence is objective but actually it provides an important opinion about the screen of the phone. Thus, subjectivity classification poses as a challenge task.

The second problem is the sentiment classification which aims at finding the opinion orientation of each sentence by classifying them into positive, negative or neutral sentiment.

- **Aspect or Feature Level:** This level has gained a lot of popularity and several researchers are using this level in their study. It is the best way of discovering what people actually like or dislike. It demonstrates the most important features of an entity by determining the sentiment of each aspect (Hu & Liu, 2004) . For example-"The size of the camera is quite small". This sentence has an aspect "size" of the entity "camera". The orientation of the opinion is negative . An another example can be cited from the movie domain as" I didn't like the storyline yet the movie was scintillating". In this, although the orientation of "storyline" is" negative" but the "movie" has an orientation "positive". Feature level allows to classify different features into different polarities-mainly positive and negative.

Approaches in OM

1. **Sentiment Classification:** In this approach, the whole document will be classified into two groups-positive or negative. It is the technique of classifying the polarity with supervised learning. It is basically a text classification approach so any supervised learning approach can be pertained to it. Example-Naïve Bayes classification algorithm, Support Vector Machines etc.
   a. Naïve Bayes Algorithm

   Suppose the document d of the class c has to be derived using the Naive Bayes (NB) classifier. This can be achieved by using Bayes' rule, (Pang et al.,2002)

   $P(c \mid d) = P(c)P(d \mid c) \, P(d)$

   To calculate the term $P(d \mid c)$, Naive Bayes decomposes it by finding the conditional probability given d' s class.

   $P_{NB}(c/d) := (P(c)(\pi_{i=1}^{m} p(f_i/c)^{n_i(d)}))/p(d)$ (Pang et al.,2002)
   b. Support Vector Machine

   It is an another technique of text classification problem for classifying the sentiments at document level. The main task is to search for a hyperplane constituted by w vector which classifies the document vectors in two different classes possibly positive and negative for which the margin, is quite large . let $c_j \in \{1, -1\}$ (corresponding to positive and negative) be the correct class document d_i, the solution can be written as $w := \sum_j \alpha_j c_j d_j$ where the $\alpha_j >= 0$ and is obtained by solving a dual optimization problem(Pang et al.,2002).

Those d_j such that α_j is greater than zero are called support vectors, since they are the only document vectors contributing to ~w. Classification of test instances consists simply of determining which side of w's hyperplane they fall on.

2. **Subjectivity Analysis:** Another technique that arises at the sentence level is subjectivity classification. There are two types of sentences –objective and subjective. The objective sentences are the factual ones and subjective sentences are those which express opinions, sentiments and emotions .The issue of subjectivity classification can be handled by two recent bootstrapping algorithms which have been used to impart different patterns. These two algorithms are Meta bootstrapping and a semantic lexicon using unannotated texts, and seed words as input.(Wiebe et al, 2003)

3. **Lexicon Based:** Opinion words are the words for which orientation is measured . Basically, there are two types of opinion words-positive and negative. Opinion lexicon is the group of words or idioms for which polarity is found. There are some Manual methods for calculation of orientation which are a little cumbersome so various automated methods are employed for this. Two automated methods are described below.

   a. **Dictionary Based:** In dictionary based approach, SentiWordNet and WordNet (Miller & Fellbaum, 1991) are used to find the polarity of the words by finding the synonyms and antonyms of the words whose orientation is already found. The limitation is that it can't find polarity for those words which are domain specific. For example-Product based documents.

   b. **Corpus Based:** In this, polarity of the opinion word is calculated using the context or the domain of the word. Different rules for conjunction are applied to find the orientation of the opinion word. For example-"The phone is excellent and cost-friendly." In this, it is assumed that the orientation of the opinion word "cost –friendly" is positive . The reason for this is that it is conjoined with opinion word 'excellent' which is a positive word using 'and' conjunction. Hence, it removes the anomaly of the dictionary based approach by finding the orientation of word using different conjunction rules like 'but', or', 'either-or' etc

4. **Statistical Based:**This method uses the formula for calculating the orientation and feature selection which are based on the probability of the occurrence of that word in the review or document. There are three statistical approaches PMI(Point Wise Mutual Information),Chi-Square and LSI (Latent Semantic Indexing).The method PMI will be discussed in detail.

   a. **PMI Method:**It is generally seen that two words occurring together frequently in a domain or corpus are likely to have the same orientation. The relative co-occurrence of frequency of an unknown word with known word can be calculated using PMI.(Wu & Wen, 2010)

   PMI(c,positive)=log (P(c,positive)/(p(c)p(positive)))

   PMI(c,negative)=log (P(c,negative)/(p(c)p(negative)))

   SO(c)=PMI(c,positive) – PMI(c,negative)

   Where P(c,positive) is the probability of a character c in the positive category ;p(c) is the probability of the character c in the sentiment lexicon ;p(positive) is the probability of the positive category in the sentiment lexicon.PMI(c,negative) has the similar meaning. (Wu & Wen, 2010)

5. **Semantic Based Approach:** In this method, the orientation of the word is found by finding the similarity between two words. The words which are semantically closest are given the same polarity.

Recommendation Systems

The recommendation system helps in suggesting the users about the different services and products based on the users' ratings. The two types of recommendation systems are content based filtering and CF. CF can be divided into three types-

1. **Memory Based CF**: It is the traditional way of CF by observing the rating matrix. It predicts the preferences of users based on related preferences of other users. It has its limitation that it recommends the same thing again and doesn't recommend anything new.(Resnick et al.,1994). It is not scalable for high volumes of datasets and its performance decreases when data are sparse.
2. **Model Based CF:** This model overcomes the limitations of memory based CF. It is based on the model which can be a data mining or machine learning algorithm. In Model-based approach, data mining or machine learning techniques are used to develop models to search patterns based on training set. Test data will use these models to make predictions . Model-Based CF is classified based on the algorithm used.(Kim and Kumoh, 2004) Model based has its own advantage such as- better address the sparsity, improve prediction performance, and give an intuitive rationale for the recommendations. The limitations are that the model building is a little expensive.
3. **Hybrid CF**: CF and content-based filtering methods are combined to make recommendation systems. It works in one of the following ways:
    a. Memory-Based and Model-Based CF techniques are combined together in a system to make recommendations.
    b. CF can be combined with Content-based systems to provide recommendations or predictions.
    c. Although it has a lot of advantages, but it has some shortcomings as well. It is expensive to implement and has increased complexity.

Applications of Collaborative Filtering in Opinion Mining

- **E-Commerce:** E-commerce website, such as Amazon and Flipkart make use of CF techniques to suggest items to the user which are both unknown and interesting to the user at the same time.
- **Social Network:** CF techniques provide tools for social network systems for finding the similar user-profiles. Hannon, et al., (2010) gave architecture for giving a recommendation to Twitter users for whom to follow based on CF techniques. It provides opportunity to find mood of users by finding the opinion from the social text.
- **Mobile Recommender System:** Mobile RS refers to the system, recommending things for a mobile-user. With advent of technology, Smartphone s and other portable digital devices equipped with Global positioning System (GPS) and internet have become part of everyday life. The user location data can be thus be analyzed with CF techniques for making recommendations based on a geographical neighborhood of the user.
- **Web Search:** Web search engines index the websites and retrieve the results matching the keyword pertaining to which user wants related items. There may be many matching websites pertaining to the keyword, the decision to be made is which of these websites should be recommended to the user or in what order they should be shown.

- **E-Learning:** CF techniques help to identify the active user as a part of the class, he belongs to (teacher, student, and novice) and then make provide adaptive course material and recommendations accordingly (Bobadilla, et al., 2009) in E-learning.
- **Personalized Recommendations:** Online RS which provides recommendations to user for a range of content makes use of CF techniques to give recommendations to user personalized to their likes and tastes pertaining to a particular genre. Table1 shows different methods proposed by different researchers (Medhat et al.,2014).

Analysis Based on the Classification of Articles

Classification of Papers According to the Year of Publication

The classification of the articles related to the field of OM by the Year of Publication is shown .The graph clearly indicates that the number of articles published is being increasing corresponding to the increase

Table 1. A review of application of different approaches in opinion

Reference	Year	Approach	Algorithm	Types of Level	Features/Data Scope
Fang and Zhan	2015	Lexicon based	NLP	Feature	Product reviews
Petz et al.	2014	Lexicon based	NLP	Feature	Social media channel
Martinez et al	2014	Dictionary based	NLP	Feature	Movie reviews
Marrese- Taylor et al	2014	dictionary based	NLP	feature	Tourism review
Cruz et al [64]	2013	Classification	Classifiers	Sentence	headphones, hotel, cars
Ghiassi et al	2013	Classification	SVM,NN	Sentence	Music
Chenlo et al	2013	Corpus based	semantic	Feature	Blog posts
Yu et al.	2013	Statistical	PMI based	Feature	Stock news
Pai et al.	2013	Corpus based	Semantic	Feature	Fast food reviews
Ptaszynski et al.	2013	Lexicon based	NLP	Feature	Narratives
Li et al.	2013	Classification	SVM	Document	Tweets
Rui et al.	2013	Classification	NB,SVM	Document	Movie review, tweets
Moraes et al.	2013	Classification	SVM,ANN	Document	Movie, camera, reviews
Reyes and Rosso	2013	Corpus based	Semantic	Feature	News, articles
Wogenstein et al.	2013	Lexicon based	NLP	feature	Insurance domain
Van de camp et al.	2012	Classification	SVM	Document	Relationship, biography
Lane Peter et al.	2012	Classification	KNN	Document	Media
Balahur et al.	2012	Classification	SVM,lexicon base	Feature	Emotion corpus
Walker et al.	2012	Classification	NB,SVM	Feature	2 sided debate
Keshtkar et al.	2012	Corpus based	Corpus based	feature	Blog data
Boldrini et al.	2012	Lexicon based	NLP	Feature	Blogs
Min and Park	2012	Lexicon based	NLP	Feature	Product reviews
Zhang et al.	2012	statistical based	PMI, semantic	Feature	Product reviews
Gupta et al.	2012	Corpus based	Lexicon	Feature	News
Kang et al.	2012	Classification	NB,SVM	Feature	Restaurant reviews
Hu et al.	2011	Statistical	PMI based	Document	Book reviews
Zirn et al.	2011	Corpus based	Semantic	Feature	Product reviews
Heerschop et al.	2011	Corpus based	Semantic	Feature	Movie review
Zhou et al.	2011	Corpus based	Semantic	Feature	Chinese training data
Fan and Chang	2011	classification	SVM	document	Buyers web pages
Chin and Tseng	2011	classification	Multiclass SVM	document	Digital cameras
Cao et al.	2011	lexicon based	Semantic, LSA	feature	Software program feedback
Zhao et al.	2010	classification	NB,SVM	document	camera review
Bai X	2010	classification	NB,SVM	document	movie review
Neviarouskaya et al.	2010	corpus based	Semantic	feature	personal stories
Lu et al.	2010	corpus based	semantic	feature	web pages

(Adopted from Medhat et al.,2014)

in the year. This implies that this topic for research is emerging widespread in different domains due its different applications and challenges. The Figure 2 exemplifies this in an easy way.

Distribution of Papers According to the Levels of OM

The papers were distributed on the basis of the different levels of OM .These levels are Document Level, Sentence Level and Aspect Level. It is important to understand the classification of articles based on the different levels of OM to provide an overall view of the growing trend in the research area. It is being implied that Feature or Aspect level has taken a big leap to the other levels of OM. Thus, this level is becoming popular in the recent 21st century. The Figure 3 illustrates it in a different way

Figure 2. CLASSIFICATION of papers according to the year of publication

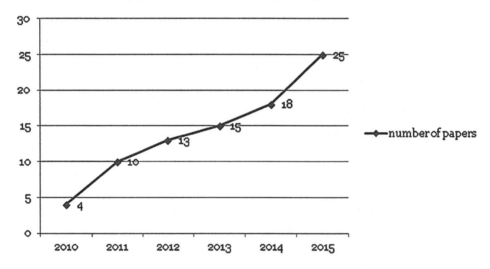

Figure 3. Distribution of papers according to the levels of OM

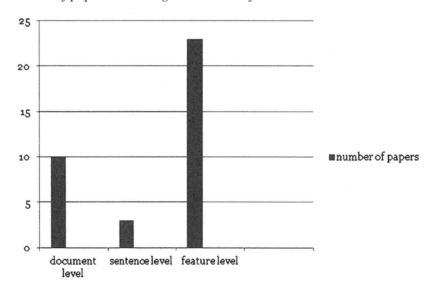

INFERENCE OF RESEARCH

1. The extensive research is going on in the field of Sentiment Analysis in different application areas like elections and stock market.
2. It is evident from our study that the level of OM which attracts the most researchers is an aspect or Feature level.
3. It can also be implied from our research that although different techniques can be used for Sentiment Analysis, NLP has emerged to be the hottest OM technique.
4. Sentiment Analysis can be combined with different fields like collaborative filtering to give an efficient recommendation system.
5. It can be seen from the research that OM is not restricted to a single domain but is predominant among different new domains like Tourism and News.
6. The value of sentiment measured can provide valuable advancements in both the personal and corporate view.

LIMITATION

1. The main limitation of the research is that the various papers related to the different levels of opinion mining are limited to a few authors.
2. It was tried to cover all the available papers of the mentioned authors, but we cannot claim encompassing research as there may be some other techniques and applications available for our study.
3. A lot of unusual opinion mining techniques and algorithms have not been touched as they don't fit with the three levels of opinion mining
4. In this study, the application of Opinion mining has not been discussed related to the papers published in non-English languages.
5. The introduction and abstract of the papers are read where a comprehensive study could not be possible and conclusions are drawn from it.

CONCLUSION AND FUTURE RESEARCH

It is quite clear from this research that Opinion Mining is an ongoing field that has attracted a lot of researchers and academicians in the recent times. The classification by the author will make new avenues for the researchers to gain insight knowledge about the subject. The existing research will be beneficial for the other authors to implement their requirements in an easy manner . The authors had identified different techniques of opinion mining, which are practiced in different applications according to the three levels of the Opinion Mining .The future work which can be done is as follows:-

*   Research on the techniques which do not cover the three levels of opinion mining.
*   Exploration of other applications can also be included.
*   The existing work will be compared with the new and improved technology to prove our work.

REFERNCES

Balahur, A., Hermida, J. M., & Montoyo, A. (2012). Detecting implicit expressions of emotion in text: A comparative analysis. *Decision Support Systems*, *53*(4), 742–753. doi:10.1016/j.dss.2012.05.024

Boldrini, E., Balahur, A., Martínez-Barco, P., & Montoyo, A. (2012). Using EmotiBlog to annotate and analyse subjectivity in the new textual genres. *Data Mining and Knowledge Discovery*, *25*(3), 603–634. doi:10.1007/s10618-012-0259-9

Cao, Q., Duan, W., & Gan, Q. (2011). Exploring determinants of voting for the "helpfulness" of online user reviews: A text mining approach. *Decision Support Systems*, *5*(2), 511–521. doi:10.1016/j.dss.2010.11.009

Chen, C. C., & Tseng, Y. D. (2011). Quality evaluation of product reviews using an information quality framework. *Decision Support Systems*, *50*(4), 755–768. doi:10.1016/j.dss.2010.08.023

Cruz, F. L., Troyano, J. A., Enríquez, F., Ortega, F. J., & Vallejo, C. G. (2013). Long autonomy or long delay?'The importance of domain in opinion mining. *Expert Systems with Applications*, *40*(8), 3174–3184. doi:10.1016/j.eswa.2012.12.031

Ding, X., Liu, B., & Philip, S. Y. (2008). A Holistic Lexicon-Based Approach to Opinion Mining.*Proceedings of the first ACM International Conference on Web search and Data Mining (WSDM'08)*,California, USA (pp. 231-240).

Fan, T. K., & Chang, C. H. (2011). Blogger-centric contextual advertising. *Expert Systems with Applications*, *38*(3), 1777–1788. doi:10.1016/j.eswa.2010.07.105

Fang, X., & Zhan, J. (2015). Sentiment analysis using product review data. *Journal of Big Data*, *2*(1), 1–14. doi:10.1186/s40537-015-0015-2

Ghiassi, M., Skinner, J., & Zimbra, D. (2013). Twitter brand sentiment analysis: A hybrid system using n-gram analysis and dynamic artificial neural network. *Expert Systems with Applications*, *40*(16), 6266–6282. doi:10.1016/j.eswa.2013.05.057

Gupta, S. K., Phung, D., Adams, B., & Venkatesh, S. (2013). Regularized nonnegative shared subspace learning. *Data Mining and Knowledge Discovery*, *26*(1), 57–97. doi:10.1007/s10618-011-0244-8

Hannon, J., Bennett, M., & Smyth, B. (2010).Recommending twitter users to follow using contentand collaborative filtering approaches.*Proceedings of the fourth ACM conference on Recommender systems* (pp. 199-206).

He, Y., & Zhou, D. (2011). Self-training from labeled features for sentiment analysis. *Information Processing & Management*, *47*(4), 606–616. doi:10.1016/j.ipm.2010.11.003

Heerschop, B., Goossen, F., Hogenboom, A., Frasincar, F., Kaymak, U., & de Jong, F. (2011, October). Polarity analysis of texts using discourse structure.*Proceedings of the 20th ACM international conference on Information and knowledge management* (pp. 1061-1070). ACM doi:10.1145/2063576.2063730

Hu, N., Bose, I., Koh, N. S., & Liu, L. (2012). Manipulation of online reviews: An analysis of ratings, readability, and sentiments. *Decision Support Systems*, *52*(3), 674–684. doi:10.1016/j.dss.2011.11.002

Kang, H., Yoo, S. J., & Han, D. (2009). Accessing positive and negative online opinions. In *Universal Access in Human-Computer Interaction* (pp. 359–368). Applications and Services.

Kang, H., Yoo, S. J., & Han, D. (2012). Senti-lexicon and improved Naïve Bayes algorithms for sentiment analysis of restaurant reviews. *Expert Systems with Applications, 39*(5), 6000–6010. doi:10.1016/j.eswa.2011.11.107

Khan, K., Baharudin, B., Khan, A., & Ullah, A. (2014). Mining opinion components from unstructured reviews: A review. *Journal of King Saud University-Computer and Information Sciences, 26*(3), 258–275. doi:10.1016/j.jksuci.2014.03.009

Kim, B. M., & Kumoh, Q. L. (2004). Probabilistic Model Estimation for Collaborative Filtering Based on Items Attributes. *Proc. of the IEEE/WIC/ACM International Conference on Web Intelligence* (pp. 185-191).

Kontopoulos, E., Berberidis, C., Dergiades, T., & Bassiliades, N. (2013). Ontology-based sentiment analysis of twitter posts. *Expert Systems with Applications, 40*(10), 4065–4074. doi:10.1016/j.eswa.2013.01.001

Lane, P. C., Clarke, D., & Hender, P. (2012). On developing robust models for favourability analysis: Model choice, feature sets and imbalanced data. *Decision Support Systems, 53*(4), 712–718. doi:10.1016/j.dss.2012.05.028

Li, Y. M., & Li, T. Y. (2013). Deriving market intelligence from microblogs. *Decision Support Systems, 55*(1), 206–217. doi:10.1016/j.dss.2013.01.023

Liu, B. (2012). Sentiment analysis and opinion mining. *Synthesis Lectures on Human Language Technologies, 5*(1), 1–167. doi:10.2200/S00416ED1V01Y201204HLT016

Lu, C. Y., Lin, S. H., Liu, J. C., Cruz-Lara, S., & Hong, J. S. (2010). Automatic event-level textual emotion sensing using mutual action histogram between entities. *Expert Systems with Applications, 37*(2), 1643–1653. doi:10.1016/j.eswa.2009.06.099

Marrese-Taylor, E., Velásquez, J. D., & Bravo-Marquez, F. (2014). A novel deterministic approach for aspect-based opinion mining in tourism products reviews. *Expert Systems with Applications, 41*(17), 7764–7775. doi:10.1016/j.eswa.2014.05.045

Medhat, W., Hassan, A., & Korashy, H. (2014). Sentiment analysis algorithms and applications: A survey. *Ain Shams Engineering Journal, 5*(4), 1093–1113. doi:10.1016/j.asej.2014.04.011

Miller, G. A., & Fellbaum, C. (1991). Semantic networks of English. *Cognition, 41*(1), 197–229. doi:10.1016/0010-0277(91)90036-4 PMID:1790654

Min, H. J., & Park, J. C. (2012). Identifying helpful reviews based on customer's mentions about experiences. *Expert Systems with Applications, 39*(15), 11830–11838. doi:10.1016/j.eswa.2012.01.116

Moraes, R., Valiati, J. F., & Neto, W. P. G. (2013). Document-level sentiment classification: An empirical comparison between SVM and ANN. *Expert Systems with Applications, 40*(2), 621–633. doi:10.1016/j.eswa.2012.07.059

Neviarouskaya, A., Prendinger, H., & Ishizuka, M. (2010). Recognition of affect, judgment, and appreciation in text. *Proceedings of the 23rd International Conference on Computational Linguistics* (pp. 806-814).

Pai, M. Y., Chu, H. C., Wang, S. C., & Chen, Y. M. (2013). Electronic word of mouth analysis for service experience. *Expert Systems with Applications, 40*(6), 1993–2006. doi:10.1016/j.eswa.2012.10.024

Pang, B., Lee, L., & Vaithyanathan, S. (2002, July). Thumbs up?: sentiment classification using machine learning techniques.*Proceedings of the ACL-02 conference on Empirical methods in natural language processing* (pp. 79-86). doi:10.3115/1118693.1118704

Peñalver-Martinez, I., Garcia-Sanchez, F., Valencia-Garcia, R., Rodríguez-García, M. Á., Moreno, V., Fraga, A., & Sánchez-Cervantes, J. L. (2014). Feature-based opinion mining through ontologies. *Expert Systems with Applications, 41*(13), 5995–6008. doi:10.1016/j.eswa.2014.03.022

Petz, G., Karpowicz, M., Fürschuß, H., Auinger, A., Stříteský, V., & Holzinger, A. (2014). Computational approaches for mining user's opinions on the Web 2.0. *Information Processing & Management, 50*(6), 899–908. doi:10.1016/j.ipm.2014.07.005

Ptaszynski, M., Dokoshi, H., Oyama, S., Rzepka, R., Kurihara, M., Araki, K., & Momouchi, Y. (2013). Affect analysis in context of characters in narratives. *Expert Systems with Applications, 40*(1), 168–176. doi:10.1016/j.eswa.2012.07.025

Resnick, P., Iacovou, N., Sushak, M., Bergstrom, P., & Riedl, J. (1994).Grouplens: An Open Architecture for Collaborative Filtering of Netnews.*Proc. of Computer Supported Collaborative Work Conf.* (pp. 175-186). doi:10.1145/192844.192905

Reyes, A., & Rosso, P. (2012). Making objective decisions from subjective data: Detecting irony in customer reviews. *Decision Support Systems, 53*(.4), 754-760.

Riloff, E., & Wiebe, J. (2003, July). Learning extraction patterns for subjective expressions.*Proceedings of the 2003 conference on Empirical methods in natural language processing* (pp. 105-112). doi:10.3115/1119355.1119369

Rui, H., Liu, Y., & Whinston, A. (2013). Whose and what chatter matters? The effect of tweets on movie sales. *Decision Support Systems, 55*(4), 863–870. doi:10.1016/j.dss.2012.12.022

Tsytsarau, M., & Palpanas, T. (2012). Survey on mining subjective data on the web. *Data Mining and Knowledge Discovery, 24*(3), 478–514. doi:10.1007/s10618-011-0238-6

Van De Camp, M., & Van Den Bosch, A. (2012). The socialist network. *Decision Support Systems, 53*(4), 761–769. doi:10.1016/j.dss.2012.05.031

Walker, M. A., Anand, P., Abbott, R., Tree, J. E. F., Martell, C., & King, J. (2012). That is your evidence?: Classifying stance in online political debate. *Decision Support Systems, 53*(4), 719–729. doi:10.1016/j.dss.2012.05.032

Wogenstein, F., Drescher, J., Reinel, D., Rill, S., & Scheidt, J. (2013, August). Evaluation of an algorithm for aspect-based opinion mining using a lexicon-based approach.*Proceedings of the Second International Workshop on Issues of Sentiment Discovery and Opinion Mining*. doi:10.1145/2502069.2502074

Wu, Y., & Wen, M. (2010, August). Disambiguating dynamic sentiment ambiguous adjectives.*Proceedings of the 23rd International Conference on Computational Linguistics* (pp. 1191-1199). Association for Computational Linguistic.

Yan-Yan, Z., Bing, Q., & Ting, L. (2010). Integrating intra-and inter-document evidences for improving sentence sentiment classification. *Acta Automatica Sinica*, *36*(10), 1417–1425.

Ye, Q., Zhang, Z., & Law, R. (2009). Sentiment classification of online reviews to travel destination by supervised machine learning approaches. *Expert Systems with Applications*, 2009, 1–9.

Yu, L. C., Wu, J. L., Chang, P. C., & Chu, H. S. (2013). Using a contextual entropy model to expand emotion words and their intensity for the sentiment classification of stock market news. *Knowledge-Based Systems*, *41*, 89–97. doi:10.1016/j.knosys.2013.01.001

Zhang, W., Xu, H., & Wan, W. (2012). Weakness Finder: Find product weakness from Chinese reviews by using aspects based sentiment analysis. *Expert Systems with Applications*, *39*(11), 10283–10291. doi:10.1016/j.eswa.2012.02.166

Zhou, L., Li, B., Gao, W., Wei, Z., & Wong, K. F. (2011, July). Unsupervised discovery of discourse relations for eliminating intra-sentence polarity ambiguities.*Proceedings of the Conference on Empirical Methods in Natural Language Processing* (pp. 162-171). Association for Computational Linguistics

Zirn, C., Niepert, M., Stuckenschmidt, H., & Strube, M. (2011, November). *Fine-Grained Sentiment Analysis with Structural Features* (pp. 336–344). IJCNLP.

ADDITIONAL READING

Amatriain, X., Lathia, N., Pujol, J. M., Kwak, H., & Oliver, N. (2009, July). The wisdom of the few: a collaborative filtering approach based on expert opinions from the web.*Proceedings of the 32nd international ACM SIGIR conference on Research and development in information retrieval* (pp. 532-539). ACM. doi:10.1145/1571941.1572033

Leung, C. W., Chan, S. C., & Chung, F. L. (2006, August). Integrating collaborative filtering and sentiment analysis: A rating inference approach.*Proceedings of the ECAI 2006 workshop on recommender systems* (pp. 62-66).

Pappas, N., & Popescu-Belis, A. (2016). Adaptive sentiment-aware one-class collaborative filtering. *Expert Systems with Applications*, *43*, 23–41. doi:10.1016/j.eswa.2015.08.035

Resnick, P., Iacovou, N., Suchak, M., Bergstrom, P., & Riedl, J. (1994, October). GroupLens: an open architecture for collaborative filtering of netnews.*Proceedings of the 1994 ACM conference on Computer supported cooperative work* (pp. 175-186). ACM. doi:10.1145/192844.192905

Sarwar, B., Karypis, G., Konstan, J., & Riedl, J. (2001, April). Item-based collaborative filtering recommendation algorithms.*Proceedings of the 10th international conference on World Wide Web* (pp. 285-295). ACM.

Su, Q., Xu, X., Guo, H., Guo, Z., Wu, X., Zhang, X., & Su, Z. et al. (2008, April). Hidden sentiment association in chinese web opinion mining.*Proceedings of the 17th international conference on World Wide Web* (pp. 959-968). ACM. doi:10.1145/1367497.1367627

KEY TERMS AND DEFINITIONS

Collaborative Filtering: It is a technique used by recommender system.

Data Mining: It is a process to extract patterns and knowledge from large amounts of data.

Machine Learning: It is a field of computer science that deals with the learning theory in artificial intelligence and construction of algorithms for making predictions on data.

Natural Language Processing: It is a field of computer science that deals with the interaction between human language and computer.

Opinion Mining: It is the field of study that analyzes people's opinions, sentiments, evaluations, attitudes, and emotions of different entities.

Recommendation System: It is an information filtering system that predicts the rating of an item.

Chapter 11

Combining User Co-Ratings and Social Trust for Collaborative Recommendation:
A Data Analytics Approach

Sheng-Jhe Ke
National Sun Yat-Sen University, Taiwan

Wei-Po Lee
National Sun Yat-Sen University, Taiwan

ABSTRACT

Traditional collaborative filtering recommendation methods calculate similarity between users to find the most similar neighbors for a particular user and take into account their opinions to predict item ratings. Though these methods have some advantages, however, they encounter difficulties in dealing with the problems of cold start users and data sparsity. To overcome these difficulties, researchers have proposed to consider social context information in the process of determining similar neighbors. In this chapter, we present a data analytics approach that combines user preference and social trust for making better collaborative recommendation. The proposed approach regards the collaborative recommendation as a classification task. It includes a data analysis procedure to explore the target dataset in terms of user similarity and trust relationship, and a data classification procedure to extract data features and build up a model accordingly. A series of experiments are conducted for performance evaluation. The results show that this approach can be used to enhance the recommendation performance in an adaptive way for different datasets without an iterative parameter-tuning process.

INTRODUCTION

Recommender systems have been advocated in different service domains for years (Adomavicius & Tuzhilin, 2005; Bobadilla, et al., 2013; Lu, et al., 2015; Ricci, et al., 2011). Traditional recommender systems address two entities for application services: the users and the items. Initially, the systems collect some ratings specified by users. Based on these rating records, these systems estimate the rating

DOI: 10.4018/978-1-5225-0489-4.ch011

function R: *Users* $\times$ *Items* $\rightarrow$ *Ratings*. Once the utility function R is constructed, the system can predict the rating of unfamiliar items and recommend the highest-rating ones to users. Various methods have been developed to find effective solutions that require less computational effort. These methods range from content-based user modeling to group-based collaboration (that is, collaborative filtering or CF). Generally speaking, the group-based approach is more efficient and effective than content-based user modeling (Bobadilla, et al., 2013; Koren & Bell, 2011).

Many collaborative recommender systems have tried to predict the rating of an item for a particular user based on how other users previously rated the same item. Algorithms for collaborative recommendations can be grouped into two classes in general: memory-based and model-based methods. Memory-based algorithms (also called neighborhood or k-nearest neighbor methods) are heuristics that make rating predictions based on the entire collection of items previously rated by the users. The neighborhood methods are popular because they are intuitive and relatively simple to implement. Moreover, these neighborhood methods offer useful and important properties: explicit explanation of the recommendations and easy inclusion of new ratings. Because our major goal in this work is to investigate how to incorporate different types of information and to analyze their effects on recommendation, we thus choose this easy-to-implement approach in our experiments.

Standard CF methods calculate user similarity to find neighbors and their opinions to make decisions. Though similarity-based neighborhood methods have some advantages, there also occur several issues to consider. For example, if the interactions among the neighbors are not considered, and some users have rated only a very small number of items (i.e., the cold-start problem), such information is not enough for making helpful recommendation. Also this method has a problem of sparsity: in real-world applications, most items are not widely rated by users. The latter problem may decline the recommendation performance (Aha, 2008; Guo, et al., 2014). To overcome these problems, researchers have suggested the inclusion of contextual information for building more accurate recommender systems, for example (Chen, et. al., 2012; Chen, et al., 2014; Lee and Lee, 2014; Ma, et al., 2011). One kind of contextual information, the social context information collectable from online communities (i.e., social networks), is useful and important for recognizing the users' situation that can influence his decision (Qian, et al., 2014; Samah, et al., 2012; Yang, et. al. 2013). Social network theory suggests that the positions of users in a web of relationships influence their access to resources, friends, and information. Social influence can be used to create intention for people to consume a product so that everyone's social relationship is one of the key factors for predicting the potential customer intention. Researchers have indicated that the relationships among friends and friends of friends within a social network are crucial when referencing trustworthy and reliable information (Golbeck & Hendler, 2006; Jamali & Ester, 2009; Ray & Mahantirt, 2010).

In this work, we present a data analytics approach that combines user preference and social trust for making better collaborative recommendation. The user preference here means the co-rating-based similarity measurement between users, and the social trust means the trust relationships derived from the users (including direct specifications by the users and indirect inference obtained from the calculation of trust transitivity). The proposed approach regards the collaborative recommendation as a classification task. It includes two phases to improve the recommendation performance. In the first phase, a data analysis procedure is performed to explore the target dataset in terms of user similarity and trust relationship. Based on the results of data analysis, a neighborhood method is used to evaluate the effects of the similarity-based and trust-based neighbors for the available user-item rating records. The second phase is to train and to test a classification model. Different features (such as the variance of user ratings) extracted from the data analysis procedure are used to build up a model that can recognize which of the similarity-based neighbors or the trust-based neighbors is more suitable (i.e., to produce a more precise rating prediction) for a particular user-item record. A series of experiments are conducted for performance evaluation. The results show that our presented approach can obtain good results in more objective experimental conditions. It also shows that this approach can be used to enhance the recommendation performance in an adaptive way for different datasets without an iterative parameter-tuning procedure.

BACKGROUND AND RELATED WORKS

The most popular CF methods calculate similarity between users to find the most similar neighbors for a particular user and take into account their opinions to predict item ratings. That is, the value of the unknown rating $r_{u,i}$ for user u and item i is usually computed as an aggregate of the ratings of the top-k most similar users for the same item i. There are many methods to calculate the similarity among users (such as Cosine similarity and Euclidean distance), and one often used method is the Pearson correlation coefficient. The similarity between the two users u and v is defined as below:

$$Sim(u,v) = \frac{\sum_{i \in Ic}(r_{u,i} - \overline{r}_u)(r_{v,i} - \overline{r}_v)}{\sqrt{\sum_{i \in Ic}(r_{u,i} - \overline{r}_u)^2}\sqrt{\sum_{i \in Ic}(r_{v,i} - \overline{r}_v)^2}} \qquad (1)$$

In equation (1), $r_{u,i}$ is the rating of user u on item i; I_c is the set of items that users u and v have already rated (i.e., the co-rated items). $\overline{r}_u$ (or $\overline{r}_v$) is the average rating of user u (or user v) regarding all items he has rated. This coefficient is between 1 (when the preferences of both users are the same) and -1 (when their preferences are opposite); a value of zero means their preferences are not correlated. For user u, other users with the most similar preferences are chosen as a set of neighbors $Neig(u)$, and their collective opinions on a certain item m are used to predict whether u will like the item. The rating of the preference of a specific item m is defined as:

$$p_{u,m} = \frac{\sum_{v \in Neig(u)} Sim(u,v) \cdot r_{v,m}}{\sum_{v \in Neig(u)} Sim(u,v)} \qquad (2)$$

In this equation, $p_{u,m}$ represents the predictive rating of user u on item m; $r_{v,m}$ is the rating of user v who is a neighbor of user u.

Because user preferences are changing from time to time, this user-based approach must repeatedly calculate the similarity of different users in real time to consider the most up-to-date referring opinions. This calculation is computationally inefficient for a dataset that includes a large number of users. To overcome this problem, the item-based (item-item) model was proposed (Sarwar, et al., 2001) that measured the similarity between items (rather than users). In their work, the similarity measurement between two users was modified to two items. However, it is notable that the item similarity is not always available (depending on the dataset used) and the prediction performance is case-dependent, determined by the dataset used.

These neighborhood methods are popular because they are intuitive and relatively simple to implement. In addition, these neighborhood methods offer useful and important properties: explicit explanation of the recommendations and easy inclusion of new ratings. However, as indicated in the above section, standard neighborhood-based methods raise several concerns (i.e., cold-start and sparsity problems). These problems could affect the precision of the recommendation results. As mentioned above, social trust has been proposed to overcome the difficulties of the similarity-based CF method (Bernardes, et al., 2014, Ma, et al., 2011; O'Donovan & Smyth, 2005). It is clear that establishing a trust network among users can be helpful to the success of recommender systems. Some works have been carried out by eliciting trust values into collaborative recommender systems; they have improved the accuracy of predictions, offered more robustness against profile attacks, and tackled the problems of sparsity and cold start (Sherchan, et al., 2013; Yang, et al., 2014).

Trust information can be explicitly collected from users (i.e. specified directly by users themselves) or implicitly inferred from user behaviors. Using trust-enhanced recommendation, the system can ask the users to rate other users. In this way, a user can express his level of trust in another user he has interacted with. The system can then aggregate all the trust statements in a single trust networks. In such a network, users are represented as nodes and trusted neighbors are connected with each other by trust links (i.e., arcs). Because the trust relationship is not symmetric, the resulting network is thus directed. Figure 1 (left) shows an example of trust network in which each arc is specified by a particular user and an arc from node i to node j indicates that user i trusts user j. The above trust relationship can be further quantified to a numerical value representing the importance of each arc. That is, the strength of the link indicates the trustworthiness (degree of trust) between two users. Figure 1 (middle) presents an example of eliciting trust values for a network.

The most popular trust measurement in a trust network is Jaccard coefficient or its variants. Without losing generality, we explain the trust measurement modified from one useful example provided in (Samah, et al., 2012), which defined a normalized Jaccard coefficient as the weight of the link between two user nodes in the network. Here, the measurement describes the explicit trust value as:

Figure 1. The explicit trust network (left), the network with trust measurement (middle), and the network with implicit trust (right)

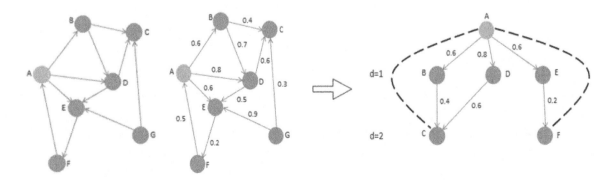

$$T_{u,v} = \frac{1}{\max T_{u,k}} \times \frac{max(|O(u) \cap O(v)|,\ 1)}{|O(u) \cup O(v)|},\ \ k \in O(u) \tag{3}$$

In the above equation, $T_{u,v}$ represents the degree of trust of user u to user v, and this value is between 0 and 1 inclusively. $maxT_{u,k}$ is the maximal degree of trust among user u to all his connected neighbors. $O(u)$ and $O(v)$ are the out-neighbors of nodes u and v, respectively (nodes that are linked from u to v). The conjunction used for two connected nodes u and v means to take into account their common out-neighbors. To preserve the explicit trust relationship indicated by the user, a lowest default value 1 is used in this equation.

Some studies have also indicated that a user is much more likely to believe a trusted user's statements rather than a stranger's. And recursively, because a trusted user will also trust his friends' opinions, trusts may propagate through the relationship network (Massa & Avesani, 2007; Guha, et al., 2004; Guo, et al., 2015a; Ziegler & Golbeck, 2015). Therefore, in addition to the explicit trust relationships specified by the users, algorithms have been developed to search for trustable users by exploiting trust propagation over the trust network. For example, in the work by Massa and Avesani (2007), the authors adopted a depth-first search to search indirect neighbors. They also used a pre-defined depth limit to constrain the search. Figure 1 (right) shows an example of using this method to find more neighbors (implicit ones). In this example network, the trust relationship between user A and user C (from A to C) does not exist in the original network. After calculating of trust propagation (with a search depth of 2), we can then construct a new arc between A and C using their connections with node B. This algorithm has been widely employed (and modified) to calculate the implicit trust value as below:

$$T_{u,v} = \frac{1}{d} \times \frac{\sum_{i \in \mathrm{Pred}(u)} T_{u,i} \times T_{i,v}}{\sum_{i \in \mathrm{Pred}} T_{u,i}} \tag{4}$$

In this equation, d is the search limit; $Pred(u)$ represents the predecessors of user u in the network. A propagation threshold is also specified for the search to determine if trust can be propagated through an intermediate node (such as B in the figure). For example, in the network shown in Figure 1, if the propagation threshold is 0, the implicit trust value of user A to user C is $1/2*[(0.6*0.4+0.8*0.6)/(0.6+0.8)]$ $= 0.257$.

To obtain the advantages of both similarity-based and trust-based strategies, some hybrid methods have been proposed, for example (Chen, et al., 2009; Golbeck, 2009; Lee & Brusilovsky, 2010; Qin, et al., 2014). In the hybrid recommender systems, there are two kinds of input information: the ratings matrix (representing all the ratings given by users to items), and the trust matrix (representing all the community trust statements). The output is a matrix of predicted ratings that users would assign to items. The focus is now on how to incorporate the two types of information to obtain the most promising results. The most popular technique is to aggregate the two measurements in one equation (e.g., a linear combination (Guo et al., 2015b)). In addition, some studies considered the combination of similarity and trust as an optimization problem and used the analytic hierarchy process (AHP) technique to solve it (e.g., (Li, et al., 2013)). Different from most of the present works in combining both similarity and trust for CF recommendation, we regard item recommendation as a classification task taking a data analytics prospective. We also adopt a learning method to build a model for data classification. The details are described in the following sections.

COMBINING USER SIMILARITY AND SOCIAL-TRUST FOR CF RECOMMENDATION

Overview of the Proposed Approach

To obtain better recommendation performance, this work presents a hybrid approach that considers recommendation as a classification task, and takes into account user similarity and social trust to train a model for data classification. The proposed approach includes two major phases: a data analysis procedure and a model learning procedure. The former is to investigate the data characteristics so that important data features can be extracted and used to constitute a new training dataset; and the latter, is to construct a learning model for classification.

As shown in Figure 1, in the first phase three types of analyses are performed. The first type is user co-rating analysis. It is to calculate the user-user similarity through their co-rated items. The second type is social relationship analysis. It involves the trust calculation of a user to other users in the same community (dataset). The relevant data obtained from the above analyses are then used, with a memory-based CF method, to perform similarity-based and trust-based rating prediction, and the results are compared (and used to determine the class of each data record). Because the proposed hybrid approach means to classify which of the strategies (similarity-based or trust-based) is the best for each data record in rating prediction, a new training dataset is prepared to construct a classification model. Finally, the third type is to extract several data features from the results of the above analyses, and compose them as a feature vector of a data record (user-item). Based on the newly formed dataset, a classification model is built. The model is then used to recognize which strategy could perform the best when a user is rating an item. The details are described as below in Figure 2.

Data Analysis

In this work we used the Epinions dataset (Massa & Avesani, 2007) to verify the presented approach. The main reason of using this dataset is that it contains both types of information often used in CF recommendation: user ratings and user trust. Because the original dataset is very large (664,824 user ratings and 487,181 trust statements), using the entire dataset to investigate this proposed approach is thus very time consuming. To enhance the effectiveness of the experiments, we randomly divide the dataset into ten folds, and at the same time ensure each fold has the same ratios of sparsity and cold start users as the original dataset. Meanwhile, the percentages of each level of users (with the same rating) are the same as the original dataset. In this way, the results can be consistent with the original dataset, while the computation cost, reduced.

As mentioned above, our approach performs a series of analyses to observe the original dataset from different perspectives. The first step is to calculate the user-user similarity as the traditional CF method does (note that the item properties are not available here so that the item-item similarity cannot not be

Figure 2. The main flow of the proposed approach

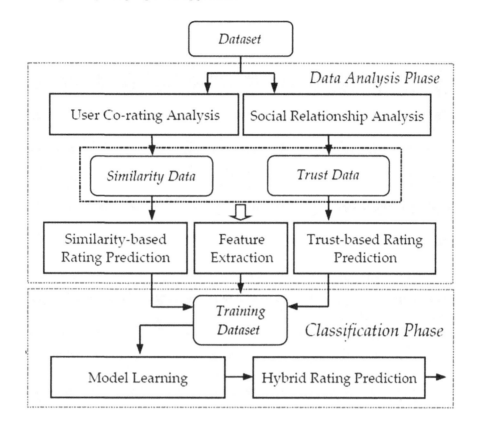

used). Once the similarity between any two users is obtained, the top-*k* nearest neighbor method is employed for item-rating prediction. In this work, the similarity between two users, *u* and *v* is calculated by the Pearson Correlation Coefficient described in Equation (1). Using this top-*k* method, two parameters need to be determined: the number of neighbor (i.e., *k*) and the similarity threshold. A large *k* accounts for more users' opinions but it also means that the less similar users are included. Therefore, a threshold T_s is required to ensure the minimal similarity between the target user and each selected neighbor. The choices of suitable *k* and T_s are dataset-dependent. For the case here, an empirical study is performed in the experimental section for better selection.

The second step is to derive the trust relationship between users and use the social trust (instead of similarity) with the top-*k* nearest neighbor method to carry out item-rating prediction. In this work, the explicit trust and implicit trust between users are both taken into account. As described above, we first construct a directed network from the trust relationships indicated by the users in the original dataset, then calculate the Jaccard Coefficient (i.e., Equation (2)) between any two nodes (users) in this network as the explicit user trust. This coefficient is taken to be the trust weight between two nodes. With the weighted (and directed) network, we adopt the *MoleTrsut* algorithm to infer the implicit trust between users (Massa & Avesani, 2007), in which a depth-first search (with a limited depth) is employed to determine neighbor nodes and a first degree transition is performed. Then, Equation (3) is used to calculate the implicit trust. Similar to the similarity-based CF recommendation, a top-*k* method is used for trust-based recommendation. Again, the choices of the number of neighbor k and the trust threshold T_t are dataset-dependent, and an empirical study is conducted in the experimental section to determine the suitable values.

This work considers the hybrid recommendation as a classification task, so that it adopts a learning method to derive a model for data classification. After the similarity and trust between users are derived and the corresponding rating predictions are performed, the original dataset is divided into two subsets for training and testing. The class label for each data record is determined by the prediction performance of the similarity-based and trust-based CF methods described above. That is, each record is attached with a label indicating which of the strategies can result in a smaller prediction error for this data. Moreover, some features are induced from the results of data analysis and are used as attributes for model construction and data classification. The relevant details on feature extraction and model building are described in the section below.

Classification Model for Strategy Selection

To employ a memory-based approach for collaborative filtering recommendation, one of the most important issues is to develop a distance measurement to quantify the relationship between two users. At present, user similarity and social trust are two factors widely adopted for distance measurement in CF recommendation. The strategies based on them have some advantages and disadvantages. Notably they are not exclusive to each other and no need to be used independently for neighbor selection. On the contrary, they can be used together as complements to make better recommendation. This work thus develops a hybrid approach to include their advantages in an adaptive way. According to the availability of the user similarity and social trust for the target group of people, we can categorize the situations for using similarity-based or trust-based strategies when a user v is rating an item i as the following:

$$p_{v,i} = \begin{cases} 0, & \text{if both } s_{based} \text{ and } t_{based} \text{ fail;} \\ s_{based}, & \text{if } s_{based} \text{ succeeds and } t_{based} \text{ fails;} \\ t_{based}, & \text{if } t_{based} \text{ succeeds and } s_{based} \text{ fails;} \\ h(s_{based}, t_{based}), & \text{if both } s_{based} \text{ and } t_{based} \text{ succeeds;} \end{cases} \tag{5}$$

The four situations indicate that if both similarity-based (s_{based}) and trust-based (t_{based}) strategies fail to find neighbors for user v to rate item i, they cannot be used for CF (other measurement is needed); if one of the strategies can find the neighbors (the second and the third situations), these neighbors are then considered. The last situation means when both strategies can find some useful neighbors, a heuristic method h is needed to combine their opinions. Figure 3 illustrates the situations in which neighbors exist, and the method needs to infer a rating decision from the neighbors belonging to the conjunction region.

It is notable that due to the ambiguity of similarity and friendship (trust): users with similar tastes might not trust each other, while trusted users might have different preferences. In other words, the trust and social similarity may be noisy and inaccurate. Therefore, researchers start to merge the preference and trust information to improve the overall performance of recommendations and to ameliorate the data sparsity and cold-start problems of CF. The focus is now on how to incorporate the two types of information to obtain the most promising results. After performing the above data analysis procedure to examine these data from different viewpoints, we can confirm the inconsistency of similarity and

Figure 3. Distribution of the similarity-based and trust-based neighbors

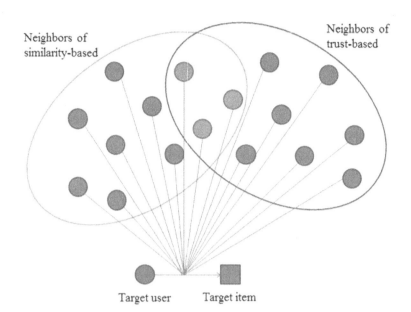

trust as indicated above: a neighbor with a large value in similarity does not guarantee a large value in trust and vice versa. With the above observations, we develop a classification approach to combine both similarity and trust, by recognizing which of the two strategies should be applied when a user is rating an item. A training dataset is prepared for the classification task, in which each original data record with two components (i.e., user and item) is expanded to include several features extracted from the results obtained from the above data analysis procedure. In addition, a class label (similarity or trust) is attached to each data as indicated in the above procedure. Ten possible features are extracted and considered. The features and the corresponding descriptions are listed in Table 1.

Table 1. Possible features extracted from the dataset

Feature	Description
user rated count	the number of items rated by a user
user rated mean	the average rate given by a user
user_rate_std_dev	deviation of the rates made by a user
item_rate_count	the number of rates made by users for an item
item_mean	average rate of an item
item_rate_dev	standard deviation of the rates obtained for an item
sim_neighbor_count	number of similar neighbors
trust_neighbor_count	number of trust neighbors
similarity rating average	rate average of the similar neighbors
Trust rating average	rate average of the trust neighbors
recommend type	label (class)

Before conducting the experiments for data classification, we carry out a small set of data analysis for feature selection. The information gain is measured for each possible feature and the results are presented in Figure 4. Here some features (including user rated count, user rated mean, and user_rate std-dev) have very small information gains (which are less than 0.015). They are disregarded in the classification task afterward. With the selected data features and the correct classes, the data records belonging to, we use a decision tree method (i.e., J48) to perform data classification.

EXPERIMENTS AND RESULTS

Evaluation Criteria

In this work, the recommendation is evaluated by two standard criteria: the mean absolute error (MAE) and the rating coverage (RC). MAE is the average of the absolute difference between the predicted and actual ratings over all items. It is defined as

$$\text{MAE} = \frac{1}{N} \sum_u \sum_i \left| p_{u,i} - r_{u,i} \right| \tag{6}$$

where $p_{u,i}$ and $r_{u,i}$ are the actual and predicted ratings for user i on item i, respectively, and N is the number of items. The other criterion RC measures the degree to which the testing ratings can be predicted and covered relative to the whole testing ratings. It is defined as:

$$\text{RC} = \frac{M}{N} \tag{7}$$

Figure 4. Information gains of the possible data features

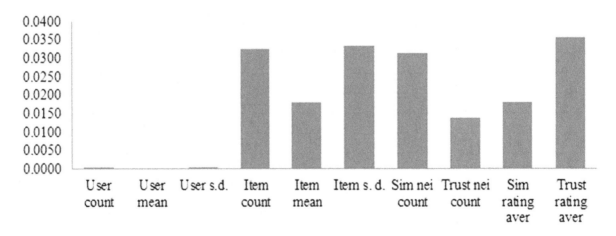

where M is the number of predictable ratings and N is the number of all testing ratings. The two criteria are used below to compare recommendation performance of different methods.

Results for Similarity-Based and Trust-Based Strategies

Results

To perform performance comparison, the two popular CF methods (similarity-based and trust-based) were taken independently to conduct CF recommendation and a ten-fold validation method was used for evaluation. For the similarity-based strategy, Pearson correlation–based similarity measurement was used as mentioned above. For trust-based recommendation, two methods (for explicit and implicit trust calculations) were employed, in which the *MoleTrust* algorithm was adopted for trust calculation. They are named mole-1 trust-based (explicit trust only) and mole-2 trust-based (both explicit and implicit trust) afterward. Doing depth-first search to find implicit neighbors, we limited the trust transition threshold to 0.6 and the search depth to 2, as suggested in the original algorithm.

Table 2 presents the results of MAE for the above three strategies, in which different k were applied to neighbor selection and a fixed threshold 0 (T_s and T_t) was used. Here when the value for k is (or exceeds) 5 for the three strategies mentioned above, the error can be reduced to a lower level. Table 3 lists the other set of results, in which k was set to a fixed value 5 and different thresholds were used to examine the error variations. The results show that though RC decreases along with the increasing threshold, MAE remain similar level (only a small change is observed).

Results of the similarity-based strategy in Table 2 show that the increase of k (the neighbors to be considered) results in differences on rating prediction, but RC is not changed because the number of neighbors (with a similarity larger or equal to the pre-defined threshold) for each user remains the same. In Table 3, a higher threshold finds more similar but fewer neighbors for each target user that causes the decrease of rating coverage. As can be observed, the MAE for all different k are similar. It indicates that the threshold is not sensitive in neighbor selection for this dataset and a value within the specified range can obtain similar results. Figure 5 presents the distribution of the similarity between any two users. It shows that most of the user-pairs have a relatively high similarity (i.e., large than 0.5). This explains the similar results (on MAE) obtained in Table 3 in which a threshold between 0 and 0.5 was chosen.

Table 2. MAE for different k with a pre-defined threshold

	sim-based	mole-1 trust-based	mole-2 trust-based
$k = 1$	0.991	0.908	0.917
$k = 3$	0.907	0.864	0.868
$k = 5$	0.890	0.861	0.861
$k = 7$	0.884	0.860	0.860
$k = 10$	0.880	0.860	0.859
$k = 15$	0.878	0.860	0.859
$k = 20$	0.877	0.860	0.859
RC	53.43%	25.39%	30.70%

Table 3. MAE and RC for different thresholds with a pre-defined k

		sim-based	mole-1 trust-based	mole-2 trust-based
threshold = 0	MAE	0.890	0.861	0.861
	RC	53.43%	25.39%	30.70%
threshold = 0.1	MAE	0.889	0.859	0.861
	RC	52.56%	23.50%	29.05%
threshold = 0.2	MAE	0.889	0.860	0.862
	RC	51.67%	20.85%	26.76%
threshold = 0.3	MAE	0.890	0.858	0.867
	RC	50.66%	18.33%	23.28%
threshold = 0.4	MAE	0.892	0.858	0.866
	RC	49.52%	15.72%	17.47%
threshold = 0.5	MAE	0.891	0.854	0.854
	RC	48.04%	12.92%	12.92%

Figure 5. The distribution of similarity between any two users

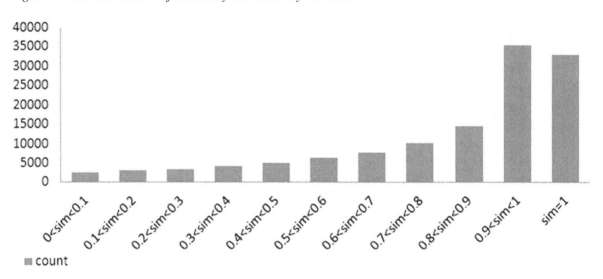

As can be observed in the above tables, when the threshold is less than 0.5, RC of mole-2 trust strategy is higher than that of mole-1 trust strategy. It indicates that using trust transition can indeed increase the number of neighbors to be considered. When the threshold reaches to a level of 0.5, the two trust strategies have the same RC. It means the selected neighbors were all explicit in this situation, and the implicit neighbors with lower trust values were all discarded. Figure 6 presents the distribution of the trust between any two users. It echoes the results described above (Table 3): when a small threshold was used, more neighbors (implicit) can be included for the mole-2 trust-based strategy to improve the performance.

Figure 6. The distribution of trust between any two users.

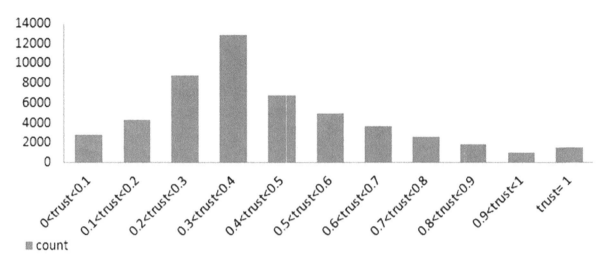

As mentioned above, many collaborative filtering studies focus on the problem of cold start users. It means that for the users only rated a very small amount (i.e., less than 5) of items, it is difficult to find similar neighbors for them through the co-rating strategy, in order to make more precise recommendation. To compare the cold start effect occurring in the similarity-based and trust-based methods, we conducted a set of trials and observed the results. Table 4 lists MAE and RC for three strategies, including similarity-based (sim), explicit trust-based (mole-1 trust), and implicit trust-based (mole-2 trust). In this table, "all user" means to consider all users in the dataset. They can be divided into two groups: "normal user" and "cold start user". As can be seen in Figure 6, both trust-based methods have better results (MAE) than the traditional similarity-based method, especially on cold start users. Meanwhile, the trust-based methods have high rating coverage (RC) than the similarity-based method. These results indicate that in the used dataset (i.e., Epinions), with the similarity-based method we were not able to find enough similar neighbors for cold start users; whereas with the trust-based methods we were able to find more neighbors for them in making recommendation, and the error was thus reduced.

Table 4. MAE and RC of the all users, normal users and cold start users.

		sim	mole-1 trust	mole-2 trust
all user	MAE	0.890	0.861	0.861
	RC	53.42%	25.39%	30.70%
normal user	MAE	0.890	0.862	0.862
	RC	53.30%	25.09%	30.31%
cold start user	MAE	1.131	0.762	0.791
	RC	0.13%	0.30%	0.39%

Analysis and Discussion

From the above implementations for the two types of CF methods and the corresponding results, we can observe (for this dataset) that:

1. Under the same experimental conditions, trust-based methods obtain better MAE;
2. Similarity-based method has a higher rating coverage;
3. Implicit (transitive) trust can improve rate coverage;
4. Trust-based method can mediate the cold start problem.

Though these observations are dataset-dependent, the data analysis techniques can help to understand the data characteristics of the target dataset in general and to develop useful strategies accordingly for rating prediction.

To further investigate the relationship between user similarity and social trust (produced by the mole-2 trust method to deliver the best performance), we conducted two sets of analyses that examined the average trust for those users selected as similar neighbors (subject to each user) with the similarity-based method (the first set), and the average similarity for those users selected as trusted neighbors with the trust-based method (the second set), respectively. Figure 7 presents the first set of results (distribution of the average trust of similar neighbors). As can be observed clearly, trust values for those neighbors with a high rating similarity are mostly low and the values are between 0 and 0.1. To inspect the distribution of these trust values, we divide the values of user similarity (for those selected as similar neighbors) into 4 intervals (0~0.25, 0.25~0.5, 0.5~0.75, 0.75~1), and the distributions of the social trust for the four groups of similar neighbors are illustrated in Figure 8. They are consistent with the results obtained above.

The second set of results is presented in Figure 9. Similar to the first set of experiments, the similarity values of the trust neighbors are mostly low and the values are between 0 to 0.1. To examine the distribution of these similarity values, we again divide the values of social trust (for those selected as

Figure 7. Distribution of the average trust of the selected similar neighbors.

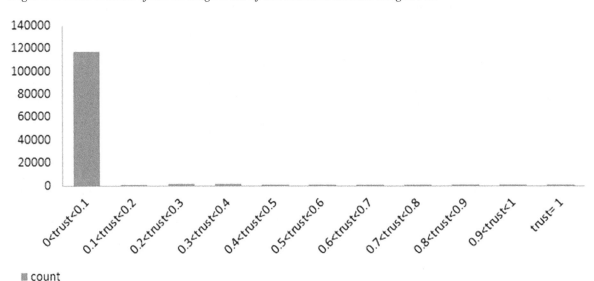

Figure 8. Distributions of the social trust for the similar neighbors within each interval

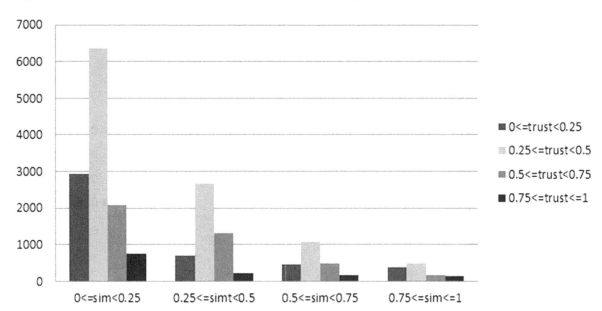

Figure 9. Distribution of the average similarity of the selected trusted neighbors

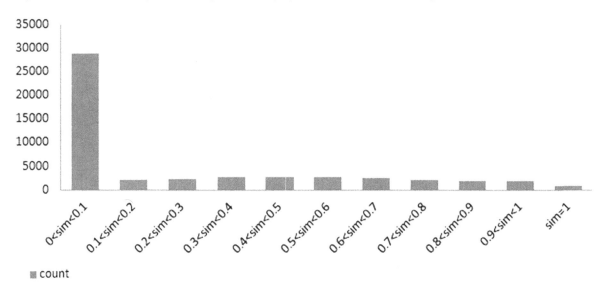

similar neighbors) into 4 intervals as in the first set of experiments. The distributions of the similarity values for these trusted neighbors within each interval is illustrated in Figure 10 and they are compatible with the results in Figure 9.

The above empirical analyses demonstrate that the rating similarity and social trust are not necessarily consistent. For any user, the persons with similar tastes (high co-rating similarity neighbors) might not be trustworthy; on the contrary, the most trusted persons (high trust values neighbors) might not have similar preferences. Ideally, the conjunction of the two sets of persons are the best references for mak-

Figure 10. Distributions of the similarity for the trusted neighbors within each interval

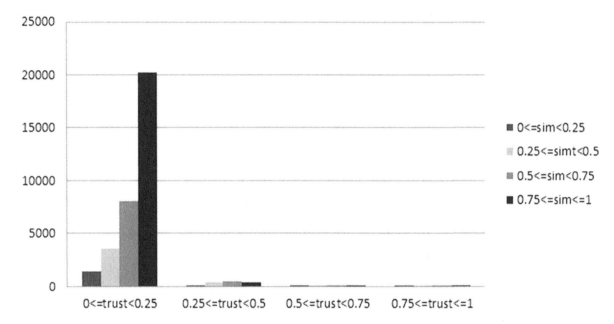

ing prediction. Nevertheless, in the real world cases, it is difficult to find those neighbors as references for most of the users. Therefore a hybrid approach is needed to integrate both strategies and account for advantages for making better recommendation. This also indicates that a more flexible and adaptive method rather than a set of fixed weighting factors to combine the two strategies would be more suitable.

Results for Combining Similarity and Trust Measurements in CF

We have also carried out a set of experiments to investigate the performance of linear combination based on the similarity-based and trust-based rating prediction. The following equation is used to combine two types of ratings:

$$Rating_{predict} = \alpha \times \mathrm{Pr}\, edict_{sim} + \beta \times \mathrm{Pr}\, edict_{trust} \qquad (8)$$

In this equation, $Predict_{sim}$ is the rating score made by the similarity based measurement; and $Predict_{trust}$, by the trust-based measurement. The parameters α and β ($\alpha + \beta = 1$) are weighting factors representing the corresponding importance of the two measurements. The results for different parameter combinations are listed in Table 5. It shows that the best result (0.826) can be obtained when the two weighting factors are both set to 0.5; however, this result is in fact far from the optimal prediction (0.59, obtained by an exhaustive calculation for all data). Meanwhile the computational effort for trying different combinations to derive the best weighing factors is high (in this case, ten trials were performed). It means that there is much room for improvement and a classification method can achieve the improvement as shown in the section below.

Table 5. MAE of different weighting factor combinations

(α, β)	MAE
0.9, 0.1	0.8490
0.8, 0.2	0.8385
0.7, 0.3	0.8313
0.6, 0.4	0.8273
0.5, 0.5	0.8267
0.4, 0.6	0.8296
0.3, 0.7	0.8356
0.2, 0.8	0.8441
0.1, 0.9	0.8542

Results of Model Training and Data Classification

After showing the performance of using a linear combination method to integrate similarity-based and trust-based strategies, in this section we present another set of experiments by building a classifier to recognize which of the strategies can deliver best result for each data. In this set of learning experiments, a ten-fold criterion was used for validation.

In addition to the accuracy, three other criteria often used in binary classification (with positive and negative classes) are taken for evaluation and the corresponding results are also presented. First of all, precision that is defined as the fraction of relevant retrieved instances. Second, recall, defined as the fraction of relevant instances retrieved. Although often in conflict in nature, the measures of precision and recall are both essential in evaluating the performance of a prediction approach. Therefore, these two measures can be combined with equal weights to obtain the third metric, *F*-measure. Evaluation of the three metrics are defined as follows:

$$precision = \frac{TP}{TP + FP} \tag{8}$$

$$recall = \frac{TP}{TP + FN} \tag{9}$$

$$F\text{-}measure = \frac{2 \times precision \times recall}{precision + recall} \tag{10}$$

In these measures, *TP* is true positive (the number of items correctly labeled as belonging to the positive class); *FP* is false positive (the number of items incorrectly labeled as belonging to the positive class); and *FN* is false negative (the number of items incorrectly labeled as belonging to the negative class).

The results show that the accuracy rate is 66.61%, which is not high enough for a general classification task. Other performance indices also show similar results (precision is 0.662, recall is 0.666, and F-measure is 0.661). We then performed a set of further analyses to examine the results in detail. Figure 11 illustrates some of the distributions of the features used in the classification, in which x-axis is the feature value, and y-axis, the number of data records with a feature value specified. In this figure, trust data are marked in deep color and similar data, light color. As can be seen, in such a dataset, the distributions for trust and similar types of data are very similar, and this characteristic makes it difficult to classify the two classes of data through these features. However, as shown below, this accuracy rate is enough to enhance the recommendation performance.

Results of the proposed approach are listed in Table 6. Compared to the above implemented similarity-based and trust-based strategies (Table 4), our overall performance (for all users) is better than the above two strategies: MAE of all users is lower than the two strategies and the coverage rate, higher. To examine the details, we can observe that for the cold start users the MAE obtained from our classification-based approach is higher than that of the trust-based strategy. The reason is that most of the cold start users in this dataset have only trusted neighbors and thus cannot be classified correctly by the presented approach. For those small number of cold start users with two types of neighbors (the last category in Table 6), our approach is able to obtain better performance than the trust-based strategy.

Figure 11. Data distribution along with different features

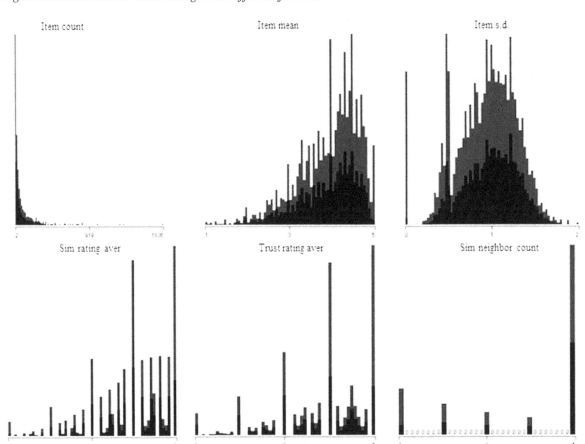

Table 6. Results of the classification-based approach

		Proposed method
all users	MAE	0.846
	RC	56.86%
normal users	MAE	0.846
	RC	56.36%
cold start users	MAE	0.866
	RC	0.50%
cold start users (two types of neighbors)	MAE	0.646
	RC	0.02%

CONCLUSION

Standard similarity-based CF methods are popular because they are intuitive, relatively simple to implement, and easy to include new ratings. However, these methods raise several issues that could affect the precision of recommended results. Social trust has been proposed to tackle such problems. Clearly it is considered helpful to establish a trust network among users that can bring about successful recommender systems. To exploit the advantages of both similarity-based and trust-based strategies, we hereby present a data analytics approach that combines user preference and social trust for making better collaborative recommendation. Different from other studies, the proposed approach regards the collaborative recommendation as a classification task. It includes two phases to improve the recommendation performance. A data analysis procedure is carried out to explore the target dataset in terms of user similarity and trust relationship. The results of data analysis are used to label the records. Then, a training and testing procedure is performed to extract features from the data analysis procedure and to build up a model for data classification. Experiments have been conducted to evaluate performance. The results show that the presented approach has better performance in more objective experimental conditions. It also shows that our approach can be operated to enhance the recommendation performance in an adaptive way for different datasets without an iterative parameter-tuning procedure.

The experiments conducted were restricted to the available dataset because the approach presented requires both types of information on user ratings and social trust. We are currently collecting more datasets to perform extensive evaluations for the proposed approaches. Meanwhile, we have been investigating further other methods for large datasets, including adopting the Hadoop cloud framework for parallelism, and accelerating the calculation of similarity and trust among users. In the near future, we will investigate more data analysis techniques and classification methods for even better recommendation performance.

REFERENCES

Adomavicius, G., & Tuzhilin, A. (2005). Toward the next generation of recommender systems: A survey of the state-of-the-art and possible extensions. *IEEE Transactions on Knowledge and Data Engineering*, *17*(6), 734–749. doi:10.1109/TKDE.2005.99

Ahn, H. J. (2008). A new similarity measure for collaborative filtering to alleviate the new user cold-starting problem. *Information Sciences, 178*(1), 37–51. doi:10.1016/j.ins.2007.07.024

Bernardes, D., Diaby, M. Fournier, R., FogelmanSoulié, F. & Viennet, E. (2014). A Social formalism and survey for recommender systems. *ACM SIGKDD Explorations Newsletter, 16*(2), 20-37.

Bobadilla, J., Ortega, F., Hernando, A., & Gutiérrez, A. (2013). Recommender systems survey. *Knowledge-Based Systems, 46,* 109–132. doi:10.1016/j.knosys.2013.03.012

Chen, C., Zheng, X., Wang, Y., Hong, F., & Lin, Z. (2014) Context-aware collaborative topic regression with social matrix factorization for recommender systems.*Proceedings of the Twenty-Eighth AAAI Conference on Artificial Intelligence* (pp. 9-15). AAAI Press.

Chen, K., Chen, T., Zheng, G., Jin, O., Yao, E., & Yu, Y. (2012) Collaborative personalized tweet recommendation.*Proceedings of ACM SIGIR International Conference on Research and Development in Information Retrieval*, pp 661-670. ACM Press.

Chen, S., Luo, T., Liu, W., & Xu, Y. (2009). Incorporating similarity and trust for collaborative filtering.*Proceedings of the Sixth International Conference on Fuzzy Systems and Knowledge Discovery* (pp. 487-493). IEEE Press. doi:10.1109/FSKD.2009.720

Golbeck, J. (2009). Trust and nuanced profile similarity in online social networks. *ACM Trans. on the Web, 3*(4).

Golbeck, J., & Hendler, J. (2006). FilmTrust: Movie recommendations using trust in web-based social networks.*Proceedings of the Third IEEE International Conference on Consumer Communications and Networking Conference* (pp. 282-286). IEEE Press. doi:10.1109/CCNC.2006.1593032

Guha, R., Kumar, R., Raghavan, P., & Tomkins, A. (2004). Propagation of trust and distrust.*Proceedings of the Thirteenth International Conference on World Wide Web* (pp. 403-412). ACM Press.

Guo, G., Zhang, J., & Thalmann, D. (2014). Merging trust in collaborative filtering to alleviate data sparsity and cold start. *Knowledge-Based Systems, 57,* 57–68. doi:10.1016/j.knosys.2013.12.007

Guo, G., Zhang, J., & Yorke-Smith, N. (2015a). TrustSVD: Collaborative filtering with both the explicit and implicit influence of user trust and of item ratings.*Proceedings of the Twenty-Ninth AAAI Conference on Artificial Intelligence*. AAAI Press.

Guo, G., Zhang, J., & Yorke-Smith, N. (2015b). Leveraging multiviews of trust and similarity to enhance clustering-based recommender systems. *Knowledge-Based Systems, 74,* 14–27. doi:10.1016/j.knosys.2014.10.016

Jamali, M., & Ester, M. (2009). Using a trust network to improve top-N recommendation.*Proceedings of the Third ACM International Conference on Recommender Systems* (pp. 181-188). ACM Press. doi:10.1145/1639714.1639745

Koren, Y., & Bell, R. (2011). Advances in collaborative filtering. In F. Ricci, L. Rokach, B. Shapira, & P. Kantor (Eds.), *Recommender Systems Handbook* (pp. 1–42). Springer. doi:10.1007/978-0-387-85820-3_5

Lee, D. H., & Brusilovsky, P., P. (2010). Social networks and interest similarity: the case of CiteULike. *Proceedings of the 21st ACM conference on Hypertext and Hypermedia* (pp. 151-156). ACM Press doi:10.1145/1810617.1810643

Lee, W.-P., & Lee, K.-H. (2014). Making smartphone service recommendations by predicting users' intentions: A context-aware approach. *Information Sciences, 277*, 21–35. doi:10.1016/j.ins.2014.04.033

Li, Y.-M., Wu, C.-T., & Lai, C.-Y. (2013). A social recommender mechanism for e-commerce: Combining similarity, trust and relationship. *Decision Support Systems, 55*(3), 740–752. doi:10.1016/j.dss.2013.02.009

Lu, J., Wu, D., Mao, M., Wang, W., & Zhang, G. (2015). Recommender system application developments: A survey. *Decision Support Systems, 74*, 12–32. doi:10.1016/j.dss.2015.03.008

Ma, H., Zhou, T. C., Lyu, M. R., & King, I. (2011). Improving recommender systems by incorporating social contextual information. *ACM Trans. on Information Systems, 29*(2).

Massa, P., & Avesani, P. (2007). Trust-aware recommender systems. *Proceedings of the ACM International Conference on Recommender Systems* (pp. 17-24). ACM Press.

O'Donovan, J., & Smyth, B. (2005). Trust in recommender systems. *Proceedings of the Tenth International Conference on Intelligent User Interfaces* (pp. 167-174). doi:10.1145/1040830.1040870

Qian, X., Feng, H., Zhao, G., & Mei, T. (2014). Personalized recommendation combining user interest and social circle. *IEEE Transactions on Knowledge and Data Engineering, 26*(7), 1487–1502. doi:10.1109/TKDE.2013.168

Qin, J., Zheng, Q., Tian, F., & Zheng, D. (2014). An emotion-oriented music recommendation algorithm fusing rating and trust. *International Journal of Computational Intelligence Systems, 7*(2), 371–381. doi:10.1080/18756891.2013.865405

Ray, S., & Mahantirt, A. (2010). Improving prediction accuracy in trust-aware recommender systems. *Proceedings of the 43rd Hawaii International Conference on System Sciences* (pp. 1-9). doi:10.1109/HICSS.2010.225

Ricci, F., Rokach, L., & Shapira, B. (2011). Introduction to recommender systems handbook. In F. Ricci, L. Rokach, B. Shapira, & P. Kantor (Eds.), *Recommender Systems Handbook* (pp. 1–35). Springer. doi:10.1007/978-0-387-85820-3_1

Samah, A., Kim, H.-N., & Saddik, A. E. (2012). A group trust metric for identifying people of trust in online social networks. *Expert Systems with Applications, 39*(18), 13173–13181. doi:10.1016/j.eswa.2012.05.084

Sarwar, B., Karypis, G., Konstan, J., & Riedl, J. (2001). Item-based collaborative filtering recommendation algorithms. *Proceedings of the Tenth International World Wide Web Conference* (pp. 285-295). ACM Press. doi:10.1145/371920.372071

Sherchan, W., Nepal, S., & Paris, C. (2013). A survey of trust in social networks. *ACM Computing Surveys, 45*(4), 47. doi:10.1145/2501654.2501661

Yang, B., Lei, Y., Liu, D., & Liu, J. (2013). Social collaborative filtering by trust.*Proceedings of the 23rd International Joint Conference on Artificial Intelligence* (pp. 2747-2753).

Yang, X., Guo, Y., Liu, Y., & Steck, H. (2014). A survey of collaborative filtering based social recommender systems. *Computer Communications*, *41*, 1–10. doi:10.1016/j.comcom.2013.06.009

Ziegler, C. N., & Golbeck, J. (2015). Models for trust inference in social networks. In D. Król et al. (Eds.), *Propagation Phenomena in Real World Networks, Intelligent Systems Reference Library* (Vol. 85, pp. 53–89). Springer. doi:10.1007/978-3-319-15916-4_3

KEY TERMS AND DEFINITIONS

Collaborative Filtering: It is a method of making automatic predictions about the interests of a user by collecting preferences or taste information from many users. Collaborative filtering explores techniques for matching people with similar interests and making recommendations on this basis.

Data Analytics: It refers to qualitative and quantitative techniques and processes used to enhance productivity and business gain. It examines raw data and focuses on inference, statistical and quantitative analysis, explanatory and predictive models, to drive conclusions and decisions.

Data Classification: The problem of identifying to which of a set of categories a new instance belongs, on the basis of a training set of data containing instances on whose category membership is known.

Feature Extraction: When the data is too large to be processed, the data will be transformed into a reduced representation set of features. The process of transforming the input data into the set of features is called feature extraction.

*k***-Nearest Neighbors Algorithm:** It is a type of instance-based learning, or lazy learning, where the function is only approximated locally and all computation is deferred until classification. The neighbors are taken from a set of objects for which the class is known. This can be thought of as the training set for the algorithm, though no explicit training step is required.

Trust Network: It typically refers to a situation characterized by the aspect that one party with a set of properties which another party willing to rely on. Trust can be attributed to relationships between people. This information can be used to establish a directed network, where the nodes are individual users with the relationship of one user trusts the other resulting in an edge directed from one node to the other.

Chapter 12
Visual Data Mining for Collaborative Filtering:
A State-of-the-Art Survey

Marenglen Biba
University of New York Tirana, Albania

Narasimha Rao Vajjhala
University of New York Tirana, Albania

Lediona Nishani
University of New York Tirana, Albania

ABSTRACT

This book chapter provides a state-of-the-art survey of visual data mining techniques used for collaborative filtering. The chapter begins with a discussion on various visual data mining techniques along with an analysis of the state-of-the-art visual data mining techniques used by researchers as well as in the industry. Collaborative filtering approaches are presented along with an analysis of the state-of-the-art collaborative filtering approaches currently in use in the industry. Visual data mining can provide benefit to existing data mining techniques by providing the users with visual exploration and interpretation of data. The users can use these visual interpretations for further data mining. This chapter dealt with state-of-the-art visual data mining technologies that are currently in use apart. The chapter also includes the key section of the discussion on the latest trends in visual data mining for collaborative filtering.

INTRODUCTION

Researchers are struggling to explore large volumes of data as the volume of data generated increased exponentially over the last few years. The traditional data mining techniques are not adequate to analyze and explore these large volumes of data as the available data is available in different dimensions and varying formats, including multimedia, geographical, and temporal data. Visual data mining techniques and

DOI: 10.4018/978-1-5225-0489-4.ch012

approaches supplementing traditional data mining techniques can help in dealing with the large volume of data. Data Mining is defined as the process of analyzing large information repositories for deriving and discovering useful patterns and identifying hidden relationships among the data (Siguenza-Guzman, Saquicela, Avila- Ordóñez, Vanderwalle & Cattysse, 2015). Data mining is used for knowledge classification and exploring consistent patterns from large volumes of collected data. Visual data mining can be quite useful and helpful in designing models for practical solutions for complex problems (Kashwan &Velu, 2012). Visual data mining has the potential to simplify and ease exploration of these large volumes of data as the user is directly involved in the data mining process (Keim, 2002).

Classification of visual data mining techniques is based on three criteria, namely, the data to be visualized, the technique of visualization, and the adopted distortion technique (Keim, 2002). Visual data mining methods can be categorized into two categories, namely, data visualization and information visualization (Kashwan &Velu, 2012). Data visualization involves the presentation of data in schematic forms, including histograms, scatter plots, and charts. Information visualization is suitable for datasets that lack standard mapping of abstract data onto the physical screen space and include visualization techniques (Keim, 2002).The data mining process includes a sequence of steps, the first of which deals with integration of raw data from different data sources, including data in data formats. Data cleaning process follows the data integration process. During data cleansing, noise, duplication and inconsistent data are removed (Siguenza-Guzman et al., 2015). The third phase is transformation into other formats that can be interpreted by various data mining tools which apply filtration and aggregation to derive summarized data. The data analyst can now derive meaningful patterns using these data mining tools. Visualization can be applied to present data to the user in a comprehensible manner.

Collaborative filtering also referred to as social information filtering, is a variant of memory-based reasoning that is suitable for application of providing personalized recommendations (Linoff & Berry, 2011). Collaborative filtering methods utilize the past ratings of users to predict or recommend new contact that the user might like (Nilashi et al., 2013). Collaborative filtering methods are often classified into two categories, namely, user-based collaborative filtering and item-based collaborative filtering. Collaborative filtering is based on the concept of similarity coupled with preferences.

Traditional recommendation systems have used collaboration filtering for making recommendations to users on the basis of how other users have rated the items. Collaborative filtering uses a three-step process for preparing recommendations for new customers (Linoff & Berry, 2011). The customer profile is first built followed by a comparison of the new customer profile with profiles of other customers using some measure of similarity. Such similar profiles are referred to as neighbor profiles in collaborative filtering. Recommendations are then made based on the predictions from the combination of customer ratings with those of the neighbor profiles (Bobadilla, Hernando, Ortega, & Gutiérrez, 2012). Collaborative filtering techniques are normally applied on large data sets consisting of different kinds of data. Visual data mining techniques, when applied for collaborative filtering could help in discovering implicit knowledge in visual forms from these large data sets. Several visualization techniques have been applied in collaborative filtering, including Multi-Dimensional Scaling (MDS), Spring Embedder, and the Navigating Exhibitions, Annotations and Resources (NEAR).

BACKGROUND

Visual Data Mining

The exponential growth in information technology in the last two decades has created efficient ways of collecting and storing large volumes of data. From a research point of view, large volumes of data are certainly quite useful, but this situation has also brought forward challenges on how to deal and identify meaningful and useful patterns from such huge volume of data. Kashwan and Velu (2012) suggest the use of visualization techniques to represent useful information extracted from massive data sources because of its instantaneous interpretational characteristics. Data mining techniques offer several advantages; including providing marketing analysts with a better understanding of the customer buying habits allowing marketing managers to develop planned marketing campaigns for new products. Visual data mining techniques can help managers, especially nontechnical business managers to understand and quickly retrieve data as well as make informed decisions (Soukup & Davidson, 2002).

Data mining is defined as the extraction of patterns or models from observed data (Oliveira & Levkowitz, 2003). Data mining is used for knowledge classification and exploring consistent patterns from large volumes of collected data. Data mining is part of the Knowledge Discovery in Databases (KDD), which involves extracting high-level data from low-level data (Fayyad, Piatetsky-Shapiro, & Smyth, 1996). Visual data mining can be quite useful and helpful in designing models for practical solutions of complex problems (Kashwan & Velu, 2012). Visual data mining has the potential to simplify and ease exploration of these large volumes of data as the user is directly involved in the data mining process (Keim, 2002).

One of the key advantages of visual data mining is that there is always human involvement i.e. the involvement of the data analyst in the exploration process (Keim, 2002). The three step process used in visual data exploration includes overview first, zoom and filter, and details-on-demand (Keim, 2002). The data analyst identifies patterns in the data and focuses on it followed by the zoom process during which the analyst explores further details. Visual data mining techniques allows the analyst to focus on details about the data. The application of visual data mining techniques allows data analysts to offer faster data exploration as data analysts can best benefit from these techniques along with traditional data mining techniques. Visual data exploration is quite useful when little is known about the data and the goals of exploration are unclear (Keim, 2002). As there is constant user interaction and involvement in the visual data exploration process, the exploration goals are automatically adjusted when necessary. The visual data interaction process is seen as a hypothesis-generation activity and the user explores the data visualization to gain new insights into the data and to come up with new hypothesis (Keim, 2002).

Data mining algorithms and information visualization share a common goal of building tools and developing new techniques for dealing with large amounts of data (Yu, Zhong, Smith, Park, & Huang, 2009). Information visualization and data mining techniques can complement each other in discovering complicated patterns. According to Oliveira and Levkowitz (2003), visual data mining tools can help domain experts in quickly examining what-if scenarios as well as interact with multivariate visual displays. Visual data mining is a complementary step to the process of knowledge discovery and data mining as this process can help in interpretation of three key aspects, namely, the integration of data, mining of data and peer evaluation (Chen, Zheng, Thorne, Zaiane, & Goebel, 2013). Visual data mining allows the users to gain new information that can help in the formulation of hypotheses there by giving them opportunity for verifying the hypotheses using visual data mining methods (Chen et al., 2013).

D. A. Keim (2002) discusses several advantages of visual data mining techniques over traditional data mining techniques. The first advantage of visual data mining techniques is that these techniques can deal easily with noisy, multidimensional, and non-homogeneous data. In contrast to traditional data mining techniques and approaches, visual data mining can be done by data analysts with limited understanding of complex mathematical algorithms. Visual data mining also provides a quantitative overview of the data and the analysts can continue with further analysis of the data.

State-Of-The-Art in Visual Data Mining

Accuracy of data in mapping is quite critical as visualization involves mapping of data into some types of graphical objects. The categorization of visual data mining systems has been done using different approaches. According to one of the most commonly referred categorization approach, the classification is based on three criteria, namely, the data to be visualized, the technique of visualization, and the adopted distortion technique (Keim, 2002). According to this approach, the visual data mining methods can be categorized into two categories, namely, data visualization and information visualization (Kashwan & Velu, 2012). Data visualization involves presentation of data in schematic forms, including histograms, scatter plots, and charts. Information visualization is suitable for datasets that lack standard mapping of abstract data onto the physical screen space and include visualization techniques (Keim, 2002).

Visual data mining makes use of visualization to act as the communication channel between the user and the computer for generating interpretable patterns (Chen et al., 2013). According to Chen et al. (2013), there are three categories of visual data mining, namely, visualization of data mining results, visualization of the data mining process, and the visualization of data. Visualization of data mining results makes the extracted patterns more understandable, while visualization of the data mining process helps in discovery of patterns (Chen et al., 2013).

According to another categorization approach advocated by Keim (2002), visual data exploration techniques can be grouped into six classes, namely, graph-based, geometric projection, icon-based, pixel-based, hierarchical, and hybrid (Keim & Kriegel, 1996; Oliveira & Levkowitz, 2003). Graph-based visual data mining involves the automatic extraction of useful knowledge from the graphical representation of the data (Quirin, Cordón, Vargas-Quesada, & de Moya-Anegón, 2010). Graph-based visual data mining approaches offer the advantage of allowing an expressive document encoding with enhanced classification accuracy (Jiang, Coenen, Sanderson, & Zito, 2010). According to Quirin et al. (2010), the knowledge retrieved from the data during graph-based visual data mining is masked inside the data and is not directly encoded in the data. Geometric projection techniques include techniques used for data processing, including factor analysis, component analysis, scatterplots, projection matrices, and parallel coordinates (Hinneburg, Keim &Wawryniuk, 2003; Oliveira & Levkowitz, 2003).

Icon-based visual data mining techniques involves mapping of each multidimensional data item to an icon (Keim & Kriegel, 1996). Iconic display approaches include techniques such as Chernoff faces, shape-coding approach, and stick figure technique. Large data sets are creating increasing problems for visualization and exploratory data analysis. Hierarchical visual data mining techniques are comparatively more suitable to handle large data sets as compared to other traditional visual data mining techniques (Ward, Peng & Wang, 2004). Large data sets need not necessarily be identified by large number of records; they could also consist of a large number of attributes or contain one or more nominal dimensions having a large number of unique values (Ward et al., 2004). Hierarchical visual data mining systems can simplify the task of visualizing large data sets. Some of the popular representations of hierarchical techniques include the n-vision technique, dimensional stacking, and tree maps (Keim & Kriegel, 1996). Hybrid visual data mining techniques involve the integration of multiple visualization approaches with the purpose of enhancing the expressiveness of the visualizations (Oliveira & Levkowitz, 2003).

As per another popular taxonomy of visual data mining systems proposed by Card, Mackinlay, and Shneiderman (1999), there are four levels of visual data mining systems. The first level of tools provides users with visual access to collection of information that is external to their environment, including online databases (Oliveira & Levkowitz, 2003). The second level includes visual tools that can support users in creating highly interactive visual representations using workspace tools (Card et al., 1999). The third level includes visual knowledge tools depicting visual representation of data including support for extracting relationships from the data. The last level includes visually enhanced objects focusing on identifying information about intrinsic visual forms (Oliveira & Levkowitz, 2003).

Visual data mining can be extensively used in several key application areas including life sciences, intelligent retail, customer relationship management, finance, banking, weather forecasting, and surveillance (Kumar & Bharadwaj, 2011). Visual data mining can help in making sense of what is happening between users in collaborative filtering systems and subsequently derive meaningful graphical depiction of data relation. Significant advances have been made over the last decade in the state-of-art in visual data mining in development of several visual data mining systems, tools, and applications. Several visual data mining techniques have been recommended by researchers over the last few years for visualizing massive data. These techniques include techniques such as scatterplots for dealing with low-dimensional data as well as techniques such as parallel coordinates, radial and icon-based visualizations, and Chernoff faces. According to Saraswathi and Babu (2015), a complete visual data mining system must be syntactically simple to learn, apply, retrieve, and execute as well be reliable and secure. The visual data mining system should be adaptable and scalable to a wide range of systems and environments to reduce the need for customization and facilitate portability. With advances in computing technology as well high usage of social networks, the volume of high-quality multimedia data has increased exponentially over the last decade. Traditional data mining techniques cannot handle these volumes of multimedia data, as most of the state-of-the-art data mining techniques can extract predefined patterns from heterogeneous sources of data. Yu (2009) recommends the adoption of a hybrid approach involving use of data mining in the first round followed by a visual analysis of the data, the results of which could further be explored by data mining (Hiremath & Kodge, 2010).

Several sophisticated state-of-the-art visualization techniques can be used for visualizing data, including geometrically-transformed displays, iconic displays, dense pixel display, and stacked displays (Pham, Hess, Ju, & Zhang, 2010; Keim, 2002). Geometrically-transformed displays can map one object to a set of points and lines in either two-dimensional or three-dimensional space. One of the most commonly used forms of geometrically-transformed displays is coordinate-based visualizations in which standard two-dimensional or three dimensional displays are extended through geometric transformations and projections of data on coordinate axes (Pham et al., 2010). Geometrically transformed displays involve the projection into a 2D plane of all the dimensions of the data (Collins, Hussell, Hettings, Powell, Mane & Martinez, 2007). Another example of geometrically transformed displays is the parallel coordinate visualization technique (Collins et al, 2007).Some of the other visualization techniques including iconic or icon-based displays such as Chernoff faces use certain features of icons such as color with greater attention as compared to other attributes (Pham et al., 2010). Stacked display techniques use space-filling approaches where the hierarchy of data is nested and are suitable for hierarchical data.

Some of the popular visual data mining tools include Clementine, Time Searcher, Theme River, Viz Tree, and Xmdv Tool (Chen et al., 2013; Kimani, Lodi, Catarci, Santucci & Sartori, 2004; Xiang, Niansu & Min, 2014; Yu et al., 2009). Clementine is a visual data mining tool supporting several mining techniques, including sequential patterns, factor analysis, neural networks, and clustering (Kimani et al., 2004). Clementine is one of the three most popular visual data mining tools that are currently in use. Clementine can help discover and predict valuable relationships present in the data using a powerful and easy to use data mining workbench (Xiang et al., 2014). The visual interface of Clementine assists the users in understanding the data flow and mining process. Clementine allows users to construct map of the data mining model and represent the steps in the data mining process using nodes (Kimani et al., 2004).

Time series is a collection of chronological observations including large-sized data with high dimensionality (Fu, 2011). Time series data is not only large in the context of the size of the data but also in the context of the number of observed attributes. One of the key problems with time series data mining is identifying mechanisms of representing the time series data (Fu, 2011). With the increasing availability and use of temporal and time-series data, visual data mining techniques can provide a solution for the representation of complex temporal and time series data. Time Searcher is an information visualization tool written in Java using Piccolo for rendering of graphics, which uses time box queries along with query-by-example (QBE) facilities and also provides support for overview displays (Hochheiser & Shneiderman, 2004). Time Searcher is an exploratory visualization tool that can be used to retrieve time series by querying. The modified version of this tool, TimeSearcher2, uses a new search interface which uses both pattern searching as well as filter searching (Fu, Chung, Kwok, & Ng, 2008). Time boxes are rectangular widgets for specifying query constraints on time series data sets (Hochheiser & Shneiderman, 2004).

Visualization tools provide various views that let users gain insight in a system or answer targeted questions. Visual data mining could help analyzing massive data on human behavior collected through social networks and web usage. Researchers have been facing the challenges associated with analyzing the big data. The power of visual data mining and visualization provides valuable analysis tools and techniques that were not available to researchers earlier. One of the challenges that users face is to integrate data mining and data visualization.

Visual data mining tools can also be quite useful for representing and depicting relationships among documents or group of documents representing unstructured textual data (Yu, 2009). Theme River visual data mining tool helps in depiction of thematic variations over time within a large collection of documents (Havre, Hetzler, Whitney, Nowell, 2002).Theme River can help in visualizing thematic changes in large document collections (Yu, 2009). VizTree is another visual data mining tool that can be used to mine and monitor large amounts of time series data (Yu, 2009). Viz Tree is a time series pattern discovery and visualization system that works by transforming the time series into a symbolic representation and then encoding data in a modified suffix tree (Lin, Keogh & Leonardi, 2005). Xmdv Tool is another public-domain visual data mining tool that allows interactive visual exploration of multi-variate data sets (Elke, Matthew, Jing, & Doshi, 2002). This tool supports an active process of pattern discovery, trends, and outliers in large-scale high-dimensional datasets (Elke et al., 2002).

State-Of-The-Art in Collaborative Filtering

The concept of collaborating filtering has derived from the real world domain. Recommendations from other users are highly considered by users. They base their behavior by making choices through word of mouth, reference letters, news, media, public opinion, surveys, guide, etc. Recommender systems facilitate and alleviate people digging through a large amount of information to find the most appropriate and useful information. Recommender systems can provide personalized recommendations through different types of algorithms, including content based filtering, demographic filtering, collaborative filtering, and hybrid filtering methods (Bobadilla et al., 2012). In content-based filtering systems, recommendations are provided to users based on the information related to items that other users have rated previously (Bobadilla et al., 2012). This technique is quite useful for making recommendations for instance that of an adventure movie based on other users who have bought similar category of movies. Demographic filtering techniques on the other hand make recommendations to users taking the positive ratings made by other users who have shared demographic information such as age, gender, qualifications etc. This might help provide recommendations to users based on demographic information and could help provide culturally appropriate information. Collaborative filtering methods allow providing recommendations to users based on how other users have rated items. Hybrid filtering methods allow recommender systems to provide recommendations through techniques based on both collaborative and demographic filtering methods (Bobadilla et al., 2012).

One of the most prominent approaches of recommender systems is collaborative filtering (CF), which uses the known preferences of several users in order to build predictions or valuable recommendations for other novel users. Collaborative filtering consists of various people collaborating in order to help each other to conduct filtering by taking notes of their reactions. The reactions are dubbed as annotations. In other words, collaborative filtering facilitates individuals in the decision making process based on the other people point of view. This method focuses on learning predictive models of user preferences, interests, attitudes, or various behaviors from community data.

The first recommender system dubbed as Tapestry (Goldberg et.al., 1992) has introduced for the first time the keyword "collaborative filtering (CF)". This phrase has been vastly used from the research community even though recommenders may not specifically collaborate with other preferences. The basic assumption of collaborating filtering is that if the user X and Y rate "n" items in the same way or have related preferences, they will behave alike even for new activities or items. CF consists of a user preferences database to predict further products or items that a new user might like.

Collaborating filtering incorporates many challenges that the research community must address. CF approaches are required to have the capability of managing highly sparse data, to scale with the large amount of users and items, to provide the appropriate and valuable recommendation and prediction in a short period. In contrast, content-based algorithms do not make use of any information or details about the items; items are handled as abstract entities. Therefore, collaborating filtering cannot predict items that have not been previously rated. On the other hand, content-based systems do not experience the issue dubbed as the cold-start problem because they benefit from the intrinsic item attributes. While collaborative filtering can develop recommendation to any pair of items as given an amount of sufficient training data, content-based algorithms treat items with similar attribute as similar. Collaborative Filtering techniques are categorized in three kinds of major techniques, namely, memory-based collaborative filtering, model-based collaborative filtering, and hybrid collaborative filtering (Su & Khoshgoftaar, 2009).

Memory-based collaborative filtering employs the whole item-database of user for generating a prediction. Every user is part of a group of people having alike behaviors. A prediction can be elaborated by the system when identifying the neighbors of individuals of a novel user. Memory-based algorithms foretell the rating of items obtained by a user through aggregating the rating of other items generated by the same user or aggregate the other users' rating for the same item. These techniques make use of a similarity metric to figure out several fixed number of items rated by people that are more comparable to the specific item explored by the recommendation system. The most popular similarity metrics aiming to rate vectors are the Pearson correlation coefficient and the cosine-based similarity metric (Adomavicius & Tuzhilin, 2005).Memory-based CF algorithms are easy to implement and perform well for highly dense datasets. Major challenges of this technique are the dependence on user-ratings and their performance deterioration on sparse data. Another memory-based shortcoming is being heuristics-based; they entail extensive hand-tuning upon novel datasets. Moreover, they demand more memory than model-based techniques because of their requirement of accessing the whole dataset when developing recommendations.

Model-based collaborative filtering has been studied and investigated to deal with the drawbacks that memory based incorporates. The development of machine learning models can make the system learn to distinguish complex patterns by training the system and being able to intelligently predict items for collaborating filtering purposes. Model-based methods develop recommendations for rating by using parametric or semi-parametric model and training on the rating data.

Hybrid collaborative filtering combines CF with other recommender systems approaches just like content-based filtering systems to overcome the shortcoming of pure systems. Therefore, they enhance the performance and the prediction process. They are based on the external content that generally is not available and has increased complexity.

Herein the chapter, authors have explored the most significant pure and hybrid techniques of collaborating filtering. Employing both collaborating filtering and content-based techniques can help in alleviating many recommender system problems, rather than employing only one of respective methods.

Some researchers have pointed out that the first recommender system was Grundy (Rich, 1979), which advocated the utilization of stereotypes to build user models relying on limited information of each indvidual. These user models were exploited for recommending related books to each user and the recommendation appeared to be effective. The definition collaborative filtering was used for the first time by Goldberg et al. (1992). They have founded an experimental mail system dubbed Tapestry developed at the Xerox Palo Alto Research Center. They assumed that filtering of information can be more effective when human beings are included in the process of filtering. Tapestry was based in both content-based and collaborative methods. It aimed to deal with any incoming stream of electronic documents. It was a framework composed of an indexer, document store, annotation store, filterer, little box, remailer, appraiser, and reader/browser. The reason why researchers developed tapestry relies on the dramatic growth of electronic mail usage. Users were faced with large incoming documents. In order to exploit this bundle of documents, mailing lists were created. The mailing list orientates users to select only those lists, which might have been of their interest. This filtering approach could be further ameliorated when users specified a filter that scans all lists. The major principle that Tapestry constitutes is that filtering can be more effective when humans engage in the filtering process.

Group Lens (Resnick et.al, 1994) and Video Recommender (Hill et al, 1995) were the first recommender systems, which have incorporated collaborative filtering algorithms intended to automate predictions. The method proposed in Aggarwal et al. (1999) is based on the graph-theoretic approach and can estimate the nearest neighbor of user. There are works that have used person correlation coefficient to measure the similarity (Resnick et.al., 1994), however there are other cosine-based approaches (Breese et al., 1998) where the two users are considered as two vectors in a multi-dimensional space. The similarity between users can be estimated by calculating the cosine angle of two vectors.

Bilsus and Pazzani (1998) have introduced a collaborative filtering technique where several machine learning methods just like Artificial Neural Networks are combined with feature extraction techniques.

This technique outperformed the memory-based in terms of prediction accuracy and relevance. In Sarwar et al. (2001), the authors pointed out that item-based techniques can have better computation performance compared to traditional user-based collaborative methods. In addition, they appear to perform in comparable or better quality than best of user-based algorithms.

Many several algorithms have tackled the new user problem. Mainly they are based in the hybrid recommender systems. An interesting approach is introduced by Rashid et al. (2002), where various techniques are investigated to decide which is the best and relevant item for a new user. In order to avoid the new user problem, these approaches have made use of different scenarios like item entropy or user personalization.

In regards to the sparsity problem that collaborative techniques face, many significant methods have been explored. In order to mitigate the sparsity rating problem, the collaborating system can utilize the information of the user profile to calculate user similarity. Pazzani (1999) have included gender, age, area code, education and employment information to develop effective recommendation and to enhance the problem of sparsity. In this case, this methodology of using not only user-rating, but other demographic information is dubbed as demographic filtering. The sparsity problem have been tackled from Huang et.al. (2004), too. They have mitigated the sparsity issue by carring out the associative retrieval framework and related algorithms to explore transitive assocations through their past feedback.

A significant piece of work was presented in Pennock et al. (2000). They have proposed a novel method named as Personality Diagnosis (PD). In this research work the probability whether users have the same "personality type" when having the same user preference profile for some specific items was calculated. The recommender system can make further predictions, if users like the new arriveditems. The PD approach comprises some traditional similarity-weighting techniques where novel data can be included easily. Subsequently, personality diagnosis approach has a significant probabilistic interpretation, which may be utilized in order to analyze and interpret resulting predictions. They have undertaken the experimental phase by providing empirical results on the EachMovie dataset of user-ratings. Data of user profile have been collected by CiteSeer digital library. The Collaborating technique called PD can be viewed as hybrid method of memory-based and model-based algorithms. It has inherented the advantages of memory-based approaches by being fairy straiforward and recording all the data. In addition, it does not demand a compilation step in order to include new data. On the other hand, like other model-based approaches, its predictions are precise and the recommendations have a consequential interpretation. Every user's preference is treated as manifestation of their personality type. The personality type is materilized in a vector of the user's ratings in the database. After the system has obtained the active user's known ratings, authors have calculated the probability of having the same personality with every other user. PD makes better predictions than four other algorithms respectively two memory-based and two model-based approaches.

An interesting approach regarding hybrid collaborative filtering was proposed in (Melville et.al, 2002). They have introduced an elegant and effective approach in which was combined component of content and collaborative techniques. It was incorporated a content-based predictor in order to improve the existing user data and to generate personalized predictions via collaborative filtering. Theircontent-boosted collaborative filtering approach have given evidence to outperform the pure content-based predictor, the pure collaborative filter and even a naive hybrid approach. In order to mitigate the drawbacks of collaborating filtering algorithms, it was exploited content information of the items already rated. The content-based prediction is employed in order to convert the sparse matrix of user-ratings into a complete matrix. The framework was carried out in a domain of movie recommendation. They have utilized the user-movie rating from the EachMovie dataset (available from the Compaq Systems Research Center). The dataset is composed of a user-ratings data with the rating profile of each user and each movie. Regarding the methodology framework carried out in this research paper, they have compared their hybrid approach with a pure-based predictor and a naive hybrid approach. In order to perform comparison, it was incorporated a subset of rating data from the EachMovie dataset. Recommendation were developed for the withdrawn movie using the different predictors. The quality of the different recommendation algorithms was evaluated throughout the comparison of the predicted values for the withheld rating to the current ratings. They have addressed the sparsity problem by using the pseudo rating matrix, which embody a full user-rating matrix containing ratings for all movies. Therefore, it was aroused the probability of finding similar users with similar preference profile. Regarding the first-rater problem, the recommendation was developed using a content-based predictor for the user. They have further enhanced the process of generating effective prediction by using content-based recommendation even for the other users.

Another body of work in the area of collaborative filtering was proposed by Canny (2002). This article has presented a novel collaborative method, which is inteded to protect the privacy of user data. It has supported the Probabilistic Factor-analysis Model (PFM). In this approach the protection of data is carried out by a peer to peer protocol. Moreover, it deals with missing data and does not demand their default value. The novel approach exhibits advantages in speed and storage when compared to the preceding works. There are some significant contributions that this research paper has provided to the body of knowledge. First, this paper has presented the privacy-preserving scheme and explained the protocol generally. The second contribution consists of the new collaborative filtering that appears to be the most accurate CF comparing to the previous one, to their best knowledge. And the third is conducting testing and experiments in order to evaluate the accuracy, speed and storage.

Traditional collaborative filtering methods are based on the postulation that real-world data are stationary. Motivated by the sale prediction problem, Xiong et al (2010) introduced to the research community a factor-based algorithm that has the capability to take into consideration the time component when developing predictions. This paper has treated tensor factorization problem with a specific time dimension constraint. In addition, it is conducted a fully Bayesian treatment in order to attain automatic model complexity control. Sampling procedures are performed in order for the system to learn the model. The novel approach dubbed as Bayesian Probabilistic Tensor Factorization (BPTF) is tested in real world data ratings. Real relational data are in process of evolving and experience strong temporal patterns. This proposed framework is able to model time evolving relational data. This paper has tackled the overfitting problem by extending the approach with Bayesian algorithms. In regard to scalability function, authors have incorporated Markov Chain Monte Carlo (MCMC) process to perform the learning task.

Marlin et. al (2011) discussed the key problem in rating-based collaborative filtering: the possibility of a fundamental incompatibility among the features of recommender data sets and the supposition of valid estimation of statistical model experiencing missing data. In this research paper, it is explained and explored in depth the missing data process in the recommender systems and their influence in the standard statistical model estimation. The paper described components of recommender datasets linking them to the statistical theory of the model estimation. Authors have proposed a framework together with a set of modified evaluation protocols, which handle non-random missing data. Rating prediction provided by this paper, give strong evidence that their developed model can perform better than the standard models.

In closing of Collaborating Filtering section, we must emphasize that because of artificial data are usually not reliable due to the properties of CF tasks, it is more suitable to undertake live experiments with real world dataset regarding CF research.

Visual Data Mining for Collaborative Filtering

This section of the chapter will disclose some of the most compelling research works in regards to visual data mining techniques employed in the collaborative filtering domain.

Mei and Shelton (2010) have discussed the visualization problem of information. When given all the ratings they place users' items in only one area of Euclidian space. In other words, they indented to set near the user, items that have high ratings. Authors address this collaborative filtering problem by employing Markov Chain Monte Carlo and considering this issue as real-valued non-linear Bayesian Network. In this paper, it is provided a metric or criterion to evaluate the quality of a visualization and comparison of the results against Eigentaste, which is a locally linear embedding in the real-world dataset. The major task of this approach is to extract the similar and dissimilar object relating the users and their items and to characterize them in significant graph. One shortcoming been alleviated from the underlying approach regards collaborative filtering, which does not perform well in the browsing process of online collection. Instead, their framework builds a fixed graph composed of the entire items and provides zoom and scroll for the purchaser in order to inspect and to have a detailed overview of the objects that might be of his interest. Thus, the approach aims to build correctly the items that will be near to the users so that they will increase the buyer interest. Furthermore, it is taken a D-dimensional Euclidian Space dubbed as embedded space. Every user is determined as a point pertaining at this space. When two data points are close, consequently the two users corresponding to these data points are assuming to have alike user-profiles. The distance between the point characterized by the user and the point of the item must correspond to the respective rating of the item. The collaborative visualization is deemed appropriate not only in online shopping, but even in music navigation or photography as well.

Boner (2001) presented an interesting work regarding the evaluation and implementation of the 3-dimensional collaborative information visualization (CIVs). The author has motivated its work by claiming that 3-D CIVs can be meaningfully adjusted in terms of single users and users of large groups so far. They have introduced a virtual document space, which allows accessing various files that are disposed online in Library school. In the second space, is embedded the user interaction data, which is visualized. The major concern of this paper is addressing the level of adaptability of the 3D space in the single user and at the same time the space of the associated single user, which is considered 2-dimesional.

Another significant paper regarding visual data mining techniques incorporated for collaborative filtering is Chen et al (2007). They proposed a novel approach namely as NEAR (navigating exhibitions, annotations and resources) panel representing a method, which manages digital collections and users' ratings on behalf of collaborative filtering. Moreover, this approach discloses through graphs the relationship of data and their similarity items. They have build an online media repository, which involves several resources and comments. This repository is updated and renewed by the daily contribution of the users, which are pushed and motivated to add their annotation, and their analysis related to the source and to the objects. The framework of NEAR is inspired from some existing concepts of visualization and its sound theoretical background. The user logs and their rating are stored and kept as evidence of trends. The NEAR approach allows undertaking new navigation supporting the discover of data relations. It is advised for the researchers to take advantage of the function of recommendation, which discovers relationship between data based on similarity, co-reference and inclusion between neighbors. This can help in making sense of what is happening between users and subsequently, derive in a meaningful graphical depiction of data relation. By making use of the NEAR panel, users can not only discover underlying relationship, but also can even discover potential relations between various data points. One major drawback of the framework stated by authors is its lack of self-explanatory property, which is encouraged to be developed in the future and to be overcome by using rich human interaction information.

Xiong et al (1998) advocated a method aiming to build visualization of social interaction in the social network. They discussed the application of their framework in the Usenet and specified the level of improvement that can induce in previous systems. They mainly focus on incorporating visualization as interface tool to facilitate the simple users to access the collaborative filtering information rather than visualizing large of commercial or technical data. In this paper, collaborative filtering can be viewed through object-to-object diagram identifying like-minded user by the distance of their corresponding data points. Their research work can be viewed as new way to conduct visual collaborative filtering by exploring the People-to-Object graph.

A general graphical model incorporating visual content for collaborative filtering was discussed in (Boutemedjet & Ziou, 2006). The relevance of visual documents, which embodies the visual features, is predicted from the construction of the preference profile of the users with similar behavior and taste. Authors have addressed this task coming up with a probabilistic latent variable model where the preferences of user are mixed with items. In addition, they create a framework for deriving in an accurate generative model that alleviates the problem of the new item, which is one of the popular shortcomings that collaborative filtering techniques pose.

Gruvstad et al. (2009) have designed a data mining system of a movie search as a recommendation system, which captures similar movies with movies that have been search from users. They have incorporated the Netflix prize dataset. Their approach resembles to some extend to the Amazon recommendation system. Users are enabled to have a full overview of the results thanks to the result visualization provided from their approach. Results can be inspected efficiently and quickly when possessing strong data mining element, which can be joined with usable visualization methods. Based on user logs and preference the system can enforce or mitigate the score depending on the user ratings. User is provided with an appealing property of being capable to change the results. The recommender system designed in this paper generates recommendations of the points, which appear to be nearer, but at the same time the user has the right to modify it by renewing the graphical presentation. This leads to a self-enhanced system from time to time. One additional characteristic that previous existing methods do not have, is the participation of users in giving their feedbacks and contributing in making the system more accurate and efficient. Authors' intention is to facilitate users in the process of discovering movies they have never heard of them before that can accommodate their preference.

Heckerman et al (2001) have presented a graphical model regarding the probabilistic relation dubbed as the dependency network. This approach represents an alternative over Bayesian Network and in addition, it is potentially cyclic. The property of probability is specified as a set of conditional distribution assigned for each node when it is provided its parents. In this paper, it is explained and it is characterized the process of graph learning. Major focus in this paper it is given to the application of the representation of the probabilistic inference, collaborative filtering and the visualization of data relations. The graph structure is learned through conducting classification/ regression for every variable in the local distribution of the respective variable. This leads to making the dependency network inconsistent, meaning that local distribution can be yielded throughout the inference from only one joint distribution. However, when it is appeared to have adequate data, the local distribution can be approximately stable because it is learned from the same data. It is provided strong evidence that the approach of dependency network can be applied efficiently in collaborative filtering and for visualization of predictive relationship. One of the major purposes of this paper is to describe profoundly the basic concepts of dependency networks.

Dependency network is practical for collaborative filtering due to the network storing the probabilistic quantities in the local distribution. It is proposed to be created a query network which can learn the probabilities of a given set of the queries.

Vlachos and Svonava (2012) have presented a novel approach, which aimed to visualize neighborhood and the cluster relationship in the graphical structures. Its focus relies on describing the way this scenario can be applicable to the recommender systems domain. The idea of the technique is to map the original object distance onto two dimensions by maintaining the core of the important distance. Their approach is composed of a subset of essential distances pertaining to the minimum spanning tree graph. Moreover, this work constitutes a novel scenario of having object relationship and cluster information at the same time. In this framework, there are carried out two-dimensional mapping techniques with dendograms for obtaining solution for the cluster structure when viewed at various granularities. The cluster information is represented on the dendosgram, which is overlayed in the third dimension. The general user can view the cluster information at different granularities. Moreover, he can take part on the process by choosing the cluster resolution from the low level to the higher one that multi-resolution features provide for the user. A substantial benefit of this approach is it property of making use of both metric and non-metric distance functions. In addition, this piece of work is implemented significantly to a visual recommender system for movies and facilitates examination of the actor-movie bipartite graph in the graph space. The collaborative filtering system generates accurate movie prediction and recommendation according to a selected pivot movie. It is explored in depth in order to have a understanding of how the proposed high dimensional data embedding approach can be applied in the movie recommendation system. In few words, this framework incorporates a movie repository specified by the graph structure. When given a set of movies, the recommender system can yield a set of similar movies that are projected and grouped in two dimensions. Additional feature is provided from this approach such as automatic streaming of movie trailer picked from users.

Igo Jr. et al. (2002) have proposed a recommendation system for movies that exhibit an incremental SVD prediction algorithm at the same time it reveals a multidimensional visualization of the recommendation results. This proposed system can generate effective prediction and allow update of daily basis in the real time. Recommendations combined with various features of the movies are portrayed in parallel bar grams by making use of the multidimensional visualization tools. The user can interactively explore short list of results by a low number of clicks. Another additional feature that this approach comprises is demonstrating that the system can generate recommendation and prediction at the same convenience for group of users as for the single users. Therefore, the recommender system can be transformed in a recommender system for a group of users. The recommendations generated for group of users can be displayed as parallel dimensions along with the recommendations of individual users. This can lead to facilitation for users in order to filter by utilizing a long list of attributes and recommendation in order to select the items of interest to the whole group. Therefore, in this paper, it is strongly advocated that the movie recommender system can be substantially enhanced when addition of multidimensional visualization is added.

Kermarrec & Moin (2012) reported some methods for global and personalized visualization CF data. User and items are combined into a high dimensional latent feature space according to predictor function particularly projected to comply with the visualization criteria. Data is mapped into a two dimensional space through the Principal Component Analysis PCA and Curvilinear Component (CCA). PCA sets all the items in a Global Item MAP in order for the correlation between latent features to be optimally. On the other hand, CCA designs Personalized Item Maps (PIMs) for specifying a small subset to a respective user. The two algorithms are applied in three versions of the MovieLens and the Netflix dataset. Thus, they have demonstrated they can incorporate good accuracy with compelling visual properties. The most significant feature that this novel approach provides is its ability to communicate latent information, which can be cumbersome to be interpreted to some extent. The graphical maps inherit the collective intelligence of large amount of users. These methods can be applied to different recommendation scenario. While GIM can be employed for monitoring purposes of public opinion about various products, on the other hand PIMs can help in visualizing comparison and difference among digital catalogue items.

CONCLUSION

Visualization techniques are very important for data analysis. Visual data mining is a powerful tool that allows users to extract and explore visual patterns in data. Visualization in data mining process is increasingly used a tool for supporting user interaction and for displaying data. Visual data mining addresses the major drawback of traditional non-visual data mining techniques that allow users to discover meaningful predefined patterns in data but do not provide visual forms of interpretation. Visual data mining is not a replacement for traditional data mining techniques; rather it augments the non-visual data mining approaches. Visual data mining can provide benefit to existing data mining techniques by providing the users with visual exploration and interpretation of data. The users can use these visual interpretations for further data mining. This chapter dealt with state-of-the-art visual data mining technologies that are currently in use apart. The advantages of visual data mining techniques were discussed extensively in this chapter and the benefit these techniques can provide when they are used in conjunction with traditional data mining techniques was emphasized throughout this chapter. The purpose of visual data mining and exploration is to integrate the data analysts in the data exploration process, so that the data analyst can get an insight into the data from the visual output provided by the visual data mining tools. Visual data mining tools have demonstrated high potential in exploring large databases.

Recommender systems facilitate and alleviate people digging through a large amount of information in order to find the most appropriate and useful information. One of the most prominent approaches of recommender systems is collaborative filtering (CF), which uses the known preferences of several users in order to build predictions or valuable recommendations for other novel users. Collaborative Filtering techniques are categorized in three kinds of major techniques namely, memory-based collaborative filtering, model-based collaborative filtering and hybrid collaborative filtering. Collaborating Filtering incorporates many challenges that the research community must address. CF approaches are required to have the capability of managing highly sparse data, to scale with the large amount of users and items, to provide the appropriate and valuable recommendation and prediction in a short period. Combining visual data mining techniques for collaborative filtering has lead to substantial improvement of the overall systems and can alleviate the shortcomings of traditional collaborative filtering techniques. The power of visual data mining and visualization provides valuable analysis tools and techniques that were not available to researchers earlier. Visual data mining can help in making sense of what is happening between users in collaborative filtering systems and subsequently derive meaningful graphical depiction of data relation.

REFERENCES

Adomavicius, G., & Tuzhilin, A. (2005). Toward the next generation of recommender systems: A survey of the state-of-the-art and possible extensions. *IEEE Transactions on Knowledge and Data Engineering*, *17*(6), 734–749. doi:10.1109/TKDE.2005.99

Aggarwal, C. C., Wolf, J. L., Wu, K. L., & Yu, P. S. (1999). Horting hatches an agg: A new graph-theoretic approach to collaborative. *Proceedings of theFifth ACM SIGKDD Int'l Conf. Knowledge Discovery and Data Mining*, ACM Digital Library.

Bilsus, D., & Pazzani, M. (1998). Learning Collaborative Information Filters. *Proceedings of theInt'l Conf. Machine Learning*.

Bobadilla, J., Hernando, A., Ortega, F., & Gutiérrez, A. (2012). Collaborative filtering based on significances. *Information Sciences*, *185*(1), 1–17. doi:10.1016/j.ins.2011.09.014

Börner, K. (2001). Adaptation and evaluation of 3-dimensional collaborative Information visualizations. *Proceedings of Workshop on Empirical Evaluations of Adaptive Systems*.

Boutemedjet, S. & Ziou, D. *(2006).* A Generative graphical Model for Collaborative Filtering of Visual Content. In *Advances in Data Mining. Applications in Medicine, Web Mining, Marketing, Image and Signal Mining* (pp. 404-415).

Breese, J., Heckerman, D., & Kadie, C. (1998). Empirical Analysis of predictive algorithms for collaborative filtering.*Proceedings of the 14th Conference on Uncertainty in Artificial Intelligence*.

Canny, J. (2002). Collaborative filtering with privacy via factor analysis. *Proceedings of the 25th annual international ACM SIGIR conference on Research and development in information retrieval SIGIR '02*, Tampere, Finland (pp. 238-245).

Card, S. K., Mackinlay, J. D., & Shneiderman, B. (Eds.). (1999). *Readings in Information Visualization—Using Vision to Think*. San Francisco: Morgan Kaufmann.

Chen, J., Zheng, T., Thorne, W., Zaiane, O., & Goebel, R. (2013). *Visual data mining of web navigational data*. Paper presented at the 17th International Conference on Information Visualisation.

Chen, V. Y., Oian, Ch. Z., & Woodbury, R. F. (2007). Visualizing collaborative filtering in digital collections. *Presented at11th International Conference Information Visualization (IV'07)*.

Collins, L. M., Hussell, J., Hettinga, R., Powell, J., Mane, K., & Martinez, M. L. (2007). Information visualization and large-scale repositories.*Library HiTech*, *25*(3), 366–378. doi:10.1108/07378830710820943

Elke, A. R., Matthew, O. W., Jing, Y., & Doshi, P. R. (2002). XmdvTool: Visual interactive data exploration and trend discovery of high-dimensional data sets. *Paper presented at theProceedings of the 2002 ACM SIGMOD international conference on Management of data*, Madison, Wisconsin.

Fayyad, U. M., Piatetsky-Shapiro, G., & Smyth, P. (1996). From data mining to knowledge discovery: An overview. In M. F. Usama, P.-S. Gregory, S. Padhraic, & U. Ramasamy (Eds.), *Advances in knowledge discovery and data mining* (pp. 1–34). American Association for Artificial Intelligence.

Fu, T. (2011). A review on time series data mining. *Engineering Applications of Artificial Intelligence*, *24*(1), 164–181. doi:10.1016/j.engappai.2010.09.007

Fu, T., Chung, F., Kwok, K., & Ng, C. (2008). Stock time series visualization based on data point importance. *Engineering Applications of Artificial Intelligence*, *21*(8), 1217–1232. doi:10.1016/j.engappai.2008.01.005

Goldberg, D., Nichols, D.; Oki, B. M, & Terry, D. (1992). Using collaborative filtering to weave an information Tapestry. *Communications of the ACM*, p61(10)

Gruvstad, F., Gupta, N. & Agrawal, Sh. (2009). Shiniphy - Visual Data Mining of movie recommendations.

Havre, S., Hetzler, E., Whitney, P., & Nowell, L. (2002). ThemeRiver: Visualizing Thematic Changes in Large Document Collections. *Visualization and Computer Graphics*, *8*(1), 8–20. doi:10.1109/2945.981848

Heckerman, D., Chickering, D. M., Meek, Ch., Rounthwaite, R., & Kadie, C. (2001). Dependency Networks for Inference, Collaborative Filtering and Data Visualization. *Journal of Machine Learning Research*, *1*, 49–75.

Hill, W., Stead, L., Rosenstein, M., & Furnas, G. (1995). *Recommndeing and Evaluating Choices in a Virtual Community of Use*. Conf. Human Factors in Computing Systems.

Hinneburg, A., Keim, D., & Wawryniuk, M. (2003). Using projections to visually cluster high-dimensional data. *Computing in Science & Engineering*, *5*(2), 14–25. doi:10.1109/MCISE.2003.1182958

Hiremath, P. S., & Kodge, B. G. (2010). Visualization techniques for data mining of Latur district satellite imagery. *Advances in Computational Research*, *2*(1), 21–24.

Hochheiser, H., & Shneiderman, B. (2004). Dynamic query tools for time series data sets: Timebox widgets for interactive exploration. *Information Visualization*, *3*(1), 1–18. doi:10.1057/palgrave.ivs.9500061

Huang, Z., Chen, H., & Zeng, D. (2004). Applying Associative Retrieval Techniques to Alleviate the Sparsity Problem. *ACM Transactions on Information Systems*, *22*(1), 116–142. doi:10.1145/963770.963775

Igo, F. Jr, Brand, M., Wittenburg, K., Wong, D., & Azuma, Sh. (2002). *Multidimensional Visualization for Collaborative Filtering Recommender Systems*. Mitsubishi Electric Research Laboratories.

Jiang, C., Coenen, F., Sanderson, R., & Zito, M. (2010). Text classification using graph mining-based feature extraction. *Knowledge-Based Systems*, *23*(4), 302–308. doi:10.1016/j.knosys.2009.11.010

Kashwan, K. R., & Velu, C. M. (2012). Performance analysis for visual data mining classification techniques of decision tree, Ensemble, and SOM. *International Journal of Computers and Applications*, *57*(22), 65–71. doi:10.5120/9426-3874

Keim, D., & Kriegel, H. (1996). Visualization techniques for mining large databases: A comparison. *IEEE Transactions on Knowledge and Data Engineering*, *8*(6), 923–938. doi:10.1109/69.553159

Keim, D. A. (2002). Information visualization and visual data mining. *IEEE Transactions on Visualization and Computer Graphics*, *8*(1), 1–8. doi:10.1109/2945.981847

Kermarrec, A. M., & Moin, A. (2012). *Data visualization via collaborative filtering* [Research Report]. (p. 23).

Kimani, S., Lodi, S., Catarci, T., Santucci, G., & Sartori, C. (2004). VidaMine: A visual data mining environment. *Journal of Visual Languages and Computing*, *15*(1), 37–67. doi:10.1016/j.jvlc.2003.06.005

Kumar, D., & Bharadwaj, D. (2011). Rise of data mining: Current and future application areas. *International Journal of Computer Science Issues*, *8*(5), 256–260.

Lin, J., Keogh, E., & Lonardi, S. (2005). Visualizing and discovering non-trivial patterns in large time series databases. *Information Visualization*, *4*(2), 61–82. doi:10.1057/palgrave.ivs.9500089

Linoff, G. S., & Berry, M. J. (2011). *Data Mining Techniques. For Marketing, Sales, and Customer Relationship Management* (3rd ed.). New York, NY: John Wiley & Sons Inc.

Marlin, M. B., Zemel, R., Roweis, S. T., & Slaney, M. (2011). Recommender Systems: Missing Data and Statistical Model Estimation.*Proceedings of the Twenty-Second International Joint Conference on Artificial Intelligence* (pp. 2686-2691).

Melville, P., Mooney, R. J., & Nagarajan, R. (2002). Content-Boosted Collaborative Filtering for Improved Recommendations. *Proceedings of the Eighteenth National Conference on Artificial Intelligence*, Edmonton, Canada (pp. 187-192).

Nilashi, M., Bagherifard, K., Ibrahim, O., Alizadeh, H., Nojeem, L. A., & Roozegar, N. (2013). Collaborative filtering recommender systems. *Research Journal of Applied Sciences. Engineering and Technology*, *5*(16), 4168–4182.

Oliveira, M. C., & Levkowitz, H. (2003). From visual data exploration to visual data mining: A survey.*IEEE Transactions on Visualization and Computer Graphics*, *9*(3), 378–394. doi:10.1109/TVCG.2003.1207445

Pazzani, M. (1999). A Framework for Collaborative, Content-Based, and Demographic Filtering. *Artificial Intelligence Review*, *13*(5/6), 393–408. doi:10.1023/A:1006544522159

Pennock, D. M., Horvitz, E., Lawrence, S. & Giles, C. L. (2000). Collaborative Filtering by Personality Diagnosis: A Hybrid Memory. In *Uncertainty in Artificial Intelligence* (pp. 473-480).

Pham, T., Hess, R., Ju, C., Zhang, E., & Metoyer, R. (2010). Visualization of diversity in large multivariate data sets. *Visualization and Computer Graphics*, *16*(6), 1053–1062. doi:10.1109/TVCG.2010.216 PMID:20975143

Quirin, A., Cordón, O., Vargas-Quesada, B., & de Moya-Anegón, F. (2010). Graph-based data mining: A new tool for the analysis and comparison of scientific domains represented as scientograms. *Journal of Informetrics*, *4*(3), 291–312. doi:10.1016/j.joi.2010.01.004

Rashid, A. M., Albert, I., Cosley, D., Lam, S. K., McNee, S. M., Konstan, J. A., & Riedl, J. (2002). Getting to know you: Learning new user preferences in recommender systems.*Proc. Int'l Conf. Intelligent.* doi:10.1145/502716.502737

Resnick, P., Iakovou, N., Sushak, M., Bergstrom, P., & Riedl, J. (1994). GroupLens: An open architecture for collaborative filtering of NetNews. *Computer Supported Cooperative Work*.

Saraswathi, K., & Babu, V. G. (2015). A survey on data mining trends, applications and techniques. *Discovery*, *30*(135), 383–389.

Sarwar, B., Karypis, G., Konstan, J. & Riedl, J. (2001). Item-Based Collaborative Filtering Recommendation Algorithms. *Proceedings of the 10th Int'l WWW*.

Shardanand, U., & Maes, P. (1995). Social information filtering, algorithms for automating - Word of Mouth. Proceedings of theConf. Human Factors in Computing Systems.

Shneiderman, B. (1996) The Eyes Have It: A Task by Data Type Taxonomy for Information Visualizations.*Proceedings of the IEEE Symposium on Visual Languages*, Silver Spring, MD (pp. 336–343). doi:10.1109/VL.1996.545307

Siguenza-Guzman, L., Saquicela, V., Avila-Ordóñez, E., Vandewalle, J., & Cattrysse, D. (2015). Literature review of data mining applications in academic libraries. *Journal of Academic Librarianship*, *41*(4), 499–510. doi:10.1016/j.acalib.2015.06.007

Simoff, S. J., Bohlen, M. H., & Mazeika, A. (2008). Visual data mining: An introduction and overview In Visual data mining, LNCS (Vol. 4404, pp. 1–12). Berlin, Heidelberg: Springer. doi:10.1007/978-3-540-71080-6_1

Soukup, T., & Davidson, I. (2002). *Visual Data Mining: Techniques and Tools for Data Visualization and Mining*. John Wiley & Sons, Inc.

Su, X., & Khoshgoftaar, T. M. (2009). *A survey of collaborative filtering techniques* (Vol. 2009). Advances in Artificial Intelligence.

Vlachos, M. & Svonava, D. (2012). Recommendation and visualization of similar movies using minimum spanning dendrograms. In *Information Visualization*, 1–17.

Ward, M., Peng, W., & Wang, X. (2004). Hierarchical visual data mining for large-scale data. *Computational Statistics*, *19*(1), 147–158. doi:10.1007/BF02915281

Xiang, W., Niansu, H., & Min, H. (2014). Application of Association Rules Data Mining in the Determination the Operation Target Values in the Thermal Power Plant. *Paper presented at theInternational Conference on Computer Science and Service System*, Bangkok, Thailand.

Xiong, L., Chen, X., Huang, T., Schneidery, J., & Carbonellz, J. G. (2010). Temporal collaborative filtering with Bayesian probabilistic tensor. In SIAM Data Mining.

Xiong, R., Smith, M. A., & Drucker, S. M. (1998). Visualizations of collaborative information for end-users.*Ministry of Research and Information Technology*. Retrieved from http://www.fsk.dk/fsk/publ/elcom/

Yu, C., Zhong, Y., Smith, T., Park, I., & Huang, W. (2009). Visual data mining of multimedia data for social and behavioral studies. *Information Visualization*, *8*(1), 56–70. doi:10.1057/ivs.2008.32

KEY TERMS AND DEFINITIONS

Collaborative Filtering: Collaborative filtering allows recommendations to users taking into account how other users have rated items. Collaborative filtering needs an extensive database containing exclusively the ratings made by users over the items (Bobadilla et al., 2012).

Content-Based Filtering: Content-based filtering systems allow recommender systems to provide recommendations to users based on the information related to items that other users have rated previously.

Data Mining: Data Mining is defined as the process of analyzing large information repositories for deriving and discovering useful patterns and identifying hidden relationships among the data (Siguenza-Guzman et al., 2015).

Hybrid Collaborative Filtering: Hybrid filtering methods allow recommender systems to provide recommendations through techniques based on both collaborative and demographic filtering methods (Bobadilla et al., 2012).

Recommender Systems: Recommender systems are software tools and techniques for suggesting items to users by considering their preferences in an automated fashion (Nilashi et al., 2013).

Visual Data Mining: Visual data mining combines data mining methods and computer-aided, interactive visual techniques to discover novel and interpretable patterns with the help of human perception abilities (Chen et al., 2013).

Chapter 13
Data Stream Mining Using Ensemble Classifier:
A Collaborative Approach of Classifiers

Snehlata Sewakdas Dongre
Ghrce Nagpur, India

Latesh G. Malik
Ghrce Nagpur, India

ABSTRACT

A data stream is giant amount of data which is generated uncontrollably at a rapid rate from many applications like call detail records, log records, sensors applications etc. Data stream mining has grasped the attention of so many researchers. A rising problem in Data Streams is the handling of concept drift. To be a good algorithm it should adapt the changes and handle the concept drift properly. Ensemble classification method is the group of classifiers which works in collaborative manner. Overall this chapter will cover all the aspects of the data stream classification. The mission of this chapter is to discuss various techniques which use collaborative filtering for the data stream mining. The main concern of this chapter is to make reader familiar with the data stream domain and data stream mining. Instead of single classifier the group of classifiers is used to enhance the accuracy of classification. The collaborative filtering will play important role here how the different classifiers work collaborative within the ensemble to achieve a goal.

INTRODUCTION

The necessity to handle large amount of data has given birth to the data mining field where it analyzes the processing time and memory for the static data sets. Larger data sets can be handled by the data mining approach but it fails when dealing with the continuous data. Usually, a previously trained model cannot be updated when new type of data arrives, at that time model cannot handle the new data and model should be retrained using new data. This is a very tedious process to retrain model whenever the

DOI: 10.4018/978-1-5225-0489-4.ch013

new data arrives. In response to the continuous supply of data, stream data mining approach has recently emerged. The data stream algorithms are capable to deal with huge volume of data even with the changing nature of the data which are not addressed by the data mining.

Data stream is giant amount of data which is generated in uncontrolled manner at a quick rate from many applications like call detail records, log records, sensors applications, emails, blogging, twitter posts and etc. Data stream mining has gained the attention of so many researchers, so it has become a latest topic of research. As this is huge in the volume it is very difficult to store all data and analyze them and use their characteristics in the future. Massive volume and high speed are the characteristics which make the data stream difficult to handle by the traditional data mining techniques. In the data mining the underline data distribution is static which is not happened in data stream. In data stream the underline data distribution is changing as the data may span long time and the sources which generates may undergo some changes. Data stream is not stable but dynamic in the nature it means it changes with time and these changes are known as concept drift. A rising problem in data streams is the handling of concept drift. The new challenges have brought the concept of stream data. Several algorithms have been developed to handle the data stream.

Generally, in data mining, data can be stored in memory as the size of data is not beyond storage as well as processing time is not an issue. But in the data stream mining the data is beyond the storage capacity as it is huge in the volume as well as it requires lot of time to process the data which is not affordable. So space and time limitation is there in mining of the data streams. In the data streams the data may evolve as per the time so algorithm, which can adapt automatically, is required to handle the evolving data. An algorithm which can adapt the changes, takes less time & memory but gives poor accuracy will not be accepted. So the main issues related to the data stream are: - time, space, concept drift and the most important is accuracy. A good algorithm should give high accuracy, adapt the changes, requires less time to process the data and demand very less memory to store.

Data Stream Mining

The data stream classification is having simple model as it takes data streams as input to the classifier then on the basis of input the learning model is created. Once the model is created it is can predict/classify unknown data streams. The classifier should be capable to take care of data stream mining issues. The classifier can be of two types 1) Single classifier and 2) ensemble classifier

1. **Single Classifier:** Single classifier can process the data quickly and gives the result in very less amount of time. In case of data stream the single classifier's performance is going to be poor as the volume is very high. If a new data comes in the data stream, the single classifier cannot handle the concept drift properly. So the single classifier is not suitable for the data stream mining. There are number of single classifiers available in the literature like Bayesian classifier, decision trees, naïve Bayes, SVM, Nearest Neighbor etc. (Utgoff, Berkman & Clouse, 1997; Utgoff, 1989)

2. **Ensemble Classifier:** Concept of ensemble classifier is a innovation in the field of data mining. Ensemble classification method is the group of classifiers which works in collaborative manner. It has introduced the concept of collaborative filtering. All the classifiers in the ensemble work collaboratively to classify data stream. The group of classifiers gives better performance than the single classifier. Instead of using one classifier if the group of classifier is used for data stream

classification then it can handle the data streams properly as it can adapt the changes easily and gives the good accuracy. The classifiers in the ensemble can be similar type of classifiers or different classifiers.

There are number of ways to create the ensemble classifiers:

- Using single learning method with a different subset of training data.
- Using different learning methods.

The Ensemble classifier works on the simple concept shown in the *Figure 1*.

Input data stream is provided to the Ensemble classifier. Ensemble Classifier tries to classify the given input data stream using the base classifier predictions and combined their prediction and finally gives the global prediction. If the prediction given by any classifier is below the specified threshold, then update the ensemble means add a new classifier and replace the poor performing one. This will help the ensemble to improve the performance.

There are mainly two methods used in ensemble Bagging and Boosting. Each uses the number of learning methods and gives the output. They are differentiated by the way of combining the model and produce the output by combining the prediction of all the learning models. In Bagging the dataset of size S is resampling which creates the M different bootstrap training sets of size S which are further used to create M different base learners in the ensembles. In Boosting series of M base learners generated,

Figure 1. Basic structure of ensemble classification and updating

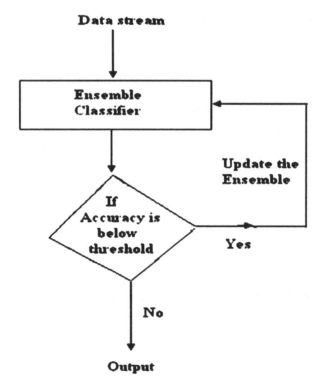

each base learner is learned from weighted training set. The misclassified examples have more weights. The concept behind using the ensemble is, group of classifiers gives better performance as compared to single classifier. Instead of single classifier the group of classifiers is used to enhance the accuracy of prediction as well as of classification. The collaborative filtering plays an important role about how the different classifiers work collaborative within the ensemble to give the better output.

Let's take an example of patient to understand the concept of bagging (Han & Kamber, 2008). A patient wants to have diagnosis, on the basis of his symptoms. Patient consults several doctors rather than a single doctor. The diagnosis that is suggested by majority of doctors will be taken as final diagnosis. Here each doctor has equal vote and the final decision made on the majority vote. Now if we substitute each doctor with a classifier. So the bagging works in the same way. Bagging is stands for bootstrap aggregation in which the training set is bootstrap sampled. A training set D_i of d tuple is sampled with replacement from original set of tuples for iteration i(i= 1, 2, ..., k).

Let's take an example to understand the concept of boosting (Han & Kamber, 2008). A patient wants to have diagnosis, on the basis of his symptoms. Patient consults several doctors rather than a single doctor. Based on the performance of previous diagnosis, the weights are assigned to each doctor's diagnosis. Grouping of the weighted diagnoses will give the final diagnosis. Substitution of each doctor with a classifier and to understand the concept of boosting is performed in a same way. Each training tuple is assigned with weight in Boosting. A group of classifier is trained. When a classifier M_i is trained the weights are updated so that next classifier M_{i+1}, will give more concentration to the examples that were incorrectly classified by M_i. Final output will be combination of each classifier's vote where the accuracy of that classifier will decide the weight of its vote.

BACKGROUND

Data stream is massive in the volume for partitioning of data and supply to the model for the classification in a proper manner is also very much important. Using the windowing concept in the data stream mining is the recently used. In ensemble, prediction from each classifier is taken and gives the combined output. Combining the predictions can be done in different ways. The researchers have done much study on ensemble classifiers. So finally we will discuss the techniques that are utilizing concept of windowing and the techniques that are using the ensemble classifier:

1.   Windowing Concept for the Data Stream Mining:
     a.   **Windowing Technique** (Dongre & Malik, 2014): Windowing is the simple technique; It captures the data in the window and supply to the learner. It keeps the new data and throw outs the older data to keep the classifier trained with the new data rather than the older data. The sliding window is the popular technique but it uses fixed size of window.
     b.   **ADWIN** (Dongre & Malik, 2014; Bifet, Frank, Holmes, & Pfahringer, 2010; Bifet & Gavalda, 2009; Bifet & Gavalda, 2007): It uses the adaptive windowing concept. ADWIN keeps the observations in the window that automatically detect the change in data and adapts. It keeps the window of recent data and discards the older one. Most of the methods use ADWIN along with the ensemble method to increase the performance.
     c.   **Instance-Based Window** (Attar, Chaudhary, Rahagude, Chaudhari & Sinha, 2011): Author has proposed a instance window of fixed size which contains the recent instances to train

the new ensemble. It stores only the instances of the latest concept. So that when the new ensemble is trained using the instances which are stored in the instance-based window that can learn the latest concept more easily and recover from it fast.

d. **Hoeffding Window Tree** (Bifet & Gavalda, 2009): Author has used the hoeffding tree with the ADWIN. Any decision tree which uses hoeffding bound along with the concept of ADWIN is known as the Hoeffding window tree.

e. **Optimal Window Size** (Yang, Yan, Han, & Wang, 2013; Kuncheva & Zliobaite, 2009; Zliobaite & Kuncheva, 2010): The window size is the one of the parameter which affects the classification accuracy. When the size of window is small then it cannot contain the sufficient instances to train a model. And when the size of window is too big, then it cannot track the change quickly in the data stream (Yang, Yan, Han, & Wang, 2013). Kuncheva & Zliobaite, 2009), have tried to get the optimal value for window size. (Zliobaite & Kuncheva, 2010), has also tried to get the optimal value for window size for the sudden concept drift.

2. Ensemble Concept for the Data Stream Mining:

a. (Zhu, Wu & Yang, 2004) have proposed the Dynamic Classifier Selection(DCS) with the attribute information. Attribute information is useful to partition the evaluation set is into disjoined subsets. This is useful to find out the classification accuracy of each classifier in the ensemble. Subset that has similar instances in the evaluation set with the test instance is constructed on the basis of attributes of test instance. The classifier which is having higher accuracy for those subsets is chosen for the classification of the test instances.

(Wu et al., 2009) have used AEC(Adaptive Ensemble Classifier) for concept drift in the data stream which uses the bagging approach with the naïve bayes classifier. This algorithm works on online and offline both modes. And three phases component classifier subset selection, ensemble classifiers and reconstruction and classifier updating. Online classification model will create the diversity between different base classifiers and then reconstructing and selecting the subset of the ensemble which contains the portion of ensemble that gives better accuracy.

(Wang, Fan, Yu & Han, 2003) have used the ensemble of different classifiers and train them with the sequential chunks of data stream. Each classifier is weighted according to their accuracy for test data classification. So the initially the data stream is divided in the same size of partitions then the each classifier is trained from the each partitions. According to their accuracy for the test data, the each classifier is weighted. There are number of classifiers, we cannot use all of them for classification. Only k classifiers which give the higher accuracy are used for prediction. They selected the k classifiers with the help of ensemble pruning. For the ensemble pruning, set of classifiers with the benefit output is used. For that every classifier is consulted for a test data.

Kuncheva (2004) has thrown the light on the need of the ensemble classifier over the single classifier and discussed the various approaches to build the ensemble. The different approaches for ensemble are grouped as follows:

1. **Dynamic Combiners:** It also known as horse racing algorithm. In this group individual experts are trained and learn the data stream.

2. **Updating Training Data:** This group uses the concept of using the new data rather than the old data to train the classifier so that the each expert in the ensemble will properly learns from the new data.

3. **Updating the Ensemble Members:** Updating of the ensemble can be done in two mode it can be online or it can be batch mode.
4. **Structural Changes of the Ensemble:** The poor performing ensemble will be replaced with a newly added expert.
5. **Adding New Features:** The new feature can be added into the ensemble to increase the performance. Author has described number of different approaches related with the ensemble classifier for the data streams.

Bifet, Holmes, Pfahringer, Kirkby and Gavalda (2009), have proposed a new approach bagging with ASHT. ASHT (Adaptive Size Hoeffding Tree) is the variation in the hoeffding tree. They have assumed that the smaller trees are best when changes in the data streams. Smaller trees can adapt the changes easily. But the larger the trees work better when less changes are there in the data stream.

Wankhade and Dongre (2011) have proposed a new algorithm named AEBC(Adaptive Ensemble Boosting Classifier), that uses the concept of Boosting, along with the Adaptive sliding window concept and naïve bayes, hoeffding tree as the base classifier. By concept of Adaptive sliding window the change has been detected. If there is a change in data an alarm has been raised and then the updating of the ensemble to improve the performance.

Learn++.NSE (Gangardiwala & Polikar, 2005; Elwell & Polikar, 2011) is a ensemble approach which uses the concept of weighted majority voting in which the weights are updated according to the changes. This algorithm is very popular as it can handle variety of concept drifts like gradual or sudden, even it can handle the variable rare drift.

(Dal et al., 2014) have proposed Hellinger weighted ensemble approach in that the Hellinger distance has been used to find the distance between two different batches. When a new batch is available then the new model is learnt and stores all the models. The weights are assigned to the models which should be inversely proportional to the distances of the batches. If the distance is less between the batches means the data are more similar. This method deals with concept drift even the skewed data problem. It also handles the instance propagation. By using this algorithm the accuracy is improved.

(Zliobaite, Bifet, Pfahringer & Holmes, 2014) have proposed a new framework that uses three active learning strategies to handle the concept drift in the data streams. When the accuracy of classifier decreases, new classifier is created on the new data. When the concept drift is detected the new classifier replaces the old one. The authors have concluded that the proposed method can handle the changes which occur in the data stream.

VFDT(Very Fast Decision Tree) has been developed by (Domingos & Hulten, 2000). VFDT is a decision tree learning system that uses Hoeffding bound. It does not store any example; it only stores the tree and statistics. It scans the examples only once and need not to store the examples for future use. The VFDT is ready to use model means it can predict at any time. It can handle the larger datasets but it cannot handle the concept drift.

(Hulten, Spencer & Domingos, 2001) have proposed a new algorithm called CVFDT which stands for Concept-adapting Very Fast Decision Tree with the aim to handle time changing data. CVFDT uses the sliding window technique for keeping the recent data. If the concept drift occurred a new subtree with best attribute is created. If the new subtree gives the better result than the old one then the new tree replaced the old one. In this way the CVFDT handles the concept drift.

(Masud, Gao, Khan, Han & Thuraisingham, 2009) have proposed the ensemble technique which uses the multi-partition multi-chunk approach. In this the consecutive data chunks with n-fold partitioning of data is used to train the classifiers in the ensemble. This technique is better than the single partition single chunk ensemble approach. There are two main reasons. First, in the ensemble updating if a classifier is removed, all information taken from that chunk is also lost in case of single partition single chunk approach. But in case of multi partition multi chunk approach, there may be one or more classifier may exist from a chunk. Second, to train the certain number of classifier, single partition single chunk ensemble approach requires more data as compared to the multi partition multi chunk approach. So the single partition single chunk approach is keeping the old & outdated classifiers which can degrade the performance of the single partition single chunk approach. So multi partition multi chunk ensemble approach minimizes the classification errors as compared with single partition single chunk ensemble approach.

(Street & Kim, 2001) has proposed SEA(Streaming Ensemble Algorithm) which uses the ensemble classifier with bagging approach and the base learner is C4.5. This approach uses the sequential chunks of training data and creates separate classifiers. All these classifiers are grouped together to build an ensemble. The number of classifier is fixed to maintain the size of ensemble. If a new classifier is added to improve the performance of ensemble then it replaces the poor classifier. The SEA can handle the large amount of data or streaming data. It also handles the concept drift.

Dynamic Weighted Majority (DWM) (Kolter & Maloof, 2007) uses the ensemble of base learners. Ensemble predicts on the basis of weighted majority vote of experts. Each expert is assigned with weight. When a new example comes, that passes to each expert. Each expert will predict for that example. The final prediction is the weighted majority vote of each expert. Expert's weight decreases if it misclassifies the example. If the final prediction of the ensemble is wrong then a classifier is added to the ensemble. The expert that has weight below the specified threshold is removed. So the DMW dynamically creates and removes the experts based on its prediction so that it can cope with the concept drift.

OzaBag is the online bagging (Oza & Russell, 2001a; Oza & Russell, 2001b), it is approximation of batch bagging. In bagging, resampling the dataset of size N to create different bootstrap of training sets of the size N. Each one dataset is used to train a base learner. So if there is M bootstrap datasets that can build M base models. Bootstrap datasets generated by the random sampling with the replacement of the original dataset.

OzaBoost (Oza & Russell, 2001a; Oza & Russell, 2001b), is a online boosting algorithm which uses the weighted training set to create M base models. The samples that are misclassified by the previous model have more weights in the training set for the current model. AdaBoost is the famous algorithm used for Boosting.

OCBoost (Pelossof, Jones, Vovsha & Rudin, 2008) is proposed in 2008. It uses the AdaBoost method. OCBoost is a boosting algorithm which updates the boosted classifier's weights. This approach tries to minimize the exponential loss function of AdaBoost. When the AdaBoost is training with the m examples, after that a single example is added to the m training examples and the retraining is provided with this m+1 examples.

ANNCAD- (Law & Zaniolo, 2005) proposed an approach ANNCAD which stands for Adaptive NN Classification Algorithm for Data-streams. This approach uses the Nearest Neighbors classifier as it is very difficult to find the value of K in KNN Algorithm. In this method author expand the test point's nearby area until the classification results obtained are satisfactory. This approach has less processing time and taking less memory. But it cannot handle the sudden concept drift.

OVA- This is One-Versus-All decision tree classification (Hashemi, Yang, Mirzamomen & Kangavari, 2009) method learns the k classifiers for k-class problem. k binary classifiers differentiate the examples from one class to the examples of other classes. A new instance classifies by running the k classifiers and the classifier who gives the highest confidence is selected. This approach is faster in training and updating and gives the good accuracy.

(Liang, Zhang & Song, 2010) have proposed UCVFDT i.e. Uncertainty-handling and Concept-adapting Very Fast Decision Tree, this method is making use of CVFDT technique. UCVFDT is based on CVFDT and DTU. UCVFDT can deal with the concept drift even it can handle the uncertainty. This approach is well suited for the real life applications.

(Zliobaite, 2007) has listed the three main problems while new expert is added in the ensemble. First, what should be the weight of the newly added expert? Second, expert should participate from the beginning or it should have some extra period for acceleration. Third, the weight associated with the expert should be variable of fixed. To solve the above three problems this technique has proposed the modification so that it can resolves the problem.

Streaming Random Forest has proposed by (Abdulsalam, Skillicorn & Martin, 2011). By using an entropy-based technique this method detects the concept. Two techniques are merged together; one is creating the decision tree from streams and second building Random forests. This produces perfect algorithm which can easily update to handle the concept drift.

(Dongre & Malik, 2013), have proposed a new ensemble algorithm which uses the concept of Boosting along with the adaptive windowing. This algorithm is giving good accuracy, requires less memory and time.

MAIN FOCUS OF THE CHAPTER

Issues, Controversies, Problems

A good algorithm handles the different issues of data stream mining. Data continually growing in volume and in speed also changing underlying concepts are the challenges in the data stream mining. There are two fundamental issues in the data stream mining:

1. **Issue Related with the Performance**: As the data stream flowing continuously and it is huge in the volume, so it requires lot of memory to store it and time to process. To give the response to the online data and limitation in of memory and time, the algorithm which is used for data stream mining should have following properties:
    a. As the data is coming continuously and rapidly so to handle this fast data, the algorithm should be capable enough to scan the data at one pass.
    b. As the data is high in volume, algorithm should not store all the data in the memory rather only important statistics related to model should be stored. Even though an algorithm is taking minimal time and memory but predicting incorrectly will not of use. So the accuracy is the main parameter. Finally there are mainly three performance issues:
        i. Accuracy
        ii. Time
        iii. Memory.

So data stream mining requires the algorithms which take less time, memory and giving good accuracy.

2. **Issues Related with the Adaptation**: In the normal data mining the data is still that is, the underlying concept that maps the features to class labels is not variable. But in the data streams the underlying concepts that maps features to the class labels is variable, this is known as concept drift. Concept drift handling is the main concern in the data stream mining. An algorithm which has learned from the data stream but concept drift may occur at any time if the algorithm is not able to adapt the changes it would not be of use. To be a good algorithm it should adapt the changes and handle the concept drift properly. There are four types of concept drift. First type of concept drift deals with noise which shows the changes that are deemed non-significant and are apparent as noise. The second type of concept drift (Blip) represents a rare event. This is very useful in some of the applications. The third type of concept drift is the gradual concept drift where the changes happens gradually where as in the fourth type of concept drift changes happens abruptly so it is known as abrupt or sudden concept drift. The first and second type of concept drift means noise. So the concept drift classify mainly in two categories in the literature: sudden and gradual concept drift.

3. **Evaluating the Accuracy of a Classifier**: There are different techniques for assessing accuracy:
   a. **Holdout Method** (Han & Kamber, 2008): The given dataset is randomly partitioned into two parts- training set and the testing set. The training set is useful to build the model where as the testing set is useful to test the model.
   b. **Random Subsampling** (Han & Kamber, 2008): It is a variation of the holdout method. The holdout method is repeated n times in the random subsampling and the average of the accuracy will give the final overall accuracy.
   c. **Cross Validation** (Han & Kamber, 2008): In the n-fold cross validation the data is randomly partitioned in the n partitions. Each partition is a subset of the dataset of equal size and mutually exclusive subsets. $D_1, D_2 \ldots D_n$. In i iteration the D_i is used as the test set and the remaining n-1 sets are used as the training the model.
   d. **Bootstrap** (Han & Kamber, 2008): In the bootstrapping the given tuples are samples uniformly with the replacement. The model can select the same tuple more than once.

4. **Limitations of Data Stream Mining:** Various issues related with the data stream mining are already discussed in the chapter. Though there would be good algorithm to deal with the different issues related with the data stream mining but there is also the limitation lies for the data stream mining:
   a. As the data is in huge in the volume we need to sampled the data. The sampling of data is very much related with the accuracy. If we choose the proper sampling method the accuracy increases.
   b. All parameters are not useful for the analysis of data. Some attributes are contributing more in the classification and some are useless. So the selection of attribute which are important for the classification is also plays the important role. If we choose the wrong attributes for classification then it will affect the accuracy of model.
   c. The time and memory requirement by the data stream mining is more than the traditional data mining for the stationary datasets.

If the Ensemble classifier used for classification of data stream, its accuracy is also affected by other parameters like how many classifiers grouped to prepare an ensemble. If number of classifiers is more it will take more time and more memory for classification as each classifier need to give their own prediction and then their predictions are combined to give the final prediction. The input parameters that used are also plays important role like selection of attribute, weights of each classifier or weight of each tuple if the boosting is used, the size of the window is very much important if the windowing technique is used.

REAL TIME APPLICATIONS

Today data mining is used in a vast array of areas:

1. **Data Mining for Financial Analysis** (Han & Kamber, 2008): Banks and the financial institutes are providing number of services like credit cards, loans, insurance and stock investment services etc. Data mining can be applied for the financial data to predict the future. With the help of Data mining they can do the analysis of financial data for that a data warehouse. Using data mining technique classification and clustering customers for targeted marketing can be identified. Financial crimes and money laundering is a big threat to financial industry but with the help of Data mining technique this can be detected and reduced as well. Similarly the credit card fraud can also be avoided by using data mining techniques. Before granting the loan, the analysis is done for the loan payment prediction.
2. **Data Mining for Retail Industry** (Han & Kamber, 2008): Now the online shopping became a trend. There are number of websites who offers the online shopping. This leads to a huge volume of data. Data mining on this retail data discloses the customer's choice, customer buying behaviors, customer shopping patterns and trends. This will help to increase the quality of customer services, goods consumption ratio is increased, customer satisfaction and retention also reduced the cost of business.
3. **Data Mining and Recommendation Systems** (Han & Kamber, 2008): When a customer does online shopping, there are number of products available in the websites. Recommender systems, recommends different products to the consumers related to their choice like online news articles, CD, Books etc. Recommender systems may use either a content- based approach, a collaborative approach, or a hybrid approach that combines both content- based and collaborative methods. In the content based approach, the items are recommended to the user on the basis of query entered by user in the past. In the collaborative methods the recommendations are given to the user based on the other user's choice that has similar interests. In the hybrid approach it will take the combination of content- based approach and a collaborative approach. Data mining techniques are useful to recommends the user different items according to their interest.
4. **Data Mining for Intrusion Detection**: Security is the primary requirement by all networks. There is huge volume of data which is generated by the networks. So the data mining techniques comes into the picture to deal with it. To preserve the data security and to prevent the attack Intrusion Detection System (IDS) is used. Classification technique of data mining is frequently used for the Intrusion Detection System. There are standard datasets are also available for Intrusion Detection System like KDD CUP 99 Dataset. Most of the researchers make use of this standard dataset and apply number of data mining techniques for the practical experimental purpose. In (Dongre &

Wankhade, 2012) author has also implemented the Intrusion Detection System and used the ensemble classifier for it.

5. **Data Mining for Heath Care**: Health care is another area where the data mining techniques are playing important role. There are number of decision support systems that give the assistance to the doctors to maximize the accuracy level. Analysis can be done for different types of symptoms of diseases and find the exact diagnosis based on different data mining techniques. But it is difficult to analyze the continuous data like ECG in an electrical signal which is generated by the heart of a human. Wireless sensors can be used to monitor signals like ECG, EEG and BP. These sensors generate the continuous data that is continuously flowing and dynamic in nature so to handle this type of data stream mining algorithms are useful. In (Thombre & Dongre, 2013) authors have applied the different data stream algorithms and uncovered the important patters and results.

FUTURE RESEARCH DIRECTIONS

The authors have suggested that a new classifier can be proposed to deal with data stream and different issues related to it. That can use the concept of ensemble classifier with windowing techniques.

CONCLUSION

The authors have discussed the issues related to the data stream mining. The selection of data from the data stream through windowing techniques is also having its own advantage. Also discussed different approaches used in the data stream classification. We have seen the collaborative approach of the ensemble classifier that improved the classification accuracy also handle the concept drift properly. Ensemble classifier has given the new meaning to the data stream mining. Data Stream Mining involves so many issues but if uses the suitable methodology, it will try to minimize time and memory requirement and maximize the accuracy.

REFERENCES

Abdulsalam, H., Skillicorn, D., & Martin, P. (2011). Classification using Streaming Random Forests. *IEEE Transactions on Knowledge and Data Engineering*, *23*(1), 22–36. doi:10.1109/TKDE.2010.36

Attar, V., Chaudhary, P., Rahagude, S., Chaudhari, G., & Sinha, P. (2011). An Instance-Window Based Classification Algorithm for Handling Gradual Concept Drifts. *Proceedings of the International Workshop on Agents and Data Mining Interaction* (pp. 156-172).

Bifet, A., Frank, E., Holmes, G., & Pfahringer, B. (2010), Accurate Ensembles for Data Streams: Combining Restricted Hoeffding Trees using Stacking. *Proceeding of 2nd Asian Conference on Machine Learning, Tokyo, Japan* (pp. 226-240).

Bifet, A., & Gavalda, R. (2007). Learning from time-changing data with adaptive windowing. *Proceedings of the SIAM International Conference on Data Mining* (pp. 443-448).

Bifet, A., & Gavalda, R. (2009). Adaptive Parameter-free Learning from Evolving Data Streams.

Bifet, A., Holmes, G., Pfahringer, B., Kirkby, R., & Gavalda, R. (2009). New Ensemble Methods for Evolving Data Streams. *Proceedings of International Conference on Knowledge Data Discovery* (pp. 139-148).

Dal Pozzolo, A., Johnson, R., Caelen, O., Waterschoot, S., Chawala, N. V., & Bontempi, G. (2014). Using HDDT to avoid instance propagation in unbalanced and evolving data streams, *In the Proceedings of International joint Conference on Neural Networks.* 588-593

Domingos, P., & Hulten, G. (2000). Mining high-speed data streams. *Proceedings of the sixth ACM SIGKDD international conference on Knowledge discovery and data mining* (pp. 71-80). doi:10.1145/347090.347107

Dongre, P., & Malik, L. (2014). A Review on Real Time Data Stream Classification and Adaptiing to various Concept Drift Scenarios. *Proceedings of the IEEE International Advance Computing Conference*, 533-537.

Dongre, S., & Malik, L. (2013). Algorithm for Concept Drifting Data Stream Mining. *International Journal of Computer Science and Network*, 2(1), 107–111.

Dongre, S., & Wankhade, K. (2012). Intrusion Detection System Using New Ensemble Boosting Approach. *International Journal of Modeling and Optimization*, 2(4), 488–492. doi:10.7763/IJMO.2012.V2.168

Elwell, R., & Polikar, R. (2011). Increamental Learning of Concept Drift in Non stationary environments. *IEEE Transactions on Neural Networks*, 22(10), 1517–1531. doi:10.1109/TNN.2011.2160459 PMID:21824845

Gangardiwala, A., & Polikar, R. (2005). Dynamically Weighted Majority Voting for incremental Learning and Comparison of three Boosting Based approaches. *Proceedings of International joint Conference on Neural Networks* (pp. 1131-1136).

Han, J., & Kamber, M. (2008). *Data Mining: Concepts and Techniques* (2nd ed.). San Francisco: Morgan Kaufmann Publishers-An imprint of Elsevier.

Hashemi, S., Yang, Y., Mirzamomen, Z., & Kangavari, M. (2009). Adapted One-versus-All Decision Trees for Data Stream Classification. *IEEE Transactions on Knowledge and Data Engineering*, 21(5), 624–637. doi:10.1109/TKDE.2008.181

Hulten, G., Spencer, L., & Domingos, P. (2001). Mining time-changing data streams. *Proceedings of the seventh ACM SIGKDD international conference on Knowledge discovery and data mining* (pp. 97-106). doi:10.1145/502512.502529

Kolter, J., & Maloof, M. (2007). Dynamic weighted majority: A new ensemble method for tracking concept drift. Proceedings of the Third IEEE International Conference on Data Mining ICDM '03 (pp. 123-130). IEEE.

Kuncheva, L. I. (2004). Classifier Ensembles for Changing Environments. *Proceedings of the International Workshop on multiple classifier systems, Italy.*

Kuncheva, L. I., & Zliobaite, I. (2009). On the window size for Classification in Changing Environments. *Journal of Intelligent Data Analysis, 13*(6), 314–323.

Law, Y., & Zaniolo, C. (2005). An Adaptive Nearest Neighbor Classification Algorithm for Data Streams. *Proceedings of 9th European Conference on Principals and Practice of Knowledge Discovery in Databases* (pp. 108-120). Springer-Verlag. doi:10.1007/11564126_15

Liang, C., Zhang, Y., & Song, Q. (2010). Decision Tree for Dynamic and Uncertain Data Streams. *Proceedings of 2nd Asian Conference on Machine Learning* (pp. 209-224).

Masud, M., Gao, J., Khan, L., Han, J., & Thuraisingham, B. (2009). A multi partition multi chunk ensemble technique to classify concept drifting data streams. *Proceedings of the 13th Pacific-Asia Conf. on Knowledge Discovery and Data Mining (pp. 363-375). Springer-Verlag Berlin*, Heidelberg.

Oza, N., & Russell, S. (2001). Online bagging and boosting. In *Artificial Intelligence and Statistics* (pp. 105-112).

Oza, N., & Russell, S. (2001). Experimental comparisons of online and batch versions of bagging and boosting. *Proceedings of the seventh ACM SIGKDD International Conference on Knowledge discovery and data mining* (pp. 359-364). doi:10.1145/502512.502565

Pelossof, R., Jones, M., Vovsha, I., & Rudin, C. (2009). Online coordinate boosting (Technical Report TR2009-086).

Street, W., & Kim, Y. (2001). A streaming ensemble algorithm (SEA) for large-scale classification, *Proceedings of the seventh ACM SIGKDD International Conference on Knowledge discovery and data mining* (pp. 377-382). doi:10.1145/502512.502568

Thombre, S., & Dongre, S. (2013). Data Stream Mining for Health Care Application, *International Journal of Management. IT and Engineering, 3*(9), 96–105.

Utgoff, P. E. (1989). Incremental induction of decision trees. *Proceedings of the Fifth International Conference on Machine Learning* (pp. 161-186).

Utgoff, P. E., Berkman, N. C., & Clouse, J. A. (1997). Decision tree induction based on efficient tree restructuring. *Journal of Machine Learning, 29*(1), 5–44. doi:10.1023/A:1007413323501

Wang, H., Fan, W., Yu, P., & Han, J. (2003). Mining Concept Drifting Data Streams using Ensemble Classifiers. *Proceedings of the ninth ACM SIGKDD international conference on Knowledge discovery and data mining* (pp. 226 – 235). doi:10.1145/956750.956778

Wankhade, K. K., & Dongre, S. S. (2011). A New Adaptive Ensemble Boosting Classifier for Concept Drifting Stream Data. *Proceedings of The 3rd International Conference on Computer Modeling and Simulation* (pp. 417-421).

Wu, D., Liu, Y., Gao, G., Mao, Z., Ma, W., & He, T. (2009). An Adaptive Ensemble Classifier for Concept Drifting stream. *Proceedings of the IEEE Symposium on Computational Intelligence and Data Mining.*

Yang, J., Yan, X., Han, J., & Wang, W. (2013). Discovering Evolutionary Classifier over High Speed Non-static Stream. doi:10.1145/2499907.2499909

Zhu, X., Wu, X., & Yang, Y. (2004). Dynamic Classifier Selection for Effective Mining from Noisy Data Streams. *Proceedings of the IEEE International Conference on Data Mining.*

Zliobaite, I. (2007). Ensemble Learning for Concept Drift Handling-the Role of New Expert.*Proceedings of the 5th International Conference on Machine Learning and Data Mining in Pattern Recognition* (pp. 251-260).

Zliobaite, I., Bifet, A., Pfahringer, B., & Holmes, G. (2014). Active Learning With Drifting Streaming Data. *IEEE Transactions on Neural Networks and Learning Systems, 25*(1), 27–39. doi:10.1109/TNNLS.2012.2236570 PMID:24806642

Zliobaite, I., & Kuncheva, L. I. (2010). Theoretical window size for classification in the presence of sudden Concept drift (Technical Report Number BCS-TR-001-2010).

KEY TERMS AND DEFINITIONS

ADWIN: It uses the adaptive windowing concept. ADWIN keeps the observations in the window and it can automatically detect current pace of change and adapts it.

Bagging: In Bagging firstly the dataset of size S is resample which creates the M different bootstrap training sets of size S which are further used to create M different base learners in the ensembles.

Boosting: In Boosting series of M base learners generated, each base learner is learned from weighted training set.

Concept Drift: The underlying concept that maps the features to class labels is variable. This is known as concept drift.

Data Stream: Data stream is giant amount of data which is generated uncontrollably at a quick rate from many applications like call detail records, log records, sensors applications, emails, blogging, twitter posts and etc.

Data Stream Mining: Mining the Data Streams.

Ensemble Classifier: Ensemble classification method is the group of classifiers which works in collaborative manner.

Chapter 14

Statistical Relational Learning for Collaborative Filtering a State-of-the-Art Review

Lediona Nishani
University of New York Tirana, Albania

Marenglen Biba
University of New York in Tirana, Albania

ABSTRACT

People nowadays base their behavior by making choices through word of mouth, media, public opinion, surveys, etc. One of the most prominent techniques of recommender systems is Collaborative filtering (CF), which utilizes the known preferences of several users to develop recommendation for other users. CF can introduce limitations like new-item problem, new-user problem or data sparsity, which can be mitigated by employing Statistical Relational Learning (SRLs). This review chapter presents a comprehensive scientific survey from the basic and traditional techniques to the-state-of-the-art of SRL algorithms implemented for collaborative filtering issues. Authors provide a comprehensive review of SRL for CF tasks and demonstrate strong evidence that SRL can be successfully implemented in the recommender systems domain. Finally, the chapter is concluded with a summarization of the key issues that SRLs tackle in the collaborative filtering area and suggest further open issues in order to advance in this field of research.

INTRODUCTION

With the dramatic spread of Internet, many connections and interactions have taken place in the networks. Therefore, information relying on people reactions has experienced a dramatic growth. Social Networks, which are named due to the crucial role of humans, are concentrated in the social relations that people have among them. In order to exploit these large amounts of data, it is required designing new algorithms and appropriate techniques for gathering valuable information. The field of expertise,

DOI: 10.4018/978-1-5225-0489-4.ch014

which deals with the aforementioned challenges, is Social Network Mining *(SNM)*. Its major purpose is to extract information about network objects, behaviors and activities that cannot be yielded if the entities were to be examined individually.

A social network represents a social structure of entities known as nodes, which are related by one or more specific types of interdependency, such as friendship, common interests or same opinions. Social network analysis considers social relationships based on the network theory perspective; nodes represent people, whereas ties represent relations between them. Together they form a graph-based structure, which experiences significant complexity. Social networks can be categorized in four significant types due to various domains on which they operate:

1. **Citation Networks:** Deal with storing scientific papers, the relation of their subjects across their paper and corporate authors or joint paper reference
2. **SNS (Semantic Network Service) Websites**: Concern the organization of people and their related friends or professional contact for example: Facebook, LinkedIn, Instagram, twitter, etc
3. **Social Shopping Websites**: Related to e-commerce and opinion mining exploring products
4. **Social Media Websites**: Concern the suggestions about movies, music relying on user preference

Social Network Analysis has appeared to be one of the major techniques in social networks (Wasserman & Faust, 1994) intending to establish a model that can map entities and the relations between them. The probability of two entities to build a link between them may depend on the likelihood of having similar attributes. On the other hand, two entities that have developed a connection or link between them have good probability to have similar attributes.

One of the most compelling techniques of Social Network Analysis is the Statistical Relational Learning, which have emerged when traditional statistical approaches could not treat relational and complex data. Traditional approaches consider only independent and fully distributed data; therefore, they do not take into account dependent and complex relational structure of data. Furthermore, traditional Inductive Logic Programming (ILP) and relational learning do not model noisy data, hence do not perform in the presence of uncertainty. Nowadays, systems generate real world datasets, which represent multi–relational, heterogonous and semi structured data. Data mining systems deal everyday with noisy data and uncertainty. Hence, statistical relational learning approaches help to overcome these issues. Statistical relational learning can be implemented in different domains. One important task of the SRL is dealing with the recommender systems problem. Recommender systems are personalized information tools that generate recommendations, suggestions and predictions. They are employed in different areas where users might want suggestions in order to select among many various objects. For example, online portals of news provide headlines where the reader can focus. Moreover, in e-commerce perspective, online sites generally display a short list of the products in order for the user to have an overview of what the online shop provides. Subsequently, the user can select the product and explore it in more details either purchasing it.

A web page is linked with the web server, which contains a database with items available from the site. Due to the large number of items in the database, it is deemed appropriate to show the object list, which can be selected by the user. Recommender systems employ various algorithms in order to perform recommendation tasks. The algorithms aggregate items from like-minded users, thus by eliminating the item, which have been selected before and suggest the items, which have not been rated by the user. The most well-known algorithms deployed in recommender systems are collaborative filtering and content-based filtering. Collaborative Filtering is concentrated on figuring out similar items; for each user that has rated items, the algorithm finds out the similar items, subsequently it aggregates and suggests them to the user.

This review chapter presents a comprehensive scientific survey from the basic and traditional techniques to the-state-of-the-art of SRL algorithms implemented for collaborative tasks. Authors throughout this chapter aim to disclose the most prominent methods and body of work related to Statistical Relational Learning combined with collaborative filtering techniques. These approaches combined together intend to alleviate the shortcomings of previous techniques. It is claimed that the research work can serve as a helpful roadmap for further researches and practice area.

The research chapter is structured as follows. First, it is provided an introduction to Statistical Relational Learning approaches (SRL). Along the chapter, the recommender systems are examined by focusing specifically at one of the most popular recommender system method: the collaborating filtering. In addition, authors have deepened their survey with the most significant research works that have combined SRL with Collaborating Filtering (CF). Finally, authors summarize and identify open issues in this area of research while providing significant findings for the aforementioned collaborative filtering systems.

BACKGROUND

Statistical Relational Learning

Statistical Relational Learning (SRL) is a new branch of machine learning for representing and learning a joint distribution over relational data (Getoor & Taskar, 2007). Getoor and Mihalkova (2011) have defined that Statistical Relational Learning are: "Methods that combine expressive knowledge representation formalisms such as relational and first-order logic with principled probabilistic and statistical approaches to inference and learning". There are some strong reasons why Statistical Relational Learning approaches have experienced a dramatic success and have become an emerging research area in the research community. SRLs constitute an important role in data mining. These algorithms are introduced with a set of candidate features and a model of selection process. The process of feature is decupled from modeling. Usually it can be performed manually. This comprises the most important challenge to the fully integrated application in real world practice where data is recorded in a relational way. Therefore, it is of paramount importance to employ statistical modeling techniques to explore richer data structures and to identify new and complex sources of evidence.

Statistical methods can effectively handle large quantities of noisy data. SRLs are widely exploited from the research community; this fact has given rise to a wide variety of different formalisms, models and probabilistic programming languages. Probability logic-based formalism determines probabilities in two kind of different methodologies: direct and indirect techniques. In the direct technique, probabilities are provided clearly for each probabilistic fact. In the indirect approach, formalisms are not associated to their probability. In this case, the probability is defined from an associated real-valued parameter.

As learning is a fundamental part of the SRL formalism-based system, authors have deemed appropriate to introduce herein two major problems that might be taken into account: parameter estimation and structure learning (Esposito et al., 2009). When the observed data are obtained from an unknown distribution or behavior, the aim is to make sense of this novel distribution. Usually both structure and model parameters must be learned. The parametric SRL approach concentrates on probabilistic model with many finitely parameters by selecting a single model that outperforms the others. There are other nonparametric techniques, which employ probabilistic models with infinitely many parameters and multi-relational process models.

The major difference between traditional statistical approaches and statistical relational learning techniques is the fact that SRL deals with relational data while traditional models deal with propositional data. Therefore, data can be categorized as follows:

- **Propositional Data:** the data mining approaches systems mostly have focused on propositional data and rather in relational data. Propositional data (Khosravi & Bina, 2010) constitutes identically structured entities that are supposed to be independent.
- **Relational Data:** comprise different types of entities and each entity is distinguished by different attributes sets. They are complex and reflect better our real world large-scale systems where data are modeled in multiple related databases.

State-of-the-Art in Statistical Relational Learning

Probabilistic Graphical Models (PGMs) comprise joint probability distributions throughout graph tools and encode a complex distribution over high dimensional space (Chulyadyo & Leray, 2013). Regarding Probabilistic Graphical Models, nodes define the random variables in domain while edges define the probabilistic relationship among variables. Bayesian Networks and Markov Networks are two different classes of PGMs. While Bayesian networks incorporate directed acyclic graph and represent the joint probability distribution as a product of conditional probabilities, Markov Networks employ undirected graph by representing the joint probability distribution as a product of potentials.

Bayesian Networks (BNs)

The structure of a Bayesian Network (BN) (Kersting & De Raedt, 2007) is composed of directed acyclic graph and its nodes constitute a set of random variables. A Bayesian Network has a set of parameter values that determine the probability distribution of each node based on a conditional probability. The conditional probabilities are defined in a conditional probability table (Khosravi & Bina, 2010) for each variable. The assignment's joint probability is computed by multiplying the conditional probabilities of each node value assignment when it is provided the value assigment of its parent. Bayesian Logic Programming (BLPs) are models, which underlie the Bayesian Networks. They incorporate logic programmming. BLPs mitigate the propositional character of BNs, therefore, they are treated as one of the most succcesful model employed in SRL. The major principle of BLPs is to set one to one mapping between ground atoms in the least Herbrand model together with the random variables (Kersting & De Raedt, 2007). The least Herbrand model and its direct relation of influence embody the Bayesian Network. BPLs derive the same benefit of the Bayesian networks and the advantage of definite clause logic. BLPs can facilitate the graphical representation due to the strict separation. In addition, they can easily model any kind of Bayesian Network including those with pure Prolog program.

Probabilistic Relational Models (PRM)

Bayesian Networks have been very successful due to their simplicity. However, one of their major limitations is having difficulty in establishing and maintaining a model in large-scale systems. Complex systems are mostly made of repetitive patterns and they can be viewed in terms of object and relations. Bayesian model lacks the concept of objects and relations; in addition, it cannot model relational data. Hence, Bayesian model is intended to work with single tables of independent and identically distributed data. The task of converting relational real world data into flat propositional data may experience statistical skew and loss of significant data. In order to learn statistical models, PRMs were emerged as substitution of BNs for SRL.

Probabilistic Relational Models represent the first successful model belonging to the group of Statistical Relational Learning (SRLs). They represent a combination of frame-based systems with Bayesian Networks (Friedman et al., 1999). PRMs represent an extension of Bayesian Networks aiming to handle and explore relational data.

Markov Logic Networks (MLNs)

Markov Logic Networks have been one of the most successful techniques attempted to perform statistical relational learning. From the syntax perspective, they widen the first-order logic and establish weight for every formula. On the other hand, from the semantic point of view, they embody a probability distribution for possible worlds by incorporating formulas and their respective weights.

First-order knowledge base (KB) is a set of sentences or formulas in the first order logic (Genesereth & Nilsson, 1987). Formulas are created by incorporating four types of symbols: constants, variables, functions and predicates. A first-order KB is assumed to be a set of hard contraints on the set of possible worlds: if a world breaks just one formula, it is assigned to have zero probability. The motivation behind MLN was to mitigate these contraints. Thus, when a world has broken one formula in the knowledge base first-order, it has low probability, however, it is not impossiple to happen. Formulas are linked with weight in order to reveal the constraint strength.

Domingos and Richardson (2004) attempted to propose Markov logic as a unifying framework due to the need of facilitating knowledge transfer through tasks and approaches. Syntactically speaking, Markov logic can be differentiated from the first-order logic only from the formula to be weighted. In their research work, they exemplify the way certain distinct approaches like probabilistic relational model, knowledge-based construction and stochastic logic programs can be formulated into Markov Logic. Moreover, they have developed algorithms for learning and inference purposes.

Singla and Domingos (2005) have introduced a discriminative approach aiming to train MLN. Their research work intended to optimize the conditional likelihood of query predicates. They have carried out experiments regarding entity resolution and link prediction, which indicate the benefits of their approach if compared to the generative MLN training and even when compared to pure probabilistic models and logical ones.

Wong (2015) has addressed the limitation that Markov Logic Networks pose: the demand for substantial amount of training data. This downside leads to time consuming efforts from the human kind to develop and prepare the required training examples. This derives from the fact that MLN pertain to the supervised approaches. This paper attempts to come up with a semi-supervised mechanism for MLN.

Researchers aim to maximize the likelihood function of the observation rather than maximizing the likelihood function of the labeled training data; the latter is broadly used in the MLN supervised learning. Throughout various experiments, this novel approach appears to perform better than the existing frameworks, which exploit labeled training examples.

Relational Markov Networks (RMNs)

A Relational Markov Network identifies a conditional distribution over all entities labels given the relational structure and their content attributes (Taskar et al, 2002). It indicates the cliques, potentials and atributes of entities that are related. Hence, a single model specifies a logic and a relational distribution for any collection of instance. A relational clique template consists of cliques constructed in an instantiation. RMNs are mostly spread to many relational field of interest specifically in social networks. They give extensive information regarding people relations and certain links. Relational Markov Networks incorporate conjuctive database queries dubbed as clique template. Every possible state of cliques must have a feature aimed to reduce the complexity of dependecies. Markov logic undertakes first-order logic in order to describe features. Markov logic allows the presence of uncertainty against arbitrary relation and thus making RMNs more general. Generally, RMNs have been trained in a discriminative way.

An interesting piece of work regarding Relational Markov Network is proposed in (Taskar et al, 2002). Their work introduces a technique that establishes Markov Networks by addressing the shortcomings of undirected models. Undirected models do not impose acyclicity constraints and their limitations are well approppriate for discriminative training. Researchers have enhanced the conditional likelihood of the labels when features are provided. This work gives strong evidence of how to make use of approximate probabilistic inference for the collective classification task of entities related in multiple way with each other. Finally, they show that classification accuracy can be enhanced through incorporating these algorithms.

Assis Costa and Oliveira (2014) have tackled the problem integrating different data set in Linked Data Cloud, which comprises challenges due to incomplete and incosistent data containing outliers. Therefore, they have presented a novel method relying on the relational learning algorithms by incorporating statistical approximation techniques. They have viewed the problem as a relational machine learning task to be solved. This approach is founded in a sparse structure that has the significant capability to scale effectively large datasets.

RECOMMENDER SYSTEMS

A recommender system consists of a personalized information agent, which provides recommendations and suggestions for objects and items that one user might prefer (Burke, 2007). The difference between the recommender systems and information retrieval systems stands in the semantics of user interactions. A result from a recommender system is taken as a suggestion while in information retrieval systems the result is presented as the best match to the respective query. A recommender system varies from an information retrieval system even in terms of personalization and agent (Burke, 2007). A recommender system customizes its responses to a particular user according to user preferences. Rather than providing matches to user queries, it aims to embody an information agent. One compelling property of recommender systems is to alleviate the information overload by suggesting personalized recommendation for each user due to user's previous likes and dislikes. There are many approaches proposed for recommendation systems. The recommendation method can be distingueshed based on the knowledge of the source. Previous research works have categorized recommender systems techniques as below (Burke, 2002):

- **Collaborative Techniques:** The recommender system operates by providing suggestions only via rating profiles of various users; they generate the items to the like-minded users by locating them with the same preference profile.
- **Content-Based Techniques:** The recommender system recommends an item to a user based upon a description of the item and the interest profile of the user (Pazzani & Billsus, 2007).
- **Knowledge Based:** The recommender system is based on knowledge, proposes items based on the inference about the preference of what a user needs (Burke, 2002).
- **Demographic Techniques:** This type of recommender systems works by generating recommendations through the demographic user profile. These methods have the capacity of indicating cross-genre niches and can withdraw the user to overcome and to try new items or products.

All of the four aforementioned techniques have their advantages and shortcomings; collaborative recommender systems have their own limitations, too. The most important challenges that collaborative techniques face when generating recommendations are:

- **New-User Problem:** In order to make sure that the generated recommendation is relevant to users, the system must learn the preference of user from the rating data that user generates by rating various items (Adomavicius & Tuzhilin, 2005). When the user is new, he does not have a rating preference, and the system is not able to recommend any items. This problem can be tackled by using strategies based on item popularity, item entropy, user personalization, etc (Rashid et al, 2002).
- **New-Item Problem:** This happens when an item cannot be recommended when no user has rated it before. Generally, new items face difficulties in being recommended to users. Collaborative systems only make use of the user's preference to develop recommendations. Hence, until a considerable number of users can rate the new item, the recommender system cannot develop a recommendation.
- **Sparsity:** Generally, the number of ratings obtained from users is much smaller than the ratings that must be predicted from the system. Recommender Systems do not perform well when the rating data of product is sparse. Mostly, users lack in rating items. Therefore, the matrix containing the user rating for each item is generally sparse. Hence, the systems have difficulty on finding out a set of users with similar rating. This challenge is of paramount importance when the system is in the first step of usage. It is crucial for systems to effectively predict rating from small number of samples.

Zhu et al., (2015) introduced an approach, which deals with recommender top-N queries in the relational databases. This methodology yields the top-N results for queries conducted by various users. Afterwards, the mechanism determines the linked keywords by computing respective weights of the related keyword. Thus, the approach proposed in this paper can be able to figure out new query words, which are connected to the prior queries and therefore can come up with a recommender query. The associated information of tuples is stored in a knowledge base database in order to evaluate and to examine the recommender query. The advantage of this approach relies on the improving the classic ranking strategy in Information retrieval. The knowledge base, associated interchangeably as the index is the key component of this novel approach.

State-of-the-Art in Collaborative Filtering

The concept of collaborating filtering has derived from the real world domain. Recommendations from other users are highly considered by users. They base their behavior by making choices through word of mouth, reference letters, news, media, public opinion, surveys, guide, etc. Recommender systems facilitate and alleviate people digging through a large amount of information to find the most appropriate and useful information. Recommender systems can provide personalized recommendations through different types of algorithms, including content based filtering, demographic filtering, collaborative filtering, and hybrid filtering methods (Bobadilla et al., 2012). In content-based filtering systems, recommendations are provided to users based on the information related to items that other users have rated previously (Bobadilla et al., 2012). This technique is quite useful for making recommendations for instance that of an adventure movie based on other users who have bought similar category of movies. Demographic filtering techniques on the other hand make recommendations to users taking the positive ratings made by other users who have shared demographic information such as age, gender, qualifications etc. This might help provide recommendations to users based on demographic information and could help provide culturally appropriate information. Collaborative filtering methods allow providing recommendations to users based on how other users have rated items. Hybrid filtering methods allow recommender systems to provide recommendations through techniques based on both collaborative and demographic filtering methods (Bobadilla et al., 2012).

One of the most prominent approaches of recommender systems is collaborative filtering (CF), which uses the known preferences of several users in order to build predictions or valuable recommendations for other novel users. Collaborative filtering consists of various people collaborating in order to help each other to conduct filtering by taking notes of their reactions. The reactions are dubbed as annotations. In other words, collaborative filtering facilitates individuals in the decision making process based on the other people point of view. This method focuses on learning predictive models of user preferences, interests, attitudes, or various behaviors from community data.

The first recommender system dubbed as Tapestry (Goldberg et al., 1992) has introduced for the first time the keyword "collaborative filtering (CF)". This phrase has been vastly used from the research community even though recommenders may not specifically collaborate with other preferences. The basic assumption of collaborating filtering is that if the user X and Y rate "n" items in the same way or have related preferences, they will behave alike even for new activities or items. CF consists of a user preferences database to predict further products or items that a new user might like.

Collaborating filtering incorporates many challenges that the research community must address. CF approaches are required to have the capability of managing highly sparse data, to scale with the large amount of users and items, to provide the appropriate and valuable recommendation and prediction in a short period. In contrast, content-based algorithms do not make use of any information or details about the items; items are handled as abstract entities. Therefore, collaborating filtering cannot predict items that have not been previously rated. On the other hand, content-based systems do not experience the issue dubbed as the cold-start problem because they benefit from the intrinsic item attributes. While collaborative filtering can develop recommendation to any pair of items as given an amount of sufficient training data, content-based algorithms treat items with similar attribute as similar. Collaborative Filtering techniques are categorized in three kinds of major techniques, namely, memory-based collaborative filtering, model-based collaborative filtering, and hybrid collaborative filtering (Su & Khoshgoftaar, 2009).

Memory-based collaborative filtering employs the whole item-database of user for generating a prediction. Every user is part of a group of people having alike behaviors. A prediction can be elaborated by the system when identifying the neighbors of individuals of a novel user. Memory-based algorithms foretell the rating of items obtained by a user through aggregating the rating of other items generated by the same user or aggregate the other users' rating for the same item. These techniques make use of a similarity metric to figure out several fixed number of items rated by people that are more comparable to the specific item explored by the recommendation system. The most popular similarity metrics aiming to rate vectors are the Pearson correlation coefficient and the cosine-based similarity metric (Adomavicius & Tuzhilin, 2005). Memory-based CF algorithms are easy to implement and perform well for highly dense datasets. Major challenges of this technique are the dependence on user-ratings and their performance deterioration on sparse data. Another memory-based shortcoming is being heuristics-based; they entail extensive hand-tuning upon novel datasets. Moreover, they demand more memory than model-based techniques because of their requirement of accessing the whole dataset when developing recommendations.

Model-based collaborative filtering has been investigated to deal with the drawbacks that memory-based incorporates. The development of machine learning models can make the system learn to distinguish complex patterns by training the system and being able to intelligently predict items for collaborating filtering purposes. Model-based methods develop recommendations for rating by using parametric or semi-parametric model and training on the rating data.

Hybrid collaborative filtering combines CF with other recommender systems approaches just like content-based filtering systems to overcome the shortcoming of pure systems. Therefore, they enhance the performance and the prediction process. They are based on the external content that generally is not available and has increased complexity.

Herein the chapter, authors have explored the most significant pure and hybrid techniques of collaborating filtering. Employing both collaborating filtering and content-based techniques can help in alleviating many recommender system problems, rather than employing only one of respective methods.

Some researchers have pointed out that the first recommender system was Grundy (Rich, 1979), which advocated the utilization of stereotypes to build user models relying on limited information of each indvidual. These user models were exploited for recommending related books to each user and the recommendation appeared to be effective. The definition, collaborative filtering was used for the first time by Goldberg et al. (1992). They have founded an experimental mail system dubbed Tapestry developed at the Xerox Palo Alto Research Center. They assumed that filtering of information can be more effective when human beings are included in the process of filtering. Tapestry was based in both content-based and collaborative methods. It aimed to deal with any incoming stream of electronic documents. It was a framework composed of an indexer, document store, annotation store, filterer, little box, remailer, appraiser, and reader/browser. The reason why researchers developed tapestry relies on the dramatic growth of electronic mail usage. Users were faced with large incoming documents. In order to exploit this bundle of documents, mailing lists were created. The mailing list orientates users to select only those lists, which might have been of their interest. This filtering approach could be further ameliorated when users specified a filter that scans all lists. The major principle that Tapestry constitutes is that filtering can be more effective when humans engage in the filtering process.

GroupLens (Resnick et.al, 1994) and Video Recommender (Hill et al, 1995) were the first recommender systems, which have incorporated collaborative filtering algorithms intended to automate predictions. The method proposed in Aggarwal et al. (1999) is based on the graph-theoretic approach and can estimate the nearest neighbor of user. There are works that have used person correlation coefficient to measure the similarity (Resnick et.al., 1994), however there are other cosine-based approaches (Breese et al., 1998) where the two users are considered as two vectors in a multi-dimensional space. The similarity between users can be estimated by calculating the cosine angle of two vectors.

Billsus and Pazzani (1998) have introduced a collaborative filtering technique where several machine learning methods just like Artificial Neural Networks are combined with feature extraction techniques. This technique outperformed the memory-based in terms of prediction accuracy and relevance. In Sarwar et al. (2001), the authors pointed out that item-based techniques can have better computation performance compared to traditional user-based collaborative methods. In addition, they appear to perform in comparable or better quality than best of user-based algorithms.

Many several algorithms have tackled the new user problem. Mainly they are based in the hybrid recommender systems. An interesting approach is introduced by Rashid et al. (2002), where various techniques are investigated to decide which is the best and relevant item for a new user. In order to avoid the new user problem, these approaches have made use of different scenarios like item entropy or user personalization.

In regards to the sparsity problem that collaborative techniques face, many significant methods have been explored. In order to mitigate the sparsity rating problem the collaborating system can utilize the information of the user profile to calculate user similarity. Pazzani (1999) have included gender, age, area code, education and employment information to develop effective recommendation and to enhance the problem of sparsity. In this case, this methodology of using not only user-rating, but other demographic information is dubbed as demographic filtering. The sparsity problem have been tackled from Huang et.al. (2004), too. They have mitigated the sparsity issue by carrying out the associative retrieval framework and related algorithms to explore transitive associations through their past feedback.

A significant piece of work was presented in Pennock et al. (2000). They have proposed a novel method named as Personality Diagnosis (PD). In this research work the probability whether users have the same "personality type" when having the same user preference profile for some specific items was calculated. The recommender system can make further predictions, if users like the new arrived items. The PD approach comprises some traditional similarity-weighting techniques where novel data can be included easily. Subsequently, personality diagnosis approach has a significant probabilistic interpretation, which may be utilized in order to analyze and interpret resulting predictions. They have undertaken the experimental phase by providing empirical results on the EachMovie dataset of user-ratings. Data of user profile have been collected by CiteSeer digital library. The Collaborating technique called PD can be viewed as hybrid method of memory-based and model-based algorithms. It has inherited the advantages of memory-based approaches by being fairy straight forward and recording all the data. In addition, it does not demand a compilation step in order to include new data. On the other hand, like other model-based approaches, its predictions are precise and the recommendations have a consequential interpretation. Every user's preference is treated as manifestation of their personality type. The personality type is materialized in a vector of the user's ratings in the database. After the system has obtained the active user's known ratings, authors have calculated the probability of having the same personality with every other user. PD makes better predictions than four other algorithms respectively two memory-based and two model-based approaches.

An interesting approach regarding hybrid collaborative filtering was proposed in (Melville et al., 2002). They have introduced an elegant and effective approach in which was combined component of content and collaborative techniques. It was incorporated a content-based predictor in order to improve the existing user data and to generate personalized predictions via collaborative filtering. Their content-boosted collaborative filtering approach have given evidence to outperform the pure content-based predictor, the pure collaborative filter and even a naive hybrid approach. In order to mitigate the drawbacks of collaborating filtering algorithms, it was exploited content information of the items already rated. The content-based prediction is employed in order to convert the sparse matrix of user-ratings into a complete matrix. The framework was carried out in a domain of movie recommendation. They have utilized the user-movie rating from the EachMovie dataset (available from the Compaq Systems Research Center). The dataset is composed of a user-ratings data with the rating profile of each user and each movie. Regarding the methodology framework carried out in this research paper, they have compared their hybrid approach with a pure-based predictor and a naive hybrid approach. In order to perform comparison, it was incorporated a subset of rating data from the EachMovie dataset. Recommendation were developed for the withdrawn movie using the different predictors. The quality of the different recommendation algorithms was evaluated throughout the comparison of the predicted values for the withheld rating to the current ratings. They have addressed the sparsity problem by using the pseudo rating matrix, which embody a full user-rating matrix containing ratings for all movies. Therefore, it was aroused the probability of finding similar users with similar preference profile. Regarding the first-rater problem, the recommendation was developed using a content-based predictor for the user. Another body of work in the area of collaborative filtering was proposed by Canny (2002). This article has presented a novel collaborative method, which is intended to protect the privacy of user data. It has supported the Probabilistic Factor-analysis Model (PFM). In this approach the protection of data is carried out by a peer to peer protocol. Moreover, it deals with missing data and does not demand their default value. The novel approach exhibits advantages in speed and storage when compared to the preceding works. There are some significant contributions that this research paper has provided to the body of knowledge. First, this paper has presented the privacy-preserving scheme and explained the protocol generally. The second contribution consists of the new collaborative filtering that appears to be the most accurate CF comparing to the previous one, to their best knowledge. And the third is conducting testing and experiments in order to evaluate the accuracy, speed and storage.

Marlin et al. (2011) discussed the key problem in rating-based collaborative filtering: the possibility of a fundamental incompatibility among the features of recommender data sets and the supposition of valid estimation of statistical model experiencing missing data. In this research paper, it is explained and explored in depth the missing data process in the recommender systems and their influence in the standard statistical model estimation. The paper described components of recommender datasets linking them to the statistical theory of the model estimation. Authors have proposed a framework together with a set of modified evaluation protocols, which handle non-random missing data. Rating prediction provided by this paper, give strong evidence that their developed model can perform better than the standard models.

Big data have emerged substantially in our technology-based area, therefore some gaps and issues have emerged in the recommender systems. Liu & Li (2015) have addressed these issues by designing parallel recommendation algorithms, which constitute an enhanced parallel item-based collaborative filtering founded on Hadoop. Studies according to parallel recommender systems have not been explored in depth so far. The novel parallel item-based collaborative filtering introduced here aims to enhance the performance of the recommendation due to introducing soft punishment on active users. The user-rating model is considered as a prediction model. Authors provide strong evidence that this novel parallel approach outperforms the previous algorithms in terms of speed and scalability.

In closing of Collaborating Filtering section, we must emphasize that because artificial data are usually not reliable due to the properties of CF tasks, it is more suitable to undertake live experiments with real world dataset.

STATISTICAL RELATIONAL LEARNING FOR COLLABORATIVE FILTERING

In this section, this research chapter will disclose herein the most prominent approaches, which combine various statistical relational learning methods in the collaborating filtering domain.

Latent structure of data has been taken into account in order to predict links that have been cumbersome to be analyzed from existing approaches. Hence, machine-learning research communities have examined the latent class model in combination with Bayesian nonparametric methods. Blei et al. (2003) discussed Latent Dirichlet Allocation (LDA), which constitutes a generative probabilistic model for collections of discrete data such as text corpora. LDA belongs to the three-level hierarchical Bayesian model where each item is modeled as a finite mixture over a corresponding set of topics. They introduce an efficient approximate inference technique based on variation methods and EM algorithm for empirical Bayesian parameter estimation. This approach is undertaken in document modeling, text classification and collaborative filtering. This chapter is interested to review collaborative filtering with LDA. Throughout their experimental phase, authors have made use of EachMovie collaborative filtering data. Regarding the collaborative filtering perspective, the model is trained on fully observed set of users. Then for each unobserved user, all movies are displayed except of the user's preferred one. The various algorithms are assessed due to the possibility that they assign to held-out movie. Furthermore, with a 1600 movies vocabulary, authors have found predictive perplexities, however the LDA model provides the best perplexities.

Miller et al. (2009) discussed a latent variable approach making use of Bayesian nonparametric techniques to infer the numbers of features at the same time when learning the respective entities with its corresponding feature. Each entity of the Bayesian nonparametric model has binary valued latent features that affect the relations depending on a set of known covariates. The authors claimed that their approach enables to simultaneously infer the number of the latent features and at the same time to infer the way these features influence observations. Their framework joins inferred features with known covariates aiming to predict the link prediction task. Previous existing class-based frameworks infer latent structure; consequently, proposed model is deemed more expressive than traditional methods and can utilize the output of previous approaches for initialization of its work. This chapter provides insightful evidence that their novel approach can perform well regarding link prediction tasks upon various dataset even on dataset that used to argue for class-based models. This approach exhibits expressiveness, therefore this lead to an enhancement of its performance in the datasets. Moreover, its advantage relies on its richer representations, which enable to mine patterns of interaction compared to class-based models.

Traditional collaborative filtering methods are based on the postulation that real-world data are stationary. Motivated by the sale prediction problem, Xiong et al (2010) introduced to the research community a factor-based algorithm that has the capability to take into consideration the time component when developing predictions. This paper has treated tensor factorization problem with a specific time dimension constraint. In addition, it conducted a fully baysian treatment in order to attain automatic model complexity control. Sampling procedure are performed in order for the system to learn the model. The novel approach dubbed as Bayesian Probabilistic Tensor Factorization (BPTF) is tested in real world data-ratings. Real relational data are in process of evolving and experience strong temporal patterns. This proposed framework is able to model time evolving relational data. This paper has tackled the overfitting problem by extending the approach with Bayesian algorithms. In regard to scalability function, authors have incorporated Markov Chain Monte Carlo (MCMC) process to perform the learning task.

Another domain where SRLs for collaborative filtering have been implemented is the Customer Relationship Management (CRM) field of interest. Customer modeling in CRM can be defined as a special case of a relational learning problem. Perlich and Hung (2010) have presented a connection between relational learning domain and CRM analysis particularly in customer classification and product recommendation. This work has been evaluated in seven-real world CRM datasets where empirical results have been gathered. This paper illustrated that relational learning techniques can be useful in addressing CRM modeling tasks. Authors have focused on predictive customer modeling underlying classification and probability estimation for cost-sensitive, decision-making and product recommendation. Relational learning can explore large-scale set of models, thus having the capability to capture predictable dependencies. This paper has modeled CRM with statistical relational learning techniques for product recommendation task. This tool was not meant to model all CRM, but it focused on performing exploration and capturing relevant information. The illustrated example in this paper was the bookstore dataset. They have utilized this dataset to examine the relational learning capability regarding the recommendation aspect. It is implemented the unified recommendation framework based on the extension of a relational learning, known as Probabilistic Relational Model (PRMs). In order to address the recommendation tasks, they have included a special existence attribute into the order table and obtained dependency frameworks relevant to order table attribute. The performance is evaluated with well-studied metrics including precision, recall F-measure and rank score.

Xu et al. (2010) have investigated complex social networks with Infinite Hidden Relational Models (IHRMs) for tasks of community detection, link prediction and product recommendation. A social network based IHRM employs edges associated with random variables. Probabilistic dependencies between these variables are determined based on the relational structure model. The hidden variables can transfer information in order to obtain non-local probabilistic dependencies. This model can serve for predicting entity attributes. In addition, it conducts a significant cluster analysis.

Statistical relational learning in the domain of collaborative filtering has been employed also to tackle the learning of trust. Rettinger et al. (2011) have pointed out that from a trustee perspective; trust is described as many relations happening among the agent to be trusted and the state of environment. They exemplify how to apply and learn context sensitive trust by employing SRL in the form of Dirichlet process model dubbed as Infinite Hidden Relational Trust Model (IHRTM). Several experiments are carried out in the user-ratings data from the eBay platform. Authors have demonstrated with empirical results that the trustee is enabled to specify the structure of the trust-situation by the inherent clustering process. Authors have highlighted that the employment of collaborative filtering combined with relational data can lead to an improvement of the trust assessment performance. Moreover, one other contribution of this framework is to enhance the cold start performance due to the learning and transferring knowledge faster. Dealing better with dynamic behavior in an open multi-agent system is another benefit that this approach provides, which is illustrated by records interaction generated from a scenario composed of two players.

A method for modeling large-scale multi-relational dataset was discussed in Jenatton et al. (2012). Their framework represents a bilinear structure capturing several orders of data interaction. Furthermore, it shares latent factors through various relations. Authors have employed their approach on a standard tensor-factorization dataset. Their application across various experiments provides evidence that can efficiently learn semantically meaningful representations. The model for relational data is appropriate to be deployed in multi-relational graphs and in natural languages. Regarding the algorithmic approach, in order to speed up the optimization, they have utilized several scenarios. They have claimed that cannot treat the NLP application as a standard tensor factorization problem. The proposed framework is deemed probabilistic and can be a benefit for the accounting domain because of the uncertainty presence of data. The paper empirically has demonstrated that this approach outperforms the previous existing frameworks.

One of the most well-known SRL approaches, Probabilistic Relational Model (PRMs) have been employed for collaborative filtering in (Newton & Greiner, 2014). For experimental purposes, they have exploited the EachMovie dataset. First, they have learned standard PRM, then they have specified the hierarchical PRMs, which comprise an extension of standard PRM throughout refining classes into hierarchies. It is shown that this approach allows greater presence of context sensitivity compared to standard PRM, thus being more expressive. This piece of work provides strong evidence that PRMs can be effectively employed in the collaborative filtering area. They have discussed the performance of standard PRMs deployed in the EachMovie dataset and then compared it with the effectiveness of hierarchical PRMs (Getoor, 2002).

Chulyadyo and Leray (2014) proposed a novel method to establish a personalized recommendation model based on PRM incorporating user's preferences. The paper demonstrates that carrying out PRM for collaborative filtering can mitigate the cold start problem and thus making able to generate personalized recommendations. This work has emerged from the need of intelligent recommender system in professional community and in large-scale systems where the system does not have the user profile, which is composed of incomplete and inconsistent data. This work intends to serve as a help for users by showing their search queries listed by relevance. Previous techniques could not address the problem of real world applications that demanded personalized recommendation, therefore, lacking the user profile existence.

Yuan et al. (2015) have examined the importance of retrieving the contextual information of users. Contextual information stands for the time and the locations of various users. These key terms are applied in the micro-blogging services and location-based social networks domain. In this paper, authors deal with contextual recommendation tasks and contextual search. User mobility behavior is associated with four major questions: who visits, which place, what time and for what activity. Thus, addressing these topical issues demand for effective methods in examining the mobility behavior. The underlying approach introduces a nonparametric Bayesian model, which does not require any parameter tuning. When given one out of the four aspects, the mechanism itself can provide the remaining others. A variety of experiments demonstrates that the novel model is truly effective in unveiling user's spatial temporal topic. In this paper it is implemented a novel probabilistic generative model based on non-parametric Bayesian in order to represent the mobility behavior of users in terms of spatial, temporal and activity. The key contribution of this new model is to disclose spatial temporal matters for each user by making recommendations aware in terms of context and search.

SUMMARY

This chapter provided a comprehensive overview of the most compelling research papers that combine statistical relational learning for collaborative filtering tasks. Authors have conceptualized this research work by exploring first statistical relational learning and all the techniques that it comprises. Moreover, the chapter has explored the recommendation systems, its categorizations in three major approaches collaborative-based, content-based, knowledge-based, and demographic-based. Regarding collaborative techniques, the chapter has provided a profound classification, which include memory-based, model-based, and hybrid approaches. Authors have claimed that model-based techniques outperform memory-based. However, it is demonstrated in various previous researches that the hybridization of the two techniques can alleviate some limitation that each method imposes if they are employed purely. SRL have been combined for collaborative filtering purposes in recommender systems particularly for the product recommendation tasks. The most popular approaches for relational data are the PRM (an extension of Bayesian traditional Networks) and Rational Markov Networks (RMN).

In this survey work are introduced three tables, which summarize and categorize the whole research work that has been conducted throughout research chapter. Respectively, Table 1 describes the categorization of the statistical relational learning frameworks, Table 2 exhibits the classification and the state-of-the-art in collaborative filtering techniques, and finally the Table 3 refers to an overview of the research examples, which have combined techniques of statistical relational learning with collaborative filtering.

CONCLUSION AND FURTHER WORK

Collaborating Filtering incorporates many challenges that the research community must address. CF approaches are required to have the capability to manage highly sparse data, to scale with the large amount of users and items, to provide the appropriate and valuable recommendation and prediction in a short period, etc. Throughout the survey of SRL for CF approaches, it is demonstrated that carrying out PRM for collaborative filtering can mitigate the cold start problem and thus making able of generating personalized recommendations. Previous research works have addressed the sparsity problem by using the pseudo rating matrix, which enbody a full user-rating matrix containing ratings for all movies.

Table 1. Categorization of statistical relational learning techniques

	Types of Statistical Relational Learning Techniques		
	PRM	**MLN**	**BLN**
Class level model	Directed GM	Logical clauses	Bipartite directed
Parameter estimation	Machine Learning to fill CPT	Machine learning to Weights	Machine Learning to fill CPT
Structure learning	Score Based learning	ILP methods	ILP methods
Inference Graph	Bayesian network	Markov model	Bayesian network
Autocorrelation	Self-loops in class level model	Additional variables needed	It is not discussed in the research this feature

Table 2. Classification of collaborative filtering techniques

	Heuristic based	Model Based	Hybrid-based combining content-based with collaborative filtering
Collaborative Filtering	Commonly used techniques -Nearest neighbor -Clustering -Graph theory -Representative Corresponding research works; -(Rich, 1979), - Goldberg et al. (1992) -Resnick et al. (1994) -Hill et al. (1995) -Shardanand & Maes 1995 -Aggarwal et al. 1999 -Pennock & Horwits (2000) -Sarwar et al. (2001)	Commonly used techniques -Bayesian -Clustering -Artificial Neural Networks -Linear regression -Probabilistic models Corresponding research works; -Goldberg at al. (1992) -Breese et al. (1998) -Pennock & Horwits (2000) Huang et.al. (2004), -Pazzani and Billsus (2007) -Yu et al. (2002) - Canny (2002). -Marlin et al. 2011 - Liu & Li (2015)	-Linear combination of predicted ratings -Various voting schemes -Incorporating one component as a part of the heuristic for the other Corresponding research works; -Pazzani (1999) -Billsus & Pazzani (2000) -Mellville et al. (2002) - Rashid et al. (2002)

Table 3. Overview of statistical relational learning for collaborative filtering

SRL for Collaborative Filtering	PRM for CF	MLN for CF	BLN for CF
	Representative research examples: - Getoor (2002) -Perlich and Hung (2010) - Jenatton et al. (2012) -Newton & Greiner (2014) -Chulyadyo and Leray (2014)	Representative research examples: - Xu et al. (2010) - Rettinger et al. (2011)	Representative research examples: - Blei et al. (2003) -Miller et al. (2009) - Xiong et al (2010) - Yuan et al. (2015)

Sparsity rating problem can be addressed even by utilizing the information of the user profile to calculate user similarity. It is included gender, age, area code, education and employment information in order to develop effective recommendations and to overcome the problem of sparsity. In this case, this methodology of using not only user-ratings, but other demographic information is dubbed as demographic filtering. Regarding the first-rater problem, the recommendation must be developed using a content-based predictor for the user. The recommendation process has been further enhanced by generating effective prediction through using content-based prediction even for the other users. Several papers have illustrated that relational learning techniques can be useful in addressing CRM modeling tasks, too. In regards to collaborating filtering, it is emphasized that because artificial data are usually not reliable, it is more suitable to undertake live experiments with real world dataset.

In concluding this chapter, one open issue that can be suggested for future work is regarding the limitation that IHRTM impose on the process of not handling the trustees with strategies. An adaptive learning strategy can be implemented in the future. This is a domain that cannot be addressed by propositional machine learning algorithms; hence, statistical relational model would be appropriate for this problem. Finally, the combination of SRL for CF opens up new doors to many further applications in the future research. Open gaps can be tackled and future refinement of existing methods can be provided in order to advance in this new field of interest.

REFERENCES

Adomavicius, G., & Tuzhilin, A. (2005). Toward the Next Generation of Recommender Systems: A Survey of the State-of-the-Art and Gediminas AdPossible Extensions. *IEEE Transactions on Knowledge and Data Engineering*, *17*(6), 734–749. doi:10.1109/TKDE.2005.99

Aggarwal, C. C., Wolf, J. L., Wu, K. L., & Yu, P. S. (1999). Horting hatches an agg: A new graph-theoretic approach to collaborative. *Proceedings of theFifth ACM SIGKDD Int'l Conf. Knowledge Discovery and Data Mining*, ACM Digital Library.

Assis Costa, G., & Oliveira, J. M. (2014). A Relational Learning Approach for Collective Entity Resolution in the Web of Data. *Proceedings of theFifth International Workshop on Consuming Linked Data*.

Bilsus, D., & Pazzani, M. (1998). Learning Collaborative Information Filters. *Proceedings of theInt'l Conf. Machine Learning*.

Blei, D. M. (2003). Latent Dirichlet Allocation. *Journal of Machine Learning Research*, *3*, 993–1022.

Bobadilla, J., Hernando, A., Ortega, F., & Gutiérrez, A. (2012). Collaborative filtering based on significances. *Information Sciences*, *185*(1), 1–17. doi:10.1016/j.ins.2011.09.014

Breese, J., Heckerman, D., & Kadie, C. (1998). Empirical Analysis of predictive algorithms for collaborative filtering.*Proceedings of the 14 th Conference on Uncertainty in Artificial Intelligence* (pp. 1-10).

Burke, R. (2002). Hybrid Recommender Systems: Survey and Experiments. *UMUAI*, *12*, 331–270.

Burke, R. (2007). Hybrid Web Recommender Systems. In The Adaptive Web (pp. 377 – 408). Berlin Heidelberg: Springer Verlag.

Canny, J. (2002). Collaborative Filtering with Privacy via Factor Analysis. *Proceedings of the 25th annual international ACM SIGIR conference on Research and development in information retrieval SIGIR '02,* Tampere, Finland (pp. 238-245).

Chulyadyo, R., & Leray, P. (2013). *Probabilistic Relational Models for Customer Preference*. Modelling and Recommendation.

Chulyadyoa, R., & Leraya, P. (2014). A personalized recommender system from probabilistic relational. *Proceedings of the18th International Conference on Knowledge-Based and Intelligent* (pp. 1063 – 1072). Elsevier B.V.

Della Pietra, S., Della Pietra, V., & Lafferty, J. (1997). Inducing features of random fields. *IEEE Transactions on Pattern Analysis and Machine Intelligence*, *19*(4), 380–392. doi:10.1109/34.588021

Domingos, P., & Richardson, M. (2004). Markov Logic: A unifying framework for statistical relational learning. *Proceedings of the ICML-2004 Workshop on Statistical Relational Learning and its Connections to other Fields.*

Esposito, F., Ferilli, T., Basile, M.A., & Di Mauro, N. (2009). Social Networks and Statistical Relational. *Int. J. of Social Network Mining.*

Friedman, N., Linial, M., Nachman, I. & Pe'er, D. (1999). Using Bayesian Networks to Analyze. *Journal of Computational Biolog*, 1999, 601–620.

Genesereth, M.R., & Nilsson, N.J. (1987). Logical Foundations of Artificial Intelligence.

Getoor, L., & Taskar, B. (2007). *Introduction to Statistical Relational Learning*. London: The MIT Press.

Getoor, L. (2002). *Learning statistical models from relational* [Doctoral dissertation]. Stanford University.

Getoor, L., & Mihalkova, L. (2011). *Learning Statistical Models*. SIGMOND.

Goldberg, D., Nichols, D. Oki, B. M, & Terry, D. (1992). Using collaborative filtering to weave an information Tapestry. *Communications of the ACM*.

Hill, W., Stead, L., Rosenstein, M., & Furnas, G. (1995). *Recommndeing and Evaluating Choices in a Virtual Community of Use*. Conf. Human Factors in Computing Systems.

Huang, Z., Chen, H., & Zeng, D. (2004). Applying Associative Retrieval Techniques to Alleviate the Sparsity Problem. *ACM Transactions on Information Systems, 22*(1), 116–142. doi:10.1145/963770.963775

Jenatton, R., Le Roux, N., Bordes, A., & Obozinski, G. (2012). *A latent factor model for highly multi-relational data*. In Advances in Neural Information Processing Systems (p. 19). NIPS.

Kersting, K., & De Raedt, L. (2007). Bayesian Logic Programming: Theory and Tool. In *L. a. Getoor (Ed.), An Introduction to Statistical Relational Learning*. MIT Press.

Khoshneshin, M. (2012). *Latent feature networks for statistical relational learning [PHD]*. Iowa Research Online.

Khosravi, H., & Bina, B. (2010). A Survey on Statistical Relational Learning. In *Advances in Artificial Intelligence* (pp. 256–268).

Liu, Q., & Li, X. (2015). A New Parallel Item-Based Collaborative Filtering Algorithm Based on Hadoop. *Journal of Software, 10*(4), 416–426. doi:10.17706/jsw.10.4.416-426

Marlin, M. B., Zemel, R., Roweis, S. T., & Slaney, M. (2011). Recommender Systems: Missing Data and Statistical Model Estimation. *Proceedings of the Twenty-Second International Joint Conference on Artificial Intelligence* (pp. 2686-2691).

Melville, P., Mooney, R. J., & Nagarajan, R. (2002). Content-Boosted Collaborative Filtering for Improved Recommendations. *Proceedings of theEighteenth National Conference on Artificial Intelligence(AAAI-2002)* (pp. 187-192). Edmonton, Canada: American Association for Artificial Intelligence.

Miller, K. T., Griffiths, T. L., & Jordan, M. I. (2009). Nonparametric Latent Feature Models for Link Prediction. *Proceedings of the 23rd Annual Conference on Neural Information Processing Systems 2009*, Vancouver, Canada.

Neville, J., Rattigan, M., & Jensen, D. (2003). Statistical Relational Learning: Four Claims and a Survey. *Proceedings of the Workshop on Learning Statistical Models from Relational Data, 18th International Joint Conference on Artificial Intelligence* (p. 5).

Newton, J., & Greiner, R. (2004). Hierarchical Probabilistic Relational Models for Collaborative Filtering.*Workshop on Statistical Relational Learning, 21st International Conference on Machine Learning* (pp. 1-6).

Nilashi, M., Bagherifard, K., Ibrahim, O., Alizadeh, H., Nojeem, L. A., & Roozegar, N. (2013). Collaborative filtering recommender systems. *Research Journal of Applied Sciences, Engineering and Technology*, *5*(16), 4168–4182.

Pazzani, M. (1999). A Framework for Collaborative, Content-Based, and Demographic Filtering. *Artificial Intelligence Review*, *13*(5/6), 393–408. doi:10.1023/A:1006544522159

Pazzani, M. J., & Billsus, D. (2007). Content-based Recommendation Systems. In The Adaptive Web (pp. pp. 325-341). Berlin Heidelberg: Springer. doi:10.1007/978-3-540-72079-9_10

Pennock, D. M., Horvitz, E., Lawrence, S., & Giles, C. L. (2000). *Collaborative Filtering by Personality Diagnosis: A Hybrid Memory- and* (pp. 473–480). Uncertainty in Artificial Intelligence.

Perlich, C., & Huang, Z. (2010). Relational Learning for Customer Relationship Management. *Information Systems*.

Rashid, A. M., Albert, I., Cosley, D., Lam, S. K., McNee, S. M., Konstan, J. A., & Riedl, J. (2002). Getting to Know You: Learning New User Preferences in Recommender Systems.*Proc. Int'l Conf. Intelligent.* doi:10.1145/502716.502737

Resnick, P., Iakovou, N., Sushak, M., Bergstrom, P., & Riedl, J. (1994). GroupLens: An Open Architecture for Collaborative Filtering of NetNews. *Computer Supported Cooperative Work*.

Rettinger, A. (2009). Statistical Relational Learning with Formal Ontologies. In Machine Learning and Knowledge Discovery in Databases (pp. 286-301). doi:10.1007/978-3-642-04174-7_19

Rettinger, A., Nickles, M., & Tresp, V. (2011). Statistical relational learning of trust. *Machine Learning*, *82*(2), 191–209. doi:10.1007/s10994-010-5211-x

Rich, E. (1979). User Modeling via Stereotypes. *Cognitive Science*, *3*(4), 329–354. doi:10.1207/s15516709cog0304_3

Siguenza-Guzman, L., Saquicela, V., Avila-Ordóñez, E., Vandewalle, J., & Cattrysse, D. (2015). Literature review of data mining applications in academic libraries. *Journal of Academic Librarianship*, *41*(4), 499–510. doi:10.1016/j.acalib.2015.06.007

Sarwar, B., Karypis, G., Konstan, J. & Riedl, J. (2001). Item-Based Collaborative Filtering Recommendation Algorithms. *Proceedings of the 10th Int'l WWW*.

Shardanand, U., & Maes, P. (1995). *Social Information Filtering, Algorithms for Automating 'Word of Mouth*. Conf. Human Factors in Computing Systems.

Singla, P., & Domingos, P. (2005). *Discriminative Training of Markov Logic Networks*. American Association for Artificial Intelligence.

Su, X., & Khoshgoftaar, T. M. (2009). *A Survey of Collaborative Filtering Techniques*. Advances in Artificial Intelligence.

Taskar, B., Abbeel, P., & Koller, D. (2002). Discriminative Probabilistic Models for Relational Data. *Proceedings of the Eighteenth conference on Uncertainty in artificial intelligence UAI'02* (pp. 485-492).

Wasserman, S., & Faust, K. (1994). *Social Network Analysis: Methods and Applications*. Cambridge, UK: Cambridge University Press. doi:10.1017/CBO9780511815478

Winkler, W. (1999). *The state of record linkage and current research problems*. U.S: Statistical Research Division, Census Bureau.

Wong, T. (2015). Learning Markov logic networks with limited number of labeled training examples. *International Journal of Knowledge-based and Intelligent Engineering Systems*, *18*(2), 91–98.

Xiong, L., Chen, X., Huang, T., Schneidery, J., & Carbonellz, J. G. (2010). Temporal Collaborative Filtering with Bayesian Probabilistic Tensor. In SIAM Data Mining.

Xu, Z., Tresp, V., Rettinger, A., & Kersting, K. (2010). Social Network Mining with Nonparametric relational Models. *Advance in Social Network Mining An Analysis*, 77-96.

Yuan, Q., Cong, G., Zhao, K., Ma, Z., & Sun, A. (2015). Who, where, when and what: A Nonparametric Bayesian approach to context-aware recommendation and search for twitter users. *ACM Transactions on Information Systems*, *33*(1), 1–33. doi:10.1145/2699667

Zhu, L., Lei, Q., Liu, G., & Liu, F. (2015). Processing Recommender Top-*N* Queries in Relational Databases. *Journal of Software*, *10*(2), 162–171. doi:10.17706/jsw.10.2.162-171

KEY TERMS AND DEFINITIONS

Collaborative Filtering: Collaborative filtering allows recommendations to users taking into account how other users have rated items. Collaborative filtering needs an extensive database containing exclusively the ratings made by users over the items (Bobadilla et al., 2012).

Content-Based Filtering: Content-based filtering systems allow recommender systems to provide recommendations to users based on the information related to items that other users have rated previously.

Data Mining: Data Mining is defined as the process of analyzing large information repositories for deriving and discovering useful patterns and identifying hidden relationships among the data (Siguenza-Guzman et al., 2015).

Hybrid Collaborative Filtering: Hybrid filtering methods allow recommender systems to provide recommendations through techniques based on both collaborative and demographic filtering methods (Bobadilla et al., 2012).

Recommender Systems: Recommender systems are software tools and techniques for suggesting items to users by considering their preferences in an automated fashion (Nilashi et al., 2013).

Social Network Mining (SNM): Its major purpose is to extract information about network objects, behaviors and activities that cannot be yielded if the entities were to be examined individually.

Compilation of References

Abdulsalam, H., Skillicorn, D., & Martin, P. (2011). Classification using Streaming Random Forests. *IEEE Transactions on Knowledge and Data Engineering, 23*(1), 22–36. doi:10.1109/TKDE.2010.36

Adomavicius, G. & Zhang, J. (2012). Stability of recommendation algorithms. *ACM Trans. Inf. Syst., 30*(4), 23:1-23:31.

Adomavicius, G., & Tuzhilin, A. (2005). Toward the next generation of recommender systems: A survey of the state-of-the-art and possible extensions. *IEEE Transactions on* Knowledge and Data Engineering, *17*(6), 734–749.

Adomavicius, G., & Tuzhilin, A. (2005). Toward the next generation of recommender systems: A survey of the state-of-the-art and possible extensions. *IEEE Transactions on Knowledge and Data Engineering, 17*(6), 734–749. doi:10.1109/TKDE.2005.99

Agarwal, R., & Srikant, R. (1994), Fast algorithms for mining association rules. *Proc. 20th int. conf. very large data bases, VLDB* (Vol. 1215 pp. 487-499).

Aggarwal, C. C., Wolf, J. L., Wu, K. L., & Yu, P. S. (1999). Horting hatches an agg: A new graph-theoretic approach to collaborative. *Proceedings of theFifth ACM SIGKDD Int'l Conf. Knowledge Discovery and Data Mining*, ACM Digital Library.

Aggarwal, R., & Srikant, R. (1994). Fast algorithms for mining association rules. In J. B. Bocca, M. Jarke, & C. Zaniolo (Eds.), *Proceedings of the 20th International Conference on Very Large Data Bases* (*VLDB 1994*) (pp. 487-399). San Francisco, CA: Morgan Kaufmann.

Ahn, H. J. (2008). A new similarity measure for collaborative filtering to alleviate the new user cold-starting problem. *Information Sciences, 178*(1), 37–51. doi:10.1016/j.ins.2007.07.024

Al-Jarrah, O. Y., Yoo, P. D., Muhaidat, S., Karagiannidis, G. K., & Taha, K. (2015). Efficient Machine Learning for Big Data: A Review. *Big Data Research, 2*(3), 87–93. doi:10.1016/j.bdr.2015.04.001

Aloui, A., & Touzi, A. G. (2015). A Fuzzy Ontology-Based Platform for Flexible Querying. *International Journal of Service Science, Management, Engineering, and Technology, 6*(3), 12–26.

Amatriain, X., Jaimes, A., Oliver, N. & Pujol, J.M. (2011). Data Mining Methods for Recommender Systems,, *by Springer*

Amatriain, X. (2013). Mining large streams of user data for personalized recommendations. *ACM SIGKDD Explorations Newsletter, 14*(2), 37–48. doi:10.1145/2481244.2481250

Anitha, A., & Krishnan, N. (2011). A Dynamic Web Mining Framework for E-Learning Recommendations using Rough Sets and Association Rule Mining. *International Journal of Computers and Applications, 12*(11), 36–41. doi:10.5120/1724-2326

Arthur, D., & Vassilvitskii, S. (2007). *k*-means++: The advantage of careful seeding. *Proc. ofSymposium of Discrete Analysis* (pp. 1027-1035).

Assis Costa, G., & Oliveira, J. M. (2014). A Relational Learning Approach for Collective Entity Resolution in the Web of Data. *Proceedings of theFifth International Workshop on Consuming Linked Data.*

Attar, V., Chaudhary, P., Rahagude, S., Chaudhari, G., & Sinha, P. (2011). An Instance-Window Based Classification Algorithm for Handling Gradual Concept Drifts. *Proceedings of the International Workshop on Agents and Data Mining Interaction* (pp. 156-172).

Aye, K. N., & Thein, T. (2015). A platform for big data analytics on distributed scale-out storage system. *International Journal of Big Data Intelligence.*, *2*(2), 127–141. doi:10.1504/IJBDI.2015.069088

Azar, A.T. & Hassanien, A.E. (2014). Dimensionality reduction of medical big data using neural-fuzzy classifier. *Soft computing.* 19(4), 1115-1127. DOI:.10.1007/s00500-014-1327-4

Baharudin, B. (2010, December). Sentence based sentiment classification from online customer reviews.*Proceedings of the 8th International Conference on Frontiers of Information Technology* (p. 25). ACM.

Baker, R. S., & Yacef, K. (2009). The State of Educational Data Mining in 2009: *A Review and Future Visions. Journal of Educational Data Mining*, *1*(1), 3–17.

Balahur, A., Hermida, J. M., & Montoyo, A. (2012). Detecting implicit expressions of emotion in text: A comparative analysis. *Decision Support Systems*, *53*(4), 742–753. doi:10.1016/j.dss.2012.05.024

Barker, K. J., Amato, J., & Sheridon, J. (2008). Credit card fraud: Awareness and prevention. *Journal of Financial Crime*, *15*(4), 398–410. doi:10.1108/13590790810907236

Barracosa, J. I. M. S. (2011). *Mining Behaviors from Educational Data* [Doctoral Thesis].

Bellaachia, A., & Vommina, E. (2006), MINEL: A framework for mining e-learning logs. *Proceedings of theFifth IASTED International Conference on Web based Education*, Mexico (pp. 259-263).

Ben-Gal, I. (2005). Outlier detection. In *Data Mining and Knowledge Discovery Handbook: A Complete Guide for Practitioners and Researchers*. Kluwer Academic Publishers. doi:10.1007/0-387-25465-X_7

Bernardes, D., Diaby, M. Fournier, R., FogelmanSoulié, F. & Viennet, E. (2014). A Social formalism and survey for recommender systems. *ACM SIGKDD Explorations Newsletter, 16*(2), 20-37.

Berry, M. J. A., & Linoff, J. S. (2004). *Data Mining Techniques for Marketing, Sales and customer Relationship Management* (2nd ed.). Wiley.

Bhanu, S. K., & Tripathy, B. K. (2016). Rough Set Based Similarity Measures for Data Analytics in Spatial Epidemiology. *International Journal of Rough Sets and Data Analysis*, *3*(1), 114–123. doi:10.4018/IJRSDA.2016010107

Bhargava, H. K., Sridhar, S., & Herrick, C. (1999). Beyond spreadsheets: Tools for building decision support systems. *IEEE Computer*, *32*(3), 31–39. doi:10.1109/2.751326

Bifet, A., & Gavalda, R. (2007). Learning from time-changing data with adaptive windowing. *Proceedings of the SIAM International Conference on Data Mining* (pp. 443-448).

Bifet, A., Holmes, G., Pfahringer, B., Kirkby, R., & Gavalda, R. (2009). New Ensemble Methods for Evolving Data Streams. *Proceedings of International Conference on Knowledge Data Discovery* (pp. 139-148).

Bifet, A., Frank, E., Holmes, G., & Pfahringer, B. (2010), Accurate Ensembles for Data Streams: Combining Restricted Hoeffding Trees using Stacking. *Proceeding of 2nd Asian Conference on Machine Learning, Tokyo, Japan* (pp. 226-240).

Bifet, A., & Gavalda, R. (2009). Adaptive Parameter-free Learning from Evolving Data Streams.

Bilsus, D., & Pazzani, M. (1998). Learning Collaborative Information Filters. *Proceedings of theInt'l Conf. Machine Learning*.

Blei, D. M. (2003). Latent Dirichlet Allocation. *Journal of Machine Learning Research, 3*, 993–1022.

Blitzer, J., Dredze, M., & Pereira, F. (2007, june). Biographies, Bollywood, Boom-boxes and Blenders: Domain Adaptation for Sentiment Classification. In ACL (Vol. 7, pp. 440-447).

Bobadilla, J., Hernando, A., Ortega, F., & Gutiérrez, A. (2012). Collaborative filtering based on significances. *Information Sciences, 185*(1), 1–17. doi:10.1016/j.ins.2011.09.014

Bobadilla, J., Ortega, F., Hernando, A., & Gutiérrez, A. (2013). Recommender systems survey. *Knowledge-Based Systems, 46*, 109–132. doi:10.1016/j.knosys.2013.03.012

Boldrini, E., Balahur, A., Martínez-Barco, P., & Montoyo, A. (2012). Using EmotiBlog to annotate and analyse subjectivity in the new textual genres. *Data Mining and Knowledge Discovery, 25*(3), 603–634. doi:10.1007/s10618-012-0259-9

Bollegala, D., Weir, D. J. & Carroll, J. A. (2013). Cross-Domain Sentiment Classification Using a Sentiment Sensitive Thesaurus. *IEEE transactions on Knowledge and Data Engineering, 25*(8), 1719-1731.

Bollier, D. (2010). The promise and peril of big data. Washington, DC: The Aspen Institute. Retrieved from http://www.aspeninstitute.org/sites/default/files/content/docs/pubs/The_Promise_and_Peril_of_Big_Data.pdf

Börner, K. (2001). Adaptation and evaluation of 3-dimensional collaborative Information visualizations.*Proceedings of Workshop on Empirical Evaluations of Adaptive Systems*.

Botsios, S., & Georgiou, D. (2008, July 22-25). Recent Adaptive E-Learning Contributions Towards A "Standard Ready" Architecture. *Proceedings of the IADIS International Conference e-Learning '08*, Amsterdam, The Netherlands.

Boutemedjet, S. & Ziou, D. *(2006)*. A Generative graphical Model for Collaborative Filtering of Visual Content. In *Advances in Data Mining. Applications in Medicine, Web Mining, Marketing, Image and Signal Mining* (pp. 404-415).

Bouza, A., Reif, G., Bernstein, A., & Gall, H. (2008). Semtree: ontology-based decision tree algorithm for recommender systems. *Proceedings of theInternational Semantic Web Conference*.

Bradley, P. S., Fayyad, U. M., & Reina, C. A. (1998b). Scaling clustering algorithms to large databases. *Proceedings of the4ᵗʰ International Conference on Knowledge Discovery and Data Mining* (pp. 9-15).

Breese, J., Heckerman, D., & Kadie, C. (1998). Empirical Analysis of predictive algorithms for collaborative filtering. *Proceedings of the 14 th Conference on Uncertainty in Artificial Intelligence* (pp. 1-10).

Breese, J., Heckerman, D., & Kadie, C. (1998). Empirical Analysis of Predictive Algorithms for Collaborative Filtering. *Proceedings of the 14th Conference on Uncertainty in Artificial Intelligence (UAI-98)*, (pp 43-52).

Breese, J., Heckerman, D., & Kadie, C. (1998). Empirical Analysis of predictive algorithms for collaborative filtering. *Proceedings of the 14th Conference on Uncertainty in Artificial Intelligence*.

Brody, S., & Elhadad, N. (2010, June). An unsupervised aspect-sentiment model for online reviews. *Proceedings of Human Language Technologies: The 2010 Annual Conference of the North American Chapter of the Association for Computational Linguistics* (pp. 804-812). Association for Computational Linguistics.

Brown, E., Cristea, A., Stewart, C., & Brailsford, T. (2005). Patterns in authoring of adaptive educational hypermedia: A taxonomy of learning styles. *Journal of Educational Technology & Society, 8*(3), 77–90.

Brusilovsky P. (1996a), Methods and techniques of adaptive hypermedia, *User Modeling and User Adapted Interaction* (Special issue on adaptive hypertext and hypermedia), 6(3), 87-129.

Brusilovsky, P., & Millan, E. (2007). User Models for Adaptive Hypermedia and Adaptive Educational Systems. In The Adaptive Web, LNCS (Vol. 4321, pp. 3-53). Springer-Verlag Berlin Heidelberg. doi:10.1007/978-3-540-72079-9_1

Brusilovsky, P. (1996b). *Adaptive Hypermedia: an Attempt to Analyze and Generalize Multimedia. In Hypermedia, and Virtual Reality,*LNCS (Vol. 1077, pp. 288–304). Berlin: Springer-Verlag.

Brusilovsky, P. (2001). Adaptive hypermedia. *Journal User Modeling and User Adapted Interaction, 11*(1-2), 87–110. doi:10.1023/A:1011143116306

Brusilovsky, P., & Peylo, C. (2003). Adaptive and intelligent web-based educational systems. *International Journal of Artificial Intelligence in Education, 13*, 156–169.

Burke, R. (2007). Hybrid Web Recommender Systems. In The Adaptive Web (pp. 377 – 408). Berlin Heidelberg: Springer Verlag.

Burke, R. (2002). Hybrid Recommender Systems: Survey and Experiments. *UMUAI, 12*, 331–270.

Burke, R. (2002). Hybrid recommender systems: Survey and experiments. *User Modeling and User-Adapted Interaction, 12*(4), 331–370. doi:10.1023/A:1021240730564

Burr, L., & Spennemann, D. H. (2004). Pattern of user behavior in university online forums. *International Journal of Instructional Technology and Distance Learning, 1*(10), 11–28.

Cai, D., He, X., Wen, J. R., & Ma, W. Y. (2004). Block-level link analysis. *Proceedings of the 27th annual international ACM SIGIR conference on Research and development in, information retrieval*, 440–447.

Canny, J. (2002). Collaborative filtering with privacy via factor analysis. *Proceedings of the 25th annual international ACM SIGIR conference on Research and development in information retrieval SIGIR '02,* Tampere, Finland (pp. 238-245).

Canny, J. (2002). Collaborative Filtering with Privacy via Factor Analysis. *Proceedings of the 25th annual international ACM SIGIR conference on Research and development in information retrieval SIGIR '02,* Tampere, Finland (pp. 238-245).

Cantador, I., & Cremonesi, P. (2014, October). Tutorial on cross-domain recommender systems.*Proceedings of the 8th ACM Conference on Recommender systems* (pp. 401-402). ACM.

Cao, F., Liang, J., & Jiang, G. (2009). An initialization method for the *k*-means algorithm using neighborhood model. *Journal of Computers and Mathematics with Applications, 58*, 474–483. doi:10.1016/j.camwa.2009.04.017

Cao, Q., Duan, W., & Gan, Q. (2011). Exploring determinants of voting for the "helpfulness" of online user reviews: A text mining approach. *Decision Support Systems, 5*(2), 511–521. doi:10.1016/j.dss.2010.11.009

Cardot, H., Cenac, P., & Monnez, J.-M. (2012). A fast and recursive algorithm for clustering large datasets with *k*-medians. *Computational Statistics & Data Analysis, 56*(6), 1434–1449. doi:10.1016/j.csda.2011.11.019

Card, S. K., Mackinlay, J. D., & Shneiderman, B. (Eds.). (1999). *Readings in Information Visualization—Using Vision to Think*. San Francisco: Morgan Kaufmann.

Castro, F., Vellido, A., Nebot, A., & Mugica, F. (2007). Applying Data Mining Techniques to e-Learning. *Studies in Computational Intelligence, 62*, 183–221. doi:10.1007/978-3-540-71974-8_8

Celebi, M. E., Kingravi, H. A., & Vela, P. A. (2013). A comparative study of efficient initialization methods for the *k*-means clustering algorithm. *Expert Systems with Applications, 40*(1), 200–210. doi:10.1016/j.eswa.2012.07.021

CERN. (2015). CERN data center passes 100 petabytes. Retrieved from http://home.web.cern.ch/about/updates/2013/02/cern-data-centre-passes-100-petabytes

Chand, C., Thakkar, A., & Ganatra, A. (2012), Sequential Pattern Mining: Survey and Current Research Challenges. *International Journal of Soft Computing and Engineering*, 2(1), 185-193.

Chandrashekar, G., & Sahin, F. (2014). A survey on feature selection methods. *Computers & Electrical Engineering*, 40(1), 16–28. doi:10.1016/j.compeleceng.2013.11.024

Chen, J., Zheng, T., Thorne, W., Zaiane, O., & Goebel, R. (2013). *Visual data mining of web navigational data*. Paper presented at the 17th International Conference on Information Visualisation.

Chen, T., Zhang, W., Lu, Q., Chen, K., Zheng, Z. & Yu, Y. (2012). SVDFeature: A Toolkit for Feature-based Collaborative Filtering. *Journal of Machine Learning Research*, 13, 3619-3622.

Chen, V. Y., Oian, Ch. Z., & Woodbury, R. F. (2007). Visualizing collaborative filtering in digital collections. *Presented at 11th International Conference Information Visualization (IV'07)*.

Chen, C. C., & Tseng, Y. D. (2011). Quality evaluation of product reviews using an information quality framework. *Decision Support Systems*, 50(4), 755–768. doi:10.1016/j.dss.2010.08.023

Chen, C., Zheng, X., Wang, Y., Hong, F., & Lin, Z. (2014) Context-aware collaborative topic regression with social matrix factorization for recommender systems.*Proceedings of the Twenty-Eighth AAAI Conference on Artificial Intelligence* (pp. 9-15). AAAI Press.

Cheng, N., Chandramouli, R., & Subbalakshmi, K. P. (2011). Author gender identification from text. *Digital Investigation*, 8(1), 78–88. doi:10.1016/j.diin.2011.04.002

Cheng, S.-C., Huang, Y.-M., Chen, J.-N., & Lin, Y.-T. (2005). Automatic Leveling System for E-Learning Examination Pool Using Entropy-Based Decision Tree. In *Advances in Web-Based Learning, LNCS* (Vol. 3583, pp. 273–278). Springer. doi:10.1007/11528043_27

Chen, K., Chen, T., Zheng, G., Jin, O., Yao, E., & Yu, Y. (2012) Collaborative personalized tweet recommendation. *Proceedings of ACM SIGIR International Conference on Research and Development in Information Retrieval*, pp 661-670. ACM Press.

Chen, L., Chen, G., & Wang, F. (2015). Recommender Systems Based on User Reviews: The State of the Art. *User Modeling and User-Adapted Interaction*, 25(2), 99–154. doi:10.1007/s11257-015-9155-5

Chen, M., Mao, S., & Liu, Y. (2009). Big Data: A Survey. *Springer-. Mobile Networks and Applications*, 19(2), 171–209. doi:10.1007/s11036-013-0489-0

Chen, S., Luo, T., Liu, W., & Xu, Y. (2009). Incorporating similarity and trust for collaborative filtering.*Proceedings of the Sixth International Conference on Fuzzy Systems and Knowledge Discovery* (pp. 487-493). IEEE Press. doi:10.1109/FSKD.2009.720

Chiang, M. M.-T., & Mirkin, B. (2009). Intelligent choice of the number of clusters in k-means clustering: An experimental study with different cluster spreads. *Journal of Classification*, 27(1), 3–40. doi:10.1007/s00357-010-9049-5

Chinsha, T. C., & Joseph, S. (2015, February). A syntactic approach for aspect based opinion mining.*Proceedings of the 2015 IEEE International Conference on Semantic Computing (ICSC)* (pp. 24-31). IEEE. doi:10.1109/COMSNETS.2015.7098727

ChoiceStream. (2005), ChoiceStream Personalization Survey: Consumer Trends and Perceptions. Retrieved from http://www.choicestream.com/pdf/ChoiceStream_PersonalizationSurveyResults2005.pdf

Chou, P.-H., Wu, M.-J., Li, P.-H., & Chen, K.-K. (2010). Integrating web mining and neural network for personalized e-commerce automatic service. *Journal Expert Systems with Applications: An International Journal, 37*(4), 2898–2910. doi:10.1016/j.eswa.2009.09.047

Cho, Y. H., Kim, J. K., & Kim, S. H. (2002). A personalized recommender system based on web usage mining and decision tree induction. *Expert Systems with Applications, 23*(3), 329–342. doi:10.1016/S0957-4174(02)00052-0

Chulyadyoa, R., & Leraya, P. (2014). A personalized recommender system from probabilistic relational. *Proceedings of the18th International Conference on Knowledge-Based and Intelligent* (pp. 1063 – 1072). Elsevier B.V.

Chulyadyo, R., & Leray, P. (2013). *Probabilistic Relational Models for Customer Preference*. Modelling and Recommendation.

Collins, L. M., Hussell, J., Hettinga, R., Powell, J., Mane, K., & Martinez, M. L. (2007). Information visualization and large-scale repositories. *Library Hi Tech, 25*(3), 366–378. doi:10.1108/07378830710820943

Cover, T., & Hart, P. (1967). Nearest neighbor pattern classification. *IEEE Transactions on* Information Theory, *13*(1), 21–27.

Cruz, F. L., Troyano, J. A., Enríquez, F., Ortega, F. J., & Vallejo, C. G. (2013). Long autonomy or long delay?'The importance of domain in opinion mining. *Expert Systems with Applications, 40*(8), 3174–3184. doi:10.1016/j.eswa.2012.12.031

Cuzzocrea, A., Jiang, F., Lee, W., & Leung, C. K.-S. (2014). Efficient frequent itemset mining from dense data streams. In L. Chen, Y. Jia, T. K. Sellis, & G. Liu (Eds.), *Proceedings of the16th Asia-Pacific Web Conference (APWeb 2014)* (pp. 593-601). Heidelberg, Germany: Springer. doi:10.1007/978-3-319-11116-2_56

Dal Pozzolo, A., Johnson, R., Caelen, O., Waterschoot, S., Chawala, N. V., & Bontempi, G. (2014). Using HDDT to avoid instance propagation in unbalanced and evolving data streams, *In the Proceedings of International joint Conference on Neural Networks.* 588-593

Dang, Y., Zhang, Y., & Chen, H. (2010). A Lexicon-Enhanced Method for Sentiment Classification: An Experiment on Online Product Reviews. *IEEE Intelligent Systems, 25*(4), 46–53. doi:10.1109/MIS.2009.105

Darvishi-mirshekarlou, F., Akbarpour, S. H., & Feizi-Derakhshi, M. (2013). Reviewing Cluster Based Collaborative Filtering Approaches. *International Journal of Computer Applications Technology and Research, 2*(6), 650–659. doi:10.7753/IJCATR0206.1004

Dawson, S. (2008). A study of the relationship between student social networks and sense of community. *Journal of Educational Technology & Society, 11*(3), 224–238.

De Bra, P., & Calvi, L. (1998), AHA: a Generic Adaptive Hypermedia System. *Proceedings of the 2nd Workshop on Adaptive Hypertext and Hypermedia HYPERTEXT'98*, Pittsburgh, USA (pp. 20-24). Doi:10.1145/502932.502935

Deelers, S., & Auwatanamongkol, S. (2007). Enhancing *k*-means algorithm with initial cluster centers derived from data partitioning along the data axis with the highest variance. *International Journal of Computer Science, 2*(4), 323–328.

Deepak, D., & John, S. J. (2016). Information Systems on Hesitant Fuzzy Sets. *International Journal of Rough Sets and Data Analysis, 3*(1), 55–70.

Della Pietra, S., Della Pietra, V., & Lafferty, J. (1997). Inducing features of random fields. *IEEE Transactions on Pattern Analysis and Machine Intelligence, 19*(4), 380–392. doi:10.1109/34.588021

Deshpande, M., & Karypis, G. (2004). Item-based top-N recommendation algorithms. *ACM Transactions on Information Systems*, *22*(1), 143–177. doi:10.1145/963770.963776

Despotović, M., Marković, A., Bogdanović, Z., Barać, D., & Krčo, S. (2013). Providing Adaptivity in Moodle LMS Courses. *Journal of Educational Technology & Society*, *15*(1), 326–338. doi:10.1080/0952398990360206

Ding, X., Liu, B., & Philip, S. Y. (2008). A Holistic Lexicon-Based Approach to Opinion Mining. *Proceedings of the first ACM International Conference on Web search and Data Mining (WSDM'08)*, California, USA (pp. 231-240).

Domingos, P., & Richardson, M. (2004). Markov Logic: A unifying framework for statistical relational learning. *Proceedings of the ICML-2004 Workshop on Statistical Relational Learning and its Connections to other Fields*.

Domingos, P., & Hulten, G. (2000). Mining high-speed data streams. *Proceedings of the sixth ACM SIGKDD international conference on Knowledge discovery and data mining* (pp. 71-80). doi:10.1145/347090.347107

Dongre, P., & Malik, L. (2014). A Review on Real Time Data Stream Classification and Adaptiing to various Concept Drift Scenarios. *Proceedings of the IEEE International Advance Computing Conference*, 533-537.

Dongre, S., & Malik, L. (2013). Algorithm for Concept Drifting Data Stream Mining. *International Journal of Computer Science and Network*, *2*(1), 107–111.

Dongre, S., & Wankhade, K. (2012). Intrusion Detection System Using New Ensemble Boosting Approach. *International Journal of Modeling and Optimization*, *2*(4), 488–492. doi:10.7763/IJMO.2012.V2.168

Dorrofield & Bagnall. (2007), Education for all, Education for all, Thursday, 11 October 2007, Referred from URL: http://www.iweek.co.za/special-report/education-for-all

Downs, S. (1998): The future of online learning, Retrieved from URL: http://www.atl.ualberta.ca/downes/future/home.html

Duda, R. O., & Hart, P. E. (1973). *Pattern classification and scene analysis*. New York: John Wiley & Sons.

Dunham, M. H. (2002). Data Mining: Introductory and Advanced Topics. Upper Saddle River, NJ, USA: Prentice Hall PTR.

Durairaj. M. & Suresh C. (2014). A Study on Web Usage Mining For Web Based Adaptive Educational System. *International Journal of Innovative Science, Engineering and Technology,* *1*(6).

Elahi, M., Ricci, F., & Rubens, N. (2014). Active learning in collaborative filtering recommender systems. In *E-Commerce and Web Technologies* (pp. 113–124). Springer International Publishing. doi:10.1007/978-3-319-10491-1_12

Elke, A. R., Matthew, O. W., Jing, Y., & Doshi, P. R. (2002). XmdvTool: Visual interactive data exploration and trend discovery of high-dimensional data sets. *Paper presented at the Proceedings of the 2002 ACM SIGMOD international conference on Management of data*, Madison, Wisconsin.

Elwell, R., & Polikar, R. (2011). Increamental Learning of Concept Drift in Non stationary environments. *IEEE Transactions on Neural Networks*, *22*(10), 1517–1531. doi:10.1109/TNN.2011.2160459 PMID:21824845

Erisoglu, M., Calis, N., & Sakallioglu, S. (2011). A new algorithm for initial cluster centers in *k*-means algorithm. *Pattern Recognition Letters*, *32*(14), 1701–1705. doi:10.1016/j.patrec.2011.07.011

Esposito, F., Ferilli, T., Basile, M.A., & Di Mauro, N. (2009). Social Networks and Statistical Relational. *Int. J. of Social Network Mining*.

Esslimani, I., Brun, A., & Boyer, A. (2009). A collaborative filtering approach combining clustering and navigational based correlations. In *Web Information Systems and Technologies* (pp. 364-369).

Etzioni, O. (1996). The World Wide Web: Quagmire or gold mine. *Communications of the ACM*, *39*(11), 65–68. doi:10.1145/240455.240473

Ezeife, C. I., & Lu, Y. (2005). Mining Web Log Sequential Patterns with Position Coded Pre-Order Linked WAP-Tree. *Data Mining and Knowledge Discovery*, *10*(1), 5–38. doi:10.1007/s10618-005-0248-3

Fahim, A. M., Saake, G., Salem, A. M., Torkey, F. A., & Ramadan, M. A. (2008). K-means for Spherical Clusters with Large Variance in Sizes. Proc. of the World Academy Science, Engineering and Technology (Vol. 35, pp. 177-182).

Fahim, A. M., Salem, A. M., Torkey, F. A., & Ramadan, M. A. (2006). An efficient enhanced *k*-means clustering algorithm. *Journal of Zhejiang University Science A*, *7*(10), 1626–1633. doi:10.1631/jzus.2006.A1626

Fancsali, S. (2012). *Variable Construction and Causal Discovery for Cognitive Tutor Log data: Initial Results* (pp. 238–239). EDM.

Fang, X., & Zhan, J. (2015). Sentiment analysis using product review data. *Journal of Big Data*, *2*(1), 1–14. doi:10.1186/s40537-015-0015-2

Fan, T. K., & Chang, C. H. (2011). Blogger-centric contextual advertising. *Expert Systems with Applications*, *38*(3), 1777–1788. doi:10.1016/j.eswa.2010.07.105

Fathi, E. (2010). A fully personalization strategy of E-learning scenarios. *Computers in Human Behavior*, *26*(4), 581–591. doi:10.1016/j.chb.2009.12.010

Fayyad, U. M., Piatetsky-Shapiro, G., & Smyth, P. (1996). From data mining to knowledge discovery: An overview. In M. F. Usama, P.-S. Gregory, S. Padhraic, & U. Ramasamy (Eds.), *Advances in knowledge discovery and data mining* (pp. 1–34). American Association for Artificial Intelligence.

Fedoryszak, M., Tkaczyk, D., & Bolikowski, L. (2013). Large Scale Citation Matching Using Apache Hadoop. In Research and Advanced Technology for Digital Libraries, LNCS (Vol. 8092, pp. 362-365). Springer.

Felix, U. (2005). E-learning pedagogy in the third millennium: The need for combining social and cognitive constructivist approaches., J*ournal*. ReCALL, *17*(1), 85–100. doi:10.1017/S0958344005000716

Feng, S., Zhang, M., Zhang, Y., & Deng, Z. (2010, April). Recommended or not recommended? review classification through opinion extraction. *Proceedings of the2010 12th International Asia-PacificWeb Conference (APWEB),* (pp. 350-352). IEEE. doi:10.1109/APWeb.2010.38

Feng-jung, L., & Bai-Jiun, S. (2007). Learning Activity- Based E-Learning Material Recommendation System. *Proceedings of the Ninth IEEE International Symposium on Multimedia Workshops ISMW '07.*

Frey, B. J., & Dueck, D. (2007). Clustering by passing messages between data points. *Science*, 2007, 307. PMID:17218491

Frias-Martinez, E., Chen, S. Y., & Liu, X. (2009). Evaluation of a personalized digital library based on cognitive styles: Adaptivity vs. adaptability. *International Journal of Information Management*, *29*(1), 48–56. doi:10.1016/j.ijinfomgt.2008.01.012

Frias-Martinez, E., Magoulas, G., Chen, S. Y., & Macredie, R. (2006). Automated user modeling for personalized digital libraries. *International Journal of Information Management*, *26*(3), 234–248. doi:10.1016/j.ijinfomgt.2006.02.006

Friedman, N., Linial, M., Nachman, I. & Pe'er, D. (1999). Using Bayesian Networks to Analyze. *Journal of Computational Biolog*, 1999, 601–620.

Fu, T. (2011). A review on time series data mining. *Engineering Applications of Artificial Intelligence*, *24*(1), 164–181. doi:10.1016/j.engappai.2010.09.007

Fu, T., Chung, F., Kwok, K., & Ng, C. (2008). Stock time series visualization based on data point importance. *Engineering Applications of Artificial Intelligence, 21*(8), 1217–1232. doi:10.1016/j.engappai.2008.01.005

Gangardiwala, A., & Polikar, R. (2005). Dynamically Weighted Majority Voting for incremental Learning and Comparison of three Boosting Based approaches. *Proceedings of International joint Conference on Neural Networks* (pp. 1131-1136).

Gao, T., & Lehman, J. D. (2003). The effects of different levels of interaction on the achievement and motivational perceptions of college students in a web-based learning environment. *Journal of Interactive Learning Research, 14*(4), 367–386.

Genesereth, M.R., & Nilsson, N.J. (1987). Logical Foundations of Artificial Intelligence.

George, T., & Merugu, S. (2005). A Scalable Collaborative Filtering Framework Based On Co-Clustering. *Proceedings of theData Mining Fifth IEEE International Conference.* doi:10.1109/ICDM.2005.14

Getoor, L. (2002). *Learning statistical models from relational* [Doctoral dissertation]. Stanford University.

Getoor, L., & Mihalkova, L. (2011). *Learning Statistical Models.* SIGMOND.

Getoor, L., & Taskar, B. (2007). *Introduction to Statistical Relational Learning.* London: The MIT Press.

Ghallab, S. A., Badr, N. L., Salem, A. B., & Tolba, M. F. (2014). Strictness petroleum prediction system based on fussy model. *International Journal of Service Science, Management, Engineering, and Technology, 5*(4), 44–65. doi:10.4018/ijssmet.2014100104

Ghani, R., & Fano, A. (2002). Building recommender systems using a knowledge base of product semantics. *Proceedings of the2nd International Conference on Adaptive Hypermedia and Adaptive Web Based Systems.*

Ghauth, K. I., & Abdullah, N. A. (2010). An empirical evaluation of learner performance in e-learning recommender systems and an adaptive hypermedia system. *Malaysian Journal of Computer Science, 23*(3), 141–152.

Ghiassi, M., Skinner, J., & Zimbra, D. (2013). Twitter brand sentiment analysis: A hybrid system using n-gram analysis and dynamic artificial neural network. *Expert Systems with Applications, 40*(16), 6266–6282. doi:10.1016/j.eswa.2013.05.057

Giridharan, A. (2005). Adaptive e-Learning Environment for Students with Divergent Knowledge Levels. *ELTECH INDIA.* Retrieved from www.elearn.cdac.in

Golbeck, J. (2009). Trust and nuanced profile similarity in online social networks. *ACM Trans. on the Web, 3*(4).

Golbeck, J., & Hendler, J. (2006). FilmTrust: Movie recommendations using trust in web-based social networks.*Proceedings of the Third IEEE International Conference on Consumer Communications and Networking Conference* (pp. 282-286). IEEE Press. doi:10.1109/CCNC.2006.1593032

Goldberg, D., Nichols, D. Oki, B. M, & Terry, D. (1992). Using collaborative filtering to weave an information Tapestry. *Communications of the ACM.*

Goldberg, D., Nichols, D.; Oki, B. M, & Terry, D. (1992). Using collaborative filtering to weave an information Tapestry. *Communications of the ACM,* p61(10)

Goldberg, D., Nichols, D., Oki, B. M., & Terry, D. (1992). Using collaborative filtering to weave an information tapestry. *Communications of the ACM, 35*(12), 61–70. doi:10.1145/138859.138867

Gong, S. (2010). A Collaborative Filtering Recommendation Algorithm Based On User Clustering And Item Clustering. *Journal Of Software, 5*(7), 745–752. doi:10.4304/jsw.5.7.745-752

Goyal, M., Yadav, D., & Choubey, A. (2012). E-learning: Current State of Art and Future Prospects. *IJCSI International Journal of Computer Science Issues, 9*(2), 490–499.

Grob, H. L., Bensberg, F., & Kaderali, F. (2004). Controlling Open Source Intermediaries – a Web Log Mining Approach. *Proceedings of theInternational Conference on Information Technology Interfaces*, Zagreb (pp. 233-242).

Gruvstad, F., Gupta, N. & Agrawal, Sh. (2009). Shiniphy - Visual Data Mining of movie recommendations.

Guha, R. V., Kumar, R., Raghavan, P., & Tomkins, A. (2004). Propagation of trust and distrust. *Proceedings of the 13th International World Wide Web Conference* (pp. 403–412).

Guha, R., Kumar, R., Raghavan, P., & Tomkins, A. (2004). Propagation of trust and distrust.*Proceedings of the Thirteenth International Conference on World Wide Web* (pp. 403-412). ACM Press.

Guo, G., Zhang, J., & Thalmann, D. (2014). Merging trust in collaborative filtering to alleviate data sparsity and cold start. *Knowledge-Based Systems*, *57*, 57–68. doi:10.1016/j.knosys.2013.12.007

Guo, G., Zhang, J., & Yorke-Smith, N. (2015). Leveraging multiviews of trust and similarity to enhance clustering-based recommender systems. *Knowledge-Based Systems*, *74*, 14–27. doi:10.1016/j.knosys.2014.10.016

Guo, G., Zhang, J., & Yorke-Smith, N. (2015a). TrustSVD: Collaborative filtering with both the explicit and implicit influence of user trust and of item ratings.*Proceedings of the Twenty-Ninth AAAI Conference on Artificial Intelligence*. AAAI Press.

Gupta, S. K., Phung, D., Adams, B., & Venkatesh, S. (2013). Regularized nonnegative shared subspace learning. *Data Mining and Knowledge Discovery*, *26*(1), 57–97. doi:10.1007/s10618-011-0244-8

Guttman, R. H., Moukas, A. G., & Maes, P. (1998). Agent-mediated electronic commerce: *A survey. The Knowledge Engineering Review*, *13*(2), 147–159. doi:10.1017/S0269888998002082

Guyon, I., Gunn, S., Nikravesh, M., & Zadeh, L. A. (Eds.). (2008). *Feature Extraction: Foundations and Applications* (Vol. 207). Springer.

Hall, M., Frank, E., Holmes, G., Pfahringer, B., Reutemann, P. & Witten, I. H. (2009). The WEKA data mining software: an update. *ACM SIGKDD explorations newsletter*, 11(1), 10-18.

Hamalainen, W., Suhonen, J., Sutinen, E., & Toivonen, H. (2004). Data mining in personalizing distance education courses. *Proceedings of theWorld Conference on Open Learning and Distance Education*, Hong Kong (pp. 1-11).

Hammond, N. 1989, Hypermedia and learning: Who guides whom? In Computer Assisted Learning, LNCS (Vol. 360, pp. 167-181). Berlin: Springer-Verlag.

Han, P., Du, J., & Chen, L. (2010, September). Web opinion mining based on sentiment phrase classification vector. *Proceedings of the 2010 2nd IEEE International Conference on Network Infrastructure and Digital Content* (pp. 308-312). IEEE. doi:10.1109/ICNIDC.2010.5657968

Hand, D., Mannila, H., & Smyth, P. (2001). *Principles of Data Mining*. MIT Press.

Han, J., Cheng, H., Xin, D., & Yan, X. (2007). Frequent pattern mining: Current status and future directions. *Journal of Data Mining and Knowledge Discovery*, *15*(1), 55–86. doi:10.1007/s10618-006-0059-1

Han, J., & Kamber, M. (2006). *Data Mining, Concepts and Techniques* (2nd ed.). San Francisco, CA, USA: Morgan Kaufmann Publishers Inc.

Han, J., Kamber, M., & Pei, J. (2006). *Data Mining: Concepts and Techniques* (2nd ed.). Elsevier Inc.

Han, J., Pei, J., & Yin, Y. (2000) Mining frequent patterns without candidate generation. In W. Chen, J. F. Naughton, & P. A. Bernstein (Eds.), *Proceedings of the 2000 ACM SIGMOD International Conference on Management of Data* (pp. 1-12). New York, NY: ACM. doi:10.1145/342009.335372

Hanna, M. (2004). Data Mining in the e-Learning Domain. *Campus-Wide Information Systems*, *21*(1), 29–34. doi:10.1108/10650740410512301

Hannon, J., Bennett, M., & Smyth, B. (2010).Recommending twitter users to follow using contentand collaborative filtering approaches.*Proceedings of the fourth ACM conference on Recommender systems* (pp. 199-206).

Hashem, I. A. T., Yaqoob, I., Anuar, N. B., Mokhtar, S., Gani, A., & Khan, S. U. (2015). The rise of "big data" on cloud computing: Review and open research issues. *Information Systems*, *47*, 98–115. doi:10.1016/j.is.2014.07.006

Hashemi, S., Yang, Y., Mirzamomen, Z., & Kangavari, M. (2009). Adapted One-versus-All Decision Trees for Data Stream Classification. *IEEE Transactions on Knowledge and Data Engineering*, *21*(5), 624–637. doi:10.1109/TKDE.2008.181

Hassanien, A. E., Azar, A. T., Snasel, V., Kacprzyk, J., & Abawajy, J. H. (2015). *Big Data in Complex Systems: Challenges and Opportunities. In Studies in Big Data* (Vol. 9). Springer.

Havre, S., Hetzler, E., Whitney, P., & Nowell, L. (2002). ThemeRiver: Visualizing Thematic Changes in Large Document Collections. *Visualization and Computer Graphics*, *8*(1), 8–20. doi:10.1109/2945.981848

Haythornthwaite, C. (2001). Exploring Multiplexity: Social Network Structures in a Computer- Supported Distance Learning Class. *The Information Society International Journal (Toronto, Ont.)*, *17*(3), 211–226.

Heckerman, D., Chickering, D. M., Meek, Ch., Rounthwaite, R., & Kadie, C. (2001). Dependency Networks for Inference, Collaborative Filtering and Data Visualization. *Journal of Machine Learning Research*, *1*, 49–75.

Heerschop, B., Goossen, F., Hogenboom, A., Frasincar, F., Kaymak, U., & de Jong, F. (2011, October). Polarity analysis of texts using discourse structure.*Proceedings of the 20th ACM international conference on Information and knowledge management* (pp. 1061-1070). ACM doi:10.1145/2063576.2063730

Hengsong, T., & Hong Wu Ye. (2009, May 16-17). A Collaborative Filtering Recommendation Algorithm Based on Item Classification. *Proceedings of the Pacific-Asia Conference on Circuits, Communications and Systems* (pp. 694-697).

Hennessy, J. L., & Patterson, D. A. (2011). *MapReduce: Simplified Data Processing on Large Clusters Computer architecture: a quantitative approach*. Elsevier.

Herlocker, J., Konstan, J.A. & Riedl, J. (2002). An empirical analysis of design choices in neighborhood-based collaborative filtering algorithms. *Inf. Retr.*, *5*(4), 287-310.

He, Y., & Zhou, D. (2011). Self-training from labeled features for sentiment analysis. *Information Processing & Management*, *47*(4), 606–616. doi:10.1016/j.ipm.2010.11.003

Hill, T., & Lewicki, P. (2006). *STATISTICS Methods and Applications*. StatSoft.

Hill, W., Stead, L., Rosenstein, M., & Furnas, G. (1995). *Recommndeing and Evaluating Choices in a Virtual Community of Use*. Conf. Human Factors in Computing Systems.

Hinneburg, A., Keim, D., & Wawryniuk, M. (2003). Using projections to visually cluster high-dimensional data. *Computing in Science & Engineering*, *5*(2), 14–25. doi:10.1109/MCISE.2003.1182958

Hiremath, P. S., & Kodge, B. G. (2010). Visualization techniques for data mining of Latur district satellite imagery. *Advances in Computational Research*, *2*(1), 21–24.

Hochheiser, H., & Shneiderman, B. (2004). Dynamic query tools for time series data sets: Timebox widgets for interactive exploration. *Information Visualization, 3*(1), 1–18. doi:10.1057/palgrave.ivs.9500061

Hoffmann, A. O. I., & Birnbrich, C. (2012). The impact of fraud prevention on bank-customer relationships. *International Journal of Bank Marketing, 30*(5), 390–407. doi:10.1108/02652321211247435

Hu, R., Dou, W. & Liu, J. (2014, September). ClubCF: A Clustering-Based collaborative Filtering Approach for Big Data Application. *IEEE transactions on emerging topics in computing, 2*(3).

Hu, Y., Koren, Y., & Volinsky, C. (2008). Collaborative Filtering for Implicit Feedback Datasets. *Proceedings of the2008Eighth IEEE International Conference on Data Mining.*

Huang, T., Lan, L., Fang, X., An, P., Min, J., & Wang, F. (2015). Promises and challenges of big data computing in health science. *Big Data Research, 2*(1), 2–11. doi:10.1016/j.bdr.2015.02.002

Huang, Z., Chen, H., & Zeng, D. (2004). Applying Associative Retrieval Techniques to Alleviate the Sparsity Problem. *ACM Transactions on Information Systems, 22*(1), 116–142. doi:10.1145/963770.963775

Hulten, G., Spencer, L., & Domingos, P. (2001). Mining time-changing data streams. *Proceedings of the seventh ACM SIGKDD international conference on Knowledge discovery and data mining* (pp. 97-106). doi:10.1145/502512.502529

Hu, N., Bose, I., Koh, N. S., & Liu, L. (2012). Manipulation of online reviews: An analysis of ratings, readability, and sentiments. *Decision Support Systems, 52*(3), 674–684. doi:10.1016/j.dss.2011.11.002

Hu, R., Dou, W., & Liu, J. (2014). Clubcf: A Clustering Based Collaborative Filtering Approach For Big Data Application. *IEEE Transaction On Emerging Topics In Computing, 2*(3), 302–313. doi:10.1109/TETC.2014.2310485

Hwang, G.J., Tsai, P.S., Tsai, C.C. & Tseng, J.C.R. (2008). A novel approach for assisting teachers in analyzing student web-searching behaviors. *Computer and Education Journal, 51*, 926-938.

Hwang, W., & Jun, C. (2014). Supervised Learning-Based Collaborative Filtering Using Market Basket Data For Cold-Start Problem. *Industrial Engineering And Management Systems, 13*(4), 421–431. doi:10.7232/iems.2014.13.4.421

Ibnkahla, M. (2000). Applications of neural networks to digital communications-a survey. *Expert Systems with Applications, 80*, 1185–1215.

Ibrahim, S., Jin, H., Lu, L., Qi, L., Wu, S., & Shi, X. (2009). Evaluating MapReduce on Virtual Machines: The Hadoop Case. In Cloud Computing, LNCS (Vol. 5931, pp. 519-528). Springer.

Igo, F. Jr, Brand, M., Wittenburg, K., Wong, D., & Azuma, Sh. (2002). *Multidimensional Visualization for Collaborative Filtering Recommender Systems.* Mitsubishi Electric Research Laboratories.

Ingram, A. (1999). Using web server logs in evaluating instructional web sites. *Journal of Educational Technology Systems, 28*(2), 137–157. doi:10.2190/R3AE-UCRY-NJVR-LY6F

Jacobs, A. (2009). The pathologies of big data. *Communications of the ACM - A Blind Person's Interaction with Technology. 52*(8), 36-44.

Jagadish, H. V. (2015). Big Data and Science: Myths and Reality. *Big Data Research, 2*(2), 49–52. doi:10.1016/j.bdr.2015.01.005

Jain, A. K. (2010). Data clustering: 50 years beyond *k*-means. *Pattern Recognition Letters, 31*(8), 651–666. doi:10.1016/j.patrec.2009.09.011

Jain, A. K., Murty, M. N., & Flynn, P. J. (1999). Data Clustering: A Review. *ACM Computing Surveys*, *31*(3), 264–323. doi:10.1145/331499.331504

Jamali, M., & Ester, M. (2009). Using a trust network to improve top-N recommendation.*Proceedings of the Third ACM International Conference on Recommender Systems* (pp. 181-188). ACM Press. doi:10.1145/1639714.1639745

Jenatton, R., Le Roux, N., Bordes, A., & Obozinski, G. (2012). *A latent factor model for highly multi-relational data.* In Advances in Neural Information Processing Systems (p. 19). NIPS.

Jian, C., Jian, Y., & Jin, H. (2005). Automatic content-based recommendation in e-commence. *Proceedings of the IEEE International Conference on e-Technology, e-Commerce and e-Service*, Washington, USA (pp. 748–753).

Jiang, F., & Leung, C. K.-S. (2014). Mining interesting "following" patterns from social networks. In L. Bellatreche, & M. K. Mohania (Eds.), *Proceedings of the 16th International Conference on Data Warehousing and Knowledge Discovery (DaWaK 2014)* (pp. 308-319). Heidelberg, Germany: Springer. doi:10.1007/978-3-319-10160-6_28

Jiang, C., Coenen, F., Sanderson, R., & Zito, M. (2010). Text classification using graph mining-based feature extraction. *Knowledge-Based Systems*, *23*(4), 302–308. doi:10.1016/j.knosys.2009.11.010

Jin, X., Wah, B. W., Cheng, X., & Wang, Y. (2015). Significance and challenges of big data research. *Big Data Research*, *2*(2), 59–64.

Joachims, T. (1998). *Text categorization with support vector machines: Learning with many relevant features* (pp. 137–142). Springer Berlin Heidelberg.

Julie, D. & Kumar, K.A. (2012). Optimal web service selection scheme with dynamic QoS property assignment. *Int. J. Adv. Res. Technol.*, 2(2), 69-75.

Kang, H., Yoo, S. J., & Han, D. (2009). Accessing positive and negative online opinions. In *Universal Access in Human-Computer Interaction* (pp. 359–368). Applications and Services.

Kang, H., Yoo, S. J., & Han, D. (2012). Senti-lexicon and improved Naïve Bayes algorithms for sentiment analysis of restaurant reviews. *Expert Systems with Applications*, *39*(5), 6000–6010. doi:10.1016/j.eswa.2011.11.107

Kang, U., & Faloutsos, C. (2013). Big graph mining: Algorithms and discoveries. *ACM SIGKDD Explorations Newsletter*, *14*(2), 29–36. doi:10.1145/2481244.2481249

Karamibekr, M., & Ghorbani, A. (2012, December). Verb oriented sentiment classification. *Proceedings of the 2012 IEEE/WIC/ACM International Conferences on Web Intelligence and Intelligent Agent Technology (WI-IAT)* (Vol. 1, pp. 327-331). IEEE doi:10.1109/WI-IAT.2012.122

Karamibekr, M., & Ghorbani, A. (2013, November). Sentence subjectivity analysis in social domains. *Proceedings of the 2013 IEEE/WIC/ACM International Joint Conferences on Web Intelligence (WI) and Intelligent Agent Technologies (IAT)* (Vol. 1, pp. 268-275). IEEE. doi:10.1109/WI-IAT.2013.39

Kardan, A. A., Abbaspour, S., & Hendijanifard, F. (2009) A hybrid recommender system for e-learning environments based on concept maps and collaborative tagging. *Proceedings of the 4thInternational Conference on Virtual Learning ICVL.*

Kashwan, K. R., & Velu, C. M. (2012). Performance analysis for visual data mining classification techniques of decision tree, Ensemble, and SOM. *International Journal of Computers and Applications*, *57*(22), 65–71. doi:10.5120/9426-3874

Katsavounidis, I., Kuo, C.-C. J., & Zhang, Z. (1994). A new initialization technique for generalized Lloyd iteration. *IEEE Signal Processing Letters*, *1*(10), 144–146. doi:10.1109/97.329844

Kaufman, L., & Rousseeuw, P. J. (1987). Clustering by means of medoids. In Statistical Data Analysis based on the L1 norm (pp. 405-416). Amsterdam.

Kawamae, N. (2012, September). Hierarchical Approach to Sentiment Analysis. *Proceedings of the 2012 IEEE Sixth International Conference on Semantic Computing (ICSC)* (pp. 138-145). IEEE. doi:10.1109/ICSC.2012.62

Keim, D. A. (2002). Information visualization and visual data mining. *IEEE Transactions on Visualization and Computer Graphics*, 8(1), 1–8. doi:10.1109/2945.981847

Keim, D., & Kriegel, H. (1996). Visualization techniques for mining large databases: A comparison. *IEEE Transactions on Knowledge and Data Engineering*, 8(6), 923–938. doi:10.1109/69.553159

Kermarrec, A. M., & Moin, A. (2012). *Data visualization via collaborative filtering* [Research Report]. (p. 23).

Kersting, K., & De Raedt, L. (2007). Bayesian Logic Programming: Theory and Tool. In *L. a. Getoor (Ed.), An Introduction to Statistical Relational Learning*. MIT Press.

Khan, K., Baharudin, B., Khan, A., & Ullah, A. (2014). Mining opinion components from unstructured reviews: A review. *Journal of King Saud University-Computer and Information Sciences*, 26(3), 258–275. doi:10.1016/j.jksuci.2014.03.009

Khan, S. S., & Ahmad, A. (2004). Cluster center initialization algorithm for *k*-means clustering. *Pattern Recognition Letters*, 25(11), 1293–1302. doi:10.1016/j.patrec.2004.04.007

Khoshneshin, M. (2012). *Latent feature networks for statistical relational learning [PHD]*. Iowa Research Online.

Khosravi, H., & Bina, B. (2010). A Survey on Statistical Relational Learning. In *Advances in Artificial Intelligence* (pp. 256–268).

Kibriya, A. M., Frank, E., Pfahringer, B., & Holmes, G. (2004). Multinomial naive bayes for Text Categorization Revisited. Proceedings of AI 2004: Advances in Artificial intelligence (pp. 488–499). Springer Berlin Heidelberg. doi:10.1007/978-3-540-30549-1_43

Kim, B. M., & Kumoh, Q. L. (2004). Probabilistic Model Estimation for Collaborative Filtering Based on Items Attributes. *Proc. of the IEEE/WIC/ACM International Conference on Web Intelligence* (pp. 185-191).

Kimani, S., Lodi, S., Catarci, T., Santucci, G., & Sartori, C. (2004). VidaMine: A visual data mining environment. *Journal of Visual Languages and Computing*, 15(1), 37–67. doi:10.1016/j.jvlc.2003.06.005

Kim, H. K., Kim, J. K., & Ryu, Y. U. (2009). Personalized recommendation over a customer network for ubiquitous shopping. *IEEE Transactions on Services Computing*, 2(2), 140–151. doi:10.1109/TSC.2009.7

Kim, J. K., Cho, Y. H., Kim, W. J., Kim, J. R., & Suh, J. H. (2002). A personalized recommendation procedure for internet shopping support. *Electronic Commerce Research and Applications*, 1(3-4), 301–313. doi:10.1016/S1567-4223(02)00022-4

Kim, K., Ahn, H., & Jeong, S. (2010). Context-Aware Recommender Systems Using Data Mining Techniques. *International Scholarly And Scientific Research And Innovation*, 4(4), 276–281.

Kirkwood, A., & Price, L. (2006). Adaptation for a Changing Environment: Developing learning and teaching with information and communication technologies. *International Review of Research in Open and Distance Learning*, 7(2), 1–14.

Klosgen, W., & Zytkow, J. (2002). *Handbook of data mining and knowledge discovery*. New York: Oxford University Press.

Knutov, E., De Bra, P., & Pechenizkiy, M. (2009). AH 12 years later: A comprehensive survey of adaptive hypermedia methods and techniques. *New Review of Hypermedia and Multimedia*, 15(1), 5–38. doi:10.1080/13614560902801608

Kobsa, A., Chellappa, R. K., & Spiekermann, S. (2007). Privacy-Enhanced Personalization. *Communications of the ACM*, *50*(8), 24–33. doi:10.1145/1278201.1278202

Kohavi, R., & John, G. H. (1997). Wrappers for Feature Subset Selection. *Artificial Intelligence*, *97*(1-2), 273–324. doi:10.1016/S0004-3702(97)00043-X

Kohrs, A., & Merialdo, B. (1999). Clustering For Collaborative Filtering Applications. *Intelligent Image Processing, Data Analysis & Information Retrieval*, *3*, 199.

Kolomvatsos, K., Anagnostopoulos, C., & Hadjiefthymiades, S. (2015). An Efficient Time Optimized Scheme for Progressive Analytics in Big Data. *Big Data Research*, *2*(4), 155–165. doi:10.1016/j.bdr.2015.02.001

Kolter, J., & Maloof, M. (2007). Dynamic weighted majority: A new ensemble method for tracking concept drift. Proceedings of the Third IEEE International Conference on Data Mining ICDM '03 (pp. 123-130). IEEE.

Koncz, P., & Paralic, J. (2011, June). An approach to feature selection for sentiment analysis. *Proceedings of the 2011 15th IEEE International Conference on Intelligent Engineering Systems (INES)* (pp. 357-362). IEEE.

Kontopoulos, E., Berberidis, C., Dergiades, T., & Bassiliades, N. (2013). Ontology-based sentiment analysis of twitter posts. *Expert Systems with Applications*, *40*(10), 4065–4074. doi:10.1016/j.eswa.2013.01.001

Koren, Y., & Bell, R. (2011). Advances in collaborative filtering. In F. Ricci, L. Rokach, B. Shapira, & P. Kantor (Eds.), *Recommender Systems Handbook* (pp. 1–42). Springer. doi:10.1007/978-0-387-85820-3_5

Koren, Y., Bell, R., & Volinsky, C. (2009). Matrix factorization techniques for recommender systems. *Computer*, *42*(8), 30–37. doi:10.1109/MC.2009.263

Krulwich, B. (1997). Life style finder: Intelligent user profiling using large-scale demographic data. *AI Magazine*, *18*(2), 37–45.

Kumar, A., Kansal, C., & Ekbal, A. (2015, January). Investigating active learning techniques for document level sentiment classification of tweets.*Proceedings of the 2015 7th International Conference on Communication Systems and Networks (COMSNETS)* (pp. 1-6). IEEE.

Kumar, A., & Thambidurai, P. (2010). Collaborative Web Recommendation Systems Based On An Effective Fuzzy Association Rule Mining Algorithm (FARM). *Indian Journal Of Computer Science And Engineering*, *1*(3), 184–191.

Kumaran, V. S., & Sankar, A. (2013). Recommendation System for Adaptive E-learning using Semantic Net. *International Journal of Computers and Applications*, *63*(7), 19–24. doi:10.5120/10478-5210

Kumar, D., & Bharadwaj, D. (2011). Rise of data mining: Current and future application areas. *International Journal of Computer Science Issues*, *8*(5), 256–260.

Kuncheva, L. I. (2004). Classifier Ensembles for Changing Environments. *Proceedings of the International Workshop on multiple classifier systems, Italy*.

Kuncheva, L. I., & Zliobaite, I. (2009). On the window size for Classification in Changing Environments. *Journal of Intelligent Data Analysis*, *13*(6), 314–323.

Labrinidis, A., & Jagadish, H. V. (2012). Challenges and opportunities with big data. *Proceedings of the VLDB Endowment*, 5(12), 2032-2033.

Lai, J. Z. C., & Huang, T.-J. (2010). Fast global *k*-means clustering using cluster membership and inequality. *Pattern Recognition*, *43*(5), 1954–1963. doi:10.1016/j.patcog.2009.11.021

Lai, J. Z. C., Huang, T.-J., & Liaw, Y.-C. (2009). A fast *k*-means clustering algorithm using cluster center displacement. *Pattern Recognition, 42*(11), 2551–2556. doi:10.1016/j.patcog.2009.02.014

Lane, P. C., Clarke, D., & Hender, P. (2012). On developing robust models for favourability analysis: Model choice, feature sets and imbalanced data. *Decision Support Systems, 53*(4), 712–718. doi:10.1016/j.dss.2012.05.028

Lauschke, C., & Ntoutsi, E. (2012). Monitoring user evolution in Twitter. In *Proceedings of the 2012 IEEE/ACM International Conference on Advances in Social Networks Analysis and Mining (ASONAM)*, (pp. 972-977). Los Alamitos, CA: IEEE Computer Society. doi:10.1109/ASONAM.2012.171

Law, Y., & Zaniolo, C. (2005). An Adaptive Nearest Neighbor Classification Algorithm for Data Streams. *Proceedings of 9th European Conference on Principals and Practice of Knowledge Discovery in Databases* (pp. 108-120). Springer-Verlag. doi:10.1007/11564126_15

Lee, J., Jun, C., Lee, J., & Kim, S. (2005). Classification-Based Collaborative Filtering Using Market-Basket Data. Expert Systems With Application, 29, 700-704.

Lee, D. H., & Brusilovsky, P., P. (2010). Social networks and interest similarity: the case of CiteULike.*Proceedings of the 21st ACM conference on Hypertext and Hypermedia* (pp. 151-156). ACM Press doi:10.1145/1810617.1810643

Lee, W.-P., & Lee, K.-H. (2014). Making smartphone service recommendations by predicting users' intentions: A context-aware approach. *Information Sciences, 277*, 21–35. doi:10.1016/j.ins.2014.04.033

Lee, Y., & Lee, Y. (2013). Toward scalable internet traffic measurement and analysis with Hadoop. *ACM SIGCOMM Computer Communication, 43*(1), 5–13. doi:10.1145/2427036.2427038

Letham, B. (2013). Similarity-Weighted Association Rules For A Name Recommender System.*Proceedings of European Conference on Machine Learning and Principles and Practice of Knowledge Discovery in Databases Discovery Challenge.*

Leung, C. K.-S. (2013). Mining frequent itemsets from probabilistic datasets. *Proceedings of the Fifth International Conference on Emerging Databases (EDB 2013)* (pp. 137-148).

Leung, C. K.-S. (2014b). Uncertain frequent pattern mining. In C. C. Aggarwal & J. Han (Eds.), Frequent pattern mining (pp. 417–453). Heidelberg, Germany: Springer. doi:10.1007/978-3-319-07821-2_14

Leung, C. K.-S., MacKinnon, R. K., & Jiang, F. (2014). Reducing the search space for big data mining for interesting patterns from uncertain data. *Proceedings of the 2014 IEEE International Congress on Big Data (BigData Congress)*, (pp. 315-322). Los Alamitos, CA: IEEE Computer Society. doi:10.1109/BigData.Congress.2014.53

Leung, C. K.-S., Medina, I. J. M., & Tanbeer, S. K. (2013). Analyzing social networks to mine important friends. In G. Xu & L. Li (Eds.), Social media mining and social network analysis: emerging research (pp. 90–104). Hershey, PA: IGI Global. doi:10.4018/978-1-4666-2806-9.ch006

Leung, C. K.-S., Tanbeer, S. K., & Cameron, J. J. (2014). Interactive discovery of influential friends from social networks. *Social Network Analysis and Mining, 4*(1). doi:10.1007/s13278-014-0154-z

Leung, C. K.-S. (2014a). Big data mining and analytics. In J. Wang (Ed.), *Encyclopedia of business analytics and optimization* (pp. 328–337). Hershey, PA: IGI Global. doi:10.4018/978-1-4666-5202-6.ch030

Leung, C. K.-S., Carmichael, C. L., Johnstone, P., & Yuen, D. S. H.-C. (2013). Interactive visual analytics of databases and frequent sets. *International Journal of Information Retrieval Research, 3*(4), 120–140. doi:10.4018/ijirr.2013100107

Leung, C. W., Chan, S. C., & Chung, F. (2005). A Collaborative Filtering Framework Based On Fuzzy Association Rules And Multiple-Level Similarity. *Knowledge and Information Systems, 10*(3), 357–381. doi:10.1007/s10115-006-0002-1

Li, C. S. (2011). Cluster center initialization method for *k*-means algorithm over data sets with two clusters. Proc. *International Conference on Advances in Engineering* (*Vol. 24,* pp. 324-328). Elsevier.

Li, G., & Liu, F. (2010, November). A clustering-based approach on sentiment analysis. *Proceedings of the 2010 International Conference on Intelligent Systems and Knowledge Engineering (ISKE)* (pp. 331-337). IEEE.

Li, P., Zhu, Q., & Zhang, W. (2011, July). A dependency tree based approach for sentence-level sentiment classification. *Proceedings of the 2011 12th ACIS International Conference on Software Engineering, Artificial Intelligence, Networking and Parallel/Distributed Computing (SNPD)* (pp. 166-171). IEEE. doi:10.1109/SNPD.2011.20

Liang, C., Zhang, Y., & Song, Q. (2010). Decision Tree for Dynamic and Uncertain Data Streams. *Proceedings of 2nd Asian Conference on Machine Learning* (pp. 209-224).

Liang, P. W., & Dai, B.-R. (2013). Opinion Mining on Social Media Data. *Proceedings of the 2013 IEEE 14th international Conference on Mobile Data Management (MDM)* (Vol. 2, pp. 91-96). IEEE. doi:10.1109/MDM.2013.73

Lihua, W., Lu, L., Jing, L., & Zongyong, L. (2005). Modeling user multiple interests by an improved GCS approach. *Expert Systems with Applications*, *29*(4), 757–767. doi:10.1016/j.eswa.2005.06.003

Likas, A., Vlassis, N., & Verbeek, J. J. (2003). The global *k*-means clustering algorithm. *Pattern Recognition Letters*, *36*, 451–461. doi:10.1016/S0031-3203(02)00060-2

Linden, G., Smith, B., & York, J. (2003). Amazon.com recommendations: *Item-to-item collaborative filtering. IEEE Internet Computing*, *7*(1), 76–80. doi:10.1109/MIC.2003.1167344

Lin, J., Keogh, E., & Lonardi, S. (2005). Visualizing and discovering non-trivial patterns in large time series databases. *Information Visualization*, *4*(2), 61–82. doi:10.1057/palgrave.ivs.9500089

Lin, J., & Ryaboy, D. (2013). Scaling big data mining infrastructure: The twitter experience. *ACM SIGKDD Explorations Newsletter*, *14*(2), 6–19. doi:10.1145/2481244.2481247

Linoff, G. S., & Berry, M. J. (2011). *Data Mining Techniques. For Marketing, Sales, and Customer Relationship Management* (3rd ed.). New York, NY: John Wiley & Sons Inc.

Lin, S.-H. (2012). Data mining for student retention management. *Journal of Computing Sciences in Colleges*, *27*(4), 92–99.

Liu, B. (2012). Sentiment Analysis and Opinion Mining. *Synthesis Lectures on Human Language Technologies*, *5*(1), 1–167. doi:10.2200/S00416ED1V01Y201204HLT016

Liu, Q., & Li, X. (2015). A New Parallel Item-Based Collaborative Filtering Algorithm Based on Hadoop. *Journal of Software*, *10*(4), 416–426. doi:10.17706/jsw.10.4.416-426

Liu, W., Wu, C., Feng, B., & Liu, J. (2015). Conditional preference in recommender systems. *Expert Systems with Applications*, *42*(2), 774–788. doi:10.1016/j.eswa.2014.08.044

Li, Y. M., & Li, T. Y. (2013). Deriving market intelligence from microblogs. *Decision Support Systems*, *55*(1), 206–217. doi:10.1016/j.dss.2013.01.023

Li, Y.-M., Wu, C.-T., & Lai, C.-Y. (2013). A social recommender mechanism for e-commerce: Combining similarity, trust and relationship. *Decision Support Systems*, *55*(3), 740–752. doi:10.1016/j.dss.2013.02.009

Lloyd, S. P. (1982). Least squares quantization in PCM. *IEEE Transactions on Information Theory*, *28*(2), 129–137. doi:10.1109/TIT.1982.1056489

Lu, W., & Lakshmanan, L. V. S. (2012). Profit maximization over social networks. In M. J. Zaki, A. Siebes, J. X. Yu, B. Goethals, G. I. Webb, & X. Wu (Eds.), *Proceedings of the 12th IEEE International Conference on Data Mining (ICDM 2012)* (pp. 479-488). Los Alamitos, CA: IEEE Computer Society. doi:10.1109/ICDM.2012.145

Luan, J. (2002). Data Mining and Knowledge Management in Higher Education-Potential Applications. *Paper presented at theAnnual Forum for the Association for Institutional Research*, Toronto, Ontario, Canada.

Lu, C. Y., Lin, S. H., Liu, J. C., Cruz-Lara, S., & Hong, J. S. (2010). Automatic event-level textual emotion sensing using mutual action histogram between entities. *Expert Systems with Applications*, *37*(2), 1643–1653. doi:10.1016/j.eswa.2009.06.099

Lu, J., Wu, D., Mao, M., Wang, W., & Zhang, G. (2015). Recommender system application developments: A survey. *Decision Support Systems*, *74*, 12–32. doi:10.1016/j.dss.2015.03.008

Lu, L., Medo, M., Yeung, C. H., Zhang, Y. C., Zhang, Z. K., & Zhou, T. (2012). Recommender Systems. *Physics Reports*, *519*(1), 1–49. doi:10.1016/j.physrep.2012.02.006

Lu, Y., Castellanos, M., Dayal, U., & Zhai, C. (2011, March). Automatic construction of a context-aware sentiment lexicon: an optimization approach.*Proceedings of the 20th international conference on World Wide Web* (pp. 347-356). ACM. doi:10.1145/1963405.1963456

Ma, H., Zhou, T. C., Lyu, M. R., & King, I. (2011). Improving recommender systems by incorporating social contextual information. *ACM Trans. on Information Systems, 29*(2).

Mabroukeh, N. R. & Ezeife, C. I. (2010), Taxonomy of Sequential Pattern Mining Algorithms. *ACM Computing Surveys*, 43(1).

Macfadyen, L. P., & Dawson, S. (2010). Mining LMS data to develop an "early warning system" for educators: A proof of concept. *Computers & Education*, *54*(2), 588–599. doi:10.1016/j.compedu.2009.09.008

MacQueen, J. (1967). Some methods for classification and analysis of multivariate observations.*Proc.5th Symposium Mathematical Statistics and Probability,*Berkeley, CA (Vol. 1, pp. 281-297).

Madria, S. K., Bhowmick, S. S., Ng, W. K., & Lim, E. P. (1999). *Research issues in web data mining* (pp. 303–312). Data Warehousing and Knowledge Discovery.

Mahajan, R. (2014). Real Time Analysis of Attributes Of An Indian E-Learning Site. *The International Journal of E-Learning and Educational Technologies in the Digital Media*, *1*(2), 109–114. doi:10.17781/P001706

Mahajan, R., Sodhi, J. S., & Mahajan, V. (2012). Mining User Access Pattern for Adaptive e-learning environments. *International Journal of e-Education, e-Business, e- Management Learning*, *2*(4), 277–279.

Mahajan, R., Sodhi, J. S., & Mahajan, V. (2014). Usage Patterns Discovery from a Web Log of an Indian e-learning site: A Case Study. *Education and Information Technologies*, *19*, 1–26.

Mahajan, V., Misra, R., & Mahajan, R. (2015). Review of Data Mining Techniques for Churn Prediction in Telecom. *Journal of Information and Organizational Sciences*, *39*(2), 183–197.

Maimon, O., & Rockach, L. (Eds.). (2005). *Data mining and knowledge discovery handbook* (Vol. 2). New York: Springer. doi:10.1007/b107408

Malhotra, N. K. (2007). *Marketing research: An applied orientation* (5th ed.). Pearson Education Inc. doi:10.1108/S1548-6435(2007)3

Manouselis, N., & Costopoulou, C. (2007). Experimental analysis of design choices in multiattribute utility collaborative filtering. *International Journal of Pattern Recognition and Artificial Intelligence*, *21*(2), 311–331. doi:10.1142/S021800140700548X

Marlin, M. B., Zemel, R., Roweis, S. T., & Slaney, M. (2011). Recommender Systems: Missing Data and Statistical Model Estimation.*Proceedings of the Twenty-Second International Joint Conference on Artificial Intelligence* (pp. 2686-2691).

Marrese-Taylor, E., Velásquez, J. D., & Bravo-Marquez, F. (2014). A novel deterministic approach for aspect-based opinion mining in tourism products reviews. *Expert Systems with Applications*, *41*(17), 7764–7775. doi:10.1016/j.eswa.2014.05.045

Maserrat, H., & Pei, J. (2012). Community preserving lossy compression of social networks. In M. J. Zaki, A. Siebes, J. X. Yu, B. Goethals, G. I. Webb, & X. Wu (Eds.), *Proceedings of the 12th IEEE International Conference on Data Mining (ICDM 2012)* (pp. 509-518). Los Alamitos, CA: IEEE Computer Society. doi:10.1109/ICDM.2012.14

Massa, P., & Avesani, P. (2007). Trust-aware recommender systems.*Proceedings of the ACM International Conference on Recommender Systems* (pp. 17-24). ACM Press.

Masud, M., Gao, J., Khan, L., Han, J., & Thuraisingham, B. (2009). A multi partition multi chunk ensemble technique to classify concept drifting data streams. *Proceedings of the 13th Pacific-Asia Conf. on Knowledge Discovery and Data Mining (pp. 363-375). Springer-Verlag Berlin*, Heidelberg.

McCullagh, P., & Yang, J. (2008). How many clusters? *Bayesian Analysis*, *3*(1), 101–120.

McNally, K., O'Mahony, M. P., & Smyth, B. (2014). A comparative study of collaboration-based reputation models for social recommender systems. *User Modeling and User-Adapted Interaction*, *24*(3), 219–260. doi:10.1007/s11257-013-9143-6

Mcnulty, E. (2014). Understanding Big Data: The Seven V's. *DataEconomy.com*. Retrieved from http://dataconomy.com/seven-vs-big-data/

Medhat, W., Hassan, A., & Korashy, H. (2014). Sentiment analysis algorithms and applications: A survey. *Ain Shams Engineering Journal*, *5*(4), 1093–1113. doi:10.1016/j.asej.2014.04.011

Melville, P., Mooney, R. J., & Nagarajan, R. (2002). Content-Boosted Collaborative Filtering for Improved Recommendations. *Proceedings of the Eighteenth National Conference on Artificial Intelligence*, Edmonton, Canada (pp. 187-192).

Melville, P., Mooney, R. J., & Nagarajan, R. (2002). Content-Boosted Collaborative Filtering for Improved Recommendations. *Proceedings of theEighteenth National Conference on Artificial Intelligence(AAAI-2002)* (pp. 187-192). Edmonton, Canada: American Association for Artificial Intelligence.

Melville, P., & Sindhwani, V. (2010). *Recommender Systems Encyclopedia of machine learning*.

Middleton, S. E., Shadbolt, N. R., & Roure, D. C. D. (2004). Ontological user profiling in recommender systems. *ACM Transactions on Information Systems*, *22*(1), 54–88. doi:10.1145/963770.963773

Miller, J. (2005). Usability in e-learning. Retrieved from www.learningcircuits.org

Miller, K. T., Griffiths, T. L., & Jordan, M. I. (2009). Nonparametric Latent Feature Models for Link Prediction. *Proceedings of the 23rd Annual Conference on Neural Information Processing Systems 2009,* Vancouver, Canada.

Miller, G. A., & Fellbaum, C. (1991). Semantic networks of English. *Cognition*, *41*(1), 197–229. doi:10.1016/0010-0277(91)90036-4 PMID:1790654

Min, H. J., & Park, J. C. (2012). Identifying helpful reviews based on customer's mentions about experiences. *Expert Systems with Applications*, *39*(15), 11830–11838. doi:10.1016/j.eswa.2012.01.116

Mitchell, T. J. F., Chen, S. Y., & Macredie, R. D. (2005). Hypermedia learning and prior knowledge: Domain expertise vs. system expertise. *Journal of Computer Assisted Learning*, *21*(1), 53–64. doi:10.1111/j.1365-2729.2005.00113.x

Moghaddam, S., & Ester, M. (2011 December). AQA: Aspect-based Opinion Question Answering. *Proceedings of the2011IEEE 11*th *International Conference on Data Mining Workshops (ICDMW)* (pp. 89-96). IEEE.

Montaner, M., Lopez, B., & Rosa, J. L. (2003). A taxonomy of recommender agents on the Internet. *Artificial Intelligence Review*, *19*(4), 285–330. doi:10.1023/A:1022850703159

Moraes, R., Valiati, J. F., & Neto, W. P. G. (2013). Document-level sentiment classification: An empirical comparison between SVM and ANN. *Expert Systems with Applications*, *40*(2), 621–633. doi:10.1016/j.eswa.2012.07.059

Mouthami, K., Devi, K. N., & Bhaskaran, V. M. (2013, February). Sentiment analysis and classification based on textual reviews. *Proceedings of the 2013 International Conference on Information Communication and Embedded Systems (ICICES)* (pp. 271-276). IEEE. doi:10.1109/ICICES.2013.6508366

Mukherjee, A., Liu, B., & Glance, N. (2012, April). Spotting fake reviewer groups in consumer reviews.*Proceedings of the 21st international conference on World Wide Web* (pp. 191-200). ACM. doi:10.1145/2187836.2187863

Narang, A., Srivastava, A., & Kata, N. P. K. (2012). Distributed Hierarchical Co-Clustering And Collaborative Filtering Algorithm.*Proceedings of 19th International Conference on High Performance Computing (HiPC)*. IEEE. doi:10.1109/HiPC.2012.6507497

Négrevergne, B., Dries, A., Guns, T., & Nijssen, S. (2013). Dominance programming for itemset mining. In H. Xiong, G. Karypis, B. M. Thuraisingham, D. J. Cook, & X. Wu (Eds.), *Proceedings of the 13th IEEE International Conference on Data Mining (ICDM 2013)* (pp. 557-566). Los Alamitos, CA: IEEE Computer Society. doi:10.1109/ICDM.2013.92

Neviarouskaya, A., Prendinger, H., & Ishizuka, M. (2010). Recognition of affect, judgment, and appreciation in text. *Proceedings of the 23rd International Conference on Computational Linguistics* (pp. 806-814).

Neville, J., Rattigan, M., & Jensen, D. (2003). Statistical Relational Learning: Four Claims and a Survey.*Proceedings of the Workshop on Learning Statistical Models from Relational Data, 18th International Joint Conference on Artificial Intelligence* (p. 5).

Newton, J., & Greiner, R. (2004). Hierarchical Probabilistic Relational Models for Collaborative Filtering.*Workshop on Statistical Relational Learning, 21st International Conference on Machine Learning* (pp. 1-6).

Ngai, E. W. T., Xiu, L., & Chau, D. C. K. (2009). Application of data mining techniques in customer relationship management: A literature review and classification. *Expert Systems with Applications*, *36*(2), 2592–2602. doi:10.1016/j.eswa.2008.02.021

Nguyen L., & Phung D. (2008). Learner Model in Adaptive Learning. *World Academy of Science, Engineering and Technology*, *45*(70), 395-400.

Nilashi, M., Bagherifard, K., Ibrahim, O., Alizadeh, H., Nojeem, L. A., & Roozegar, N. (2013). Collaborative filtering recommender systems. *Research Journal of Applied Sciences. Engineering and Technology*, *5*(16), 4168–4182.

Nsofor, G. C. (2006). *Comparative Analysis of Predictive Data-Mining Techniques* [Doctoral Thesis].

O'connor, M., & Herlocker, J. (1999). Clustering Items For Collaborative Filtering. *Proceedings of the ACM SIGIR workshop on recommender systems*, UC Berkeley.

O'Donovan, J., & Smyth, B. (2005). Trust in recommender systems.*Proceedings of the Tenth International Conference on Intelligent User Interfaces* (pp. 167-174). doi:10.1145/1040830.1040870

Oliveira, M. C., & Levkowitz, H. (2003). From visual data exploration to visual data mining: A survey. *IEEE Transactions on Visualization and Computer Graphics*, 9(3), 378–394. doi:10.1109/TVCG.2003.1207445

Oza, N., & Russell, S. (2001). Online bagging and boosting. In *Artificial Intelligence and Statistics* (pp. 105-112).

Oza, N., & Russell, S. (2001). Experimental comparisons of online and batch versions of bagging and boosting. *Proceedings of the seventh ACM SIGKDD International Conference on Knowledge discovery and data mining* (pp. 359-364). doi:10.1145/502512.502565

Pai, M. Y., Chu, H. C., Wang, S. C., & Chen, Y. M. (2013). Electronic word of mouth analysis for service experience. *Expert Systems with Applications*, 40(6), 1993–2006. doi:10.1016/j.eswa.2012.10.024

Palace, B. (1996). Data Mining. Retrieved from http://www.anderson.ucla.edu/faculty/jason.frand/teacher/technologies/palace/datamining.htm

Pang, B., & Lee, L. (2004, July), A sentimental education: Sentiment analysis using subjectivity summarization based on minimum cuts.*Proceedings of the 42nd annual meeting on Association for Computer Linguistics*, (p. 271). Association for Computational Linguistics. doi:10.3115/1218955.1218990

Pang, B., Lee, L., & Vaithyanathan, S. (2002, July). Thumbs up?: sentiment classification using machine learning techniques.*Proceedings of the ACL-02 conference on Empirical methods in natural language processing* (Vol. 10, pp. 79-86). Association for Computational Linguistics. doi:10.3115/1118693.1118704

Pan, P., Wang, C., Horng, G., & Cheng, S. (2010) The development of an Ontology-Based Adaptive Personalized Recommender System. *Proceedings of the2010 International Conference On*Electronics and Information Engineering (ICEIE*).

Papadimitriou, A., Symeonidis, P. & Manolopoulos, Y. (2011). *A generalized taxonomy of explanations styles for traditional and social recommender systems.* Springer.

Papagelis, M., & Plexousakis, D. (2005). D. Qualitative analysis of user-based and item-based prediction algorithms for recommendation agents. *Engineering Applications of Artificial Intelligence*, 18(7), 781–789. doi:10.1016/j.engappai.2005.06.010

Paramythis A., Loidl-Reisinger S., (2004), Adaptive Learning Environments and e-Learning Standards, *Electronic Journal of eLearning*, 2(1), 181–194.

Park, D. H., Kim, H. K., Choi, Y., & Kim, J. K. (2012). A literature review and classification of recommender systems research. *Expert Systems with Applications*, 39(11), 10059–10072. doi:10.1016/j.eswa.2012.02.038

Pazzani, M. J. (1999). A framework for collaborative, content-based and demographic filtering. *Artificial Intelligence Review*, 13(5–6), 393–408. doi:10.1023/A:1006544522159

Pazzani, M. J., & Billsus, D. (1997). Learning and revising user profiles: The identification of interesting web sites. *Machine Learning*, 27(3), 313–331. doi:10.1023/A:1007369909943

Pazzani, M. J., & Billsus, D. (2007). Content-based recommender systems. In P. Brusilovsky, A. Kobsa, & W. Nejdl (Eds.), *The Adaptive Web*. Berlin: Springer-Verlag. doi:10.1007/978-3-540-72079-9_10

Pei, J., Han, J., Lu, H., Nishio, S., Tang, S., & Yang, D. (2001). H-Mine: hyper-structure mining of frequent patterns in large databases. In N. Cercone, T. Y. Lin, & X. Wu (Eds.), *Proceedings of the First IEEE International Conference on Data Mining* (*ICDM 2001*) (pp. 441-448). Los Alamitos, CA: IEEE Computer Society. doi:10.1109/ICDM.2001.989550

Pei, J., Han, J., Mortazavi-asl, B., & Zhu, H. (2000). Mining Access Patterns Efficiently from Web Logs. *Proc. of the 2000 Pacific-Asia Conf. on Knowledge Discovery and Data Mining (PAKDD'00)*, Kyoto, Japan.

Peled, A., & Rashty, D. (1999). Logging for success: Advancing the use of WWW logs to improve computer mediated distance learning. *Journal of Educational Computing Research, 21*(4), 413–431.

Pelossof, R., Jones, M., Vovsha, I., & Rudin, C. (2009). Online coordinate boosting (Technical Report TR2009-086).

Peñalver-Martinez, I., Garcia-Sanchez, F., Valencia-Garcia, R., Rodríguez-García, M. Á., Moreno, V., Fraga, A., & Sánchez-Cervantes, J. L. (2014). Feature-based opinion mining through ontologies. *Expert Systems with Applications, 41*(13), 5995–6008. doi:10.1016/j.eswa.2014.03.022

Peng, H., Long, F., & Ding, C. (2005). Feature selection based on mutual information criteria of max-dependency, max-relevance, and min-redundancy. *IEEE Transactions on* Pattern Analysis and Machine Intelligence, 27(8), 1226–1238.

Pennock, D. M., Horvitz, E., Lawrence, S. & Giles, C. L. (2000). Collaborative Filtering by Personality Diagnosis: A Hybrid Memory. In *Uncertainty in Artificial Intelligence* (pp. 473-480).

Pennock, D. M., Horvitz, E., Lawrence, S., & Giles, C. L. (2000). *Collaborative Filtering by Personality Diagnosis: A Hybrid Memory- and* (pp. 473–480). Uncertainty in Artificial Intelligence.

Perlich, C., & Huang, Z. (2010). Relational Learning for Customer Relationship Management. *Information Systems*.

Petz, G., Karpowicz, M., Fürschuß, H., Auinger, A., Stříteský, V., & Holzinger, A. (2014). Computational approaches for mining user's opinions on the Web 2.0. *Information Processing & Management, 50*(6), 899–908. doi:10.1016/j.ipm.2014.07.005

Pham, D. T., Dimov, S. S., & Nguyen, C. D. (2004). Selection of *k* in *k*-means clustering. *Journal of Mechanical Engineering Science, 219*(1), 103–119. doi:10.1243/095440605X8298

Pham, M. C., Cao, Y., Klamma, R., & Jacke, M. (2011). A Clustering Approach For Collaborative Filtering Recommendation Using Social Network Analysis. *Journal of Universal Computer Science, 17*(14), 583–604.

Pham, T., Hess, R., Ju, C., Zhang, E., & Metoyer, R. (2010). Visualization of diversity in large multivariate data sets. *Visualization and Computer Graphics, 16*(6), 1053–1062. doi:10.1109/TVCG.2010.216 PMID:20975143

Phobun, P., & Vicheanpanya, J. (2010). Adaptive intelligent tutoring systems for e-learning systems, Innovation and Creativity in Education. *Procedia: Social and Behavioral Sciences, 2*(2), 4064–4069. doi:10.1016/j.sbspro.2010.03.641

Popescu, E. (2008). *Dynamic Adaptive Hypermedia Systems for E-Learning* [Doctoral Thesis]. University of Craiova, Romania.

Ptaszynski, M., Dokoshi, H., Oyama, S., Rzepka, R., Kurihara, M., Araki, K., & Momouchi, Y. (2013). Affect analysis in context of characters in narratives. *Expert Systems with Applications, 40*(1), 168–176. doi:10.1016/j.eswa.2012.07.025

Qian, X., Feng, H., Zhao, G., & Mei, T. (2014). Personalized recommendation combining user interest and social circle. *IEEE Transactions on Knowledge and Data Engineering, 26*(7), 1487–1502. doi:10.1109/TKDE.2013.168

Qin, J., Zheng, Q., Tian, F., & Zheng, D. (2014). An emotion-oriented music recommendation algorithm fusing rating and trust. *International Journal of Computational Intelligence Systems, 7*(2), 371–381. doi:10.1080/18756891.2013.865405

Quinlan, J. R. (1986, March). Induction of decision trees. *Machine Learning, 1*(1), 81–106. doi:10.1007/BF00116251

Quinlan, J. R. (1993). *C4.5: Programs for machine learning*. San Mateo: Morgan Kaufmann Publishers.

Quirin, A., Cordón, O., Vargas-Quesada, B., & de Moya-Anegón, F. (2010). Graph-based data mining: A new tool for the analysis and comparison of scientific domains represented as scientograms. *Journal of Informetrics*, *4*(3), 291–312. doi:10.1016/j.joi.2010.01.004

Radenkovi, B., Despotovi, M., Bogdanovi, Z., & Bara, D. (2006). Creating Adaptive Environment for e-Learning Courses. *Journal of Information and Organizational Sciences*, *33*(1), 179–189.

Raghavan N. R. S. (2005). Data mining in e-commerce: A survey. *Sadhna*, 30(Parts 2 & 3), 275–289.

Raju, R. (2014). Big Data Recommendation Systems. *Whishworks.com*. Retrieved from www.whishworks.com/blog/recommendation-systems/

Rana, C., & Jain, S. K. (2015). A study of the dynamic features of recommender systems. *Artificial Intelligence Review*, *43*(1), 141–153. doi:10.1007/s10462-012-9359-6

Rashid, A. M., Albert, I., Cosley, D., Lam, S. K., McNee, S. M., Konstan, J. A., & Riedl, J. (2002). Getting to know you: Learning new user preferences in recommender systems.*Proc. Int'l Conf. Intelligent.* doi:10.1145/502716.502737

Ray, S., & Mahantirt, A. (2010). Improving prediction accuracy in trust-aware recommender systems.*Proceedings of the 43rd Hawaii International Conference on System Sciences* (pp. 1-9). doi:10.1109/HICSS.2010.225

Ray, S., & Turi, R. (1999). Determination of number of clusters in k-means clustering and application in colour image segmentation.*Proc.4th International Conference on Advances in Pattern Recognition and Digital Techniques,*India (pp. 137-143).

Recommender System. (n. d.). Retrieved from http://en.citizendium.org/wiki/Recommendation_system

Reddy, D., & Jana, P. K. (2012). Initialization for *k*-means clustering using voronoi diagram. *Procedia Technology*, *4*, 395–400. doi:10.1016/j.protcy.2012.05.061

Redmond, S. J., & Heneghan, C. (2007). A method for initializing the *k*-means clustering algorithm using *k-d* trees. *Pattern Recognition Letters*, *28*(8), 965–973. doi:10.1016/j.patrec.2007.01.001

Resnick, P., Iakovou, N., Sushak, M., Bergstrom, P., & Riedl, J. (1994). GroupLens: An open architecture for collaborative filtering of netnews. *Proceedings of theComputer Supported Cooperative Work Conf.* doi:10.1145/192844.192905

Resnick, P., Iacovou, N., Suchak, M., Bergstrom, P., & Riedl, J. (1994, October). GroupLens: an open architecture for collaborative filtering of netnews.*Proceedings of the 1994 ACM conference on Computer supported cooperative work* (pp. 175-186). ACM.

Resnick, P., Iakovou, N., Sushak, M., Bergstrom, P., & Riedl, J. (1994). GroupLens: An open architecture for collaborative filtering of NetNews. *Computer Supported Cooperative Work*.

Resnick, P., Iakovou, N., Sushak, M., Bergstrom, P., & Riedl, J. (1994). GroupLens: An Open Architecture for Collaborative Filtering of NetNews. *Computer Supported Cooperative Work*.

Rettinger, A. (2009). Statistical Relational Learning with Formal Ontologies. In Machine Learning and Knowledge Discovery in Databases (pp. 286-301). doi:10.1007/978-3-642-04174-7_19

Rettinger, A., Nickles, M., & Tresp, V. (2011). Statistical relational learning of trust. *Machine Learning*, *82*(2), 191–209. doi:10.1007/s10994-010-5211-x

Reyes, A., & Rosso, P. (2012). Making objective decisions from subjective data: Detecting irony in customer reviews. *Decision Support Systems, 53*(.4), 754-760.

Riad M., Hamdy K. El-Minir, Haitham A. El-Ghareeb, (2009), Review of e-Learning Systems Convergence from Traditional Systems to Services based Adaptive and Intelligent Systems. *Journal of Convergence Information Technology*, 4(2).

Ricci, F., Rokach, L., & Shapira, B. (2011). Introduction to recommender systems handbook. In F. Ricci, L. Rokach, B. Shapira, & P. Kantor (Eds.), *Recommender Systems Handbook* (pp. 1–35). Springer. doi:10.1007/978-0-387-85820-3_1

Ricci, F., Rokach, L., Shapira, B., & Kantor, P. N. (2011). *Recommender Systems Handbook*. USA: Springer. doi:10.1007/978-0-387-85820-3

Rich, E. (1979). User modeling via stereotypes. *Cognitive Science*, 3(4), 329–354. doi:10.1207/s15516709cog0304_3

Riloff, E., & Wiebe, J. (2003, July). Learning extraction patterns for subjective expressions.*Proceedings of the 2003 conference on Empirical methods in natural language processing* (pp. 105-112). doi:10.3115/1119355.1119369

Rokach, L., & Maimon, O. (2008). *Data Mining with Decision Trees: Theory and Applications*. World Scientific Publishing.

Romero, C., López, M.-I., Luna, J.-M., & Ventura, S. (2013). 'Predicting students' final performance from participation in on-line discussion forums'. *Computers & Education*, 68, 458–472. doi:10.1016/j.compedu.2013.06.009

Romero, C., & Ventura, S. (2006). *Data mining in e-learning*. USA: WIT Press. doi:10.2495/1-84564-152-3

Romero, C., & Ventura, S. (2010). Educational data mining: A review of the state of the art. *Journal of IEEE Transactions on Systems, Man, and Cybernetics*, 40(6), 601–618. doi:10.1109/TSMCC.2010.2053532

Romero, C., Ventura, S., & De Bra, P. (2004). Knowledge discovery with genetic programming for providing feedback to courseware author. *User Modeling and User-Adapted Interaction: The Journal of Personalization Research*, 14(5), 425–464. doi:10.1007/s11257-004-7961-2

Romero, C., Ventura, S., & García, E. (2008). Data mining in course management systems: Moodle case study and tutorial, *Elsevier*. *Computers & Education*, 51(1), 368–384. doi:10.1016/j.compedu.2007.05.016

Romero, C., Ventura, S., Pechenizkiy, M., & Baker, R. (2010a). *Handbook of Educational Data Mining*. Taylor & Francis. doi:10.1201/b10274

Romero, C., & Ventura, S.Romero & S. Ventura. (2007). Educational Data Mining: A Survey from 1995 to 2005. *Expert Systems with Applications*, 33(1), 135–146. doi:10.1016/j.eswa.2006.04.005

Romero, C., Ventura, S., Zafra, A., & De Bra, P. (2009). Applying Web usage mining for personalizing hyperlinks in Web-based adaptive educational systems. *Computers & Education*, 53(3), 828–840. doi:10.1016/j.compedu.2009.05.003

Rong Hu. Wanchun Dou & Jianxun Liu, (2014, September). ClubCF: A Clustering-Based Collaborative Filtering Approach for Big Data Application. IEEE Transactions on Emerging Topics in Computing, 2(3), 302-313.

Rui, H., Liu, Y., & Whinston, A. (2013). Whose and what chatter matters? The effect of tweets on movie sales. *Decision Support Systems*, 55(4), 863–870. doi:10.1016/j.dss.2012.12.022

Ryan, T., & Lee, Y. C. (2015). Multi-tier resource allocation for data-intensive computing. *Big Data Research*, 2(3), 110–116. doi:10.1016/j.bdr.2015.03.001

Salah, A., Rogovschi, N., & Nadif, M. (2016). A dynamic collaborative filtering system via a weighted clustering approach. *Neurocomputing*, 175(A), 206–215.

Salton, G. (1971). *The SMART Retrieval System*. Upper Saddle River, NJ, USA: Prentice-Hall, Inc.

Salton, G., & Wong, A. (1978). Generation and search of clustered files. *ACM TODS*, 3(4), 321–346. doi:10.1145/320289.320291

Samah, A., Kim, H.-N., & Saddik, A. E. (2012). A group trust metric for identifying people of trust in online social networks. *Expert Systems with Applications*, *39*(18), 13173–13181. doi:10.1016/j.eswa.2012.05.084

Saraswathi, K., & Babu, V. G. (2015). A survey on data mining trends, applications and techniques. *Discovery*, *30*(135), 383–389.

Sarwar, B., Karypis, G., Konstan, J. & Riedl, J. (2001). Item-Based Collaborative Filtering Recommendation Algorithms. *Proceedings of the 10th Int'l WWW.*

Sarwar, B., Karypis, G., Konstan, J., & Reidl, J. (2000, August). Application of Dimensionality Reduction in Recommender Systems. *Proceedings of theACM Workshop on Web Mining for E-Commerce Challenges and Opportunities, Boston, USA.*

Sarwar, B., Karypis, G., Konstan, J., & Riedl, J. (2001). Item-based collaborative filtering recommendation algorithms. *Proceedings of the Tenth International World Wide Web Conference* (pp. 285-295). ACM Press. doi:10.1145/371920.372071

Sarwar, B., Karypis, G., Konstan, J., & Riedl, J. (2001, April). Item-based collaborative filtering recommendation algorithms. *Proceedings of the 10th international conference on World Wide Web* (pp. 285-295). ACM.

Satsiou, A., & Tassiulas, L. (2014, August). Propagating users' similarity towards improving recommender systems. *Proceedings of the 2014 IEEE/WIC/ACM International Joint Conferences on Web Intelligence (WI) and Intelligent Agent Technologies (IAT)* (Vol. 1, pp. 221-228). IEEE Computer Society.

Sayyed, M. Ali & Prof. Tuteja R.R. (2014). Data Mining Techniques. *International Journal of Computer Science and Mobile Computing*, *3*(4), 879–883. PMID:25509739

Schaal, M., O'Donovan, J., & Smyth, B. (2012). An analysis of topical proximity in the Twitter social graph. In K. Aberer, A. Flache, W. Jager, L. Liu, J. Tang, & C. Guéret (Eds.), *Proceedings of the Fourth International Conference on Social Informatics (SocInfo 2012)* (pp. 232-245). Heidelberg, Germany: Springer. doi:10.1007/978-3-642-35386-4_18

Schafer, B. J. (n. d.). The Application of Data-Mining to Recommender Systems. University of Northern Illinois. Retrieved from http://www.cs.uni.edu/~schafer/publications/dmChapter.pdf

Schafer, J. B., Joseph, A., & Riedl, J. (2001). E-commerce recommendation applications. *Data Mining and Knowledge Discovery*, *5*(1/2), 115–153. doi:10.1023/A:1009804230409

Scitovski, R., & Sabo, K. (2014). Analysis of the *k*-means algorithm in the case of data points occurring on the border of two or more clusters. *Knowledge-Based Systems*, *57*, 1–7. doi:10.1016/j.knosys.2013.11.010

Sfenrianto, Hasibuan Z. A. & Suhartanto H. (2011). The Influence Factors of Inherent Structure in e-Learning Process, *International Journal of e-Education, e-Business, e-. Management Learning*, *1*(3), 217–222.

Shabeera, T. P., & Madhu Kumar, S. D. (2015). Optimizing virtual machine allocation in MapReduce cloud for improved data locality. *International Journal of Big Data Intelligence.*, *2*(1), 2–8. doi:10.1504/IJBDI.2015.067563

Shahbaz, M., & Guergachi, A. (2014, May). Sentiment miner: A prototype for sentiment analysis of unstructured data and text. *Proceedings of the 2014 IEEE 27th Canadian Conference on Electrical and Computer Engineering (CCECE,* (pp. 1-7). IEEE. doi:10.1109/CCECE.2014.6901087

Shani, G., & Gunawardana, A. (n. d.). *Evaluating Recommendation Systems.* http://research.microsoft.com/pubs/115396/evaluationmetrics.tr.pdf

Shardanand, U., & Maes, P. (1995). Social information filtering, algorithms for automating - Word of Mouth. *Proceedings of theConf. Human Factors in Computing Systems.*

Shardanand, U., & Maes, P. (1995). Social information filtering: Algorithms for automating 'Word of Mouth'. *Proceedings of the Human Factors in Computing Systems Conf.*

Shardanand, U., & Maes, P. (1995). *Social Information Filtering, Algorithms for Automating 'Word of Mouth.* Conf. Human Factors in Computing Systems.

Sheard, J., Albrecht, D., & Butbul, E. (2005, July 2-6). ViSION: Visualizing student interactions online.*Proceedings of the 11th Australasian World Wide Web Conference (AusWeb05)*, Queensland, Australia (pp. 48–58).

Shenoy, P., Haritsa, J. R., Sudarshan, S., Bhalotia, G., Bawa, M., & Shah, D. (2000). Turbo-charging vertical mining of large databases. In W. Chen, J. F. Naughton, & P. A. Bernstein (Eds.), *Proceedings of the 2000 ACM SIGMOD International Conference on Management of Data* (pp. 22-33). New York, NY: ACM. doi:10.1145/342009.335376

Shen, R., Yang, F., & Han, P. (2002). Data analysis center based on eLearning platform. In *Workshop The Internet Challenge* (pp. 19–28). Berlin, Germany: Technology and Applications.

Sherchan, W., Nepal, S., & Paris, C. (2013). A survey of trust in social networks. *ACM Computing Surveys*, *45*(4), 47. doi:10.1145/2501654.2501661

Shishehchi, S., Banihashem, S. Y., Zin, N. A. M., & Noah, S. A. M. (2011) Review of personalized recommendation techniques for learners in elearning systems. in Semantic Technology and Information Retrieval (STAIR). *Proceedings of the2011 International Conference.*

Shneiderman, B. (1996) The Eyes Have It: A Task by Data Type Taxonomy for Information Visualizations.*Proceedings of the IEEE Symposium on Visual Languages*, Silver Spring, MD (pp. 336–343). doi:10.1109/VL.1996.545307

Shute, V., & Towle, B. (2003). Adaptive E-Learning. *Educational Psychologist*, *38*(2), 105–114. doi:10.1207/S15326985EP3802_5

Shyu, M., Haruchaiyasak, C., Chen, S., & Zhao, N. (2005). Collaborative Filtering By Mining Association Rules From User Access Sequences.*Proceedings of International Workshop on Challenges in Web Information Retrieval and Integration, WIRI'05* (pp. 128-135). IEEE. doi:10.1109/WIRI.2005.14

Siguenza-Guzman, L., Saquicela, V., Avila-Ordóñez, E., Vandewalle, J., & Cattrysse, D. (2015). Literature review of data mining applications in academic libraries. *Journal of Academic Librarianship*, *41*(4), 499–510. doi:10.1016/j.acalib.2015.06.007

Simoff, S. J., Bohlen, M. H., & Mazeika, A. (2008). Visual data mining: An introduction and overview In Visual data mining, LNCS (Vol. 4404, pp. 1–12). Berlin, Heidelberg: Springer. doi:10.1007/978-3-540-71080-6_1

Singh, V. K., Piryani, R., Uddin, A., & Waila, P. (2013, February). Sentiment analysis of Movie reviews and Blog posts. *Proceedings of the2013 IEEE 3rd InternationalAdvance Computing Conference (IACC),* (pp. 893-898). IEEE. doi:10.1109/IAdCC.2013.6514345

Singla, P., & Domingos, P. (2005). *Discriminative Training of Markov Logic Networks.* American Association for Artificial Intelligence.

Souali, K., Afia, A. E., Faizi, R., & Chiheb (2011) R. A new recommender system for e-learning environments. *Proceedings of the 2011 International Conference on Multimedia Computing and Systems (ICMCS).*

Soukup, T., & Davidson, I. (2002). *Visual Data Mining: Techniques and Tools for Data Visualization and Mining.* John Wiley & Sons, Inc.

Spacco, J., Winters, T., & Payne, T. (2006). Inferring use cases from unit testing. Proceedings of the AAAI Workshop on Educational Data Mining, New York (pp. 1-7).

Srivastava, J., Cooley, R., Deshpande, M., & Tan, P. (2000). Web usage mining: Discovery and applications of usage patterns from web data. *SIGKDD Explorations*, *1*(2), 12–23. doi:10.1145/846183.846188

Srivastava, U., & Gopalkrishnan, S. (2015). Impact of Big Data Analytics on Banking Sector: Learning for Indian Bank. *Big Data, Cloud and Computing Challenges*, *50*, 643–652.

Statista. (2015). Statistics and facts about Amazon. Retrieved from http://www.statista.com/topics/846/amazon/

Stolze, M., & Stroebel, M. (2003). Dealing with learning in e-Commerce product navigation and decision support: the teaching salesman problem.*Proceedings of the 2nd Interdisciplinary World Congress on Mass Customization and Personalization*, Munich,Germany.

Street, W., & Kim, Y. (2001). A streaming ensemble algorithm (SEA) for large-scale classification, *Proceedings of the seventh ACM SIGKDD International Conference on Knowledge discovery and data mining* (pp. 377-382). doi:10.1145/502512.502568

Sun, Y., & Han, J. (2013). Mining heterogeneous information networks: A structural analysis approach. *ACM SIGKDD Explorations Newsletter*, *14*(2), 20–28. doi:10.1145/2481244.2481248

Suppes. (n. d.). Addressing diversity in e-learning. Retrieved from http://suppes-corpus.stanford.edu/articles/comped/426.pdf

Surjono, H. D. (2011). The Design of Adaptive E-Learning System based on Student's Learning Styles. *International Journal of Computer Science and Information Technologies*, *2*(5), 2350–2353.

Su, X., & Khoshgoftaar, T. M. (2009). *A survey of collaborative filtering techniques* (Vol. 2009). Advances in Artificial Intelligence.

Su, X., & Khoshgoftaar, T. M. (2009). *A Survey of Collaborative Filtering Techniques*. Advances in Artificial Intelligence.

Su, X., & Khoshgoftaar, T. M. (2009). A survey of collaborative filtering techniques. *Advances in Artificial Intelligence*, *2009*. doi:10.1155/2009/421425

T. B. et al. (2002). A trail based internet-domain recommender system using artificial neural networks.*Proceedings of the Int. Conf. on Adaptive Hypermedia and Adaptive Web Based Systems*.

Tan, H., & Ye, H. (2009, May). A collaborative filtering recommendation algorithm based on item classification. *Proceedings of the Pacific-Asia Conference on Circuits, Communications and Systems, 2009* (pp. 694-697). IEEE. doi:10.1109/PACCS.2009.68

Taskar, B., Abbeel, P., & Koller, D. (2002). Discriminative Probabilistic Models for Relational Data. *Proceedings of the Eighteenth conference on Uncertainty in artificial intelligence UAI'02* (pp. 485-492).

Terveen, L., & Hill, W. (2001). Beyond Recommender Systems: Helping People Help Each Other. In Human Computer Interaction in the New Millennium (pp. 487-509).

Thokal, S., & Bhusari, V. (2014). Review Paper on Clustering Based Collaborative Filtering. *International Journal of Advance Research in Computer Science and Management Studies*, *2*(11), 558–561.

Thombre, S., & Dongre, S. (2013). Data Stream Mining for Health Care Application, *International Journal of Management. IT and Engineering*, *3*(9), 96–105.

Tibshirani, R., Walther, G., & Hastie, T. (2001). Estimating the number of clusters in a data set via the gap statistic. *Journal of the Royal Statistical Society. Series B. Methodological*, *63*(2), 411–423. doi:10.1111/1467-9868.00293

Tiwari, P. K., & Joshi, S. (2015). Data security for software as a service. *International Journal of Service Science, Management, Engineering, and Technology*, *6*(3), 47–63. doi:10.4018/IJSSMET.2015070104

Towle, B., & Quinn, C. (2000). Knowledge Based Recommender Systems using Explicit User Models. *Proceedings of the AAAI Workshop on Knowledge-Based Electronic Markets*, Menlo Park, CA (pp. 74-77).

Tsytsarau, M., & Palpanas, T. (2012). Survey on mining subjective data on the web. *Data Mining and Knowledge Discovery*, *24*(3), 478–514. doi:10.1007/s10618-011-0238-6

Ungar, L. H., & Foster, D. P. (1998). Clustering Methods For Collaborative Filtering. Proceedings of the AAAI workshop on recommendation systems (pp. 114-129).

Utgoff, P. E. (1989). Incremental induction of decision trees. *Proceedings of the Fifth International Conference on Machine Learning* (pp. 161-186).

Utgoff, P. E., Berkman, N. C., & Clouse, J. A. (1997). Decision tree induction based on efficient tree restructuring. *Journal of Machine Learning*, *29*(1), 5–44. doi:10.1023/A:1007413323501

Valsamidis, S., Kontogiannis, S., Kazanidis, I., & Karakos, A. (2011). E-Learning Platform Usage Analysis. *Interdisciplinary Journal of E-Learning and Learning Objects*, *7*(1), 185-204.

Van De Camp, M., & Van Den Bosch, A. (2012). The socialist network. *Decision Support Systems*, *53*(4), 761–769. doi:10.1016/j.dss.2012.05.031

Vanijja, V., & Supattathum, M. (2006). Statistical analysis of eLearning usage in a university. *Proceedings of the Third International Conference on eLearning for Knowledge-Based Society*, Bangkok, Thailand (pp. 22.1-22.5).

Vatcharaporn, E., Supaporn, L., & Clemens, B. (2009). Student Modelling in Adaptive E-Learning Systems, Knowledge Management and E-Learning. *International Journal (Toronto, Ont.)*, *3*(3), 342–355.

Veloso, M., Jorge, A., & Azevedo, P. (2004). Model-Based Collaborative Filtering For Team Building Support. *Proceedings International Conference on Enterprise Information Systems* (pp. 241-248).

Venkatadri, M., & Reddy, L.C. (2011). A Review on Data mining from Past to the Future. *International Journal of Computer Applications*, *15*(7), 19-22.

Verbert, K., Manouselis, N., Ochoa, X., Wolpers, M., Drachsler, H., Bosnic, I., & Duval, E. (2012). Context-aware recommender systems for learning: A survey and future challenges. *IEEE Transactions on Learning Technologies*, *5*(4), 318–335.

Verma, J. P., Patel, B., & Patel, A. (2015, February). Big Data Analysis: Recommendation System with Hadoop Framework. *Proceedings of the 2015 IEEE International Conference onComputational Intelligence & Communication Technology (CICT)* (pp. 92-97). IEEE.

Vlachos, M. & Svonava, D. (2012). Recommendation and visualization of similar movies using minimum spanning dendrograms. In *Information Visualization*, 1–17.

Wahi, A. K., Medury, Y., & Misra, R. K. (2014). Social Media: The core of enterprise 2.0. *International Journal of Service Science, Management, Engineering, and Technology*, *5*(3), 1–15. doi:10.4018/ijssmet.2014070101

Wahi, A. K., Medury, Y., & Misra, R. K. (2015). Big Data: Enabler or Challenge for Enterprise 2.0. *International Journal of Service Science, Management, Engineering, and Technology*, *6*(2), 1–17.

Walker, A., Recker, M., Lawless, K., & Wiley, D. (2004). Collaborative Information Filtering: A Review and an Educational Application. *International Journal of Artificial Intelligence in Education, 14*(1), 3–24.

Walker, M. A., Anand, P., Abbott, R., Tree, J. E. F., Martell, C., & King, J. (2012). That is your evidence?: Classifying stance in online political debate. *Decision Support Systems, 53*(4), 719–729. doi:10.1016/j.dss.2012.05.032

Wang, K., Tang, L., Han, J., & Liu, J. (2002). Top down FP-growth for association rule mining, In M.-S. Cheng, P. S. Yu, & B. Liu (Eds.), *Proceedings of the Sixth Pacific-Asia Conference on Knowledge Discovery and Data Mining* (*PAKDD 2002*) (pp. 334-340). Heidelberg, Germany: Springer. doi:10.1007/3-540-47887-6_34

Wang, L., Li, J., Ding, L., & Li, P. (2009), E-Learning Evaluation System Based on Data Mining. *Proceedings of the 2010 2nd International Symposium on Information Engineering and Electronic Commerce (IEEC).*

Wang, Y. & Wong, A. K. C. (2003). From Association to Classification: Inference Using weight of evidence. *Knowledge and Data Engineering., IEEE transactions on* 15(3), 764-767.

Wang, F.-H., & Shao, H.-M. (2004). Effective personalized recommendation based on time-framed navigation clustering and association mining. *Expert Systems with Applications, 27*(3), 365–377. doi:10.1016/j.eswa.2004.05.005

Wang, H., Fan, W., Yu, P., & Han, J. (2003). Mining Concept Drifting Data Streams using Ensemble Classifiers. *Proceedings of the ninth ACM SIGKDD international conference on Knowledge discovery and data mining* (pp. 226 – 235). doi:10.1145/956750.956778

Wang, J., De Vries, A. P., & Reinders, M. J. (2006, August). Unifying user-based and item-based collaborative filtering approaches by similarity fusion. *Proceedings of the 29th annual international ACM SIGIR conference on Research and development in information retrieval* (pp. 501-508). ACM. doi:10.1145/1148170.1148257

Wankhade, K. K., & Dongre, S. S. (2011). A New Adaptive Ensemble Boosting Classifier for Concept Drifting Stream Data. *Proceedings of The 3ʳᵈ International Conference on Computer Modeling and Simulation* (pp. 417-421).

Ward, M., Peng, W., & Wang, X. (2004). Hierarchical visual data mining for large-scale data. *Computational Statistics, 19*(1), 147–158. doi:10.1007/BF02915281

Wasserman, S., & Faust, K. (1994). *Social Network Analysis: Methods and Applications.* Cambridge, UK: Cambridge University Press. doi:10.1017/CBO9780511815478

Watson, S. F., Apostolou, B., Hassell, J. M., & Webber, S. A. (2007). Accounting education literature review (2003-2005). *Journal of Accounting Education, 25*(1), 1–58. doi:10.1016/j.jaccedu.2007.01.001

Wei, Y. Z., Moreau, L., & Jennings, N. R. (2005). A market-based approach to recommender systems. *ACM Transactions on Information Systems, 23*(3), 227–266. doi:10.1145/1080343.1080344

Wen Wu, Liang He, Jing Yang. (n. d.). *Evaluating Recommender Systems.*

Whyte, C. B., & Bolyard, C. (1989). Student Affairs-The Future. *Journal of College Student Development, 30,* 86–89.

Winkler, W. (1999). *The state of record linkage and current research problems.* U.S: Statistical Research Division, Census Bureau.

Witten, I. H., & Frank, E. (2002). *Data Mining: Practical Machine Learning Tools and Techniques with Java Implementations.* San Francisco, CA: Morgan Kaufmann.

Wogenstein, F., Drescher, J., Reinel, D., Rill, S., & Scheidt, J. (2013, August). Evaluation of an algorithm for aspect-based opinion mining using a lexicon-based approach. *Proceedings of the Second International Workshop on Issues of Sentiment Discovery and Opinion Mining.* doi:10.1145/2502069.2502074

Wong, B., Pun, C. F., Kit, C., & Webster, J. J. (2011, November). Lexical cohesion for evaluation of machine translation at document level. *Proceedings of the 2011 7th International Conference on Natural Language Processing and Knowledge Engineering (NLP-KE)* (pp. 238-242). IEEE.

Wong, T. (2015). Learning Markov logic networks with limited number of labeled training examples. *International Journal of Knowledge-based and Intelligent Engineering Systems, 18*(2), 91–98.

Wu, D., Liu, Y., Gao, G., Mao, Z., Ma, W., & He, T. (2009). An Adaptive Ensemble Classifier for Concept Drifting stream. *Proceedings of the IEEE Symposium on Computational Intelligence and Data Mining.*

Wu, X., Kumar, V., Quinlan, J.-R., Ghosh, J., Yang, Q., Motoda, H., & Steinberg, D. et al. (2008). Top 10 algorithms in data mining. *Knowledge and Information Systems, 14*, 1–37.

Wu, Y., & Wen, M. (2010, August). Disambiguating dynamic sentiment ambiguous adjectives.*Proceedings of the 23rd International Conference on Computational Linguistics* (pp. 1191-1199). Association for Computational Linguistic.

Xiang, W., Niansu, H., & Min, H. (2014). Application of Association Rules Data Mining in the Determination the Operation Target Values in the Thermal Power Plant. *Paper presented at theInternational Conference on Computer Science and Service System*, Bangkok, Thailand.

Xiangliang, Recommender System Introduction (n. d.). Retrieved from http://www.slideshare.net/xlvector/recommender-system-introduction 12551956? from_action=save

Xindong, W. (2014). Data Mining with Big data. *IEEE Transactions on Knowledge and Data Engineering, 26*(1), 97–107. doi:10.1109/TKDE.2013.109

Xiong, L., Chen, X., Huang, T., Schneidery, J., & Carbonellz, J. G. (2010). Temporal collaborative filtering with Bayesian probabilistic tensor. In SIAM Data Mining.

Xiong, L., Chen, X., Huang, T., Schneidery, J., & Carbonellz, J. G. (2010). Temporal Collaborative Filtering with Bayesian Probabilistic Tensor. In SIAM Data Mining.

Xiong, R., Smith, M. A., & Drucker, S. M. (1998). Visualizations of collaborative information for end-users. *Ministry of Research and Information Technology*. Retrieved from http://www.fsk.dk/fsk/publ/elcom/

Xu, Y. (2012, December). A Comparative Study on Feature Selection in Unbalance Text Classification. *Proceedings of the 2012 International Symposium on Information Science and Engineering (ISISE)* (pp. 44-47). IEEE. doi:10.1109/ISISE.2012.19

Xu, Z., Tresp, V., Rettinger, A., & Kersting, K. (2010). Social Network Mining with Nonparametric relational Models. *Advance in Social Network Mining An Analysis*, 77-96.

Xu, B., Bu, J., Chen, C., & Cai, D. (2012). An exploration of improving collaborative recommender systems via user-item subgroups.*Proceedings of the 21st international conference on World Wide Web* (pp. 21-30). ACM. doi:10.1145/2187836.2187840

Xue, G., Lin, C., Yang, Q., Xi, W., Zueng, H., Yu, Y., & Chen, Z. (2005). Scalable Collaborative Filtering Using Cluster Based Smoothing.*Proceedings Of 2005 ACM SIGIR Conference*, Salvador, Brazil (pp. 114-121). doi:10.1145/1076034.1076056

Yamashita, H. Kawamura, & K. Suzuki (2011). Adaptive fusion method for user-based and item-based collaborative filtering. *Adv. Complex Syst.*, 14(2), 133-149.

Yan, M. (2005). *Methods of Determining the Number of Clusters in a Data Set and a New Clustering Criterion* [Ph.D. Dissertation]. Faculty Virginia Polytechnic Institute and State University, Blacksburg, Virginia.

Yang, B., Lei, Y., Liu, D., & Liu, J. (2013). Social collaborative filtering by trust. *Proceedings of the 23rd International Joint Conference on Artificial Intelligence* (pp. 2747-2753).

Yang, J., Yan, X., Han, J., & Wang, W. (2013). Discovering Evolutionary Classifier over High Speed Non-static Stream. doi:10.1145/2499907.2499909

Yang, X., Guo, Y., Liu, Y., & Steck, H. (2014). A survey of collaborative filtering based social recommender systems. *Computer Communications*, *41*, 1–10. doi:10.1016/j.comcom.2013.06.009

Yan-Yan, Z., Bing, Q., & Ting, L. (2010). Integrating intra-and inter-document evidences for improving sentence sentiment classification. *Acta Automatica Sinica*, *36*(10), 1417–1425.

Ye, Q., Zhang, Z., & Law, R. (2009). Sentiment classification of online reviews to travel destination by supervised machine learning approaches. *Expert Systems with Applications*, 2009, 1–9.

Yuan, Q., Cong, G., Ma, Z., Sun, A., & Magnenat-Thalmann, N. (2013). Who, where, when and what: discover spatio-temporal topics for Twitter users. *Proceedings of the 19th ACM SIGKDD International Conference on Knowledge Discovery and Data Mining (KDD 2013)* (pp. 605-613). New York, NY: ACM. doi:10.1145/2487575.2487576

Yuan, F., Meng, Z.-H., Zhang, H.-X., & Dong, C.-R. (2004). A new algorithm to get the initial centroids. *Proc. International Conference on Machine Learning and Cybernetics* (Vol. 2, pp. 1191-1193).

Yuan, Q., Cong, G., Zhao, K., Ma, Z., & Sun, A. (2015). Who, where, when and what: A Nonparametric Bayesian approach to context-aware recommendation and search for twitter users. *ACM Transactions on Information Systems*, *33*(1), 1–33. doi:10.1145/2699667

Yu, C., Zhong, Y., Smith, T., Park, I., & Huang, W. (2009). Visual data mining of multimedia data for social and behavioral studies. *Information Visualization*, *8*(1), 56–70. doi:10.1057/ivs.2008.32

Yu, L. C., Wu, J. L., Chang, P. C., & Chu, H. S. (2013). Using a contextual entropy model to expand emotion words and their intensity for the sentiment classification of stock market news. *Knowledge-Based Systems*, *41*, 89–97. doi:10.1016/j.knosys.2013.01.001

Yusuf, N., & Al-Banawi, N. (2013). The Impact of Changing Technology: The Case of E-Learning. *Contemporary Issues in Education Research*, *6*(2), 173–180. doi:10.19030/cier.v6i2.7726

Zaiane, O. R. (2001). Web Usage Mining for a Better Web-Based Learning Environment (Technical Report TR01-05). Department of Computing Science, University of Alberta.

Zaki, M. J. (2000). Scalable algorithms for association mining. *IEEE Transactions on Knowledge and Data Engineering*, *12*(3), 372–390. doi:10.1109/69.846291

Zalik, K. R. (2008). An efficient *k*-means clustering algorithm. *Pattern Recognition Letters*, *29*(9), 1385–1391. doi:10.1016/j.patrec.2008.02.014

Zhang, W., Xu, H., & Wan, W. (2012). Weakness Finder: Find product weakness from Chinese reviews by using aspects based sentiment analysis. *Expert Systems with Applications*, *39*(11), 10283–10291. doi:10.1016/j.eswa.2012.02.166

Zhang, Y. J., & Cheng, E. (2013). An Optimized Method for Selection of the Initial Centers of *k*-means Clustering. *Integrated Uncertainty in Knowledge Modeling and Decision Making, LNCS* (Vol. 8032, pp. 149–156). doi:10.1007/978-3-642-39515-4_13

Zhang, Y., & Zhu, W. (2013). Extracting implicit features in online customer reviews for opinion mining.*Proceedings of the 22nd international conference on World Wide Web companion* (pp. 103-104). International World Wide Web Conferences Steering Committee. doi:10.1145/2487788.2487835

Zhao, Z. D., & Shang, M. S. (2010) User-based Collaborative-Filtering Recommendation Algorithms on Hadoop. *Proceedings of the 2010 Third International Conference on Knowledge Discovery and Data Mining.*

Zhao, Z. D., & Shang, M. S. (2010, January). User-based collaborative-filtering recommendation algorithms on hadoop. *Proceedings of the Third International Conference on Knowledge Discovery and Data Mining WKDD '10* (pp. 478-481). IEEE.

Zha, Z. J., Yu, J., Tang, J., Wang, M., & Chua, T. S. (2014). Product aspect ranking and its applications. *IEEE Transactions on* Knowledge and Data Engineering, *26*(5), 1211–1224.

Zheng, Z., Ma, H., Lyu, M. R., & King, I. (2011). Qos-aware web service recommendation by collaborative filtering. *IEEE Transactions on* Services Computing, *4*(2), 140–152.

Zhou, L., Li, B., Gao, W., Wei, Z., & Wong, K. F. (2011, July). Unsupervised discovery of discourse relations for eliminating intra-sentence polarity ambiguities.*Proceedings of the Conference on Empirical Methods in Natural Language Processing* (pp. 162-171). Association for Computational Linguistics

Zhu, X., Wu, X., & Yang, Y. (2004). Dynamic Classifier Selection for Effective Mining from Noisy Data Streams. *Proceedings of the IEEE International Conference on Data Mining.*

Zhu, L., Lei, Q., Liu, G., & Liu, F. (2015). Processing Recommender Top-*N* Queries in Relational Databases. *Journal of Software, 10*(2), 162–171. doi:10.17706/jsw.10.2.162-171

Ziegler, C. N., & Golbeck, J. (2015). Models for trust inference in social networks. In D. Król et al. (Eds.), *Propagation Phenomena in Real World Networks, Intelligent Systems Reference Library* (Vol. 85, pp. 53–89). Springer. doi:10.1007/978-3-319-15916-4_3

Zirn, C., Niepert, M., Stuckenschmidt, H., & Strube, M. (2011, November). *Fine-Grained Sentiment Analysis with Structural Features* (pp. 336–344). IJCNLP.

Zliobaite, I., & Kuncheva, L. I. (2010). Theoretical window size for classification in the presence of sudden Concept drift (Technical Report Number BCS-TR-001-2010).

Zliobaite, I. (2007). Ensemble Learning for Concept Drift Handling-the Role of New Expert.*Proceedings of the 5th International Conference on Machine Learning and Data Mining in Pattern Recognition* (pp. 251-260).

Zliobaite, I., Bifet, A., Pfahringer, B., & Holmes, G. (2014). Active Learning With Drifting Streaming Data. *IEEE Transactions on Neural Networks and Learning Systems, 25*(1), 27–39. doi:10.1109/TNNLS.2012.2236570 PMID:24806642

Zorrilla, M. E., Menasalvas, E., Marin, D., Mora, E., & Segovia, J. (2005). Web usage mining project for improving web-based learning sites. *Proceedings of theInternational Conference on Computer Aided Systems Theory,* Las Palmas de Gran Canaria, Spain (pp. 205-210).

About the Contributors

Vishal Bhatnagar holds a BTech, a MTech and a PhD in the engineering field. He has more than 16 years of teaching experience at various technical institutions. He is currently working as an Associate Professor in Computer Science in the Engineering Department of the Ambedkar Institute of Advanced Communication Technologies and Research (Government of Delhi), GGSIPU, Delhi, India. His research interests include: database, advance database, data warehousing, data-mining, social network analysis, and big data analytics. He has to his credit more than 80 research papers in various international/national journals and conferences.

* * *

Neethu Akkarapatty is a B.Tech graduate in Computer science from the Sahrdaya College of Engineering and Technology, Kodakara, affiliated to the University of Calicut. She is currently pursuing full time a M.Tech in Computer Science with Information Systems (CSIS) at the SCMS School of Engineering and Technology, Karukutty, Ernakulam, Kerala. Her recent publications are in the area of Machine Learning and Sentiment Analysis.

Marenglen Biba, Ph.D., in Computer Science, University of Bari, Italy; Laurea Degree (5 years degree) Cum Laude in Computer Science, University of Bari, Italy. Current Positions and Projects 2014 – present, National IT Expert for STAR – Support for Territorial and Administrative Reform, http://rat. al/en/ 2013 – present, Project Manager for University of New York in Tirana, in ADRIATinn Project in the IPA CBC Framework, http://www.adriatinn.eu/ 2013 – present, Co-Founder and Scientific Advisor of ProTech – Professional Technologies, Sh.p.k, a company in Tirana, Albania, specialized in software development, information systems, outsourcing and research in intelligent systems. 2010 – present, representing Albania in the Machine Intelligence Research Labs (MIR Labs) 2010 – present, Editor-in-Chief for International Journal of Social Network Mining (IJSNM) 2009 - present, Chair of Computer Science Department, University of New York in Tirana, affiliated with State University of New York (SUNY) Education 2008 – 2009.

Edson M. Dela Cruz is currently a student in the Department of Computer Science at the University of Manitoba, Canada. He won a Faculty of Science Undergraduate Student Research Award (USRA) to conduct full-time research in the area of data mining under the academic supervision of Prof. Leung. Dela Cruz is interested in the research area of data mining with a focus on association rule mining and collaborative filtering.

Naveen Dahiya received his B.E. in Computer Science and Engineering from Maharshi Dayanand University, Rohtak, Haryana, India in 2003 and a M.Tech in Computer Engineering from Maharshi Dayanand University, Rohtak, Haryana, India in 2005. He is currently pursuing a Ph.D from the Y.M.C.A. University of Science and Technology, Faridabad, Haryana, India. He is working as an Assistant Professor and Head of the Computer Science and Engineering Department at the Maharaja Surajmal Institute of Technology, C-4, Janak Puri, New Delhi, India. His research interests include: database systems, data warehousing, and data mining. He has supervised various undergraduate and postgraduate students in various research projects in data warehousing and data mining.

Snehlata Sewakdas Dongre received a B. E. degree in Computer Science and Engineering from Pt. Ravishankar Shukla University, Raipur, India in 2007 and a M. Tech. degree in Computer Engineering from University of Pune, Pune, India in 2010. She is currently working as an Assistant Professor the Department of Computer Science and Engineering at G. H. Raisoni College of Engineering, Nagpur, India. She has had a number of publications in reputed international conferences for the IEEE and in journals. Her research is on Data Stream Mining, Machine Learning, Decision Support Systems, ANNs and Embedded Systems. Her book titled *Data Streams Mining: Classification and Application* was published by LAP Publication House, Germany in 2010. Ms. Snehlata S. Dongre is a member of IACSIT, the IEEE and the ISTE Organization.

Vijay Sekar Elango is currently a student in the School of Computer Science and Engineering at VIT University, Vellore, India. He won a MITACS Globalink Research Internship award to conduct full-time research in the Department of Computer Science at the University of Manitoba, Canada, in the area of data mining, under the academic supervision of Prof. Leung. Elango is interested in the research area of data mining with a focus on collaborative filtering and data analytics.

Lalit Mohan Goyal has completed a Bachelor of Technology in Computer Engineering in 2002. He has done his Master of Technology in Information Technology in 2009. He has submitted his Ph.D. to the Computer Engineering department of Jamia Millia Islamia, New Delhi, INDIA in 2015. He has been teaching since 2002.

Mahima Goyal is pursuing her MTech in Information Security at GGSIPU, Delhi, India. Her research interests include databases, data mining, big data analysis and sentiment analysis.

Arushi Jain is completing her M.Tech in Information Security at the Ambedkar Institute of Advanced Communication Technologies And Research, Delhi, India. Her research interests include databases, data warehousing, data mining and big data.

Fan Jiang received his B.C.Sc. (Hons.) and M.Sc. degrees from the University of Manitoba, Canada. He is currently a Ph.D. candidate in the Department of Computer Science at the same university under the academic supervision of Prof. Leung. Jiang is interested in conducting research in the area of data mining with a focus on association rule mining, collaborative filtering, and social network analytics.

Sheng-Jhe Ke received his M.A. degree from the Department of Information Management, National Sun Yat-sen University, Kaohsiung, Taiwan. He works as a software engineer in Kaohsiung. His research interests include data mining, social media analysis and social networking.

Manish Kumar received his PhD from Indian Institute of Information Technology, Allahabad, India in Data Management in Wireless Sensor Networks. He is an Assistant Professor at the Indian Institute of Information Technology, Allahabad, India. His research interest areas are databases, data management in sensor networks, data mining and Big Data analytics.

Wei-Po Lee received his Ph.D. in artificial intelligence from the University of Edinburgh, United Kingdom. His is currently a professor in the Department of Information Management, National Sun Yat-sen University, Kaohsiung, Taiwan. He is interested in intelligent autonomous systems, data mining, mobile multimedia, and social networking.

Carson K. Leung received his B.Sc. (Hons.), M.Sc., and Ph.D. degrees all from the University of British Columbia, Vancouver, Canada. He is currently a Professor at the University of Manitoba, Canada. He has contributed more than 130 refereed publications on the topics of big data analytics, databases, data mining, social network analysis, as well as visual analytics—including papers in ACM Transactions on Database Systems (TODS), Future Generation Computer Systems (FGCS), the Journal of Organizational Computing and Electronic Commerce, Social Network Analysis and Mining, the IEEE International Conference on Data Engineering (ICDE), the IEEE International Conference on Data Mining (ICDM), the SCA 2012 Best Paper on social computing and its applications, as well as four chapters for IGI Global, published in books and encyclopedias.

Venkatesan M. is presently completing his Ph.D in P.G. and Research, Department of Computer Science, at the Government Arts College (Autonomous), Karur, Tamilnadu, India. He has received his B.Sc (Mathematics) degree from Kongu College of Arts and science, Karur, Tamilnadu, India in 2007. He received his MCA degree from Paavai Engineering College, Namakkal, Tamilnadu, India, in 2010. He has participated in workshops and published many research papers in journals, and presented many papers in national and international conferences at various colleges.

Renuka Mahajan is an assistant professor of computer science at Amity University, Uttar Pradesh. She has completed her PhD (CS&E) from Amity University, UP. Her current research interests include: educational data mining, recommender systems and e-CRM. She has published in Scopus-indexed journals such as the Springer Journal EAIT, the Inderscience IJIL, IJDATS and IJLEG, JIOS, IJEEEE and a few other professional conference proceedings.

Latesh G. Malik received a B. E. degree in Computer Science and Engineering from Rajasthan University, India, in 1996 and a M. Tech. degree in Computer Science & Engineering from Banasthali Vidyapith, India, in 2001. She is currently working as a Professor and the Head of the Department of Computer Science and Engineering at the G.H. Raisoni College of Engineering, Nagpur, India. She has had a number of publications in reputed international conferences like the IEEE and various journals. Her research is on Document Processing, Soft Computing and Image Processing. She received a Best teacher award and she is a gold medalist in M.Tech. and B.E. She also received a grant from AICTE of Rs. 7.5 lacs under RPS. Dr. Latesh Malik is a member of CSI, the IEEE and the ISTE Organization.

Mamta Mittal has completed her Ph.D. (Computer Engineering) from Thapar University Patiala, India, in 2015. She has done M.Tech. and B.Tech. in 2007 and 2001, respectively. She is currently working as an Assistant Professor at the G.B.Pant Govt. Eng. College, New Delhi. She has been teaching since 2001.

Anjaly Muralidharan is a B.Tech graduate in Information Technology from Viswajyothi College of Engineering and Technology, Vazhakulam, Kerala. She is currently pursuing full time a M.Tech in Computer Science with Information Systems (CSIS) at the SCMS School of Engineering and Technology. Karukutty, Ernakulam, Kerala. Her areas of interest are in the field of Data Mining and Computer Networking.

Lediona Nishani was born in Berat where she attended the high school. She achieved a Master and Bachelor Degrees at the Polytechnic University of Tirana, Faculty of Information technology in the Telecommunication Engineering Department. Currently, she is pursuing a PhD degree in Computer Science at the University of New York in Tirana. Regarding the Doctoral Program, her research field of interests are machine learning techniques, security engineering, intrusion detection systems, outlier detections, greedy ensemble outliers, etc. Her dissertation consists of a combination between Intrusion Detection Systems (IDS) and Data Mining models and algorithms. She has worked for two years as a full time lecturer at The Planetary University of Tirana, and for a year as a full time pedagogue at Albanian University at the Engineering Department. Currently, she is full time lecturer at the Canadian Institute of Technology (CIT) in the Engineering Faculty. She has delivered various lectures in specialty courses for the Computer Engineering Study program.

Vinod P., is a Professor in the Department of Computer Science & Engineering at the SCMS School of Engineering & Technology, Cochin, Kerala. He holds his Ph.D in Computer Engineering from the Malaviya National Institute of Technology, Jaipur, India. He has also served as programme committee member for the International Security Conference like Security of Information and Networks, ICACCI, ICISSP, etc. Dr. Vinod P's research uses feature selection and dimensionality reduction methods which is a major principle in the Machine Learning Domain as it is used in the detection of malicious application. He has more than 70 research articles published in peer-reviewed journals and international conferences. His current research is involved in the development of an offline malware scanner for mobile applications using machine learning techniques. Vinod's areas of interest are in Malware Analysis, Data Mining, Ethical Hacking and Natural Language Processing.

Amrit Pal is pursuing his PhD degree from the Indian Institute of Information Technology, Allahabad India. He has received his M.Tech degree from the National Institute of Technical Teachers' Training and Research, Bhopal, India, in 2014. His research interest includes data mining and big data analytics. He also has publications in similar areas.

Nisha S. Raj is a graduate from Cochin University of Science and Technology, Kochi Kerala and a Post graduate from the Anna University Coimbatore, Tamil Nadu. She has been working in the Dept. of Computer Science and Engineering, SCMS School of Engineering and Technology, Angamaly, for the past 10 years. Currently, she is a research scholar at the Cochin University of Science and Technology, Kochi. Her research interests are in the areas of Text Classification, Machine Learning Techniques and Deep Learning.

Anu Saini received her Ph. D. in computer science from the Jawaharlal Nehru University, New Delhi, India, in 2014; a M. Tech. degree in computer science from MDU Rohtak, India and B. Tech. from MDU, Rohtak, India. She has authored many national and international journal and conference papers. She is working as an Assistant Professor in the Computer Science and Engineering Department at the G.B. Pant Govt. Engineering College, New Delhi, India. Her current research interests include Service Oriented Architecture, Cloud Computing, Data warehouse and Big Data.

Neeti Sangwan received her B Tech. from Maharishi Dayanand University, Rohtak, in 2010 and a M Tech. from Banasthali University, Rajasthan, in 2012. Presently, she is working as an assistant professor (C.S.E) in Maharaja Surajmal Institute of Technology, Janak Puri, New Delhi. Her research interests include data mining, data warehousing, and databases.

Pulkit Sharma is student of Ambedkar Institute of Advanced Communication Technologies And Research, Delhi. He is currently pursuing his bachelors in technology (computer science and engineering) and his area of interest is in Big Data Analytics.

R. K. Sharma received his Ph.D. degree in Mathematics from the University of Roorkee (Now, IIT Roorkee), India in 1993. He is currently working as a Professor at Thapar University, Patiala, India, where he teaches, among other things, statistical models and their usage in computer science. He has been involved in the organization of a number of conferences and other courses at Thapar University, Patiala. His main research interests are Machine Learning and Natural Language Processing.

V.P. Singh did his M.E. and Ph.D. in Computer Science from Thapar University, Patiala, India. Presently, he is an Assistant Professor, Department of Computer Science and Engineering, Thapar University, Patiala. He has published many research papers in national and international journals and conferences. His areas of interest are soft-Computing and computer networks.

K. Thangadurai is presently working as an Assistant professor and the Head in the P.G. and Research Department of Computer Science, at the Government Arts College (Autonomous), Karur. He has fifteen years of rich teaching experience, along with ten years of Research experience in the field of Computer Science. He has worked as the HOD of PG Department of Computer Science at Government Arts College (Men), Krishnagiri. He has published many technical papers in National and International Conferences and Journals. His areas of interest are Software Engineering, Network Security, Data Mining, etc.

Rao Narasimha Vajjhala, Doctor of Management. Assistant Professor in Computer Science and Programme Leader for the Masters Programme in Computer Science offered by the University of Greenwich, UK.

Index

A

adaptive e-learning system 1, 8
ADWIN 249
association analysis 101, 105, 108, 110, 114
association rule 13, 25, 76-77, 82, 85, 108-109, 159-162, 165-166, 173, 175-176, 179
association rule mining 13, 25, 77, 85, 108-109, 159-162, 175-176, 179

B

bagging 27, 238-242, 249
Big Data 3, 5, 13, 16, 118, 120, 123, 128-129, 131, 133-136, 138, 140-142, 144-145, 147-150, 152, 154-156, 158, 175, 179, 222, 260
boosting 27, 94, 181, 238-239, 241-243, 245, 249

C

classification 4-5, 13, 25-27, 50-52, 55-56, 58-62, 67, 75-78, 80, 82-84, 92, 100-101, 105-106, 109-111, 114, 129, 131, 133, 136, 142, 144-145, 160, 180-184, 187-189, 195-197, 200, 202-204, 210-213, 216, 218-220, 228, 236-240, 242, 244, 246, 249, 255, 261-262, 264
clustering 4-5, 24-31, 33-34, 36, 45-46, 53, 76-77, 81-82, 84, 101, 105, 110, 114, 116, 125, 132, 140, 142-150, 152, 154-156, 158, 160, 222, 262
cold start 14-15, 54, 110, 195, 198, 200, 207, 212, 262-264
collaborative 13-14, 52-54, 71, 74-75, 79, 81, 85-89, 92, 100-103, 105, 108-111, 115-118, 120-124, 128-133, 136, 138, 140, 142, 149-152, 154-156, 158-160, 162, 166, 175-176, 179-181, 186, 194-196, 198, 202, 207, 213, 216-218, 221-230, 235-236, 239, 246, 249-250, 252, 256-264, 269

collaborative filtering 13-14, 52-54, 71, 75, 79, 81, 85-89, 92, 100-103, 105, 108-111, 115-118, 120-124, 128-133, 136, 138, 140, 149-152, 154-156, 158-160, 162, 166, 175-176, 179-181, 186, 194-196, 202, 207, 216-218, 221-230, 235-236, 239, 250, 252, 257-264, 269
compactness 28, 36, 38-39, 41-44
concept drift 236-237, 240-243, 246, 249
content-based filtering 13, 89, 92, 223-224, 235, 252, 257-258, 269
cross validation 53, 55, 62-63

D

data analytics 140, 142, 148, 155, 195-196, 200, 213, 216
data classification 195, 200, 202, 204, 211, 213, 216, 240
data exploration 219-220, 230
data mining 1-6, 9-13, 15-16, 24-25, 27, 50, 74-76, 82, 85, 100-101, 104-105, 110-111, 115, 128-129, 132-134, 136, 140, 143-144, 148, 156, 159-160, 176, 179-180, 194, 217-222, 227-228, 230, 235-237, 245, 251-252, 269
data stream 147, 236-241, 243-244, 246, 249
data stream mining 236-237, 239, 243, 246, 249
data structure 13, 162
demographic filtering 85-86, 223, 225, 235, 257, 259, 265, 269
dimensionality reduction 49, 58-59, 67, 72, 142
Dunn index 36-37, 39, 45

E

ensemble classifier 236-240, 242, 244, 246, 249

F

feature extraction 202, 216, 224, 259
features 6, 13, 49-53, 58-61, 64-65, 67, 82-83, 86, 90-91, 101, 118, 142, 146, 150, 181, 195, 197, 200, 202-204, 212-213, 216, 221, 226, 228-229, 249, 252, 255, 260-261
frequent pattern mining 5, 12-13, 15, 160-162, 167, 171, 174, 179

H

Hadoop 115, 118, 125-126, 130, 133, 147-148, 155, 158, 213, 260
HDFS 118-119, 126, 148, 155
hybrid approaches 264
hybrid collaborative filtering 101, 111, 223-225, 230, 235, 258, 260, 269

I

information filtering 13, 85, 114, 149, 194, 218
Item Based Collaborative Filtering 129, 133, 138
Itemset 179

K

k-means 24, 27-34, 36-39, 42, 45-46, 77, 84-85
k-Nearest Neighbors Algorithm 216
Knowledge-Based Filtering 90
knowledge discovery 3, 91, 133, 179, 219

M

machine learning 3, 12, 51, 58, 60, 81, 84, 86-87, 132, 141, 148, 150, 180-181, 194, 224, 252, 255, 258-259, 265
MapReduce 115, 118, 123-124, 127, 134-136, 142, 148, 155, 158
memory-based approaches 225, 259
mining 1-6, 9-13, 15-16, 24-25, 27, 49-52, 74-77, 82, 85, 100-101, 104-105, 108-111, 115, 128-129, 132-134, 136, 140, 143-144, 148, 156, 159-164, 167-168, 171, 174-176, 179-183, 186, 189, 194, 217-222, 227-228, 230, 235-237, 239, 243, 245-246, 249, 251-252, 269
model-based approaches 225, 259

N

Natural Language Processing 49-50, 180-181, 194
neural network 76-78, 84
NLP 180-181, 263

O

opinion mining 49-52, 180-183, 186, 189, 194

P

personalized adaptive e-learning systems 1-2

R

rating 14, 50, 52-54, 75, 81, 83, 87, 93, 102, 110, 114-118, 120-121, 124, 127, 130, 132-133, 151-152, 179, 194-197, 200, 202-205, 207-210, 223-227, 258-260, 264-265
recommendation 1, 9, 13-15, 52-54, 74-76, 78-81, 85-86, 89-95, 100-101, 109-110, 115, 117-118, 123, 125, 128-136, 138, 150-152, 159-160, 166, 173, 175-176, 179-183, 186, 194-198, 200-202, 204-205, 207, 210, 212-213, 218, 223-230, 250-251, 256-260, 262-265
recommendation system 13, 80-81, 93, 100, 125, 128-131, 133, 135-136, 138, 151-152, 159-160, 175-176, 179, 181-183, 186, 194, 224, 228-229, 258
recommender 1-2, 13-16, 50, 52-54, 71-72, 74-78, 80, 82, 84-87, 90-95, 100-101, 109-110, 114, 116, 150-151, 156, 181, 194-196, 198-199, 213, 223-226, 228-230, 235, 250-252, 255-260, 263-264, 269
recommender system 1, 13, 52, 74-75, 77, 80, 82, 85-87, 90-91, 94, 101, 109-110, 114, 116, 150, 194, 223-225, 228-229, 252, 255, 257-259, 263
relational data 226, 252-254, 262-264

S

Sentiment analysis 49-51, 72, 180, 182
separation 28, 36-38, 41-44, 253
similarity 24, 26-27, 31, 33-34, 36-38, 45, 53-54, 60, 87, 92-93, 109, 116-118, 120-121, 124, 127, 132-134, 142-143, 181, 195-203, 205-206, 208-210, 213, 218, 224-225, 227, 258-259, 265
single pass clustering 24, 27, 30-31, 33-34, 45
Social network analysis 78, 251
Social Network Mining (SNM) 251, 269
social networks 74, 94-95, 130, 159, 175-176, 180, 196, 221-222, 250-251, 255, 262-263
social trust 53, 195-196, 198, 200-202, 208-209, 213
sparsity 14-15, 54, 86-87, 116, 195-196, 198, 200, 202, 225-226, 250, 259-260, 264-265

T

TF-IDF 49, 59, 62, 67, 72
threshold value 31, 36, 41-46
trust network 198-199, 213, 216

U

User Based Collaborative Filtering 132, 138
user-ratings 224-226, 258-260, 262, 265

V

visual data mining 217-222, 227, 230, 235
visualization 4, 118, 133, 148, 218-222, 227-230

W

web mining 10-11, 13, 15, 50
WEKA 55, 61, 67, 72
WET 49, 59, 62, 64, 67, 72
windowing 239, 243, 245-246, 249

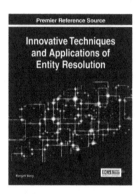

Printed in the United States
By Bookmasters